THE SEARCH FOR
FORGIVENESS

THE SEARCH FOR FORGIVENESS

Pardon and punishment in Islam and Christianity

Chawkat Moucarry

Inter-Varsity Press **ivp**

Inter-Varsity Press
38 De Montfort Street, Leicester LE1 7GP, England
Email: ivp@uccf.org.uk   Website: www.ivpbooks.com

First published 2004

British Library Cataloguing in Publication Data
A catalogue record for this book is available
from the British Library.

ISBN 1−84474−018−8

Set in Monotype Garamond 11/13pt
Typeset in Great Britain by CRB Associates, Reepham, Norfolk
Printed and bound in Great Britain by Creative Print and Design
(Wales), Ebbw Vale

Inter-Varsity Press is the publishing division of the Universities and
Colleges Christian Fellowship (formerly the Inter-Varsity Fellowship), a
student movement linking Christian Unions in universities and colleges
throughout Great Britain, and a member movement of the International
Fellowship of Evangelical Students. For more information about local
and national activities write to UCCF, 38 De Montfort Street, Leicester
LE1 7GP, email us at email@uccf.org.uk or visit the UCCF website at
www.uccf.org.uk.

I dedicate this book to
my son Christophe
and my daughters Marie, Sophie and Irène

May
the forgiving God
fill your lives with love, peace and joy

CONTENTS

TRANSLITERATION OF ARABIC WORDS

١	*a*	ض	*d̲*
ب	*b*	ط	*t̲*
ت	*t*	ظ	*z̲*
ث	*th*	ع	'
ج	*j*	غ	*gh*
ح	*h̲*	ف	*f*
خ	*kh*	ق	*q*
د	*d*	ك	*k*
ذ	*dh*	ل	*l*
ر	*r*	م	*m*
ز	*z̲*	ن	*n*
س	*s*	ـه	*h*
ش	*sh*	و	*w*
ص	*s̲*	ي	*y*
		ء	'

This simplified system does not take into account the difference between short and long vowels. However, the reader familiar with Arabic will easily identify the Arabic words. Those words that have become part of English (e.g. Hadith) have kept their usual spelling. The Prophet's name is spelt 'Muhammad', whereas the slightly different spelling 'Muhammad' is used for other Muslims who have the same name (e.g. Muhammad Shahrastani).

LIST OF TABLES

INTRODUCTION

The only true forgiveness is that which is offered and extended even before the offender has apologised and sought it.
Kierkegaard, *The Lion Christian Quotation Collection*

Do Muslims really believe in a merciful and forgiving God? Is not Allah, *their God*, revengeful and violent? I am often asked these and similar questions by Christians and non-Christians. For many years Islam has suffered a bad name in the West. The tragic events of September 11, 2001, have reinforced people's prejudice against Muslims. Their perception of Islam is usually based on what the mass media say. But, by definition, the media report what is unusual. A train or a plane crash makes the headlines, not the trains or flights that reach their destinations. Yet no-one claims that travelling by train or by air is dangerous; in fact, these forms of transport are much safer than cars and motorcycles. The public image of Islam misrepresents the religion in so far as it reflects Muslim extremists and not Muslims in general.

God's mercy and forgiveness in Islam is the focus of this book. By looking at the Islamic Scriptures (the Qur'an and the Hadith) and what they teach about God, I very much hope that the reader will have a fairer understanding of this religion. I expect Christian readers in particular to be challenged in the way they view Islam. They may well find that God's attributes in Islam and Christianity are closer than they had realized before and that Allah cannot easily be dismissed as 'an alien God'. The word Allah actually predates Islam. It is simply the word for 'God' in Arabic. It is found not only in the Qur'an but in the Arabic translations of the Bible too. All Arabic-speaking believers, Christians as well as Muslims, use it when referring to God.

Generally speaking, Muslims know very little about biblical Christianity. Their understanding is based at best on what the Qur'an says about Christ and Christians, and at worst on the assumption that Christianity and Western culture and politics are all part of the same thing. This is of course a recipe for confusion and the source of serious misunderstanding. Christianity, as taught by Jesus Christ and his disciples, remains unknown to most Muslims. Hence my earnest desire is that this book will also provide an opportunity for the Muslim reader to discover what the Christian faith is all about.

Western society is a secular society, yet it has become the home for many religious communities. This situation presents these communities with new challenges. Will they perceive each other as a potential threat? Or as an opportunity to understand and relate to each other better? Christians, Muslims and people of other faiths must, more urgently than ever, rise to this challenge. The future of society at large depends partly on their willingness and ability to engage with each other in meaningful relationships. They need not only to coexist but also to cooperate for the common good of the wider community. This book, which points out the social implications of the Muslim and Christian faiths, represents a small contribution towards this end.

A study on forgiveness

We will look into forgiveness in Islam and Christianity from different angles, and seek to answer questions such as these: Why and how does God forgive? What is the scope of his forgiveness? What are the implications and the repercussions of his forgiveness in people's lives? The study is based on a PhD dissertation, which was presented at the Sorbonne University, Paris, in 1994,[1] although the present text is very different from the original. The material has been entirely reorganized to suit a wider readership. It is intended for people who have a keen interest in interfaith issues but who do not necessarily have a degree in Islamics or theology. The subject is of course the same: God's forgiveness in Islam. The Christian perspective is incorporated mainly as a biblical response to Islamic understandings of forgiveness. An in-depth study of forgiveness in Christianity is beyond the scope of this book. The purpose of this approach is to highlight the common ground as well as the differences between the two faiths.

Part 1 sets up the theological framework within which God's forgiveness operates in Islam. Six divine attributes have been selected because they are directly related to God's pardon. In fact, these attributes, their respective importance and the ways they have been interpreted by Muslims, provide us with a basic understanding of divine forgiveness in Islam. Their meaning is explained almost exclusively in the light of God's revelation in the Qur'an and the Prophet's teaching in the Hadith. As far as Qur'anic exegesis is concerned, our main resource has been *al-Tafsir al-kabir* (the Great Commentary) by Fakhr al-Din al-Razi (606/1209). This work is acclaimed by Muslims as one of the most authoritative commentaries on the Qur'an; it is certainly the most comprehensive.[2]

Forgiveness in theology

Part 2 moves from the Islamic Scriptures to Islamic theology (*kalam*). The focus in this section is on two specific ways whereby Muslims can obtain God's pardon; that is, repentance and intercession on the Day of Judgment. Islamic theology is more diverse than is often assumed.

As far as the Muslim *community* is concerned, the main groups are the Sunnites, the Shi'ites and the Kharijites. But as far as Islamic *theology* is concerned, the main theological schools are the Sunni schools (representing mainstream Islam), the Mu'tazilite schools (characterized by rationalism) and the Kharijite school (known for its radicalism or 'fundamentalism'). There are three main Sunni schools: the Ash'arite, the Maturidite and the Hanbalite schools. Of all the theological schools, the Mu'tazilite and the Ash'arite

Community Umma	Sunnites	Shi'ites	Kharijites
Theology Kalam	**Sunni** Three main schools: • Ash'arite • Maturidite • Hanbalite Most Sunni theologians are Sunni Muslims.	**Mu'tazili** Two main schools: • Basrian • Baghdadian Mu'tazili theologians are either Sunnites or Shi'ites.	**Khariji**
Sufism Sufiyya	Sunni Sufis	Shi'i Sufis	No Sufis
Jurisprudence Fiqh	Four Sunni schools: • Hanbalite • Hanafite • Malikite • Shafi'ite	Shi'i school	Khariji school

Table 1. The diversity of the Muslim community

schools are the most elaborate and distinctive, which is why the chapters in Part 2 often examine their respective views.

The two levels of community and theology are not to be confused, although they do overlap to some degree. For instance, Sunni Muslims are not all theologically Sunnite: they can be Mu'tazilite or even Kharijite. Conversely, Mu'tazili theologians are found among both the Sunni and the Shi'i communities. A third level of differentiation within the Muslim community relates to Islamic *jurisprudence* (*fiqh*). Interpretation of Islamic law by Sunni jurists has given rise to four orthodox schools of jurisprudence (*madhahib*): Hanbalite, Hanafite, Malikite and Shafi'ite. The first school is the most rigorous, whereas the fourth is the most liberal.

In times of crisis within a Muslim country or internationally

between Muslim and non-Muslim countries, we find a number of
Muslims from both the Sunni and Shi'i communities becoming
more radical and political in their understanding of Islamic
teaching. Osama bin Laden, for example, is a Sunni Muslim but
ideologically tends towards a radical Khariji interpretation of Islam.
Being both against the West and the pro-Western regime in his
own country, Saudi Arabia, he justifies the use of violence to
achieve his aims. Other examples include Palestinian funda-
mentalists opposed to Israel (e.g. those who are members of
organizations such as Jihad or Hamas),[3] Ayatollah Khomeini (the
former Shi'i leader and founder of the Islamic Republic of Iran)
and the Egyptian Sayyid Qutb, a key figure in the Muslim
Brotherhood, whose radical teaching led to his imprisonment and
execution in 1966 in Cairo. Such extremism is not representative of
Islam but is fuelled by political, social and economic injustice. In a
sense, Islamic fundamentalism is how some Muslims respond to
the injustice they suffer: it channels their cry of anger and pain.

Forgiveness in mysticism

Part 3 looks at God's forgiveness in Sufism, or Islamic mysticism.
This spiritual trend is found right across the Muslim community.
Some Muslims (e.g. Ghazali, Qushayri) are both mystics and
theologians. Repentance is a foundational concept in Sufism, a
concept that goes far beyond divine forgiveness. It is the first and
decisive step that all people (including Muslims) need to take in
order to return to where they came from: God. Ibn 'Arabi (638/
1240) is arguably the greatest Sufi of all times and probably the
most influential in our time. The final chapters in this section
investigate the concept of 'divine mercy' (*rahma*) which plays an
eminent role in Ibn 'Arabi's mystical philosophy.

Forgiveness in daily life and ethics

Forgiveness is a divine promise that reflects who God is. It should
also be a distinctive mark of our lives. Islamic teaching urges

Muslims to seek God's forgiveness and to forgive those who have wronged them. Part 4 focuses on forgiveness in Islamic ethics. What does the *shari'a* (Islamic law) teach? How does forgiveness relate to penal law in Islam? Should Muslims forgive everyone in all circumstances?

The historical scope of this study spans the first six centuries of the Islamic era, a period that has seen the full development of Islamic theology and mysticism. Contemporary Islamic thought is still very dependent on what Muslim scholars and mystics taught and wrote during the classical age of Islam. With regard to forgiveness, the only significant development is found in the Islamic penal code. Some Muslims today observe that this code is nowhere fully implemented in the Muslim world due to the fact that our world is profoundly different from the one in which Islam was born. In the current climate of secularization and globalization Muslim societies are experiencing dramatic changes. Some are calling for Islamic law to be revisited and updated if Islam is to be relevant in the twenty-first century.

The Christian perspective on forgiveness presented in this book assumes that the Bible, both the Old and New Testaments, is reliable. Its teaching on forgiveness is summed up in Jesus' mission, which culminated in his death and resurrection. I am well aware that Islam challenges both the reliability of the Bible and the reality of Jesus' crucifixion, and have discussed these two issues in great detail in a recent book.[4] In a sense, this study builds on the argument developed in that book as regards the historicity of Jesus' crucifixion and resurrection on the one hand and the trustworthiness of the Bible on the other.

Belief in God's mercy and forgiveness is crucial for Muslims, for Christians and for all believers. This belief has, or should have, a real and profound impact on their lives. For Christians it ought to be a continually life-changing experience. As an Arab Christian, I know personally how important it is to forgive and to be forgiven, particularly in relation to Muslims and Jews. After all, whether we are believers or not, forgiveness (or the lack of it) is an integral part of our human experience. Forgiveness heals, restores and reconciles; resentment hurts, destroys and divides. We all know that forgiving can be hard, very hard. Asking for forgiveness is difficult too, perhaps more difficult than forgiving. Yet, to forgive or to ask to be forgiven is the ultimate test of one's love. 'Forgiveness is man's deepest need and highest achievement.'[5]

Notes

1. The dissertation was presented to the École Pratique des Hautes Études, Section Sciences Religieuses of Sorbonne University, Paris. The title is 'Pardon, repentir, conversion: étude de ces concepts en Islam et de leurs équivalents bibliques ('Forgiveness, repentance, conversion: study of these concepts in Islam and their biblical equivalents'). The viva (17 November 1994) resulted in the dissertation being received with distinction ('Mention très honorable avec les félicitations du Jury').

2. The modern editions of this commentary come in sixteen volumes and thirty-two parts, each volume having two parts. In the references to this work, the first figure is the volume number, and the second is the part: e.g. 'VI:11, pp. 78–83' refers to 'volume 6, part 11, pages 78–83'.

3. The word 'ḥamas' means 'boldness'. It is an acronym which stands for 'Islamic Resistance Movement'.

4. Moucarry, *Faith to Faith: Christianity and Islam in Dialogue*. Also published in the United States with the title *The Prophet and the Messiah: An Arab Christian's Perspective on Islam and Christianity*.

5. Horace Bushnell, in Castle, *Hodder Book of Christian Quotations*, p. 82.

PART ONE

FORGIVENESS
IN GOD'S ATTRIBUTES

1. GOD IS MERCIFUL

bismi-llah al-raḥman al-raḥim
In the name of God, the Ever-Merciful, the All-Merciful

These words, known as the *basmala*, are well known to Muslims and anyone familiar with the Qur'an. At the beginning of every sura except the ninth we find this proclamation of the mercy of God. The names al-Raḥman, 'the Ever-Merciful', and al-Raḥim, 'the All-Merciful', feature prominently in many other verses of the Qur'an, and belong to God's ninety-nine *asma' ḥusna* (most beautiful names).[1] Mercy is clearly one of God's key attributes.

The meaning of God's mercy

The derivation of an Arabic word is often a good starting point for investigating its meaning. The word *raḥma* (mercy) comes from the same root as *raḥim* (womb), which suggests that the relationship between a mother and her child may in some way parallel that between God and humankind. Lending weight to this argument is a tradition found in the Hadith clearly comparing God's mercy to a mother's affection for a child:

There were brought some prisoners to God's Messenger amongst whom there was also a woman, who was searching [for a baby to feed] and when she found a child amongst the prisoners, she took hold of it, pressed it against her chest and provided it suck.

The Prophet said,

– 'Do you think this woman would ever afford to throw her child in the Fire?'

We replied,

– 'By God, so far as it lies in her power, she would never throw the child in Fire.'

The Prophet then said,

– 'God is more merciful to His servants than this woman is to her child.'[2]

Mercy in this instance describes a relationship between two unequal parties, wherein a caring person provides for a subordinate's need. The caring person is characterized by the ability and willingness to help those he or she considers special. According to the Qur'an, we are all precious creatures, for God created us in 'the finest form of creaturehood' (95:4; cf. 64:3); we are his representatives on earth (2:30) and he is nearer to us than our jugular vein (50:16). The Creator God is the merciful God in that he fulfils the needs of his creatures who depend on his guidance and help. His mercy is perfect and inclusive, as Ghazali explains, for it goes beyond meeting the basic needs of his creatures:

Perfect mercy is pouring out benefaction to those in need, and directing it to them, for their care; and inclusive mercy is when it embraces deserving and undeserving alike. The mercy of God – great and glorious – is both perfect and inclusive [tamma wa-'amma]: perfect inasmuch as it wants to fulfil the needs of those in need and does meet them; and inclusive inasmuch as it embraces both deserving and undeserving, encompassing this world and the next, and includes bare necessities and needs, and special gifts over and above them. So He is utterly and truly merciful.[3]

Razi, the author of al-Tafsir al-kabir (the Great Commentary), explains that because God is merciful he does not punish people on the spot when they do wrong, but gives them respite so that they may repent. The Qur'an asserts twice that 'God has prescribed mercy unto Himself' (6:12, 54). Consider sura 6 verse 12:

> Say: 'Travel through the earth and see what was the end of those who rejected Truth.'
> Say: 'To whom belongs all that is in the heavens and on earth?'
> Say: 'To God. He has prescribed Mercy unto Himself. That He will gather you together for the Day of Judgement, there is no doubt whatever. It is they who have lost their own souls, that will not believe.' (6:11–12)

Here God's mercy is related to the Day of Judgment. Razi's interpretation is somewhat paradoxical. Without the fear inspired by the Day of Judgment, he says, life on earth would be characterized by lawlessness and, in order to restrain these excesses, by repression and violence. Since the threat of eternal judgment should prevent social disorder, it constitutes a major manifestation of God's mercy in the world. God is under no obligation to act mercifully, comments the author, but he does so because of his favour and generosity.[4] In this context Razi quotes a well-known hadith which points out that right from the beginning God decided to show his mercy: 'When God completed creating the cosmos He wrote down in a book right above his throne: "Verily, My mercy predominates My wrath".'[5]

The scope of God's mercy

According to the Qur'an (7:156), God's mercy extends to 'all things'. Muslims have interpreted this text in two ways. For some, it means that God's universal mercy in this world is shown to all people without exception, yet in the hereafter God will be merciful only with believers. Others say that this statement about God's mercy must be understood in relative rather than absolute terms (see 27:23). In other words, although God is merciful, the words 'all things' do not imply that every single creature will necessarily benefit from his mercy.[6]

The cosmos reflects God's mercy through the alternation of day and night (28:73) and that of the seasons (30:50). The wind, rain and stars, and indeed everything in creation, speak of the Creator's mercy (25:48; 27:63; 30:46). Divine mercy is also revealed through God's revelation to humankind. The Scriptures – the Torah (7:154) as well as the Qur'an (6:157) – testify to his care (7:52). Similarly, the mission of the Prophets is a token of God's concern for his human creatures. Thus the mission of Jesus (19:21) and that of Muhammad (21:107) represent powerful demonstrations of God's mercy for all the peoples of the earth. In these ways Muslims accept that his mercy is available for everyone to enjoy.

The forgiveness of sin

One of God's greatest blessings is the forgiveness of sin, for it is this blessing that will determine our destiny in the hereafter. The Qur'an makes it clear that forgiveness flows from God's mercy like a river from a mountain:

> Our Lord! ... Lay not on us a burden that we are not able to bear. Blot out our sins. Forgive us and show us Your mercy, for You are our Protector.
> (2:286)

> If you are slain, or if you die for God, [you will enjoy] God's forgiveness and mercy, which is far better than all their riches.
> (3:157)

> They [Adam and Eve] said, 'Our Lord! We have wronged our own souls. If You do not forgive us and bestow Your mercy upon us, surely we shall be among the lost ones.'
> (7:23; cf. 11:47; 23:109)

> [Moses said:] You are our Protector! So forgive us and show us Your mercy, for You are the best of those who forgive.
> (7:155)

A group of My servants used to pray, 'Our Lord! We have believed. So
forgive us and have mercy upon us, for You are the best of those who
show mercy.'
(23:109)

Say, 'My Lord! Forgive and show [Your] mercy, for You are the best of
those who show mercy.'
(23:118; cf. 7:151)

Say, 'O My servants who have transgressed against their souls! Despair
not of God's mercy. God forgives all sins, for He is the All-Forgiving,
the All-Merciful.'
(39:53)

The fact that God is merciful means that on the Day of
Judgment the reward for every good deed will be double (4:40)
and even ten times its worth (6:60; cf. 2:261). In other words, God
will take into account good deeds when considering evil ones. The
Hadith underlines that good works are weightier than bad ones:
'When someone excels in their religion, then their good deeds will
be awarded ten times to seven hundred times for each good deed
whereas a bad deed will be recorded as it is.'[7]

God's generosity is such that he is just with respect to an evil
action but gracious when rewarding a good action. Provided that
we ascribe no partner to God, nothing can limit his willingness to
forgive our sins:

Whoever comes with one good deed, there are in store for him ten like
it and even more, and whoever comes with one evil deed, it is only for it
that he will be called into account. I even forgive him [as I like].
Whoever draws close to Me by the span of a palm I draw close to him
by the cubit. Whoever draws close to Me by the cubit I draw close to
him by the space covered by two hands. Whoever walks towards Me I
rush towards him. Whoever meets Me in the state that his sins fill the
earth, but not associating anything with Me, I would meet him with the
same vastness of pardon.[8]

God's mercy is much greater than his anger. He is our Judge, but he is a merciful Judge. He knows that 'man was created weak' (4:28), and it is this weakness that explains why we find it difficult to obey his commands and to do what is good. Sufis (Muslim mystics) have an acute awareness of their shortcomings, but they also know that their failures are easily matched by God's even greater kindness. They love God for who he is and are confident that he will not disappoint them. Abu Sulayman al-Darimi takes heart in God's mercy to plead against his justice:

> My Lord! If You demand that I pay the penalty for my sins,
> I will surely ask Your pardon.
> If You demand that I pay for my meanness,
> I will surely appeal to Your generosity and large-heartedness.
> If You demand that I pay for my evil conduct,
> I will surely appeal to Your goodness.
> If You send me to hell,
> I will surely tell the people of hell that I love You.

> We [God] called Abu Sulayman and told him:
> You will not go to hell but to paradise. You will speak about Our love to the people of paradise, not to the people of hell. The rightful place for God's lovers is paradise, and the rightful place for His enemies is hell.[9]

Mercy and love may not be the same but they are certainly akin to each other. Although the Qur'an speaks far more often about God's mercy, it does have a few texts about his love, which is closely associated with his forgiveness: 'Say [O Muhammad!]: "If you love me then follow me: God will love you and forgive your sins. God is All-Forgiving and All-Merciful"' (3:31; cf. 5:57).

God is merciful and compassionate

Hebrew, like Arabic, is a Semitic language. In the Bible, God is described as *rahûm*, merciful, and *hannûn*, compassionate.[10] These attributes are parallel to God's names in Islam: *rahman* (or *rahim*), 'merciful', and _ḥannan_, 'full of pity'. Muslim scholars consider these attributes as virtually synonymous.[11]

The first occurrence of 'merciful and compassionate' is found in the context of God's revelation to Moses. The book of Exodus reports a significant event that occurred during the Israelites' journey in the desert. This episode, echoed in the Qur'an (2:51–54; 7:148–155), took place after God had made a covenant with the people of Israel (Exod. 19). Moses was on the mountain receiving the law of the covenant. After he had been there for forty days (24:18), the Israelites grew impatient and eventually chose to worship God in their own way. They represented him in the form of a golden calf (32:1–6) in stark disobedience to his command against idolatry (20:4–6). Therefore God was extremely angry with them. He wanted to destroy them completely and to make Moses the father of a new nation. But Moses declined God's offer and pleaded with him to forgive his people (32:7–34). God did punish the people by putting to death three thousand men and by sending a plague on the rest of them (32:35), but judgment was not his final word: he is a merciful God. He called Moses back and renewed the promises and the covenant he had made with the Israelites (33:12–17). He also gave Moses a fresh revelation of who God is:

> The LORD, the LORD, the merciful and compassionate God, slow to
> anger, abounding in love and faithfulness, maintaining love to
> thousands, and forgiving wickedness, rebellion and sin. Yet he does not
> leave the guilty unpunished; he punishes the children and their children
> for the sin of the fathers to the third and fourth generation.
> (Exod. 34:6–7)[12]

At such a critical moment in the history of the Israelites this revelation represents a particularly rich disclosure of God's character. Years later, Moses would refer to it when his people displayed an incredibly ungrateful attitude towards their Creator (Num. 14:18). This revelation about God's mercy, recorded in several psalms (Pss. 86:15; 103:8; 111:4; 145:8), would be remembered again and again by Israel's prophets (Joel 2:13; Jonah 4:2) and leaders (2 Chr. 30:9; Neh. 9:17, 31).

Just as with the Arabic word, the Hebrew word for 'merciful'

derives from the same root as the word for 'womb', *reḥem*. It refers
to a mother's affection for her child. In a way not dissimilar from
the hadith quoted at the beginning of this chapter God himself
compares his care for his people to a mother's care for her child.
When the people were in exile, God reassured them that his loving
care was even greater than that of a mother, despite what their
historical circumstances may have suggested:

> Can a mother forget the baby at her breast
>   and have no compassion on the child she has borne?
> Though she may forget,
>   I will not forget you!
> See, I have engraved you on the palms of my hands.
> (Is. 49:15–16a; cf. Is. 66:12–13)

If we consider again the revelation God made to Moses, we
notice a certain 'imbalance' between his mercy and his condemnation. His mercy manifests itself through his love and faithfulness to
his people. He shows his love to a thousand generations, whereas
his punishment lasts only for three or four generations. Again this
is just a different way of expressing the same truth about God. As
the above-quoted hadith says, his mercy is far greater than his
anger.

So do these similarities mean that the Islamic and Christian
understandings of God's mercy are the same? I suggest that there
are two important differences.

How God shares in our suffering

The first difference in the understanding of God's mercy is about
what prompts him to be merciful. In Islam it is his goodness and his
generosity. While affirming these attributes, Christians believe that
God's mercy is equally motivated by his sharing in human suffering. This is what he declared when he called Moses to deliver the
Israelites from Egypt: 'I have indeed seen the misery of my people
in Egypt. I have heard them crying out because of their slave
drivers, and I am concerned about their suffering' (Exod. 3:7).

Likewise, Jesus' mission expressed his deep compassion for
people. His healing and preaching ministry demonstrated his

solidarity with the needy as well as his determination to release them from their spiritual and physical oppression: 'When he [Jesus] saw the crowds, he had compassion on them, because they were harassed and helpless, like sheep without a shepherd' (Matt. 9:36). Similarly, God is portrayed as 'the Father of compassion and the God of all comfort' (2 Cor. 1:3).

As creatures we are unique because we have been created like no other creature. The first chapter in the Bible teaches that God made us in his likeness:

> God created man
>   in his own image,
> in the image of God
>   he created him;
> male and female
>   he created them.'
> (Gen. 1:27)

The way we have been made implies that God is close enough to us to feel what we feel. He is moved by our suffering. We are close enough to him and he suffers with us when our deepest needs remain unmet. His mercy is rooted in the sympathy he has for us. Thus he is not only merciful, but also *compassionate*, for compassion literally means 'to suffer with'. Because God's mercy stems from his compassion, it is more personal and more authentic. In Islam God is 'full of mercy' but not 'full of compassion', because, unlike human creatures, he is not subject to emotions. Ghazali, a Sufi and theologian, discusses this issue in his treatise on God's most beautiful names: 'Mercy is not without a painful empathy which affects the merciful, and moves him to satisfy the needs of the one receiving mercy. Yet the Lord – praise be to Him most high – transcends that, so you may think that this diminishes the meaning of mercy.'[13]

Ghazali goes on to prove why the Islamic understanding of God's mercy is perfect. He presents a threefold argument:

1. Although God's mercy is not based on compassion, it perfectly achieves its aims; that is, it meets our needs: 'the perfection of mercy depends on the perfection of its fruits'.

2. God is powerful; hence he does not suffer: 'the suffering of the merciful only stems from a weakness and defects in himself'.

3. God's mercy is pure mercy, it is only concerned with the sufferer: '[the] one who is merciful out of empathy and suffering comes close to intending to alleviate his own suffering and sensitivity by his actions, thereby looking after himself and seeking his own goals'.[14]

Ghazali's first argument is good, except that it raises the question about what our needs really are. Christianity perceives people's needs as more radical than does Islam. We need more than God's help, guidance and forgiveness. We need to be reconciled with God and to be saved by him; he is the only one who has the power to save us. Ghazali's second argument is debatable. Suffering does not necessarily point to weakness. It can point to love and to the strength of enduring suffering without being overcome by it. As human experience shows, genuine love is, more often than not, a suffering love. This is true for everyone regardless of social, religious or cultural background. Ghazali's third argument is also questionable. Why should a merciful act be seen as selfish if by meeting people's needs one demonstrates at the same time a genuine love for them? Such love can be perfect only when both sides enjoy fellowship with each other.

How God loves us

The second difference between the Christian and the Islamic understandings of God's mercy is related to *the role of love in each religion*. In the Qur'an the emphasis is on God's mercy rather than his love. In the Bible, however, the overwhelming emphasis is on God's love. 'God is love' (1 John 4:8, 16). God loves everyone, the righteous and the unrighteous; indeed, God loves the world (John 3:16).

Love in the Qur'an is conditional. God loves those who obey him (3:76, 146, 159); he does not love those who disobey him (3:32, 57). It is worth noting that *muḥibb*, 'loving', is not one of God's ninety-nine names. The nearest equivalent is the name Wadud, 'loving-kind' (11:90; 85:14). Ghazali takes this name to mean 'merciful', except that the person receiving God's mercy is not a needy one: 'Its meaning is close to "the Merciful", but mercy is linked with one who receives mercy, and the one who receives mercy is needy and poor. So the actions of the Merciful presuppose there being one who is weak to receive mercy, while the actions of the Loving-Kind do not require that.'[15] Sufis excepted, Muslims understand God's love in terms of his will to bless his people in this world and in the next.[16] Ghazali relates God's love to his mercy and explains how God shows his love in different ways: 'The Infinitely Good [*rahman*] is He who loves men, first by creating them; second, by guiding them to faith and to the means of salvation; third, by making them happy in the next world; and fourth, by granting them the contemplation of His noble face.'[17]

Thus, in Islam, God's love is not expressed directly, in terms of a personal relationship; it is mediated through his gifts. God loves his people by bestowing his blessings on them. Insofar as love is seen as an emotion, it cannot characterize God. Being transcendent, God is beyond our world of senses, feelings and emotions.

Christians, however, understand God's love as being expressed in a far more personal way. Love is mercy and much more. Love is an emotion and much more. It is a covenant relationship in which both parties are unreservedly committed to each other. This covenant between the Creator and humankind, initiated by God, is a demonstration of perfect love. To love God's way is to be willing to suffer, to forgive, to redeem, and to rebuild broken relationships. Such love is fulfilled when we respond to the loving God and are reconciled to him. 'And so we know and rely on the love God has for us. God is love. Whoever lives in love lives in God, and God in him' (1 John 4:16).

Notes

1. In addition to the *basmala*, the name al-Rahman is found fifty-seven times in the Qur'an and in most cases replaces 'Allah'. It is coupled only with *al-rahim* in five verses (1:3; 2:163; 27:30; 41:2; 59:22). *Al-rahim* occurs 115 times. With four exceptions it is always coupled with another divine name. Unlike *rahim*, *rahman* is never found as an attribute of a creature.
2. Muslim, *tawba* 22 [4947]:IV, bk 37, no. 6635, p. 1438; Bukhari, *adab* 18 [5540]:VIII, bk 73, no. 28, p. 19.

3. Ghazali, *Names*, p. 53.
4. In Arabic: *ijab al-fadli wa-l-karam*. Razi on 6:12; VI:12, p. 137.
5. Muslim, *tawba* 14 [4039]:IV, bk 37, no. 6626, p. 1437; Bukhari, *tawhid* 15 [6855]:IX, bk 93, no. 501, p. 369.
6. Razi on 7:156; VIII:15, p. 19.
7. Bukhari, *iman* 31 [40]:I, bk 2, no. 40, p. 36; Muslim, *iman* 59 [184]:I, bk 1, no. 234, p. 75.
8. Muslim, *dhikr* 22 [4852]:IV, bk 35, no. 6499, p. 1413.
9. Hurayfish, *Rawd*, II, p. 81.
10. The words *rahim* and *hannun* are each found thirteen times in the Old Testament. The two attributes are found together eleven times (Exod. 34:6; Neh. 9:17, 31; 2 Chr. 30:9; Pss. 86:15; 103:8; 111:4; 112:4; 135:8; Joel 2:13; Jonah 4:2). Except in Psalm 112:4, where they describe 'the [blessed] man who fears the Lord' (v. 1), they are always applied to God.
11. Ibn Furak, *Mujarrad*, p. 57; Gimaret, *Noms*, pp. 78, 383–384. The divine name Hannan is based on a Qur'anic text portraying the mission of John the Baptist as an expression of God's pity (19:12). It is also connected with a hadith reported by Ibn Hanbal in which a man in hell prays to God and addresses him as *ya hannan ya mannan*, 'O You who are full of pity! O You who are giver [of blessings]'. After a thousand years God responds to his prayer and lets him come to paradise (*musnad baqi al-mukthirin* 7 [12931]).
12. The translation is that of the New International Version, except that the word for *rahim* (compassionate) has been replaced with 'merciful', and the word for *hannun* (gracious) with 'compassionate'. The first word is translated as 'merciful' in some English translations (e.g. English Standard Version, New King James Version, Revised Standard Version). The two words are translated as 'merciful and compassionate' in the *Complete Jewish Bible*, tr. David H. Stern (Jerusalem: Jewish New Testament Publications, 1998). The meaning of the two words is fairly similar. They refer to God's care for his creatures, especially those who cry out to him for help.
13. Ghazali, *Names*, p. 53.
14. Ibid., pp. 53–54.
15. Ibid., pp. 118–119.
16. Gimaret, *Noms*, pp. 423–426.
17. Ghazali, *Names*, p. 55.

2. GOD IS FORGIVING

The Qur'an describes God as *ghafir*, 'the Forgiving': '[God is] the One who forgives sin and accepts repentance. He is stern in retribution and He is immensely kind' (40:3).

This verse underlines two attributes of God: he is lenient (in that he forgives sin), but he is also just (in that he punishes the sinner). Many Qur'anic texts stress these two aspects (e.g. 41:43; 57:20). Razi comments that the reference to God's punishment in this verse is preceded by two references to his clemency (he 'forgives sin and accepts repentance'), and is followed by a reminder of his kindness ('He is immensely kind'). In other words, God's justice is surpassed by his mercy and generosity.[1]

The noun *ghafir*, 'forgiving', is found only once in the Qur'an. It is derived from the verb *ghafara*, which is found frequently, and whose primary meaning is 'to hide' or 'to cover over'; hence 'to forgive'.[2] In addition to *ghafir*, two other nouns derive from the same verb: *ghafur*, 'all-forgiving', and *ghaffar*, 'ever-forgiving'.[3] They are intensive forms of *ghafir* and are both divine names; that is, they are found in the list of 'God's most beautiful names' (7:180; 59:24).

Muslims have interpreted the intensive form *ghafur* in the sense that God forgives *all* sins, and that he even forgives those who persist in wrongdoing (73:20).[4] Razi explains that God is always ready to forgive. As far as God is concerned, for him, forgiving is as easy and natural as it is for people to do their ordinary job (71:10).[5]

Another divine name describing God as the One who forgives sin is *'afuww*, which literally means 'the Effacer of sins'. Ghazali remarks that 'this name [*'afuww*] is more expressive than that [*ghafur*], for "all-forgiving" connotes concealment, while "effacer" suggests erasing, and erasing is more effectual than concealment'.[6]

Forgiveness and mercy

God is described as both *ghafur*, 'All-Forgiving', and *rahim*, 'All-Merciful', seventy-two times. Razi explains the link between God's mercy and his forgiveness in two ways. Either God is forgiving, because he covers people's evil deeds in this life; and merciful, because he forgives them in the hereafter. Or God is forgiving, as he does not punish people for their evil deeds; and merciful, as he rewards them for their good works (3:89).[7] Thus divine forgiveness and divine reward are two distinct but related blessings.

To forgive is a divine prerogative. The Qur'an asks, 'Who forgives sins apart from God?' (3:135). It is of course a rhetorical question, because ultimately only God is qualified to forgive us or to punish us for our sins. On the Day of Judgment we will be accountable only to him, our divine Judge. Thus, strictly speaking, only God is entitled to forgive (74:56). Yet God has given us the right to forgive those who do harm to us. Indeed, he has encouraged us to do so.

God will always be 'the best of those who forgive' (7:155). Addressing God, Razi explains why divine forgiveness is superior to human forgiveness:

> Everyone except You [God] forgive in order to be praised, to be rewarded or to get rid of painful feelings. In short, people forgive either to gain an advantage or to set themselves free from something harmful. As for You [God], You forgive Your servants for no other purpose or reward than bestowing Your favour and generosity.[8]

Asking for forgiveness

God's prophets proclaimed God's willingness to forgive sin (20:82;
74:56). Jesus excepted, they all asked God to forgive them their
own sins: Adam and Eve (7:23), Noah (11:47), Abraham (26:82),
Moses (7:151; 28:16), David (38:24–25), Solomon (38:35) and
Muhammad (4:106; 40:55; 110:3). In one way or another they all
transgressed God's law. The prophets also prayed on behalf of
others, asking God to forgive the sins of their people: Noah
(71:28), Abraham (9:114; 14:41; 19:47; 26:86; 60:4), Jacob (12:98)
and Jesus (5:118). Muhammad too interceded for his community:
'Know [O Muhammad], therefore, that there is no god but God
and ask forgiveness for your transgression and for the believers,
men and women. For God knows how you move about and how
you dwell in your homes' (47:19; cf. 4:64; 60:12; 63:5).

It is not only prophets who intercede for others: angels too ask
God to grant his forgiveness to those who live on earth, especially
the believers:

> And the angels celebrate the praises of their Lord, and pray for
> forgiveness for [all] beings on earth.
> (42:5)

> Those who bear up the Throne [of God] and those around it celebrate
> the praise of their Lord, and they believe in Him. They implore
> forgiveness for the believers: 'Our Lord! Your mercy and Your
> knowledge embrace all things. Forgive those that repent and follow
> Your way. Protect them from the punishment of Hell.'
> (40:7)

God promises to answer those who ask him to forgive their
wrongdoing (4:110). The fact that he is a forgiving God should encourage people to ask his forgiveness. We find in the Qur'an several
prayers in which Muslims appeal to God's mercy and clemency:

> Our Lord! Do not hold it against us if we forget and do wrong.
> Our Lord! Do not lay upon us the burden like that which You laid
> upon those who lived before us.

Our Lord! Do not lay upon us a burden that is beyond our ability to bear.

Pardon us!

Forgive us!

Have mercy upon us!

You are our Protector: grant us victory over the unbelieving people.

(2:286)

God's readiness to forgive

God invites people to come to him continually: 'Press on towards the forgiveness of your Lord and a garden as wide as the heavens and the earth, made ready for those who fear God' (3:133). He will never put off a person who appeals to his mercy. People may keep sinning, but as long as they come back to God and seek his forgiveness they will not be disappointed. Therefore no-one should despair of God's pardon, not even those who seem to be irresistibly attracted to sin. God promises that he will forgive their sins:

> If somebody commits a sin and then says, 'O my Lord! I have sinned, please forgive me!' and his Lord says, 'My servant has known that he has a Lord who forgives sins and punishes for it. I therefore have forgiven My servant [his sin].' Then he remains without committing any sin for a while and then again commits another sin and says, 'O my Lord! I have committed another, please forgive me,' and his Lord says, 'My servant has known that he has a Lord who forgives sins and punishes for it. I therefore have forgiven My slave [his sin].' Then he remains without committing any other sin for a while and then commits another sin and says, 'O my Lord! I have committed another sin, please forgive me,' and his Lord says, 'My servant has known that he has a Lord who forgives sins and punishes for it. I therefore have forgiven My servant [his sin], let him do whatever he likes.'[9]

Thus there seems to be no end to God's readiness to forgive his human creatures. It is as though God's glory requires that he is not only merciful but also forgiving. Certainly, God alone has the right to forgive, but, more than that, he ought to forgive in order to be

God. To forgive is an essential characteristic of being divine. Just as granting forgiveness gives evidence that the Creator is a merciful Judge, receiving forgiveness gives evidence that we are indeed God's creatures. Our weakness, ordained by God (4:28), and our need for forgiveness are both characteristic of being human. Thus the relationship between the Creator and his creatures ought to be that of forgiver–forgiven: 'If you were not to commit sin, God would sweep you out of existence and He would replace you by those people who would commit sin and seek forgiveness from God, and He would have pardoned them.'[10]

God will always forgive people their sins if they seek his forgiveness. Does God's readiness to forgive cause people to abuse his mercy? Is it possible that people will use it as an excuse for complacency? If they do, they will prove that they have a poor relationship with him and that they do not have true fellowship. Fear of God's judgment should deter them from being complacent. Furthermore, there is a higher motive for complying with his command. A well-known Sufi, Dhu l-Nun, refers to two different reasons for us to obey God. We are to respond to God's generosity and to fear his judgment:

> Among God's servants there are those who give up sinning because they feel shameful in relation to his generosity after they stopped sinning for fear of his judgement. Even if God told you: 'Do whatever you like, I will not hold it against you', his generosity should fill you with shame and strengthen your determination to stop disobeying him. This is how you should respond to God's generosity if you are a free, generous and grateful servant. If you do not obey God in response to his generosity, you should at least fear his judgement.[11]

God does not treat us as our sins deserve

The text from Exodus quoted in the previous chapter exalts God's mercy. Because God is merciful and compassionate, he forgives 'wickedness, rebellion and sin' (Exod. 34:7). The fact that man's disobedience is referred to in this text with three different words suggests that there is no sin beyond God's pardon. God forgives all

sins, no matter what they are. The Qur'an affirms this too: 'Say: "O
My servants who have transgressed against their souls! Despair not
of God's mercy. God forgives all sins, for He is the All-Forgiving,
the All-Merciful" ' (39:53).

The revelation given to Moses concerning God's forgiveness
nurtured the faith of the Israelites down the centuries. It became
part of their faithful response to God. When they were overwhelmed by the awareness of their guilt, they took heart in the fact
that God did not treat them as their sins deserved. God's pardon
demonstrated his compassion for his people: a compassion
comparable to that of a loving father for his children:

> [The LORD] made known his ways to Moses,
> > his deeds to the people of Israel:
> The LORD is compassionate and gracious,
> > slow to anger, abounding in love.
> He will not always accuse,
> > nor will he harbour his anger for ever;
> he does not treat us as our sins deserve
> > or repay us according to our iniquities.
> For as high as the heavens are above the earth,
> > so great is his love for those who fear him;
> as far as the east is from the west,
> > so far has he removed our transgressions from us.
> As a father has compassion on his children,
> > so the LORD has compassion on those who fear him;
> for he knows how we are formed,
> > he remembers that we are dust.
> (Ps. 103:7–14; cf. Pss. 32:1–2; 65:3; 78:38; 130:3–4)

Although God is in no way tolerant of or indulgent towards sin,
he is nevertheless eager to forgive and not to hold our sins against
us. He holds his people accountable for their transgressions; not
in order to humiliate, punish or destroy them, but that they might
acknowledge their wrongdoing and be forgiven:

> 'Come now, let us reason together,'
> > says the LORD.

'Though your sins are like scarlet,
    they shall be as white as snow;
Though they are red as crimson,
    they shall be like wool.'
(Is. 1:18; cf. Is. 57:16; Mic. 7:18–20)

Being merciful and forgiving is indeed a prominent aspect of
God's glory. As human beings we depend on our Creator and it is
our duty to be grateful for all his blessings – especially his pardon.
It reveals the extent of his love, demonstrates his sovereignty as
supreme Judge, and discloses his majesty:

I, even I, am he who blots out
    your transgressions, for my own sake,
    and remembers your sins no more.
(Is. 43:25; cf. Ezek. 20:44)

Yet, unlike what the aforementioned hadith suggests, God does
not *need* to forgive in order to be fully God. Neither do we need to
be forgiven in order to be fully human. This suggestion does justice
neither to God nor to us. Rather, it appears to justify evil and to
diminish both the seriousness of sin and our own responsibility
for it.

Forgiveness is at the heart of the gospel. In the only recorded
prayer Jesus taught his disciples he urged them to seek God's
pardon: 'Forgive us our sins as we forgive those who sin against us'
(Matt. 6:12). It is worth noting that asking God's forgiveness is not
part of the equivalent Islamic prayer, al-Fatiha (1:1–7). However,
we do find such prayers in other parts of the Qur'an:

Our Lord! We heard someone calling us to faith, 'Believe in your Lord.'
We have believed.
Our Lord! Forgive us our sins and pardon our evil deeds.
Accept us with the righteous ones.
(3:193)

Not only did Jesus teach his disciples to seek God's forgiveness;
he granted God's pardon to several people during his mission. He

did that even before people made their request. In doing so he was making a point. God is so forgiving that he offers his forgiveness even before people repent. God's initiative in forgiving people is meant to cause them to repent and to adopt a new lifestyle. Jesus said to the woman who was accused of adultery, 'Go now and leave your life of sin' (John 8:11).

What about Razi's comment that, unlike us, God forgives for no other reason than his generosity? It is helpful and even necessary to be aware that when we forgive others, our motivation is not always pure. We often seek our own well-being as much if not more than the well-being of the offender. From a Christian perspective, forgiving others in the same way God does, means taking the initiative to forgive. It also means forgiving in order to re-establish the broken relationship with the other party. In this sense, forgiving is only the first step towards reconciliation. God's forgiveness is unselfish but it does have a purpose. We are precious in God's sight, more precious than children in the eyes of their parents. This is why, through forgiving our sins, God wants to bring us back to himself and to restore his friendship with us.

Is it as easy and natural for God to forgive as Razi suggests? If forgiving were as natural for God as building a house is for a builder, would we have reason to praise him for doing what he is expected to do? In fact, because he is just and holy, it would be just as natural for him to punish us for our sins. For God to forgive our sins without denying his justice and holiness is not as easy as it may seem, yet this is exactly what he has done through the mission of Jesus Christ. This mission was powerful but also costly. It perfectly fulfilled both God's love for us and his condemnation of our sin. Jesus described his mission to his disciples as follows:

> Greater love has no-one than this, that he lay down his life for his friends ... I no longer call you servants, because a servant does not know his master's business. Instead, I have called you friends, for everything that I learned from my Father I have made known to you. (John 15:13, 15)

Notes

1. Razi on 40:3; XIV:27, pp. 24–26.

2. Basically four verbs refer to God's forgiveness: *ghafara*, *'afa*, *kaffara* and *taba*. The verb *safaha* is only used for human forgiveness; i.e., people forgiving each other. *Ghafara* and *kaffara* literally mean 'to hide', whereas *'afa* means 'to erase' and *taba* 'to return'. The verb *kaffara 'an* is used only with God as the subject (fourteen times). The noun *kaffara* designates a reparative (atoning, expiatory) deed such as forgiving an offence (5:45), feeding or clothing the poor, fasting, setting free a slave (5:89, 95). The noun *'afuww*, 'pardoning', is a divine name and so is *tawwab*, 'returning'. The first occurs five times in the Qur'an and the second twelve.

3. *Ghafir* is found only once in the Qur'an (40:3), *ghafur* ninety-one times and *ghaffar* five times (20:82; 38:66; 39:5; 40:42; 71:10).

4. Razi on 73:20; XV:30, p. 166.

5. Razi on 71:10; XV:30, p. 122.

6. Ghazali, *Names*, pp. 138–139.

7. Razi on 3:89; IV:8, p. 113.

8. Razi on 7:155; VIII:15, p. 18.

9. Bukhari, *tawhid* 35 [6953]:IX, bk 93, no. 598, p. 440; Muslim, *tawba* 29 [4953]:IV, bk 37, no. 6642, p. 1439.

10. Muslim, *tawba* 11 [4934]:IV, bk 37, no. 6622, p. 1436.

11. Sulami, *Tabaqat*, p. 30.

3. GOD IS JUST

At the same time as being merciful and forgiving, God is sovereign and just. The question is, how to reconcile his mercy with his justice. For, although on the one hand his divine mercy leads him to forgive us; on the other hand, his divine justice requires that we be punished.

This dilemma divides Muslim theologians into two major groups. The Sunnites emphasize that God is sovereign, and thus he does whatever he chooses. He has the absolute right to forgive

Sunni theologians	Mu'tazili theologians
Emphasize that God is *sovereign*.	Emphasize that God is *just*.
God has the right to forgive or punish us as he chooses.	God must treat us as we deserve. He will reward faith and obedience. He will punish sins.

Table 2. Sunni and Mu'tazili theologians: differences in emphasis

or to punish. If he forgives, no-one can doubt his justice; and if he punishes, no-one can question his mercy. We will look briefly at their teaching in the next chapter. The Mu'tazilites take the view that, first and foremost, God is just. He shows his mercy only in as much as his justice is not undermined. Hence divine justice controls and restricts divine mercy. The fact that God's justice is his overriding attribute means that he deals with us in full accord with this attribute.

God gives us what we deserve

In this chapter we will focus on the Mu'tazili position. The Qur'an points out that on the Day of Judgment God's retribution will be exactly what people deserve: 'On that Day humankind will proceed in successive groups to be shown their deeds. Then whoever has done an atom's weight of good shall see it; whoever has done an atom's weight of evil shall see it too' (99:7–8; cf. 10:61; 21:47; 34:3).

Because God is just, he will punish every single transgression (10:27; 40:40). Thus God requires not only faith but also obedience to his law. Without meeting this double condition no-one can expect to be admitted into paradise. Only those who obey God's laws revealed through his Prophet will be blessed in the hereafter (4:13–14; 48:17). God promises his eternal blessing exclusively to people who believe and do good works.[1] His forgiveness depends therefore on whether or not Muslims have given evidence, by performing good works, that their faith is genuine. Deserving Muslims will no doubt be rewarded, and this reward is associated with God's pardon: 'God has promised forgiveness and a great reward to those who believe and practise good deeds' (5:9; cf. 8:4, 74: 11:11; 22:50; 34:4; 35:7; 48:29).

The Arabic word for 'reward' in this verse, *ajr*, literally means 'wages', 'salary' or 'pay'.[2] Razi comments that this double promise of forgiveness and reward corresponds to the two characteristics by which people are described in this verse: divine forgiveness is related to people's faith, and great reward to their deserving acts.[3]

What obedience means

Obeying God's laws means, first, performing what are known as 'the Pillars of Islam'. The *shahada*, 'confession of faith', is the first pillar. God's pardon will be the reward of those who exalt God in their prayer by declaring who he is:

> He who uttered these words, 'There is no god but God, the One, who has no partner; sovereignty belongs to Him, all praise is due to Him and He is powerful over everything,' one hundred times every day, he will be rewarded as though he had set free ten slaves. He will be credited one hundred good deeds and one hundred evil deeds will be removed from his record ...
>
> He who utters these words, 'Glory and praise to God,' one hundred times a day, his sins will be wiped out even if they are equal to the extent of the foam of the ocean.[4]

Prayer is the second pillar. By performing their 'ritual prayer', *salat*, five times a day, Muslims obtain God's forgiveness for the sins they have committed between successive prayers: 'If a person performs ablution and does it well and offers prayer, all his sins during the period from one prayer to another would be pardoned by God.'[5]

The Hadith reports the following story, which explains the circumstances in which the Qur'anic verse 'the good deeds remove the evil ones' (11:114) was revealed:

> A person came to God's Apostle and said: 'I have sported with a woman in the outskirts of Medina, and I have committed an offence short of fornication. Here I am before you, kindly deliver verdict about me which you deem fit.' 'Umar said: 'God concealed your fault. You had better conceal it yourself also.' God's Apostle, however, gave no reply to him. The man stood up and went away.
>
> God's Apostle sent a person after him to call him and he recited this verse: *'Perform the rite of prayer at each end of the day, as well as during the early hours of the night. Surely, good deeds take away evil ones. That is a reminder for the mindful.'* A person amongst the people asked: 'God's Apostle, does it concern this man only?' Thereupon he replied: 'No, but the people at large.'[6]

God's pardon can also be obtained through *zakat*, 'almsgiving'; *sawm*, 'fasting'; and *hajj*, 'pilgrimage':

> Whoever observes fasting during the month of Ramadan out of sincere faith, and hoping to attain God's reward, then all his past sins will be forgiven.[7]

> Whoever came to this house [the Ka'ba] on pilgrimage and neither spoke indecently nor did he act wickedly, would return free from sin as on the day he was born.[8]

People who commit themselves to God unreservedly will also be treated mercifully by him. They agree to give everything to God, including their wealth and even their lives. This total commitment is what is meant by *jihad*. Those who die fully committed to God's cause will be granted his pardon:

> Believers! Shall I indicate to you a transaction that will save you from a painful punishment? You believe in God and in His Apostle, you strive in the way of God with your property and with your selves: that is best for you, if only you realised. He will forgive you your transgressions and bring you into gardens with flowing streams, into fine mansions in the gardens of Eden. That is the ultimate triumph.
> (61:11–12; cf. 3:195; 4:95–96)

Praying for forgiveness

God's forgiveness is promised to those who fulfil their religious duties; but, being who we are, we will never completely meet the requirements of God's law. We are liable to fall into sin willingly or unwillingly. Our first obligation then is to turn to God and implore his pardon. If we do so, we can expect God to be merciful with us:

> Those who, having committed some shameful act or done some evil against themselves, remember God and seek His forgiveness for their transgressions – for who forgives sins apart from God? – and who do

not knowingly persist in their wrongdoing. These have their reward:
forgiveness from their Lord and gardens with flowing streams where they
will dwell for ever. How surpassing is the reward of those who do so.
(3:135–136)

In addition to the 'ritual prayer', _salat_, Muslims ask God's
forgiveness through 'personal prayers', _du'a'_. The Hadith provides
some examples of such prayers. The following quotes sura 3 verse
135 ('Who forgives sins apart from God?'):

> When seeking God's forgiveness, _sayyidu l-istighfar_, one should say:
>> O God! You are my Lord. There is no god except You.
>> You have created me and I am Your servant.
>> I am faithful to Your covenant and Your promise as much as I can.
>> I seek refuge with You from the evil I have done.
>> I acknowledge before You the blessings You have bestowed upon me.
>> I confess my sin to You.
>> So please forgive me – for no-one forgives sin except You.
> Whoever recites this prayer during the day with full conviction, and
> dies on the same day before the evening, he will go to paradise; and
> whoever recites it at night with full conviction, and dies before the
> morning, he will go to paradise too.[9]

Thus God's justice plays a key role in Islamic theology,
especially in the Mu'tazili school. It requires that we comply with
God's law in general and with the five pillars in particular. For
Mu'tazili theologians divine justice takes precedence over divine
mercy (as we shall see in more detail in Part 2). This means that
God deals with us on the basis of our merits. Consequently, God
forgives only minor sins. If he were to forgive Muslims who
committed a major sin, he would deny his justice. In other words,
God's forgiveness is both conditional and limited. It will be shown
only to _practising_ Muslims who have obeyed God's commands. But
do such deserving Muslims really need to be forgiven? The answer
provided by the Mu'tazilites is that even practising Muslims have
their shortcomings. They are not immune from failure. Provided
they have not committed any major sin for which they have not
repented, God will forgive them their minor sins.

God does not leave the guilty unpunished

In the revelation Moses received at Sinai God portrayed himself as
compassionate and forgiving. But he also declared that he is just
and that he tolerates no sin whatsoever: 'he does not leave the
guilty unpunished; he punishes the children and their children for
the sin of the fathers to the third and fourth generation' (Exod.
34:7; cf. Exod. 20:7; 23:7; Num. 14:18; Deut. 5:11; Nah. 1:3).

God does not always punish sin immediately as he did when the
Israelites worshipped the golden calf. His judgment is often
delayed, though it is never cancelled. Moreover, the above text
indicates that God's punishment is not restricted to the people who
commit the sin. It involves their descendants up to the fourth
generation. But how are we to understand such a statement? Is it
fair for God to punish people for a sin committed by their parents
or their grandparents? The Qur'an highlights the principle of
personal responsibility by repeating that 'no one bears the burden
of another' (6:164; 17:15; 38:18; 39:7; 53:38).

This doctrine of personal responsibility is also taught in the
Bible. After the Israelites made the golden calf, Moses pleaded on
their behalf. He asked God to forgive them or else to punish him
instead. God's response was that he would punish only those
people who had sinned against him (Exod. 32:31–34). Similarly,
the penal law states that 'Fathers shall not be put to death for their
children, nor children put to death for their fathers; each is to die
for his own sin' (Deut. 24:16). We should therefore (as suggested in
chapter 1) take Exodus 34 verse 7 as a literary device, an expression
meant to underline how great God's love is in comparison with
his judgment. The former spans over a thousand generations, so to
speak, whereas the latter is limited to three or four (Exod. 20:5–6;
Deut. 5:9–10).

Moreover, Exodus 34 verses 6 and 7 should be interpreted in
its historical context; namely, God's covenant with Israel. Under
the Old Covenant, Israel was chosen by God as a people, not
as individuals; although inevitably, individual Israelites suffered
because of the punishment God inflicted on their nation when
they disobeyed him (e.g. the exile). In the New Covenant people
are called out of many nations (including Israel) to form God's

new people. Unlike the kingdom of Israel, God's kingdom is spiritual and eternal. Membership does not depend on one's ethnic background but on one's personal response to God's revelation in Christ. If we have faith in Christ, nothing can undermine our eternal salvation – even if we belong to the most sinful nation on earth. If our faith is not in Christ, we will have every reason to fear God's judgment, although we might have the most godly parents or children. Thus personal responsibility is what characterizes the New Covenant. It shows its superiority over the Old Covenant, according to the prophet Jeremiah (Jer. 31:29–30). In God's kingdom people will be treated individually: 'The soul who sins is the one who will die. The son will not share the guilt of the father, nor will the father share the guilt of the son. The righteousness of the righteous man will be credited to him, and the wickedness of the wicked will be charged against him' (Ezek. 18:20).

Thus God's justice is one of his major attributes in both the Bible and the Qur'an. In order to please a just God, we need to comply with his law. It is no use believing in God if our faith does not produce good deeds: 'faith by itself, if it is not accompanied by action, is dead' (Jas. 2:17).

Three essential differences

Christian doctrine is consonant with Islamic teaching in pointing out that God is just and that our response to him should be characterized by obedience. However, there are three essential differences. The first is found in *the importance of love*. Jesus summed up God's law in a twofold command: ' "Love the Lord your God with all your heart and with all your soul and with all your mind." This is the first and greatest commandment. And the second is like it: "Love your neighbour as yourself." All the Law and the Prophets hang on these two commandments' (Matt. 22:37–40). In doing so, Jesus stresses that loving God and our neighbour should be the motivation and the purpose of our lives. Unless our good deeds express our love for our Creator and for our fellow human beings, they are useless: 'If I give all I possess to the poor and surrender my body to the flames, but have not love, I gain nothing' (1 Cor. 13:3). Indeed, without love our good deeds can result in self-righteousness and spiritual arrogance.

Second, the distinction that Mu'tazili theologians draw between major and minor sins is unconvincing. Jesus teaches *that sin is sin in all its forms*:

> You have heard that it was said to the people long ago, 'Do not murder, and anyone who murders will be subject to judgement.' But I tell you that anyone who is angry with his brother will be subject to judgement. (Matt. 5:21–22)

> You have heard that it was said, 'Do not commit adultery.' But I tell you that anyone who looks at a woman lustfully has already committed adultery with her in his heart. (Matt. 5:27–28)

Evil is the root cause for sin, whether it is a 'small sin' or a 'big sin'. Consequently, God's justice requires that all sins be punished. If God were to forgive sin instead of punishing it, he would compromise his justice. In other words, God's justice from a Christian perspective is even stricter than in Mu'tazili thought.

Finally, the Bible teaches that *our acts of obedience do not make up for our sins*. Our only hope is God's mercy. God commands us to do good deeds, but this does not mean that they can wipe away our evil deeds. On the contrary, we are warned that what may seem to us to be good deeds may well be corrupted by sin. As the prophet Isaiah declares, 'All of us have become like one who is unclean,/ and all our righteous acts are like filthy rags' (Is. 64:6). This is why our only hope is in God's mercy. The merciful God is willing to forgive us our sins if we humbly confess them instead of trying to make up for them. In the parable of the Pharisee and the tax collector Jesus explains that God's mercy is all we need to have our sins forgiven:

> Two men went up to the temple to pray, one a Pharisee and the other a tax collector. The Pharisee stood up and prayed about himself: 'God, I thank you that I am not like other men – robbers, evildoers, adulterers –

or even like this tax collector. I fast twice a week and give a tenth of all
I get.'

But the tax collector stood at a distance. He would not even look up
to heaven, but beat his breast and said, 'God, have mercy on me, a
sinner.'

I tell you [Jesus concluded] that this man, rather than the other, went
home justified before God. For everyone who exalts himself will be
humbled, and he who humbles himself will be exalted.

(Luke 18:10–14)

Notes

1. 2:25, 82; 4:57, 122; 11:23; 14:23; 29:58; 18:107; 22:14; 23:56; 31:8; 32:19;
   42:22; 47:12; 65:11; 85:11.
2. The word *ajr* occurs about one hundred times in the Qur'an. Its meaning
   is very similar to *rizq*, which is used less frequently.
3. Razi on 35:7; XII:26, p. 6.
4. Muslim, *dhikr* 28 [4857]:IV, bk 35, no. 6508, p. 1415; Tirmidhi, *da'awat*
   24 [3390].
5. Muslim, *tahara* 5 [333]:I, bk 2, no. 440, p. 150.
6. Muslim, *tawba* 39 [4964]:IV, bk 37, no. 6658, p. 1442.
7. Bukhari, *iman* 28 [36]:I, bk 2, no. 37, p. 34.
8. Muslim, *hajj* 438 [2404]:II, bk 7, no. 3129, p. 680; Bukhari, *hajj* 4 [1424];
   Tirmidhi, *hajj* 2 [739]; Nasa'i, *hajj* 4 [2580].
9. Bukhari, *da'awat* 2 [5831]:VIII, bk 75, no. 318, p. 212; Abu Dawud, *adab*
   109 [4408]:III, bk 36, no. 5052, p. 1407; Tirmidhi, *da'awat* 15 [3315];
   Nasa'i, *isti'adha* 57 [5427].

4. GOD IS SOVEREIGN

God is merciful and forgiving. These attributes prompt Muslims to seek his forgiveness, knowing that granting forgiveness is one of his exclusive privileges. But isn't God's justice compromised if he forgives people who deserve to be punished? And does not divine justice require that sinful Muslims be punished just as much as godly Muslims be rewarded? Sunni theologians, who represent mainstream Islam, believe that such questions are meaningless in the light of God's sovereignty.

God forgives whom he chooses

Sunni theology emphasizes that God is entirely free to do whatever he chooses. He has every right to show mercy as well as to punish. He does not need to justify or explain his actions, and people have no right to challenge him. It is unfitting for us, his creatures, to question his justice if and when he decides to grant forgiveness to those who deserve to be punished. A well-known Qur'anic text describes God's absolute authority as follows: 'He will not be questioned for his acts but they will be questioned for theirs' (21:23; cf. 2:105; 3:74; 7:155; 12:56; 17:54; 29:21; 42:8). Thus God is not accountable to us but we are accountable to him. On the Day of Judgment we will have to give account to our Creator for what we have done with our lives. He will then decide whether to forgive or punish us.

God's supreme authority means that he has the right and the power either to forgive or to condemn any person regardless of his or her deeds. In other words, God's decisions are not determined by his creatures. Neither good works nor evildoing compel God to act in one way or another: 'He will forgive whom He will and He will punish whom He will. For God has supreme power over all things' (2:284; cf. 3:129; 5:20, 43; 48:14).

However, the fact that human merit or guilt does not determine God's forgiveness or punishment does not mean that he deals with us arbitrarily. The Qur'an states that, broadly speaking, God's judgment will be related to our attitude towards him. Thus he has sovereignly decided not to grant his forgiveness to the 'unbelievers', *kafirun*.

Who are the unbelievers?

Muslim theologians see all non-Muslims as unbelievers in one way or another. Non-Muslims fall under four main categories.

1. *The Polytheists, al-mushriqun* (lit. 'those who associate'). The Qur'an singles out their sin as follows: 'God does not forgive that partners be associated with Him, but He forgives any other sin to whom He pleases. Those who associate partners with God commit a great sin' (4:48; cf. 4:116).

This text suggests that the only unforgivable sin consists of ascribing partners to God. This is why Muhammad and Muslims were commanded not to pray for polytheistic Arabs (9:113). If they do not believe in the one and only God, God will not forgive them their sins even if the Prophet were to pray seventy times for them (9:80; 63:6). When Abraham interceded for his father, he did so before it was revealed to him that his father was God's enemy (9:114).

2. *The Apostates, al-murtaddun*. Unless they repent and come back to Islam, Muslims who abandon their faith will surely be sent to hell on the Day of Judgment. God's pardon will not be available to them: 'Should any of you turn back from their religion and die in unbelief – their works will come to nought in this present world and in the next. They will be sent to fire where they will stay forever' (2:217; cf. 3:85–90; 4:137; 5:5).

3. *'The last-minute believers'*. These are those who repent knowing that they are soon going to die. Such people are driven by fear of God's judgment rather than by a genuine conviction that Islam is the true religion. God will not accept their repentance because it is insincere: 'Repentance does not avail in the case of those who do evil deeds right up to the approach of death, and then one says, "Now I repent," nor yet for those who die in unbelief. For these We have prepared a painful punishment' (4:18; cf. 23:99–100; 63:10–11).

Pharaoh represents the archetype of unbelieving people. According to the Qur'an, he professed faith when he realized he was going to die. His faith was hypocritical since it was motivated not by a sense of guilt but by a desperate and last-minute attempt to escape God's punishment. God prevented his body from being swallowed by the sea so that his example would serve as a warning for all unbelievers:

> We conveyed the children of Israel through the sea. Pharaoh and his armies followed after them in hot, impetuous pursuit until, on the point of drowning, Pharaoh cried: 'I believe that there is no god but He in whom the children of Israel believe. I, too, am with those who yield to Him.'
>
> What? Now! You who were up to this point a rebel, one of the foul dealers? This day We will save your body to be a sign to those who come after you. Most people take no heed of the things We reveal. (10:90–92; cf. 40:84–85)

4. *Jews and Christians*. Although described in the Qur'an as 'the People of the Book', they are nevertheless unbelievers. Because they have not accepted Muhammad as God's Prophet, their faith is invalid (2:105; 3:70; 5:72–73; 9:30; 98:1). Jews are accused of breaking the covenant God made with them (4:155). Christians are

blamed for making a man (Jesus) into a god and believing in three gods (4:171). One Qur'anic text appears to suggest that Jews and Christians will enjoy God's blessing in the hereafter (2:62), yet in many other texts they are promised the same fate as the polytheistic Arabs: 'Those of the People of the Book who disbelieved, together with the Polytheists, will be in hell-fire forever. They are the worst of creatures' (98:6).

Will all Muslims be forgiven?

God's pardon will be granted only to Muslims who by definition ascribe no partner to God. So, does monotheistic faith *guarantee* eternal happiness? And what about Muslims who transgress God's laws? If they do not pray or fast, if they commit serious sins, will they still be saved?

Sunni theologians consider that disobedience does not seriously undermine eternal salvation. They argue that sinful Muslims are still genuine believers and that they will eventually go to paradise. Because God is both merciful and sovereign, and because polytheism is the only unforgivable sin, all Muslims will be admitted to paradise in the end. They back up their claim with Prophetic sayings reported in the Hadith, such as this dialogue between Muhammad and one of his companions:

> Abu Dharr said: 'I came to the Prophet while he was wearing white clothes and sleeping. Then I went to him when he was awaken.'
>
> He said, 'Nobody says, "None has the right to be worshipped but God," and then died believing in that, but he will enter Paradise.'
>
> I said, 'Even if he had committed illegal sexual intercourse and theft?'
>
> He said, 'Even if he had committed illegal sexual intercourse and theft.'
>
> I said, 'Even if he had committed illegal sexual intercourse and theft?'
>
> He said, 'Even if he had committed illegal sexual intercourse and theft.'
>
> I said, 'Even if he had committed illegal sexual intercourse and theft?'
>
> He said, 'Even if he had committed illegal sexual intercourse and theft whether Abu Dharr likes it or not.'[1]

However, Sunni scholars do not assert that all Muslims will enter paradise *immediately* after the Day of Judgment. Disobedient Muslims in particular may well go to hell first, in order to atone for their sins. Unless God forgives their transgressions, they will be punished temporarily in hell. Thus God will use his discretionary power either to forgive or to condemn. If he decides to punish sinful Muslims, their punishment will not be eternal. Once they have paid the penalty they deserve, they will be given access to paradise. Their faith will prevail over their disobedience. They will then be united with their fellow Muslims to enjoy God's eternal blessing. This doctrine of *temporary punishment* is based on several hadiths such as this one:

> Whoever declares, 'None has the right to be worshipped but God' and has in his heart faith equal to the weight of a grain of barley will be taken out of hell. Whoever declares, 'None has the right to be worshipped but God' and has in his heart faith equal to the weight of a grain of wheat will be taken out of hell. Whoever declares, 'None has the right to be worshipped but God' and has in his heart faith equal to the weight of an atom will be taken out of hell.[2]

How can God be both merciful and just?

In the Bible too, sovereignty is a prominent attribute of God. God said to Moses after the Israelites worshipped the golden calf, 'I will have mercy on whom I will have mercy, and I will have compassion on whom I will have compassion' (Exod. 33:19). In the New Testament, Paul elaborates on the implications of God's sovereignty as illustrated in God's words to Moses. Paul points out that God's blessings are free. They have nothing to do with our merits; they are clear evidence of who God is: 'It does not, therefore, depend on man's desire or effort, but on God's mercy' (Rom. 9:16).

However, God's sovereign will is displayed in Christianity differently from how it is in Islam. The Qur'an states that God is free to forgive and free to punish. Sunni theologians understand God's sovereignty at the expense of his justice, whereas Mu'tazili theologians conceive of God's justice in a way that makes little room for his mercy and sovereignty. But, according to the Bible, God demonstrated his sovereign power in that he met the requirements of both his justice and his mercy. He showed his mercy through saving us from sin and death instead of condemning us. He proved his commitment to save humankind by sending Jesus Christ. Jesus himself defined his mission with the words 'I did not come to judge the world, but to save it' (John 12:47; cf. John 3:17).

Why do people need, not only to be *forgiven*, but to be *saved*? The answer is that God's justice requires that our sins be adequately punished. This means eternal punishment. Therefore, the only way for God to forgive sinful people was to send us a Saviour; that is, Jesus Christ who died for all our sins. John the Baptist described Jesus as 'the Lamb of God, who takes away the sin of the world' (John 1:29). Jesus, through his sacrificial death, demonstrated both God's justice and mercy. He fulfilled God's justice towards sin (taking the punishment upon himself) and God's mercy towards sinners (bringing forgiveness and salvation). Jesus' mission represents a powerful demonstration of God's sovereignty over evil.

Thus our salvation does not depend on our merits but on Jesus' death and resurrection. The gospel is all about forgiveness of sins, promised to those who put their trust in Jesus Christ (Luke 24:46). We do not have to wait until the Day of Judgment to know God's verdict on our lives. We can have the assurance of God's forgiveness in this life. We can enjoy fellowship with God now as a token of the eternal life Jesus promises: 'I tell you the truth, whoever hears my word and believes him who sent me has eternal life and will not be condemned; he has crossed over from death to life' (John 5:24).

How does the promise of forgiveness of sins, based on the atoning death of Christ, fit with the principle of personal responsibility? The fact that God sent Jesus to be 'the Saviour of the world' (John 4:42) does not mean that everyone is saved. We still need to respond to God's offer. This response, whether positive or negative, can be made only by us individually and for no-one other than ourselves. It involves making an informed, free and personal decision as to who Jesus really is. It also involves a lifelong commitment to walk in Jesus' footsteps.

Notes

1. Bukhari, *libas* 24 [5379]:VII, bk 72, no. 717, p. 481; Muslim, *iman* 40 [137]:I, bk 1, no. 172, p. 54; *zakat* 10 [1654]:II, bk 5, no. 2175, p. 476.
2. Bukhari, *iman* 33 [42]:I, bk 2, no. 42, p. 37. The same hadith has a slightly different version. Instead of 'faith', *iman*, it has *khayr*, 'something good'. Cf. Muslim, *iman* 39 [132]:I, bk 1, no. 165, p. 54; Ibn Majah, *muqaddima* 9 [58]:I, fwd, no. 59, p. 33.

5. GOD IS PATIENT

God is described as _ḥalim_ eleven times in the Qur'an, a word that means 'patient' or 'forbearing'. This divine name is associated with _ghafur_, 'all-forgiving', in six verses.[1] 'Know that God knows what is in your hearts, and take heed of Him; and know that God is All-Forgiving, Forbearing' (2:235).

Judgment delayed

Razi explains God is patient and forbearing in the sense that he does not hasten his judgment on those who disobey him. He gives them respite so that they may repent and, as a result, gain paradise.[2] God's forbearance is a consequence of his boundless mercy.[3] Ghazali defines the word _ḥalim_ as referring to one who is not easily incited to wrath or vengeance: '[God] observes the disobedience of the rebellious and notices the opposition to the command, yet anger does not incite him nor wrath seize him, nor do haste and recklessness move him to rush to take vengeance, although he is utterly capable of doing that.'[4]

The Qur'an praises God's patience with the evildoers. Because of God's forbearance people are not punished according to their evil deeds. If God were not patient with them, they all would have been under his condemnation: 'If God were to treat people according to their evildoing, no creature would escape His punishment; but He gives them a fixed respite. When it is over they will not be able to delay nor to anticipate [God's judgement] one single hour' (16:61).

Razi explains that the postponement of divine judgment reveals God's 'favour' (*fadl*), 'mercy' (*rahma*) and 'generosity' (*karam*). When will God's patience come to an end? Some Muslims think it will be over on the Day of Judgment when sinful people will be condemned and sent to hell. But other Muslims believe that God's forbearance expires when people die and depart from this life.[5]

Muhammad is described in the Qur'an as a messenger of 'good news' (*bashir*) and a 'warner' (*nadhir*). This double message corresponds to two categories of people. On the Last Day God will reward those who do good and condemn those who do evil. Polytheistic Arabs dismissed the Qur'anic warning, ridiculed the Prophet and argued sarcastically with him. They urged him to ask God not to delay his judgment any longer. The Prophet responded that, sooner or later, God's judgment would fall upon them and no-one would be able to escape:

> They ask you to hasten the punishment. [Tell them that] God will not fail in what He promises. A day with your Lord is like a thousand years as you reckon. How many a city, given to evil, have I borne with before I destroyed its people. [They will be punished when] they are brought back to Me.
> Say: 'O People! I have been sent to you as a messenger with plain warning. For those who believe and do good deeds there is forgiveness and generous provision. But those who strive to thwart Our Signs, hell is their final destiny.'
> (22:48–51; cf. 38:16)

God keeps his word. Eternal judgment will take place in due course. It will happen according to God's timing. God will judge those who refuse to listen to his warning. What do the words 'a day with your Lord is like a thousand years' mean? Razi suggests three interpretations. According to the first, which Razi favours, God's judgment will be far more rigorous than what people imagine: one day of suffering will feel like a thousand years. The second interpretation is similar: God's judgment will not only be intense, but also endless. Not only will one day of suffering feel like an eternity, but people will also suffer infinitely longer than they had imagined. The severity of eternal judgment is such that no sensible person would want Judgment Day to be hastened. Finally, there is no difference in God's sight between one day and a thousand years. When it comes to judgment, it makes no difference to God whether the respite he grants humankind lasts for one day or for a thousand years.[6]

People who heed God's warning, believe in him and commit themselves to doing good works will receive God's forgiveness and enjoy eternal blessing. People who dismiss God's message will be punished, certainly in the hereafter if not already in this life. God will accomplish what he has promised and he will do it at the appointed time without any delay: 'Your Lord is swift in retribution, yet He is All-Forgiving and All-Merciful' (6:165; 7:167). Not only is God's punishment swift; it is also strict. Thus the Qur'an holds together God's justice and his mercy: 'Be aware that God is strong in retribution and that God is also All-Forgiving and All-Merciful' (5:101; cf. 2:196, 211; 3:11; 5:2; 8:52; 41:43; 57:20; 59:7).

Patience in the face of unbelief

When God reveals to Moses that he is merciful and compassionate, he also tells him that he is 'slow to anger' (Exod. 34:6).[7] God's patience with sinners is an expression of his mercy towards them. It is meant to spur them on to repentance and to restore their relationship with him. The apostle Paul challenges those who pass judgment on others and warns them that they too stand under God's judgment: 'Do you show contempt for the riches of his kindness, tolerance and patience, not realising that God's kindness leads you towards repentance?' (Rom. 2:4).

The same attitude shown by polytheistic Arabs towards the Prophet was found among those who opposed the message of the gospel in the first century AD. The Christian response to unbelief is similar to the Qur'anic response. Not only is the argument of the same kind, but the words are also very much alike. God's timing is not ours, and if there seems to be a delay in the judgment to come it is for our own sake:

> you must understand that in the last days scoffers will come, scoffing and following their own evil desires. They will say, 'Where is this "coming" he promised? Ever since our fathers died, everything goes on as it has since the beginning of creation' ... With the Lord a day is like a thousand years, and a thousand years are like a day. The Lord is not slow in keeping his promise, as some understand slowness. He is patient with you, not wanting anyone to perish, but everyone to come to repentance ... Bear in mind that our Lord's patience means salvation ...
> (2 Pet. 3:3–4, 8–9, 15)

Zero tolerance for sin

The major difference between Islamic teaching and Christian doctrine with regard to God's patience pertains to his attitude to sin. In Islam *God is not bound to punish sin*. He may forgive any sin, except polytheism (for the Sunnites), or at least minor sins (for the Mu'tazilites). In Christianity *God requires that all sin is punished*, and yet paradoxically, he offers his forgiveness freely to all sinners. While God's forbearance with sinners will last (as in Islam) until the Day of Judgment, he has zero tolerance for sin (unlike Islam). Indeed, he tolerated sin only for a time, and then provided a way for it to be punished, condemning it through the death of Jesus on the cross:

> God presented him [Jesus Christ] as a sacrifice of atonement, through faith in his blood. He did this to demonstrate his justice, *because in his forbearance he had left the sins committed beforehand unpunished* – he did it to demonstrate his justice at the present time ...
> (Rom. 3:25–26a; my italics)

On the cross Jesus was suffering the punishment for sin, thus demonstrating God's justice, his intolerance of sin, and at the same time his incredible love for sinners.

God tolerates no sin at all, yet his patience with sinners seems unlimited. While he delays his judgment, it may result in his people suffering at the hands of evildoers. Thus he let the Israelites suffer as slaves in Egypt for more than four hundred years. He did not want them to take possession of the land prematurely; that is, before the sin of its inhabitants had reached its full measure (Gen. 15:16). Many prophets were persecuted by their people. Jeremiah is a prime example. He was aware that his suffering was a result of God's patience with his persecutors. He knew that his life was under threat because of God's goodness towards his enemies. Even so, he pleaded with God to step in and bring his suffering to an end:

> You understand, O LORD;
>> remember me and care for me.
>> Avenge me on my persecutors.
> You are long-suffering – do not take me away;
>> think of how I suffer reproach for your sake.
> (Jer. 15:15)

Notes

1. God is patient and 'all-forgiving', *ghafur* (2:225, 235; 3:155; 5:101; 17:44; 35:21), patient and 'all-knowing', *'alim* (4:12; 22:59; 33:51), patient and 'rich', *ghani* (2:263), patient and 'grateful', *shakur* (64:17). Three prophets are also described as patient: Abraham (9:114; 11:75), his (unnamed) son (37:101) and Shu'ayb, the prophet sent to Madian (11:87).

2. Razi on 22:59; XII:23, p. 52.

3. See Razi's exegesis of 6:147; VII:13, p. 184.

4. Ghazali, *Names*, p. 99.

5. According to Islamic teaching, 'the punishment in the tomb', *'adhab al-qabr*, anticipates eternal punishment. People suffer this temporary punishment shortly after they have been buried.

6. Razi on 22:47–49; XII:23, p. 41.

7. The attribute 'slow to anger' is found fourteen times in the Old
   Testament. It describes the wise man (Prov. 14:29; 15:18; 16:32; Eccles.
   7:8), but is more often applied to God. It is linked with God as the
   merciful and the compassionate seven times out of ten.

6. GOD IS RETURNING

In the Qur'anic account of the Israelites' making of the golden calf (2:51–54; cf. Exod. 32), we find another divine name closely connected with God's forgiveness: *tawwab*, 'Most-Returning':

> Moses said to his people: 'You have wronged yourselves, my people, in worshipping the calf. *Turn* [in repentance] to your Maker and slay yourselves. That will be best for you in His sight'. And He *turned* to you [in mercy], for He is *Most-Returning* and All-Merciful.
> (2:54; my italics)[1]

The divine name *tawwab* is not easy to translate into English. It usually means 'repentant', but could be rendered as 'ever-relenting' or 'most-returning'. It derives from the verb *taba*, which literally means 'to return', 'to come back'. The verb is used for God and for man, as in the above verse.[2] God turns to man and man turns back to God.[3] Sin alienates man from God, God turns away from man and man runs away from God. Forgiveness of sin restores the relationship between man and his Lord. Forgiveness is thus the meeting point between the Creator who grants it and people who

receive it. God turns mercifully to us and we turn repentantly to
God.

The word *tawwab* is found twelve times in the Qur'an. With one
exception it is always used for God.[4] It is linked with 'all-merciful'
(*rahim*) in nine texts (2:37, 54, 128, 160; 4:16, 64; 9:104, 118; 49:12),
and with 'all-wise' (*hakim*) in just one (24:10). It stands on its own in
one text that portrays God as the One who always responds when
people confess their sins:

> When God's triumph comes about, and victory,
> And you see people embrace God's religion in multitudes,
> Then give glory to your Lord, praise Him and ask pardon of Him.
> For He is Most-Returning.
> (110:1–3)

The victory referred to in this sura is the conquest of Mecca by
Muslims in 630. Following this victory many Arab tribes converted
to Islam. The Prophet was urged to praise God for this event and
to seek his forgiveness.

The Hadith too highlights that God is always ready to welcome
people who turn to him. He is willing to accept their repentance at
any time: 'God stretches out His hand during the night so that the
people repent for the fault committed from dawn to dusk, and He
stretches out His hand during the day so that people repent for the
fault committed from dusk to dawn.'[5]

The lost camel

God rejoices when people come back to him. Indeed, his joy is
compared to that of a bedouin who has come through a life-
threatening experience in the wilderness:

> God is more pleased with the repentance of His believing servant than a
> person who loses his riding camel carrying food and drink. He sleeps
> and then gets up and goes in search for that, until he is stricken with
> thirst, then comes back to the place where he had been before and goes
> to sleep completely exhausted placing his head upon his hands waiting

for death. And when he gets up, lo! There is before him his riding camel
and his provisions of food and drink. God is more pleased with the
repentance of His servant than the recovery of his riding camel along
with the provisions of food and drink.[6]

The fact that God is a Most-Returning God means that he wants
to turn mercifully to believers, men and women, who have
transgressed his laws (4:26–27; 33:73). Ever since God created
Adam he has turned graciously to people. He did so with Adam
(2:37; 20:122), with Abraham (2:128), with the Israelites (2:54; 5:74)
and with Muhammad and his companions (2:187; 9:117; 58:13;
73:20). God turns to people when he accepts their repentance. He
is indeed 'the One who accepts people's repentance' (40:3).

Those who sin in ignorance

The Qur'an goes as far as to say that 'God ought to turn [in mercy]
to those who do evil in ignorance and turn [in repentance] to Him
soon afterwards' (4:17; cf. 6:54; 16:119). Does God have to accept
people's repentance? Razi's answer is that God is bound to accept it
because this is what he has promised. This obligation is therefore
based on God's graciousness rather than on the merits of those who
repent. However, the promise applies only, first, to 'people who do
evil in ignorance' and, second, provided they turn to God 'soon
afterwards'; that is, before the time when their death is drawing near.
    The question is, who are 'those who do evil in ignorance'? Razi
lists three different interpretations.

1. There is a sense in which all sinners are ignorant. Indeed, the
   Qur'an equates sin with an act of ignorance (2:67; 11:46;
   12:33, 89). Although people know about God's reward (if
   they obey) and punishment (if they disobey), they do not live
   accordingly. If they were consistent with what they knew,
   they would not commit sin.
2. People who knowingly commit sin are not fully aware how
   terrible their punishment will be; hence they are described as
   ignorant.

3. People disobey in ignorance when they commit evil
   unknowingly. In other words, they are unaware that their act
   is evil though it is possible for them to know that what they
   have done is wrong. A Jew, for instance, commits sin in
   following Judaism but is unaware of his sin, although Islam
   makes it clear that Judaism is no longer a religion acceptable
   to God.

Razi himself favours the third interpretation, which takes the
word 'ignorance' literally, whereas the first and second take it in a
metaphorical sense.[7]

Those who sin knowingly

What about those who, having knowingly disobeyed God's
commands, turn in repentance to him? Will God turn in mercy to
them? The Qur'anic answer is yes (2:160; cf. 2:54; 5:42). According
to Razi, however, if people do not repent promptly after they
disobey, they cannot enjoy the certainty of God's promise that he
will accept their repentance and forgive their sins (9:102).[8]

The name *tawwab*, '*most*-returning', is an intensive form. The
regular form, *ta'ib*, 'returning', is used only for people, never for
God. So why is God described with the intensive form? Razi
suggests two reasons. Unlike human kings, God is always willing to
forgive those who constantly disobey him but keep seeking his
pardon. He accepts their repentance by way of sheer 'kindness'
(*ihsan*), and 'undeserved favour' (*tafaddul*). Thus God forgives for
no other reason than his generosity. His forgiveness has nothing to
do with 'mild temperament' (*riqqatu tab'*), nor is it motivated by a
desire to gain a 'benefit' (*jalbu naf'*), nor to get rid of 'something
harmful' (*daf'u darar*). On the other hand, those who come back to
God are many and he accepts the repentance of them all. Razi
also explains why God is often called both *tawwab* and *rahim*
(all-merciful). Accepting people's repentance and cancelling their
punishment implies granting them a reward (paradise). Since this
reward is an expression of 'divine grace' (*ni'ma*), and mercy, God is
said to be not only 'most-returning' but also 'all-merciful'.[9]

The three who were left behind

For Sunni theologians, the intensive form *tawwab* points to God's initiative when people repent. They explain that it is God who makes people turn to him in repentance. God first turns to people and, as a result, they turn to him. In other words, God's action is sovereign: it causes people's repentance. Their argument is based on several Qur'anic texts (9:15, 27), and in particular this one:

> God turned [with mercy] to the Prophet, the [Meccan] Emigrants and the [Medinan] Allies who followed him in time of hardship after the hearts of some of them had nearly swerved. He turned to them [with mercy] for He is Lenient and All-Merciful.
>
> [God also turned with mercy] to the three who were left behind. They were so remorseful that the whole earth, despite its vastness, seemed like a prison for them. Such were their low feelings. They realised that there was no shelter [for them] from [the wrath of] God but [the mercy of] God. God turned [with mercy] to them so that they may turn [with repentance] to Him. God is the Most-Returning, the All-Merciful.
>
> (9:117–118)

These two verses are part of a long passage (9:101–122) about the battle of Tabuk (north of Arabia). The Hadith gives many (and sometimes contradictory) details about this battle, which Muslims fought against the Byzantine army and their Christian Arab allies in 630.[10] Initially, the battle was dreaded by all Muslims: the Prophet himself, the Emigrants (*muhajirun* – Muslims who emigrated with the Prophet from Mecca to Medina in 622), and the Allies (*ansar* – Muslims from Medina who welcomed Muhammad and his people). They all were reluctant to go on the expedition: it was in the summer heat and during the harvest period, the journey was very long and the enemy's army was much larger than the Muslim army. All this explains why the battle was referred to as *ghazwat al-'usra*, 'the raid of hardship'. Some Arabs simply refused to join in; they are described as hypocrites and are warned that they will be severely punished (9:101). Most Muslims eventually overcame their fears and laziness and marched on Tabuk. God forgave their initial reluctance (9:117). A small group of Muslims stayed behind, but promptly regretted their desertion. When the Prophet came back to Medina, after an inconclusive expedition, they confessed their sins and pledged allegiance to him. He sought God's forgiveness for them and accepted their offerings as compensation for their wrongdoing (9:102–105). However, he ordered that three men of the group be kept apart from the Muslim community until God revealed whether they should be punished or forgiven (9:106). Razi makes a suggestion as to why God did not accept the repentance of the three men. Their repentance, he says, was probably not genuine because it had wrong motivations; it was prompted either by fear of God's punishment (instead of conviction of sin) or by an attempt to get out of an embarrassing and shameful situation.[11] Fifty days later, it was revealed that 'God turned [with mercy] to them so that they may [genuinely] turn [with repentance] to Him' (9:118).

This verse proves, Sunni Muslims argue, that God's role in people's repentance is decisive in either of the two possible situations:

1. Their initial repentance was not genuine. As soon as God turned to them and granted them his pardon, his initiative aroused a genuine repentance in their heart. This interpretation is suggested by Razi.
2. Their initial repentance was genuine. Although they repented, God punished them for fifty days before he accepted their repentance. This shows that, from a rational point of view, God is under no obligation to forgive. However, thanks to God's revelation, we know that he does forgive sinners because he is a merciful and gracious God.[12]

Mu'tazili theologians believe that God would be unjust if he refused to accept people's repentance. So how do they interpret sura 9 verses 117–118? For them, God did forgive the three men as soon as they repented, but he revealed his decision only fifty days later. Why did he not reveal his decision immediately and why did he let repenting people be punished by being ostracized by the Muslim community? Mu'tazili commentators deny that the suffering of the three people was a punishment: it was a special trial ordained by God as 'a measure of reinforcing people's duty to submit to God's law'.[13] The purpose of this trial was to deter anyone else from disobeying God's command: if forgiven Muslims had to go through such a hard test as a result of their disobedience, people should think twice when they are tempted to transgress God's law. In the end, God revealed that he had accepted the repentance of the three men in order to encourage *all* disobedient Muslims to repent from their sins.[14]

God initiates repentance

God's sovereignty plays a key role in Sufism as well as in Sunni theology. Muslim mystics understand God as the One who initiates people's repentance. His merciful and sovereign act determines our coming back to him. This is illustrated by a short dialogue between a Sufi woman, Rabi'a al-'Adawiyya, and a man who was overwhelmed by his guilt: 'He said, "I have sinned much and rebelled much against God. If I turn in repentance to God will he turn in mercy to me?" She replied, "No, but if he turns in mercy to you, then you will turn in repentance to him." '[15]

Rabi'a was fully aware that her own relationship with God was the result of his grace at work in her life: 'She emphasized her conception of Repentance as a "gift from God" in another saying of hers, to the effect that "Seeking forgiveness with the tongue is the sin of lying. If I seek repentance of myself, I shall have need of repentance again" '.[16] Ibn 'Arabi's understanding of God as *tawwab*, 'Most-Returning', is the key to his mystical philosophy. We will look at his original interpretation of God's repenting in chapter 15.

Return to me!

The word *tawwab*, as a divine name, has no equivalent in the Bible. However, its meaning is found in both the Old and the New Testament. The Hebrew verb, *šûb*, carries a similar meaning to the Arabic verb *taba*. The Greek verb *metanoeō*, which is usually translated by 'to repent', also refers to the idea of change: change of direction, mindset, attitude; hence the meaning of God turning to people and people turning to God.

As in the Qur'an, the Hebrew verb *šûb* is used for both God and man. God turns to his people and they turn back to him. The people of Israel often went astray. The message of many prophets consisted in calling the Israelites to come back to him: ' "Ever since the time of your forefathers you have turned away from my decrees and have not kept them. Return to me, and I will return to you", says the LORD Almighty' (Mal. 3:7; cf. 2 Chr. 30:6; Zech. 1:3).[17]

God's call for Israel to turn back to him was rarely met with a positive response. More often than not, 'they made their faces harder than stone/and refused to repent (*šûb*)' (Jer. 5:3; cf. 8:5; Is. 9:12–13; Hos. 7:10). God sent them many warnings. Through natural disasters (famine, drought, disease) he called them to come back to him, but each time their attitude was the same: ' "yet you have not returned to me", declares the LORD' (see Amos 4:6–11). In the end, God punished them and sent them into exile in Babylon.

The plight of Israel made some people realize that the Israelites were incapable, in their own strength, of returning to God. God's initiative was indispensable, for without it there was no hope. Hence the cry for God to step in and rescue his people:

> O God of our salvation!
> Turn to us, and break up your anger with us.
> (Ps. 85:5; lit. tr.)

> Return, O Lord! How long will it be?
> Have compassion on your servants.
> (Ps. 90:13; lit. tr.)

> O Lord! Return us to you, and we will return;
> Renew our days of old.
> (Lam. 5:21; lit. tr.; cf. Jer. 17:14; 31:18)

God, who is merciful, listened to the cry of his people in exile just as he did when they were in Egypt (Exod. 3:7). He promised that he would answer their prayers by accomplishing their return to him: 'If you return – and I will turn you, you will stand before me' (Jer. 15:19; lit. tr.). As a result of God's intervention, those in exile turned back to him and repented en masse (Neh. 9; Dan. 9). Many came back to the land of their forefathers. But it was not long before they turned away from God again and returned to their old sinful ways.

God's decisive initiative took place when he sent Jesus Christ. Jesus' mission was enhanced by the fact that his coming followed nearly five hundred years during which God did not send any prophet to Israel. Immediately before Jesus, God sent John the Baptist (*Yahya* in the Qur'an) to prepare the way for him. John summed up the message of the prophets who came before him by calling his people to come back to God: 'Repent for the kingdom of heaven is near' (Matt. 3:2) and Jesus started his mission with the same call (Matt. 4:17). His message was all about God's kingdom and people's response. Thus the coming of God's kingdom through Jesus was nothing less than God returning to his people and, in this context, the people's response (their repentance) meant their coming back to God.

The lost sheep

In his preaching Jesus highlights God's initiative in rescuing his people. One of his parables, the parable of the lost sheep, has striking similarities with 'the parable of the lost camel' reported in the Hadith:

Suppose one of you has a hundred sheep and loses one of them. Does he not leave the ninety-nine in the open country and go after the lost sheep until he finds it? And when he finds it, he joyfully puts it on his shoulders and goes home. Then he calls his friends and neighbours together and says, 'Rejoice with me; I have found my lost sheep.' I tell you that in the same way there will be more rejoicing in heaven over one sinner who repents than over ninety-nine righteous persons who do not need to repent.
(Luke 15:4–7)

What stands out in both parables is God's joy over the repentance of his servants. Yet there are some significant differences between these stories. Whereas the lost camel finds its way to its exhausted owner, the lost sheep is found by the shepherd himself. In the story told by Jesus, the shepherd, who represents God, shows no exhaustion of any kind; he goes 'after the lost sheep until he finds it'. This story perfectly illustrates the fact that God's intervention in our coming back to him is decisive. In other words, we do not find God – he finds us.

We cannot come back on our own

God's sovereign initiative comes first in Christianity as it does in Sunni Islam. But why is God's intervention so crucial? From a biblical perspective, the answer lies in the fact that we are unable to come back to God by ourselves. Sin alienates us from God. Its impact on our spiritual life is such that even if we wanted to come back to God, we would fail. However, God is a loving God. He loves us more than we can possibly imagine. In fact, Jesus compares God's relationship with us to a father's relationship with his children (Luke 15:11–32; Matt. 21:28–32) and tells us that God loves us more than our parents ever could (Matt. 7:9–11). God's love for us explains that he used his sovereign power to restore our relationship with him. Jesus reveals who God is. He came *from* God so that we may return *to* God: 'This is love: not that we loved God, but that he loved us and sent his Son as an atoning sacrifice for our sins ... We love because he first loved us' (1 John 4:10, 19).

Notes

1. For an interpretation of this verse, see the section 'Apostasy' in chapter 17, pp. 272–273.
2. Two different prepositions are used for God and for man, respectively *'ala* and *ila*.
3. The Qur'an uses two other verbs with the same meaning as *taba*. The first is *aba*. God forgives those who turn to him in repentance (17:30), like David (38:17, 25), Solomon (38:30, 40) and Job (38:44). The second,

anaba, is used for Abraham (11:75), David (38:24), Solomon (38:34), Shu'ayb (11:88) and Muhammad (42:10).

4. The exception is sura 2 verse 222: 'God loves those who turn to Him [in repentance]'.

5. Muslim, *tawba* 31 [4954]:IV, bk 37, no. 6644, p. 1440.

6. Muslim, *tawba* 3 [4929]:IV, bk 37, no. 6613, p. 1434; Bukhari, *da'awat* 4 [5833]:VIII, bk 75, no. 321, p. 215.

7. Razi on 4:17; V:10, pp. 3–6.

8. Ibid.

9. Razi on 2:37; II:3, pp. 21–22.

10. See Bukhari, *maghazi* 79 [4066]:V, bk 59, no. 702, p. 493; Muslim, *tawba* 53 [4973]:IV, bk 37, no. 6670, p. 1445.

11. Razi on 9:106; VIII:16, pp. 101–103.

12. Razi on 9:118; VIII:16, pp. 172–175.

13. This concept is known as *tashdid al-taklif*, i.e. the tightening of the obligations imposed by the Lord on his subjects. Or *tashdid al-mihna*; i.e. the tightening of testing inflicted by God on his servants for a specific purpose. In this case, it was meant to deter other Muslims from following the example of the three men; i.e. staying behind while Muslims are fighting their enemies.

14. Gimaret, *Lecture*, p. 431.

15. Qushayri, *Risala*, p. 96; cf. Smith, *Rabi'a*, p. 56.

16. Smith, *Rabi'a*, p. 55.

17. God's call for Israel to turn back to him is echoed in the New Testament. Jesus commands the church to repent and come back to him (Rev. 2:5, 16; 3:3, 19).

PART TWO

FORGIVENESS
IN THEOLOGY

7. SIN: ARE ALL SINS EQUALLY SERIOUS?

Two issues condition the understanding of God's forgiveness in Islam. The first is the *definition of sin*, or more specifically whether or not there are two categories of sin; that is, major sins and minor sins. The second is the *definition of faith*. Does faith mainly consist of trusting God, or is obedience to God's law an essential part of being Muslim? These two issues are closely related. If obeying God's commands is a defining part of being Muslim, then committing sin (especially a major sin) undermines one's faith. But if faith essentially means trusting God, then disobeying God cannot seriously endanger one's faith. The question therefore is whether a disobedient Muslim is still a Muslim. The purpose of this chapter and the next is to answer this important question, which will partly determine the answers to two other questions: Will God forgive sinful Muslims? Will the Prophet intercede for them on the Day of Judgment? These questions will be addressed in the two subsequent chapters. The final chapter in Part 2 deals with the issue of God's forgiveness in relation to the prophets. Are the prophets sinless? Do they need God's pardon?

Major and minor sins

In Islam sin is usually defined as an act of disobedience to God's will. This will is expressed in his law, comprising both commands and prohibitions. The question is, are all precepts equal in terms of their importance or are some more important than others? In other words, are all sins equally serious or is there a difference to be made between acts of disobedience that are particularly sinful and other 'more ordinary' sins?

Consider the following three texts in the Qur'an.

> If you keep away from major [sins], We will pardon your [minor] sins and introduce you [to Paradise] through a gate of great honour.
> (4:31)

> ... those that keep away from major crimes and shameful deeds and forgive [others] after they have been made angry ...
> (42:37)

> Those that keep away from major crimes and shameful deeds [and fall] only into minor sins will find that Your Lord's forgiveness is all-embracing.
> (53:32)

In each of these verses the word *kaba'ir* is found, the plural form of *kabira*, which literally means 'big'. Depending on the context *kabira* refers to 'a big sin' (4:31) or 'a big deed' (18:49; 54:53) or 'a difficult deed' (2:45, 143). The opposite of *kabira* is *saghira*, which literally means 'small', 'a small thing' (9:121) or 'a small deed' (10:61; 34:3). A sin that is *kabira* is grave, gross, grievous or heinous. I have chosen the translation 'major' because of the contrast between 'major' and 'minor' sins.

Looking for a definition

In none of the above texts are major or minor sins defined. Islamic tradition has therefore sought to identify them. From the first generation, Muslims have been divided over this issue.[1]

Early definitions

Razi tells us that, for some, *all sins are major sins*. He challenges this interpretation on several grounds. First, the Qur'an does make a distinction between major and minor sins (4:31; 18:49; 54:53). Second, one Qur'anic text seems to differentiate between three categories of sins: 'God has made faith precious to you and beautified it in your hearts, rendering unbelief, wickedness and disobedience hateful to you' (49:7). Thus, according to Razi, God's 'prohibitions' (*munhayat*) in order of seriousness are 'unbelief' (*kufr*), 'wickedness' (*fisq*) and 'disobedience' (*'isyan*). This distinction, he claims, suggests that wickedness refers to major sins and disobedience to minor sins.[2] Razi's third argument is that in several sayings the Prophet refers specifically to major sins. One hadith has it that 'the major sins are: polytheism (*shirk*), perjury, rebellion against one's parents, and murder'.[3]

Razi attributes to Ibn 'Abbas the opinion that all sins are major sins. This companion of the Prophet based his judgment on two considerations. The first is that we disobey God, whose blessings are so many that, as the Qur'an says, it is impossible to count them (14:34; 16:18). The second is that we disobey God, who is the greatest and the highest Existent in the whole universe. Razi's reply to this argument is that God is also most merciful, most generous and all-sufficient. Our obedience or disobedience does not affect him. He needs neither. Consequently, although sin is serious, it is not beyond the scope of his forgiveness.[4] Finally, Razi adds, if all sins are serious, some are nevertheless more serious than others.[5]

A second group claims that there is *a clear-cut difference between major and minor sins*. Major sins are either sins for which the Qur'an promises God's punishment (*wa'id*)[6] or sins committed deliberately. Razi disagrees with these definitions. All sins deserve to be punished, he says, whether the punishment is stated explicitly or not. The evidence that a major sin is not necessarily a sin committed intentionally is that Jews and Christians do commit a major sin, since they do not believe in Muhammad as God's prophet, yet they are unaware of their sin.[7]

The Hadith attributes several sayings to Muhammad as regards major sins. One has it that there are seven major sins.[8] These sins highlight the seriousness of specific sins already mentioned in the

Qur'an: polytheism (22:31), witchcraft (10:77), murder (4:93), consuming the property of an orphan (4:10), taking of usury (2:275), desertion in a religious expedition (8:15) and falsely accusing married Muslim women of adultery (24:23).[9] Other traditions consider as major sins rebellion against one's parents (4:36), false testimony (16:91),[10] attacking pilgrims on their way to Mecca (5:3), drinking wine (2:219), despairing of God's mercy (39:53) or ignoring God's judgment (7:99).[11] Thus the figure seven is not to be taken literally. Ibn 'Abbas is believed to have said that the number of major sins is closer to seven hundred than to seven.[12] This saying would confirm his view that any act of disobedience represents a major sin.

Developments in theology

The radical view of Ibn 'Abbas that all sins are major sins has been taken up by Khariji theology. On the other side of the debate,

	Mu'tazilites	Sunnites	Kharijites
Are some sins more serious than others?	There is a clear distinction between major sins, *kaba'ir*, and minor sins, *sagha'ir*	All sins are serious, but some are more serious than others. The distinction between major and minor sins is relative.	All sins are major sins.
Which sins will God *not* forgive unless the person repents?	• Polytheism, *shirk* • Unbelief, *kufr* • Major sins, *kaba'ir*	• Polytheism, *shirk* • Unbelief, *kufr*	Any sin not repented from.

Table 3. Definitions of major and minor sins in Islamic theology

Mu'tazili theologians hold that there is a clear distinction between major and minor sins. Razi's arguments are characteristic of the Sunni position who see this distinction to be relative.

The Mu'tazili view

Mu'tazili theology is characterized by its doctrine regarding major and minor sins. Definitions of what is major and what is minor vary. There are three main definitions:

1. Major sins are those the Qur'an associates with God's punishment.
2. Major sins are those that are particularly serious regardless of whether or not they are associated with God's punishment.
3. Any sin committed deliberately is a major sin.[13]

Mankdim (a Mu'tazili theologian) considers that there is simply no scriptural evidence in favour of the third definition. Take a Jew, for example, who does not believe in Muhammad. Although he is unaware of it, he is committing the major sin of unbelief. Like Razi, Mankdim argues that what is true of unbelief is true of sin in general. The seriousness of sin is not based on people's knowledge that what they do is evil.[14]

How do we know that sins fall into two categories? Abu 'Ali al-Jubba'i, a leading Mu'tazili theologian, considers that God's revelation teaches us this truth. Without it every sin would appear to us as a major sin. Because of God's undeserved blessings, any act of disobedience would earn a double portion of punishment (one because the act is evil in itself and one because it entails ungratefulness to God), whereas a good deed would earn a simple portion of reward. Disobeying God is like a son disobeying a compassionate and dedicated father. His disobedience is far more serious than disobeying a stranger.[15]

Mankdim points to the scriptural evidence for the Mu'tazili doctrine by quoting relevant Qur'anic texts (18:49; 54:53). He draws the same conclusion as Razi from sura 49 verse 7 ('God has made faith precious to you and beautified it in your hearts, rendering unbelief, wickedness and disobedience hateful to you'). Apart from unbelief, which is the most serious disobedience, this text shows that there are major sins referred to as *fisq*, and minor sins referred to as *'isyan*. Sura 53 verse 32 states that God's forgiveness is conditional ('Those that keep away from major crimes and shameful deeds [and fall] only into minor sins will find that Your Lord's forgiveness is all-embracing'). This condition makes no sense without the implied divide between major and minor sins. Finally, sura 4 verse 48 ('God does not forgive that partners be associated with Him, but He forgives any other sin to whom He pleases') relates God's forgiveness to all sins except polytheism. In this context, Mankdim comments, forgiveness of sin can only mean forgiveness of minor sins.[16]

Abu Hashim disagrees with his father, Abu 'Ali. For him the difference between major and minor sins is not only based on God's revelation. There is a rational difference as well. Everyone knows, he says, that stealing one dirham is not the same as stealing ten. The first is a minor sin, whereas the second is a major one.[17] Although Mankdim is of the Basrian school of Mu'tazilism, on this issue he supports the view of Abu 'Ali, whose name is associated with the Baghdadian school.[18]

The difference between major and minor sins has theological implications. The person who commits a major sin becomes a sinful Muslim, and deserves eternal punishment. If his sin represents an offence (adultery, robbery, drinking wine etc.), there is a legal penalty to be carried out against him. So in the case of robbery it is very important to determine what is a major sin and what is not. In Muhammad's time, stealing a quarter of a dinar,[19] or something worth a dinar or three dirhams,[20] was seen as a crime and the criminal had his hand cut off. A major sin starts with five dirhams for Abu l-Hudhayl, with ten for Mankdim, with two hundred for Nazzam. For Ja'far bin Mubashshir any amount represents a major sin if the theft is deliberate. Abu 'Ali considers that five dirhams is the dividing line between a major and a minor sin, and he takes into account whether the theft is deliberate or not. So in the case of deliberate theft, if a robber first conceives the idea of stealing one dirham and two-thirds, then some time later he resolves to commit the theft, and finally he steals this sum, his act (done in three successive stages) amounts to a major sin, as three times one dirham and two-thirds equals five![21] Abu 'Ali considers that to resolve to commit a major sin is a major sin, and to resolve to commit a minor sin is a minor sin, and to resolve to commit an act of unbelief is an act of unbelief.[22]

Do minor sins add up to make a major sin? Some Mu'tazilites say they don't, others claim they do. For Abu 'Ali stealing five dirhams one by one amounts to stealing five dirhams at once.[23] Mankdim takes the same view (though he considers that ten dirhams is the borderline).[24] 'Abd al-Jabbar believes that persisting in a minor sin equals committing a major sin.[25]

What about sins neither associated with eternal punishment nor with legal punishment? Is it possible to know whether they are major or minor sins? All Mu'tazilites agree that it is impossible for us to know for sure whether a particular act of disobedience is a major or a minor sin. Why? Because if God were to let us know which sins are minor, we would be tempted to commit them. Since we would know that they have no damaging consequences for our eternal destiny, nothing would stop us from committing them.[26] The fact that we cannot know which are the minor sins is intended to be an incentive for us to keep away from any sin for fear that it might turn out to be a major one. It is therefore for our own sake that we are unable to distinguish between major and minor sins.

Major sins have been revealed only in part to us. Any sin could potentially be a major sin. By definition a major sin is a sin for which the punishment will outweigh the reward for all good deeds.[27] This definition is based on the belief that God will not forgive major sins unless people repent. God will forgive only minor sins (according to sura 4 verse 31: 'If you keep away from major [sins], We will pardon your [minor] sins'). Is God's forgiveness a favour or a reward granted to those who have abstained from major sins? Minor sins will be forgiven undeservedly (*tafaddul^(an)*) according to some (e.g. Abu l-Hudhayl),[28] but as an earned recompense (*bi-stihqaq*) for others (e.g. Abu 'Ali).[29]

The Sunni view

Most Muslim theologians differ with the Mu'tazilites over their doctrine on major and minor sins. The Kharijites in particular consider that all sins are major sins.[30] Sunni theologians are also of the opinion that all sins are major. Ash'ari (a great figure in Sunni theology) considers that transgressing God's commands is what characterizes all sins. Therefore all sins are to be seen as major sins. But, when compared with each other, sins can be described as major or minor (18:49; 54:53).[31] Thus when the Qur'an speaks of 'major sins' (42:37), it refers to the most grave crime, unbelief, for any 'crime' (*ithm*) is grave. Ash'ari gives a similar interpretation to sura 4 verse 31 ('If you keep away from major [sins], We will forgive your [minor] sins'). This text calls people to abandon their unbelief; in other words, to repent from their unbelief and come to faith. The Mu'tazilites are right when they claim that unbelief is a bigger sin than adultery, but this does not mean that adultery is a small sin.[32] Juwayni (an Ash'ari theologian) takes a similar view. Sin is 'great' (*'azim*) because it represents an act of disobedience towards God, who is 'the greatest' (*a'zam*). Sins bigger than others are those that reflect people's careless attitude towards religion. As a result, they undermine their 'reputation' (*'adala*).[33] Sabuni (a Maturidite theologian) points out that, compared with unbelief, which is the biggest of all sins, other sins may seem to be minor.[34]

Ash'ari, primarily using rational arguments, is very critical of Mu'tazili doctrine. They claim that minor sins will be forgiven through refraining from committing major sins. Yet how can they claim this while acknowledging that we don't even know what minor or major sins are? Ash'ari tells a story aimed at showing the irrationality of Mu'tazili beliefs. Imagine a man, he says, who rescued another man from murder several times. Later on he steals five dirhams from him to buy food for himself. He knows that the man is in no need of this money, since he possesses one hundred thousand dirhams. According to Mu'tazili doctrine, this man has committed a major sin, which will not be forgiven unless he repents! Ash'ari agrees with Abu 'Ali (at whom the story is apparently directed) that resolving to commit a sin is a sin. But, unlike his former teacher, he thinks that the resolve to commit a sin and the sin itself are two different acts. To decide to commit adultery is evil but it is not adultery. To commit adultery is an individual act and a different act to the resolve that was behind it.[35]

In brief, Sunni theologians disagree with the Mu'tazilites, in that they believe that the difference between major and minor sins is a relative one. God can forgive both, and his forgiveness is by no means conditioned by people's repentance. For them, a 'major sin' does not result in the person being condemned to eternal punishment. Neither does it mean that the person is no longer a Muslim, as we will see in the next chapter.

Sin in the Bible

The Islamic understanding of sin as disobedience to God's law is consonant with one of the definitions of sin in the Bible: 'Everyone who sins breaks the law; in fact, sin is lawlessness' (1 John 3:4). However, sin is not just a transgression of the law; it is an offence against the Lawgiver: 'Against you, you only, have I sinned/and done what is evil in your sight' (Ps. 51:4; cf. Luke 15:18, 21).

Jesus summed up the teaching of the law and the prophets with a twofold command: to love God and to love one's neighbour (Matt. 22:34–40). Sin is therefore failing to respond adequately to God's love. Because God is our loving Lord, sin harms our relationship with him and offends him personally: ' "A son honours his father, and a servant his master. If I am a father, where is the honour due to me? If I am a master, where is the respect due to me?" says the LORD Almighty' (Mal. 1:6). In Islam, by contrast, God is transcendent and self-contained. The Creator is far above his human creatures. He is not affected by our disobedience. Sin can only concern *us*. It has no impact but on ourselves: 'Whoever transgresses God's bounds does evil to himself' (65:1; cf. 2:57; 7:160; 18:35; 35:32; 37:113).

Our sinful nature
Sin is an act of disobedience, but it is more than that. What we do reflects who we are. The fact that we all sin demonstrates that we are sinful. We cannot separate what we do and who we are. Our wrongdoing has an adverse effect on our spiritual well-being. Our evil acts worsen our spiritual ill-health. Thus sin affects our deeds as well as our nature. We need to acknowledge not only that *we have sinned*, but also that *we are sinful*. God in return will forgive our sins and purify us from sin:

If we claim to be without sin, we deceive ourselves and the truth is not in us. If we confess our sins, he is faithful and just and will forgive us our sins and purify us from all unrighteousness. If we claim we have not sinned, we make him out to be a liar and his word has no place in our lives.

(1 John 1:8–10)

Islam does not share the Christian view about the sinfulness of human nature. People commit sin not because they are sinful, but because they are weak. Indeed, weakness characterizes human beings just as strength is one of God's attributes: 'God wills to make things lighter for you; for man was created weak' (4:28). Yet the Qur'an also describes human beings in such a way that their sins can hardly be attributed to sheer weakness. Man, it is said, is a creature with a restless anxiety (70:19). He is hasty (17:11), forgetful (39:8), ignorant (33:72), perverse, thankless (14:34), contentious (18:54) and rebellious (96:6). Above all, it is said that 'the soul is prone to evil' (12:53). Does this portrait not suggest that sin is ingrained in human nature? There is a saying in the Hadith which suggests that people are affected by evil right from the beginning of their existence. In other words, before they do anything in this life, good or bad, they fall victim to the evil one: 'There is none born among the offspring of Adam but Satan touches it. A child, therefore, cries loudly at the time of birth because of the touch of Satan, except Mary and her child.' [36]

The Christian belief known as 'original sin' implies that human nature is not neutral. We are predisposed to commit evil, as we all do: 'Surely I was sinful at birth,/sinful from the time my mother conceived me' (Ps. 51:5). This predisposition is the result of Adam's disobedience (Gen. 3). Because we are not just individuals, but members of the same human family, our father's personal disobedience had repercussions for all of us. It did not take long before the consequences of Adam's sin on his descendants were tragically illustrated: Cain, Adam's son, killed his own brother. The story of this gratuitous murder, recorded in both the Bible (Gen. 4:1–16; cf. Heb. 11:4; 1 John 3:12–13) and the Qur'an (5:30–34), reveals that Adam's disobedience had far-reaching implications for his offspring. Thus sin embraces all human beings.

The unforgivable sin

Unlike the Qur'an, the Bible makes no reference to minor and major sins. However, Jesus speaks of a sin that will never be forgiven. To understand his words we need to read them in their context:

> Then they brought him a demon-possessed man who was blind and mute, and Jesus healed him, so that he could both talk and see ... But when the Pharisees heard this, they said, 'It is only by Beelzebub, the prince of demons, that this fellow drives out demons' ... [Jesus replied,] 'every sin and blasphemy will be forgiven men, but the blasphemy against the Spirit will not be forgiven. Anyone who speaks a word against the Son of Man will be forgiven, but anyone who speaks against the Holy Spirit will not be forgiven, either in this age or in the age to come.'
>
> (Matt. 12:22, 24, 31–32; cf. Mark 3:22–30)

The unforgivable sin appears to be the wilful rejection of the truth about Jesus after one has been given irrefutable evidence of that truth. This sin is called 'the blasphemy against the Holy Spirit' because God's Spirit has been powerfully at work through Jesus to authenticate his claims. Yet, instead of believing in him, the Pharisees (the Jewish leaders who were members of a very strict religious party) accused Jesus of being the devil's agent. They also committed this sin when they condemned him to death. Some years later there were people who claimed to be Christians – and who were for a while members of the Christian community – who ended up denying the truth about Jesus Christ (1 John 2:18–19). The falsehood of their teaching was such that they were called 'antichrists' (1 John 2:22; 4:2–3). Their deliberate denial of the truth amounted to committing 'a sin that leads to death' (1 John 5:16). This sin, known as 'deadly (or mortal) sin', will result in eternal punishment, which is described as 'a second death' (Rev. 2:11; 20:6, 14; 21:8) in comparison with the first death; that is, the physical death.[37] Thus the unforgivable sin appears to be a hardened and deliberate refusal to believe in Christ despite one's full knowledge of who he is. Seen in this perspective, this sin is neither a specific sin (as in Mu'tazili theology) nor mere unbelief (as in Sunni theology).[38] It is a well-informed denial of the truth about Jesus Christ.

Notes

1. See Razi's treatment of this issue, found in his exegesis of sura 4 verse 31; V:10, pp. 60–64.
2. In Islamic theology the word *kufr* refers to unbelief in all its forms. Unbelievers include 'polytheists', *mushrikun*, Jews and Christians and heretic Muslims. The word *fisq* (or *fusuq*) is the technical word for 'committing a gross or major sin'. Theologians use the word *fasiq* when they refer to a Muslim who is guilty of *fisq*. I have systematically translated the word *fasiq* as 'sinful Muslim' throughout this study. The reader needs to keep in mind this specific meaning of the word. By contrast, a Muslim who commits an ordinary or minor sin is described simply as a 'disobedient Muslim'.
3. Bukhari, *shahadat* 10 [2460]:III, bk 48, no. 821, p. 499; *diyat* 2 [6362, 6363]:II, bk 83, nos. 9, 10, p. 5; *istitaba* 1 [6408]:IX, bk 84, no. 55, p. 41.
4. In Arabic: *kullu dhalika yujibu khiffata al-dhanb*.
5. Razi on 4:31; V:10, pp. 60–61.
6. Islamic theology uses two similar words for God's reward and punishment: *wa'd*, 'promise', and *wa'id*, 'threat'. These words derive from the verb *wa'ada*, 'to promise'. Thus God's promise is dual: he promises his reward to some and his punishment to others. In this study the word 'promise' means either reward or punishment. The context will determine the sense in which it is used.
7. Razi on 4:31; V:10, pp. 60–61.
8. Nasa'i, *zakat* 1 [2395], *tahrim* 3 [3947].
9. Muslim, *iman* 39 [129]:I, bk 1, no. 161, p. 52; Bukhari, *hudud* 45 [6351]:VIII, bk 81, no. 840, p. 560.
10. Bukhari, *adab* 6 [5519]:VIII, bk 73, no. 8, p. 7; Muslim, *iman* 143 [126], 144 [128]:I, bk 1, nos. 158, 160, p. 52; Tirmidhi, *shahadat* 3 [2224], *birr* 4 [1823].
11. Razi on 4:31; V:10, p. 62.
12. Ibid.
13. Ash'ari, *Maqalat*, I, p. 332.
14. Mankdim, *Sharh*, p. 634.
15. Ibid., p. 633.

16. Ibid., pp. 633–634.
17. Ibid., p. 634.
18. In Islamic theology the Mu'tazilite school has two main trends. These subgroups are identified in reference to two towns in Iraq where they developed: Baghdad (the capital) and Basra (in the south). Generally speaking, 'the Baghdadians' are closer than 'the Basrians' to Sunni theologians.
19. Bukhari, *ḥudud* 13 [6291]:VIII, bk 81, no. 781, p. 514; Muslim, *ḥudud* 1 [3189]:III, bk 17, no. 4175, p. 907; Abu Dawud, *ḥudud* 12 [3810]:III, bk 33, no. 4370, p. 1222; Tirmidhi, *ḥudud* 16 [1365]; Nasa'i, *qaṭ' al-sariq* 9 [4830].
20. Bukhari, *ḥudud* 13 [6297–6300]:VIII, bk 81, nos. 787–790, p. 516; Muslim, *ḥudud* 2 [3194]:III, bk 17, no. 4183, p. 908; Abu Dawud, *ḥudud* 13 [3812]:III, bk 33, no. 4372, p. 1222; Nasa'i, *qaṭ' al-sariq* 8 [4858].
21. Ash'ari, *Maqalat*, I, p. 334. For Mankdim's evaluation of a major sin see *Sharḥ*, p. 665.
22. Ash'ari, *Maqalat*, I, p. 332.
23. Ibid., p. 333.
24. Mankdim, *Sharḥ*, p. 800.
25. 'Abd al-Jabbar, *Mughni*, XIV, p. 323.
26. Mankdim, *Sharḥ*, p. 635. In Mu'tazilite theology minor sins have no effect at all on people's eternal destiny, according to the cancellation theory *al-iḥbaṭ*; they have only a secondary effect, according to the compensation theory *al-muwazana*. In the first theory minor sins will be forgiven if outnumbered by good deeds. In the second, the punishment for minor sins will reduce proportionately the reward for the good deeds if the good deeds outnumber the evil ones. Likewise, the reward for the good deeds will reduce proportionately the punishment for the evil deeds if the evil deeds outnumber the good ones. Thus in both theories minor sins do not determine people's eternal destiny (see chapter 11).
27. Mankdim, *Sharḥ*, p. 632.
28. Ash'ari, *Maqalat*, I, p. 330.
29. Ibid., I, pp. 331–333; II, p. 170.
30. Mankdim, *Sharḥ*, p. 632; Juwayni, *Irshad*, p. 218. Some Kharijites, however, do make a difference between major sins and minor (see Nasafi, *Tabsira*, II, p. 767).
31. Ibn Furak, *Mujarrad*, p. 157.
32. Ibid., p. 158.

33. Juwayni, *Irshad*, p. 222.
34. Ṣabuni, *Bidaya*, p. 147.
35. Ibn Furak, *Mujarrad*, p. 160.
36. Bukhari, *anbiya'* 44 [3177]:IV, bk 55, no. 641, p. 426.
37. Three main interpretations have been suggested about the 'sin that leads to death' (1 John 5:16): a specific sin, apostasy and the blasphemy against the Holy Spirit (Stott, *Epistles*, pp. 186–190).
38. Mu'tazili teaching is not dissimilar from the Catholic doctrine that distinguishes between grave (or mortal) sins and venial sins. Capital sins (a third category) are sins that give rise to the seven other sins: pride, avarice, envy, wrath, lust, gluttony and sloth or acedia (see *Catechism*, paras. 1854–1866, pp. 409–412).

8. FAITH: WHAT DOES IT MEAN TO BE A BELIEVER?

All Muslim theologians agree that God's pardon is closely related to Islamic faith. Without faith there is no pardon. But they differ as to who is a Muslim and who is not. The reason is that they hold different definitions of faith. Broadly speaking, there are three main definitions:

Kharijites and Mu'tazilites	Sunnites	
	Hanbalites	Murji'ites *(Ash'arites and Maturidites)*
Faith is obeying God's commands.	Faith is trusting God, obeying his commands and professing one's beliefs.	Faith is knowing God and trusting him.

Table 4. Definitions of faith, according to Islamic theology

Definitions of faith

Faith is obeying God's commands

Kharijite theologians consider that faith means obeying God's commands.[1] As a result, they regard sinful Muslims as 'unbelievers' (kuffar).[2] Some Kharijites go as far as to say that sinful Muslims are 'polytheists' (mushrikun), not because of what they say, but because of what they do (see 18:110). Consequently, on the Day of Judgment all sinful Muslims will receive the same punishment as unbelievers.

The Mu'tazilites have a similar definition of faith. For Abu 'Ali and Abu Hashim, faith means 'performing the religious obligations and avoiding the evil acts'. Other Mu'tazilites (Abu l-Hudhayl, 'Abd al-Jabbar and Mankdim) include in their definition the supererogatory acts (nawafil); that is, acts that are commendable but not obligatory.[3] Mu'tazili theologians differ from the Kharijites in that they do not consider sinful Muslims as unbelievers. They are not seen as believers either but have an intermediate status, al-manzila bayna l-manzilatayn.[4] On the Day of Judgment they will go to hell but their suffering will be less painful than that of the unbelievers.[5]

If sinful Muslims are not genuine believers, is it possible to consider them as Muslims? The Qur'an appears to make a distinction between iman (faith), and islam (submission): 'The Arabs of the desert declare: "We have believed." Say: "You have not believed"; say rather, "We have become Muslims", for faith has not entered your hearts' (49:14).

According to Razi this text was revealed when there was a famine in Arabia. An Arab tribe, the Banu Asad, came to Medina and professed faith in order to obtain a share of the alms. God revealed to the Prophet that their conversion to Islam was not genuine. They had surrendered to Islamic authority, but faith had not found its way into their hearts.[6]

Mankdim considers that sinful Muslims are not even entitled to be called Muslims. In the above text he takes the words 'we have become Muslims' metaphorically. That is, they do not have a religious meaning. They simply indicate that people submitted to Islamic rule. In a similar way, the Qur'an calls to faith those who are addressed as 'believers' (e.g. 4:136).[7]

Faith is trusting God, obeying him and professing one's beliefs

Sunni Muslims of the Ḥanbali school claim that faith is made up of three parts. It consists of trusting God in one's heart, obeying his commands with one's limbs and confessing one's beliefs with one's tongue.[8] The Prophet is believed to have said, 'Faith is knowing [God] with one's heart, confessing [Him] with one's tongue, and complying with the Pillars [of Islam]'.[9] The first constituent of faith, trusting God, is supported by several Qur'anic texts: 'Apostle! Do not grieve for those who hurry up into unbelief, those who declared with their lips: "We have believed." They did not believe in their hearts' (5:41; cf. 16:106; 49:14).

Another component of faith is confessing one's faith. To give evidence of the importance of declaring one's faith verbally, Ajurri quotes a well-known hadith in which the Prophet defines his mission:

> I have been commended to wage war against men as long as they do not say, 'There is no god but God'. As soon as they make this confession, I have no rights over their lives and possessions – unless they commit an offence against God's law. They are accountable only to God.[10]

The role of good deeds is to prove that the faith in the heart and the profession of the mouth are genuine.[11] Many texts urge Muslims to demonstrate their faith in practical ways; for example by almsgiving, prayer, caring for orphans and the needy and so on (e.g. 2:177; 22:77). So what if a Muslim fails to live up to his faith? Is he still a believer? The Ḥanbalites argue that sinful Muslims are no longer believers but are still Muslims. As soon as they repent, they recover their faith.[12] Failing to obey God's law results in crossing the border between faith and unbelief.[13] A saying attributed to the Prophet underlines the importance of complying with God's commands, especially prayer: 'Negligence of prayer is what stands between people and unbelief.'[14]

When asked about this subject, one Ḥanbali theologian, Abu Ja'far, drew two concentric circles. The inner circle, he explained, represents *iman*, 'faith', and the outer circle, *islam*, 'submission'.

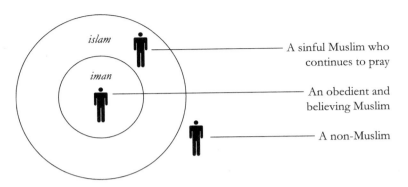

If Muslims sin (e.g. by stealing or committing adultery), they move from the inner circle to the outer circle and cease to be believers. Nevertheless, as long as they continue to pray five times a day and do not commit the sin of associating partners with God, they remain Muslims. If they repent, they return to the inner circle, *iman*.

Faith is knowing God and trusting him

Murji'ite theologians define faith first and foremost in terms of knowing God as the one and only transcendent God. This definition implies that obeying God's law is not an integral part of believing in him. They owe their name 'Murji'ite' to the fact that they attribute a secondary role to good deeds in their definition of what faith is.[15] The Murji'ites include two main groups, the Ash'arites and the Maturidites who, together with the Ḥanbalites, represent the main schools in Sunni theology.

Ash'ari explains that 'knowing God' (*al-ma'rifa bi-llah*) implies submitting to him as Creator, acknowledging him as Lord, exalting him and worshipping no-one else but him. By contrast, unbelief is 'ignorance about God' (*al-jahl bi-llah*). This ignorance takes many forms: hatred, arrogance, indifference towards God, as well as associating other gods with God.[16] Unbelief, in line with the derivation of the Arabic word *kafara*, consists in concealing God's grace (*ni'ma*) by not recognizing that he is the source of all blessings we enjoy in this life. Hence the root of unbelief is an ungrateful attitude towards God.[17]

This definition of faith means that religious obligations (e.g. prayer, almsgiving) are 'the legal expressions of faith' (*shara'i' al-iman*), not faith itself. They are the 'marks' (*'alamat*) and 'signs' (*amarat*) of faith. Therefore, it is only in a broad and weak sense that religious duties can be referred to as faith itself. The Qur'an uses such loose language when 'prayer' is called 'faith' (2:143). Thus there is a clear-cut difference to be made between *iman* (faith) and *islam* (submission). Outward submission to Islamic rule does not necessarily reflect faith in God. Therefore 'all believers are Muslims but not all Muslims (i.e. those who submit outwardly to Islamic authority) are believers'.[18]

Hanbalites	Murji'ites	
	Ash'arites	Maturidites
Sinful Muslims are Muslims but not believers (because faith includes obeying God's commands).	Sinful Muslims are seen as both Muslims and believers (because, although they have been disobedient, they still believe – which is what faith means).	
Hypocritical Muslims are Muslims but not believers.		Hypocritical Muslims are neither believers nor Muslims.

Table 5. The status of sinful and hypocritical Muslims, according to Sunni theologians

This definition of faith means that, for the Ash'arites, 'Muslims who commit sin' (*fussaq*) are both believers and Muslims (whereas for the Hanbalites, they are Muslims but not believers). 'Hypocritical Muslims' (*munafiqun*) are Muslims but not believers. On the Day of Judgment they will be treated as unbelievers because they professed to be Muslims but in fact had no faith (49:14).[19] Unlike the Ash'arites, the Maturidites make no difference at all between *iman* and *islam*. For them, hypocritical Muslims are neither believers nor Muslims. In fact, Nasafi says, hypocritical Muslims are exactly the opposite of sinful Muslims. They put up an Islamic façade but behind this veneer there is no faith. Sinful Muslims, by contrast, disobey God outwardly but in their heart of hearts they still believe in him. This explains why the former will be sent to hell whereas the latter will eventually go to paradise.[20] The Arabs referred to in sura 49 verse 14 were in reality hypocritical. Their profession of faith meant nothing more than their 'surrender' (*istislam*) to Islamic leadership. They wanted to join the Muslim camp after they realized the benefit they could gain from such a move.[21]

All Murji'ites consider that as long as Muslims continue to believe sincerely in God and the Prophet, they are true believers. Their sinful behaviour does not invalidate their faith.[22] This view appears to contradict a well-known hadith:

> He that commits adultery is not a believer when he commits adultery.
> He that commits a theft is not a believer when he commits a theft.[23]

The Murji'ites claim that this tradition is about the Muslim who is not only 'sinful' (*fasiq*), but also 'irreligious' (*mustahill*). Such a Muslim does not consider himself under the authority of God's law. He thinks he can do what he likes, that he is his own judge. In fact, such a Muslim is neither a believer nor a Muslim.[24]

The Murji'ite doctrine is criticized by both Mu'tazilites and Hanbalites. If faith only means trusting in God, claims Ajurri (who is a Hanbalite theologian), then the devil should be considered a believer! For not only does he know God, but he also addresses him as Lord (15:39; 38:79). Likewise, Jews should be seen as believers, since 'they know the Scripture as they know their sons' (2:146).[25] Even polytheists and unbelievers in general know God as their Creator and pray to him when they face hardship or danger. Mu'tazili and Hanbali theologians argue that what characterizes Muslims are in fact their deeds and their submission to God's laws.[26]

The Murji'ites are aware of the deviations to which their doctrines might lead. Nasafi, himself a Murji'ite, acknowledges that not all Murji'ites are orthodox Muslims. Most are orthodox and are well represented by Abu Hanifa – the founder of the Hanafite school of Islamic 'jurisprudence' (*fiqh*). Some, however, hold unorthodox beliefs. To this trend belong Muqatil bin Sulayman and his disciples. Muqatil claimed that Muslims will never be punished in hell, not even those who are sinful.[27] Why? Because he considered that 'just as a good deed will not benefit a polytheist, an evil deed will not harm a believer'. Sabuni criticizes this group of extremist Murji'ites by pointing out the deviations to which their doctrines will inevitably lead. Such doctrines, he says, open wide the gate to permissiveness (*ibahiyya*).[28]

Summary

In short, Muslim theologians understand faith in three different ways. The Mu'tazilites and the Kharijites define faith essentially as *obeying God*. Hence a sinful Muslim is not a genuine Muslim. The Murji'ites (Ash'arites and Maturidites) consider that believing means first and foremost *trusting God*. As long as people believe sincerely in God and his Prophet there is no reason to doubt their faith even if they do not live up to Islamic teaching. The position taken by Hanbali theologians can be seen as a compromise between the two other definitions. Faith consists in *believing in God and obeying his law*. Hence, *a non-practising Muslim is still a Muslim but not a believer*.

Kharijites	Mu'tazilites	Sunnites	
		Hanbalites	**Murji'ites** *(Ash'arites and Maturidites)*
Faith is obeying God's commands.		Faith is trusting God, obeying his commands and professing one's beliefs.	Faith is knowing God and trusting him.
Sinful Muslims are seen as unbelievers.	Sinful Muslims are nominal Muslims (neither believers nor unbelievers).	Sinful Muslims are still Muslims, but they are not believers.	Sinful Muslims are Muslims and are also seen as believers.

Table 6. Definitions of faith and the status of sinful Muslims

The faith of Abraham

The way Christians understand faith in God can be best illustrated through the example of Abraham, who is called 'the father of all believers' (Rom. 4:15–17; Qur'an 22:78). God had promised to give Abraham a son and, through this son, descendants 'as numerous as the stars in the sky and as the sand on the seashore' (Gen. 22:17). But Abraham and his wife Sarah, who were both very elderly, were childless.

> But Abram said, 'O Sovereign LORD ... You have given me no children; so a servant in my household will be my heir.'
>
> Then the word of the LORD came to him: 'This man will not be your heir, but a son coming from your own body will be your heir.' He took him outside and said, 'Look up at the heavens and count the stars – if indeed you can count them.' Then he said to him, 'So shall your offspring be.'
>
> (Gen. 15:2–5)

What was Abraham's response? He responded in faith. He believed God would fulfil his promise: 'Abram believed the LORD and he credited it to him as righteousness' (Gen. 15:6; cf. Rom. 4:18–22; Heb. 11:11–12).[29]

Thus in the Bible, as in Sunni theology, faith means trusting God. This trust-based relationship is just the kind God wants to have with his people. It implies friendship between God and those who trust him, just as Abraham was described as God's 'friend' (2 Chr. 20:7; Is. 41:8; Jas. 2:23; Qur'an 4:125).

Years later God put Abraham to the test by asking him to offer his son as a sacrifice. Abraham obeyed God, for he believed God could raise his son from the dead in order to fulfil his promise (Gen. 22:1–18; Heb. 11:11–19). At the last moment God stepped in, himself providing Abraham with 'a great sacrifice' that saved the life of his son (Qur'an 37:102–111). Thus Abraham's faith was a submissive faith. His example shows that 'faith without deeds is useless ... his faith and his actions were working together, and his faith was made complete by what he did' (Jas. 2:20–22).

Abraham's faith was remarkable, but this does not mean that his life was spotless. When there was a severe famine in the land, instead of relying on God to provide for his needs, he went to Egypt (Gen. 12:10). The Bible and the Hadith report that, when he was there, he was fearful for his life and that of Sarah his wife. He said that Sarah was his sister. God, however, disclosed his lie and rebuked him through Pharaoh himself (Gen. 12:11–20).[30] Years later, before the birth of Isaac, Abraham listened to his wife, who wanted him to give her a child through Hagar her maidservant. God promised Abraham that he would bless Ishmael, Hagar's son, yet made it clear to Abraham that Ishmael was not the promised son. He confirmed to Abraham that his wife, Sarah, would be pregnant and that her son would be called Isaac (Gen. 17:15–22).

In brief, Abraham was a genuine believer; yet he failed on more than one occasion. His example shows that no believer is perfect. Like Abraham, Christians do commit sins 'in thoughts, words and deeds'. Those Muslims who point out that all sins are major sins, because of God's greatness and generosity, are right. God is holy and his moral standards perfect: 'Your eyes are too pure to look on evil;/you cannot tolerate wrong' (Hab. 1:13). Therefore, unlike what Razi claims, God does consider sin as very serious indeed. Yet he is also merciful and forgiving. Provided we acknowledge our failures, he will forgive, restore and help us to live out our faith: 'though a righteous man falls seven times, he rises again,/but the wicked are brought down by calamity' (Prov. 24:16). Believers and unbelievers alike commit sin. What characterizes the former is that they acknowledge their sins and repent. In the next chapter we will look into what repentance means.

Notes

1. Juwayni, *Irshad*, p. 224. In Arabic: *al-imanu huwa l-ta'a*.
2. Mankdim, *Sharh*, p. 720; Sabuni, *Bidaya*, p. 140.
3. Mankdim, *Sharh*, p. 707.
4. Ibid., p. 697.
5. Ash'ari, *Maqalat*, I, p. 204.
6. Razi on 49:14; XIV:28, p. 122.
7. Mankdim, *Sharh*, p. 707.
8. Ajurri, *Shari'a*, p. 119; cf. Juwayni, *Irshad*, p. 224.

9. Ibn Majah, *muqaddima* 9 [64]:I, fwd, p. 38, no. 65. In Arabic: *al-iman ma'rifat^{un} bi-l-qalb wa qawl^{un} bi-l-lisan wa 'amal^{un} bi-l-arkan.*

10. Bukhari, *iman* 16 [24]:I, bk 2, no. 24, p. 25; *i'tisam* 28:IX, bk 92, p. 339; Muslim, *iman* 15 [31]:I, bk 1, no. 29, p. 15; Ibn Majah, *fitan* 1 [3917]:V, bk 36, no. 3927, p. 267; Tirmidhi, *tafsir* sura 88 [3264]; Nasa'i, *jihad* 1 [3042].

11. Ajurri, *Shari'a*, p. 120.

12. Ibid., p. 113.

13. Ibid., p. 114.

14. Muslim, *iman* 36 [116]:I, bk 1, no. 146, p. 48; Abu Dawud, *sunna* 12 [4058]:III, bk 35, no. 4661, p. 1311; Ibn Majah, *iqamat al-salat* 77 [1068]:II, bk 5, no. 1078, p. 133; Tirmidhi, *iman* 9 [2543]; Nasa'i, *salat* 8 [459].

15. One meaning of the verb *arja'a* is 'to move back'. The Murji'ites believe that good works come second after faith, which is understood in terms of knowing God and trusting in him. In this sense they 'move' good deeds behind faith.

16. Ibn Furak, *Mujarrad*, p. 151.

17. Ibid., p. 152. Baqillani, Juwayni, Nasafi and Sabuni take very similar views. They all define faith as 'trusting in God', *al-tasdiqu bi-llah* (see respectively *Tamhid*, p. 345; *Irshad*, p. 224; *Tabsira*, II, p. 769; *Bidaya*, p. 141).

18. Ibn Furak, *Mujarrad*, p. 155; Baqillani, *Tamhid*, p. 347.

19. Ibn Furak, *Mujarrad*, p. 152.

20. Nasafi, *Tabsira*, II, p. 770.

21. Ibid., p. 819.

22. Ibn Furak, *Mujarrad*, p. 154; Baqillani, *Tamhid*, p. 349; Nasafi, *Tabsira*, II, p. 822.

23. Bukhari, *ashriba* 1 [5150]:VII, bk 69, no. 484, p. 339; *hudud* 1 [6274], 6 [6284], 20 [6311]:VIII, bk 81, no. 763, p. 503; no. 773, p. 508; no. 800, p. 524; no. 801, p. 525; Muslim, *iman* 100 [86]:I, bk 1, no. 109, p. 40; Abu Dawud, *sunna* 16 [4069]:III, bk 35, no. 4672, p. 1313; Ibn Majah, *fitan* 3 [3926]:V, bk 36, no. 3936, p. 275; Tirmidhi, *iman* 10 [2549]; Nasa'i, *ashriba* 43 [5565], *qat' al-sariq* 1 [4787].

24. Baqillani, *Insaf*, pp. 172–173, 793.

25. Ajurri, *Shari'a*, p. 145.

26. Ibid., p. 146.

27. Nasafi, *Tabsira*, II, p. 766; cf. Ash'ari, *Maqalat*, I, p. 231.

28. Sabuni, *Bidaya*, p. 140; cf. Ash'ari, *Maqalat*, I, pp. 227–228.

29. Abraham's initial name was 'Abram'. God changed it to 'Abraham', which means 'father of many nations' (Gen. 17:5).

30. The story in the Hadith is slightly different from the one in the Bible. God rescued Sarah and vindicated Abraham, but God did not blame him for telling a lie (Bukhari, *anbiya'* 8 [3108]:IV, bk 55, no. 578, p. 368; Muslim, *fada'il* 154 [4371]:IV, bk 30, no. 5848, p. 1262). According to a Jewish tradition, reproduced in the Hadith, when Pharaoh discovered that Sarah was in fact Abraham's wife, he gave her Hagar to be her maidservant. The Jewish tradition specifies that Hagar was Pharaoh's daughter and her mother one of Pharaoh's concubines (*Encyclopaedia Judaica*, 'Hagar', VII, p. 1074).

9. REPENTANCE (*tawba*)

God is merciful and forgiving. Moreover, because of his willingness to forgive, he has revealed the means by which we can receive his pardon when we disobey his commands. Forgiveness comes through repentance. As long as we live on this side of the Day of Judgment, repentance is our surest way to benefit from his mercy.

'Repentance' (*tawba*) has two meanings in the Qur'an. It refers to the conversion of non-Muslims to Islam (5:36–37). It is also used for believing people in connection with sins they have committed and for which they need to ask God's forgiveness. Because all human beings are sinners, God entrusted his prophets with a message of repentance to be delivered to their people: Moses to the Israelites (2:54), Hud to 'Ad (11:56), Salih to Thamud (11:61), Shu'ayb to Median (11:90) and Muhammad to the Arabs (11:3). Thus Muslims are also urged to turn to God in repentance: 'O Believers! Turn to God, all of you, so that you may attain success' (24:31).

Repentance in the Qur'an and Hadith

Razi explains that, because of human weakness, we will never be able to comply with all of God's commands, no matter how hard we try. Our obedience will always be insufficient. Hence the call goes out for us to repent and to pray for God's forgiveness with the view of enjoying his blessings in this life as well as in the life to come.[1] Thus repentance characterizes the life of godly Muslims, both men (9:112) and women (66:5).

What the Qur'an says about sincere repentance
The Qur'an pleads with Muslims and encourages them to repent whenever they fall short of God's requirements. Repentance must be genuine in order to be acceptable to God:

> O believers! Turn to God with sincere repentance so that your Lord may absolve you of your evil doings and bring you into Gardens where streams flow, on the Day when God will not confound the Prophet or the believers with him.
> (66:8)

Razi comments that people repent sincerely when they profoundly regret and stop doing what was the reason for their repentance.[2] So does a sincere repentance guarantee that God will forgive our sins? This text says literally that God *may* do so; but will he? The Arabic word *'asa* usually means 'maybe', 'perhaps'. Does it have the same meaning in this verse? It occurs in a few other texts in connection with God's forgiveness (4:99; 9:102; 28:67). Razi explains that the word in itself conveys the idea of 'uncertainty' (*shakk*), but since this uncertainty is unfitting for God, it must have another meaning. Exegetes, he says, agree that when applied to God, the word implies a mandatory action, *'asa mina llahi wajib*. The evidence for this meaning is found in the Qur'an in a verse that uses the same word: 'Perhaps God will give [us] the victory' (5:55). God did indeed make Muslims triumph over their polytheistic enemies in Mecca. So why does the Qur'an use this word instead of a more straightforward one? The answer is twofold. First, because Qur'anic language complies with human conventions. A monarch

will only accept the request of those who come to him begging his
favour. In doing so he makes it clear that he is under no obligation.
His action is motivated by sheer favour and pure generosity. So it
is with God. Second, the purpose of using this language is to
highlight that people ought to seek God's pardon earnestly and
humbly.[3] Razi expands this point in another context. Arab
linguists, he observes, consider that the use of the word *'asa* aims
at spurring us on to desire something eagerly (*itma'*). To deny us
what we have been encouraged to look forward to is a shameful
act. God is too generous to deprive us of what he has incited us to
expect ardently.[4]

Thus, without having a formal promise as regards God's
pardon, Muslims can be hopeful that God will indeed forgive their
sins if they repent sincerely. But what is the proof that someone
has sincerely repented? Many Qur'anic texts associate repentance
with reform. This suggests that, unless repentance is followed by
good deeds, it is no more than a useless and superficial act. If
repentance results in a life more in tune with God's standards, then
Muslims can confidently expect God to forgive them: 'To him who
repents, believes, does good works and keeps to the right way, I
will be the Ever-Forgiving [God]' (20:82; cf. 2:160; 3:89; 4:146;
19:60; 24:4; 25:70).

What the Hadith says about the necessity of repentance

The Hadith confirms the teaching of the Qur'an and provides
additional information. Muhammad is portrayed as 'the Prophet of
mercy'.[5] This title may well refer to his mission, which is described
as a vivid expression of God's mercy: 'We [i.e. God] have sent you
as a mercy to the worlds' (21:107). At the heart of Muhammad's
message was the revelation of God's mercy. He is given another
title: 'the Prophet of repentance'.[6] This title points out that
Muhammad, like all prophets, preached repentance to his people.
He was also himself a repentant prophet: 'By God! I ask for God's
forgiveness and turn to Him in repentance more than seventy
times a day.'[7]

That all human creatures need to repent is made clear in the
Prophetic Tradition (the Sunna). This obligation is based on the fact
that everyone transgresses God's law: 'All humans are sinful and the

best among the sinful are those who repent.'[8] When people repent they recover their initial sinless state. Like Adam their father, their disobedience has no further consequence once they have repented: 'He who repents of sin is even as one who has no sin.'[9] This saying suggests that sin has no lasting impact on people: it does not affect their nature. Sin makes them sin*ners* but not sin*ful*. People's evil acts remain extrinsic: they do not change their inner being.

Repentance in theological debate

Muslim theologians have raised several questions with regard to repentance. The answers to these questions have been very different and often irreconcilable. Without going into too much detail, we need to look at some of them.

What is repentance?

According to a saying attributed to the Prophet, 'to regret is to repent' *(al-nadamu tawba)*.[10] Is this a comprehensive definition or is there more to repentance than mere regret? Abu Ya'la believes that this definition is sufficient. His main argument is based on the meaning of the verb *taba*, 'to turn away' (from sin). However, he considers that for repentance to be genuine, the repentant needs to meet two conditions: to resolve not to sin any longer and, as far as possible, to be willing to repair one's fault.[11]

For most theologians, repentance means not only to regret the wrongdoing, but also to resolve not to do it again.[12] 'Abd al-Jabbar believes that one must resolve not to sin any longer while one is still able to sin. Otherwise, God would have to accept the repentance of people in hell, for they will undoubtedly regret their evil doings, although their regret will be useless.[13] Juwayni points out that repentance is not sincere unless regret is prompted by the right motivation; that is, the conviction of having disobeyed God's law.[14] So, for instance, a robber who regrets his theft just because he was caught is by no means a repentant person. According to Juwayni, authentic regret is usually characterized by two 'attributes' *(sifat)*: sadness and sorrow for having transgressed God's command and a resolve not to commit what led to repentance.[15]

For Mankdim, regret is the 'basis' (*aṣl*) for repentance. The condition or the 'characteristic' (*sharṭ*) is 'resolve' (*ʿazm*), which demonstrates its genuineness.[16] Like Juwayni (who is a Sunni theologian), Mankdim underlines the right motivation of true repentance. But, as a Muʿtazili theologian, he considers that an evil act is inherently evil.[17] For Sunni theologians an act is evil not in itself but because it conflicts with God's law.

Muʿtazilites	Sunnites
With or without the law, good acts are inherently good and evil acts are inherently evil.	Good acts are good because God has sovereignly decreed them to be so. Similarly, evil acts are evil only because God says so.
True repentance involves being convinced that what we have done is intrinsically evil.	True repentance involves being convinced that we have disobeyed God.

Table 7. What makes an act evil, and its implications for repentance

Is it possible to repent from one sin while persisting in another?

Ashʿari believes that when people repent from one sin (e.g. drinking alcohol), their repentance is valid even if they do not repent from another sin (e.g. adultery).[18] Abu ʿAli al-Jubbaʾi takes a similar view.[19] Abu Hashim disagrees and so does Mankdim. They argue that to repent requires that one regrets the evil act and resolves to stop committing all evil acts (not just the one repented from). It is useless, Mankdim comments, to abstain from eating a poisonous meal, only to indulge in another meal equally poisonous.[20] Juwayni criticizes this view on the basis that it contradicts common sense and divine revelation as interpreted by religious leaders. These leaders consider that if someone wrongs a person several times and presents his apologies for one thing, his apologies are acceptable although he did not present his apologies for all the bad things he did.[21] Otherwise, abstaining from an evil act (e.g. robbery) should be disapproved of if one keeps doing another evil act (e.g. lying)! Similarly, an act of obedience (e.g. praying) should be invalidated if one neglects another act of obedience (e.g. fasting)![22]

Abu 'Ali al-Jubba'i takes the discussion further. He responds with a threefold argument to those who consider that a true repentant should repent from all acts of disobedience at the same time. First, he remarks that such a doctrine would require that a person should repent not only for committing an evil act, but also for doing a good and even obligatory act! For instance, consider a person who used to be a Muslim and who now holds that it is wrong to believe in Muhammad as a prophet. If this person commits a robbery, he would need to repent. But which of his sins should he repent from? If he believes he has to repent from all of them, he would repent for both the robbery and also for having believed in Muhammad (since for him this belief is wrong). Mankdim does not accept this as a valid argument and looks at it from two points of view. From the point of view of the person and the incentive that led him to repentance (*min ḥaythu al-da'i*) Mankdim concedes that what made him regret his act of robbery will also make him regret his former belief in Muhammad as a prophet. But all human beings are liable to various misgivings. From the point of view of God's commandments (*min ḥaythu al-taklif*) Mankdim deems Jubba'i's argument unconvincing. God's law, he says, allows the robber to repent from his robbery without having to repent from believing in Muhammad as a prophet (in fact, God's law forbids doing this). He can repent from his evil acts in general (*jumlat^an*) or he can repent from his act of robbery without considering his belief as regards Muhammad; or he can repent only from what he knows to be an evil act, leaving aside what he is uncertain about.[23]

Jubba'i's second argument is that there is a consensus among Muslims that an authentic repentance from an evil act does not require repentance from every other evil act. Mankdim challenges this statement by citing dissonant voices. Among those he names 'Ali, Muhammad's cousin, successor and leader of the Muslim community.[24]

Finally, Jubba'i puts forward another compelling case to make his point. Let us imagine that a Jew repents from not believing in Muhammad as a prophet. In other words, he converts to Islam.

Suppose, however, that at the same time he does not repent from a shameful act he committed while still a Jew. Should his conversion to Islam be accepted? Is it not invalidated by the fact he has not repented from his other evil act? Jubba'i observes that, on the contrary, he is seen by all Muslims as one of them. Mankdim responds by saying that the repentance of this man (his conversion to Islam) is not valid. Therefore on the Day of Judgment God will treat him as a Jew (he will send him to hell). However, the fact that his repentance (his conversion to Islam) is not valid does not mean he should be treated by Muslims as a Jew rather than as a Muslim. Why should he be treated as a Muslim if in the hereafter he will be punished as a Jew? Mankdim's answer is that the religious status all Muslims enjoy in society does not necessarily coincide with the way God sees them. Thus a hypocritical Muslim will have exactly the same punishment as a Jew on the Day of Judgment, although he is treated in Muslim society as a full member of the Muslim community. Mankdim backs up his counter-argument by quoting a well-known hadith. In this saying Muhammad declares that he has been commissioned by God to fight people until they *confess* – but not necessarily *believe* – that God is one:

> I have been commended to wage war against men as long as they do not say: 'There is no god but God.' As soon as they make this confession, I have no rights over their lives and possessions – unless they commit an offence against God's law. They are accountable only to God.[25]

Do we have to repent from every single sin?

Muslim theologians agree that we have to repent from all sins, major as well as minor. Ash'ari (who, unlike Mu'tazili theologians, makes no real difference between minor and major sins) considers that we need to repent without delay. To keep doing what is evil, in other words delaying repentance, represents another sin.[26]

What makes repentance an obligation? Muslim scholars have come up with different answers. Juwayni argues that this obligation has been established by the consensus of the Muslim community, because God has commissioned it to set up all the religious rules (*al-ahkam al-shar'iyya*) by which Muslims are to abide.[27] According to Jubba'i, the obligation to repent from minor as well as major sins is based on both God's revelation *(sam'ʿanʾ)* and human rationality *('aqlʿanʾ)*.[28] Mankdim considers that the obligation to repent from minor sins is based only on God's revelation. He argues that repentance is compulsory, because through it we escape God's eternal condemnation. Minor sins, he says (as a Mu'tazili theologian), do not affect our eternal destiny; that is, whether we go to hell or to paradise. All they can do is decrease our reward. Therefore, from a strictly human perspective, there is no real need to repent from minor sins. We have to repent from them only because God enjoins us to do so. Unlike minor sins, he adds, major sins do determine our final destiny. Repentance or non-repentance from one major sin makes the difference between going to paradise or to hell. Therefore the obligation to repent from every major sin is justified rationally and required by God's revelation.[29] Thus the only sins that people do not have to repent from are those committed by mistake; in other words, sins committed inadvertently and unwillingly *('ala ṭariq al-sahw wa l-khaṭa')*.[30]

Does God have to accept our repentance?

We have just seen that, according to all Muslim theologians, people have to repent from every sin. But does God have to accept their repentance? When looking at one of his attributes, *al-tawwab* ('the Most-Returning'), we briefly discussed this issue in connection with sura 9 verse 118. We noted that Mu'tazili theologians consider that God is duty-bound to forgive people who sincerely repent. For 'Abd al-Jabbar, the very purpose of repenting is to remove the punishment for sin.[31] This would not be true if our repentance might not be accepted. God would be unjust if he did not accept it. But what if people keep sinning and repenting? Would God still have to accept their repentance? If a son keeps offending his father, does the father have to accept his renewed apologies? 'Abd al-Jabbar's answer is as follows. The father may well have to discipline his son, but he would still have to accept his apologies, providing they are sincere. The theologian acknowledges that father–son relationships do not always follow this pattern in reality. However, despite what is seen in society, our rational judgment does tell us that a father should always be willing to forgive his disobedient, but remorseful son.[32]

Sunni theologians completely disagree with their Mu'tazili colleagues. For them, from a strictly rational perspective, God is under no obligation to accept our repentance. Having said that, Ash'ari considers that God's revelation tells us that God does accept our penitence. His acceptance is nothing other than a 'favour' (*fadl*) and is consistent with the way he deals with us. In fact, it is God who makes us turn away from disobedience to obedience. He initiates our repentance by warning us of his judgment on disobedience and by rousing in our hearts the desire to obey him.[33] Juwayni takes a slightly different approach but reaches the same conclusion. He considers that nothing can force human beings to accept the apologies of people who have wronged them. If this is true of us, it is even truer of God. Divine revelation confirms our human understanding. It exhorts us to implore God to accept our repentance. If he were under obligation to do so, we would not need to ask him. So, concludes Juwayni, without being absolutely sure of God's response, we are entitled, on the grounds of his revelation, to be hopeful and confident. If we fulfil the conditions for genuine repentance, God is most likely to accept our repentance.[34]

Mu'tazilites	Sunnites
God must accept our repentance.	God does not have to accept our repentance.
We can be sure that if we repent, God will forgive us. But, we cannot be sure we have repented from all our major sins. We may have committed a sin without knowing it, or we may have forgotten to repent from a sin.	We do not have to repent for God to forgive us – he can forgive us without it. But even if we repent, he is not bound to forgive us. Although God's revelation gives us reason to be hopeful, there will be some uncertainty until the Day of Judgment.

Table 8. Does God have to accept our repentance?

Does repentance by itself remove the punishment for sin?

Theologians disagree on whether or not the act of repentance itself removes God's punishment for sin. This issue divides them into two groups. Some argue, yes, repentance does automatically remove the punishment for sin. In this sense, the repentant man earns God's forgiveness by his own merits (*istiḥqaq^{an}*). Others insist that, despite people's repentance, the way God forgives our sins is by his favour (*tafaḍḍul^{an}*).[35]

Baṣrian Mu'tazilites	Sunnites and Baghdadian Mu'tazilites
Repentance automatically removes the punishment for sin.	Repentance does not by itself remove the punishment for sin.
God forgives sin on the basis of human merit.	God forgives sin on the basis of his favour.

Table 9. Does repentance by itself remove the punishment for sin?

The first group is represented by the Baṣrian Mu'tazilites. Mankdim, who is one of them, teaches that 'it is repentance and nothing else which removes the punishment for sin'. He draws a parallel between 'repentance towards God' (*tawba*) and 'presenting one's apologies to fellow human beings' (*i'tidhar*). As soon as the wrongdoer sincerely apologizes to the wronged person for his wrongdoing, he must no longer be blamed. Why? For no other reason than that he has presented his apologies. This proves that what removes the blame is precisely the very fact of presenting one's apologies. What is true of our relationships with each other is also true of our relationship with God.[36]

Mankdim disagrees with those who claim that it is because of his favour that God will not punish penitent people. If it is favour, then God has an equal right either to punish or to forgive, for to do someone a favour by definition means having the absolute liberty to do something or not to do it. On the other hand, if repentance did not remove by itself the punishment for sin, God would have every right to punish repentant people instead of forgiving them. Consequently, the options would not be equal: the most likely option would be to punish them for their sins. Someone may object, what if God bestows his favour on some people by not punishing them because this option corresponds to their 'best interests or advantage' (*aslah*)? Mankdim responds to this argument by saying that God acts according to his justice and not according to our best interests or advantage.[37] If repentance does not remove the punishment for sin, then God has every right to punish repentant people. The fact that God does not punish repentant people proves, he concludes, that it is repentance which removes the punishment for sin.[38]

The second group of scholars include Muʻtazilis from the Baghdadian school and Sunni theologians. Ashʻari is the best representative of this group. For him, repentance by itself does not remove God's punishment and he explains why. Repenting from a sin takes away the 'persistence' in this sin (*al-iṣrar*) but not the sin itself. Thus by repenting we spare ourselves the punishment for persistence. Yet we are still accountable for the sins committed in the past. God is by no means bound to forgive us our past sins just because we have repented. Our repenting removes neither what we did nor the punishment for what we did. However, God does forgive us these sins by way of favour (*tafaddul*[an]). Ashʻari concludes that the doctrine of God's favour tears Muʻtazili beliefs to shreds; namely, that minor sins are forgiven through keeping away from major sins and that repentance removes the punishment for sin.[39]

Repentance in the Bible

The call to repentance is a prominent feature in the Bible just as it is in the Qur'an. In the Old Testament this call was addressed primarily to Israel. Often the Israelites strayed from the teaching of the Torah. Injustice, immorality, idolatry and violence became prevalent among God's people. Their kings made alliances with unbelieving political leaders in neighbouring countries and, for many, worship consisted of rituals performed to the neglect of upholding social justice. God's judgment appeared inevitable, although it was not – and will never be – God's first choice in dealing with his people:

> Therefore, O house of Israel, I will judge you, each one according to his ways, declares the Sovereign LORD. Repent! Turn away from all your offences; then sin will not be your downfall. Rid yourselves of all the offences you have committed, and get a new heart and a new spirit. Why will you die, O house of Israel? For I take no pleasure in the death of anyone, declares the Sovereign LORD. Repent and live!
>
> (Ezek. 18:30–32; cf. Ezek. 14:6; 33:11; Jer. 3:12–14, 22; Is. 31:6; 55:7; Hos. 14:2–3)

Since God's call to repentance was motivated by the desire to forgive his people (2 Chr. 7:14), there can be no doubt that if they had responded and repented he would indeed have suspended his judgment. We can be sure of God's forgiveness, not because he is under obligation to forgive, but because he promises to do so. As Sunni theologians and some Mu'tazilites contend, God's forgiveness by no means represents our right; it is purely his free gift. The Arabic word '*asa*, 'perhaps', is parallel to the Old Testament words 'who knows?' They underline that God is sovereign when he forgives and that his people need to be humble when they ask his forgiveness:

> Rend your heart
>   and not your garments.
> Return to the LORD your God,
>   for he is gracious and compassionate,
> slow to anger and abounding in love,
>   and he relents from sending calamity.
> *Who knows?* He may turn and have pity
>   and leave behind a blessing ...
> (Joel 2:13–14; my italics; cf. Jonah 3:7–9)

The message of John the Baptist

John the Baptist (*Yaḥya* in the Qur'an), the last prophet of the Old Covenant, was sent to prepare the way for the coming of Jesus Christ. He preached the same message as the prophets who came before him. He called the Jewish people to repent. He also used the symbolic act of baptism to illustrate what repentance is all about: breaking away from sin and being cleansed from sin by God. John baptized in the river Jordan those who came to him confessing their sins. But he also sensed that many Jewish leaders were coming without really committing themselves to live a new life. He warned them that they would not escape God's judgment unless their repentance was sincere and, therefore, a life-changing experience:

> But when he saw many of the Pharisees and Sadducees coming to where he was baptising, he said to them: 'You brood of vipers! Who warned you to flee from the coming wrath? Produce fruit in keeping with repentance. And do not think you can say to yourselves, "We have Abraham as our father." I tell you that out of these stones God can raise up children for Abraham. The axe is already at the root of the trees, and every tree that does not produce good fruit will be cut down and thrown into the fire.'
>
> (Matt. 3:7–10)[40]

The mission of Jesus

John's words proved to be particularly relevant during Jesus' mission. More often than not Jesus was opposed by the religious leaders of his day. They were upset by his attitude towards those who were deemed to be the 'sinners' (prostitutes and tax collectors), the ritually unclean (lepers) or the enemies of God's people (Samaritans). These people were discriminated against and were thought to be unworthy of God's kingdom. Yet Jesus befriended and shared God's love with them in many ways. They were open to his message and more responsive to his call:

> While Jesus was having dinner at Matthew's house, many tax collectors and 'sinners' came and ate with him and his disciples. When the Pharisees saw this, they asked his disciples, 'Why does your teacher eat with tax collectors and "sinners"?' On hearing this, Jesus said, 'It is not the healthy who need a doctor, but the sick. But go and learn what this means: "I desire mercy, not sacrifice." [Hos. 6:6] For I have not come to call the righteous, but sinners.'
>
> (Matt. 9:10–13; cf. Luke 5:30–31)

Jesus' words do not mean that while some people need to repent others do not. His words simply indicate that God cares for everyone, particularly the outcast. They also suggest that God expects believers to demonstrate their faith through compassionate relationships, especially with 'non-religious' and deprived people. Jesus' reply to the Pharisees makes the point that people who are more aware of their needs, physical or spiritual, are more likely to accept the gospel than 'the righteous' who consider themselves in no need of God's grace. In fact, Jesus makes it clear that everyone needs to repent, because we are all sinners. Unless we repent we remain under God's judgment:

> Now there were some present at that time who told Jesus about the Galileans whose blood Pilate had mixed with their sacrifices. Jesus answered, 'Do you think that these Galileans were worse sinners than all the other Galileans because they suffered this way? I tell you, no! But unless you repent, you too will all perish.'
> (Luke 13:1–3)

Pontius Pilate was the Roman governor of Palestine at the time. Jesus' comment on the bloodshed Pilate perpetrated is quite unexpected. One would have thought that Jesus would condemn Pilate's criminal act and express his compassion for the victims and their relatives. Instead, Jesus takes the opportunity to issue a very solemn warning to everyone: repent or perish! To make his call to repentance stronger and more urgent he repeats it, this time referring not to Pilate's violence but to what seems to have been the loss of human lives through a tragic accident: 'those eighteen who died when the tower in Siloam fell on them – do you think they were more guilty than all the others living in Jerusalem? I tell you, no! But unless you repent, you too will all perish' (Luke 13:4–5).

The Jewish people dismissed Jesus' call to repentance, despite all the miracles accrediting his mission. They refused to repent and believe in him as God's Messiah. As a result, he told them they would have to face God's judgment on the Last Day (Matt. 11:20–24). Jesus drew a striking contrast between his people and the people of Nineveh (in present-day Iraq). Jonah was sent to Nineveh in order to announce God's imminent judgment on the city unless they repented (Jonah 3:7–9). Much to the disappointment of Jonah, the people of Nineveh, who were not God's people, did turn back and consequently God decided not to punish them. Israel, on the other hand, refused to accept the message of repentance brought by Jesus, although 'one greater than Jonah' preached it to them (Matt. 12:39–41). Therefore God's judgment was inescapable and it was not only to be on the Last Day. Jesus foretold the destruction of Jerusalem and the dispersion of its inhabitants as a direct consequence of Israel's rejection of him (Luke 19:41–44; 21:20–24).

The core of the gospel

Jesus' prophecy about Jerusalem was fulfilled in AD 70. His warning about God's eternal punishment will also become a reality for all others who do not repent. But the gospel is not primarily about God's judgment. It is about God's salvation, which Jesus achieved through his death and resurrection. Before he ascended to heaven, he entrusted the gospel to his disciples. The core of this message of good news consists of God's promise to grant forgiveness of sins to those who repent and believe in Jesus Christ:

> [Jesus] told them, 'This is what is written: The Christ will suffer and rise from the dead on the third day, and repentance and forgiveness of sins will be preached in his name to all nations, beginning at Jerusalem. You are witnesses of these things.'
> (Luke 24:46–48)

Thus the call to repentance in the Bible does not refer to any specific sin. It is a call to turn back to God and to believe in the one who made God's forgiveness possible. It is a call to enter into a new relationship with God.

Knowing that God has promised to forgive our sins results in a lifelong transforming relationship with him. His promise urges us to acknowledge our sins and to strive to live a holy life: 'just as he who called you is holy, so be holy in all you do, for it is written: "Be holy, because I am holy"' (1 Pet. 1:15–16; cf. Lev. 11:44). This rules out any complacency with sin. In fact, Christians experience a paradox in their lives as they respond to God's call to holiness. The more we live in close relationship with him, the more we are aware of our shortcomings. The sins we are aware of only represent the tip of the iceberg. We need to confess these sins but also to receive God's forgiveness for all our sins. Indeed, Jesus taught his disciples that they need God's pardon just as much as their daily food:

Our Father in heaven,
hallowed be your name,
your kingdom come,
your will be done
    on earth as it is in heaven.
Give us today our daily bread.
Forgive us our debts [i.e. our sins]
    as we also have forgiven our debtors.
(Matt. 6:9–12)

Notes

1. Razi on 24:31; XII:23, p. 183.
2. Razi on 66:8; XV:30, p. 42.
3. Razi on 9:102; VIII:16, p. 140.
4. Razi on 17:79; XI:21, p. 26.
5. Ibn Majah, *iqamat al-salat* 189 [1375]:II, bk 5, no. 1385, p. 298.
6. Muslim, *ayman* 27 [3138]:III, bk 15, no. 4091, p. 884; Abu Dawud, *adab* 124 [4497]:III, bk 36, no. 5146, p. 1427; Tirmidhi, *birr* 30 [1870].
7. Bukhari, *da'awat* 3 [5832]:VIII, bk 75, no. 319, p. 213. According to other versions of this prayer, the Prophet used to ask God's forgiveness one hundred times a day (Muslim, *dhikr* 42 [4871]:IV, bk 35, no. 6522, p. 1418). This prayer raises the question of the alleged sinlessness of Muhammad in particular and of the prophets in general. The Islamic doctrine about the sinlessness of the prophets is examined in chapter 12.
8. Ibn Majah, *zuhd* 30 [4241]:V, bk 37, no. 4251, p. 490; Tirmidhi *qiyama* 49 [2423]; Darimi, *riqaq* 18 [2611]. The Arabic words for 'all humans' are *kullu bani adam*, 'all of Adam's children'; for 'sinful', *khatta'*, an intensive form of *khati'*, 'sinner'; for 'those who repent', *tawwabun*, an intensive form of *ta'ib*, 'repentant'.
9. Ibn Majah, *zuhd* 30 [4240]:V, bk 37, no. 4250, p. 490.
10. Ibid. [4242]:V, bk 37, no. 4252, p. 491.

11. Abu Ya'la, *Mu'tamad*, p. 199.
12. Ibn Furak, *Mujarrad*, p. 166; 'Abd al-Jabbar, *Mughni*, XIV, pp. 314–315.
13. 'Abd al-Jabbar, *Mughni*, XIV, p. 346.
14. Juwayni, *Irshad*, pp. 226–227; cf. Razi on 9:102; VIII:16, p. 139.
15. Ibid.
16. Mankdim, *Sharh*, p. 792.
17. Ibid., pp. 789, 791.
18. Ibn Furak, *Mujarrad*, p. 166.
19. Mankdim, *Sharh*, p. 794.
20. Ibid., pp. 794–795.
21. Juwayni, *Irshad*, p. 229.
22. Ibid.
23. Mankdim, *Sharh*, pp. 796–797.
24. Ibid., p. 797.
25. Ibid., pp. 797–798. Cf. Bukhari, *iman* 16 [24]:I, bk 2, no. 24, p. 25; *i'tisam* 28: IX, bk 92, p. 339; Muslim, *iman* 15 [31]:I, bk 1, no. 29, p. 15; Ibn Majah, *fitan* 1 [3917]:V, bk 36, no. 3927, p. 267; Tirmidhi, *tafsir* sura 88 [3264]; Nasa'i, *jihad* 1 [3042].
26. Ibn Furak, *Mujarrad*, p. 167.
27. Juwayni, *Irshad*, p. 228.
28. Mankdim, *Sharh*, p. 789.
29. Ibid.
30. 'Abd al-Jabbar, *Mughni*, XIV, p. 415.
31. Ibid., p. 337.
32. Ibid., pp. 374–375.
33. Ibn Furak, *Mujarrad*, p. 166.
34. Juwayni, *Irshad*, p. 227.
35. Ash'ari, *Maqalat*, I, p. 231.
36. Mankdim, *Sharh*, p. 790.
37. Mankdim refers here to the doctrine of *salah* (advantage) and *aslah* (best advantage). For Sunni theologians, this doctrine means that God is free to act to the best advantage of some people by granting them a 'special blessing' (*lutf*) which enables them to believe and consequently to be saved on the Day of Judgment. Mu'tazili theologians use exactly the same words with a completely different meaning. They consider that, having imposed on us the obligation to obey his law (*taklif*), God is bound to act according to our advantage or even to our best advantage. This means granting us whatever help we need to meet his demands and,

as a result, to earn an eternal reward. See Mankdim, *Sharḥ*, pp. 518–526, 779–780; Shahrastani, *Religions*, I, pp. 112–113, 230–231.

38. Mankdim, *Sharḥ*, p. 790.

39. Ibn Furak, *Mujarrad*, p. 159.

40. The Gospel of John does not have the word 'repentance' at all. The concept of 'new birth' (John 3:1–8) is the closest equivalent to what repentance means in the Synoptic Gospels (Matthew, Mark, Luke).

10. INTERCESSION ON THE DAY OF JUDGMENT (*shafa'a*)

Repentance is the key to obtaining God's pardon. We all fall short of God's expectations as expressed in his law, yet God is always willing to accept our repentance. Islam teaches that on the Day of Judgment God will grant forgiveness to those who have sincerely repented.

But what about unrepentant Muslims? Is there any hope that they will receive forgiveness for sins from which they have not repented? Will God's mercy be displayed on the Day of Judgment? Muslim theologians have given different answers to these questions depending on their understanding of Qur'anic teaching. But they all agree that Muhammad's intercession on the Last Day will be decisive for many Muslims.

Intercession in the Qur'an

The Qur'an teaches that God's prophets lived among people who, more often than not, disobeyed God's law. The prophets proclaimed God's judgment and called people to repent. They also appealed to God's mercy and asked him to forgive the sins of their people. Thus Noah prayed for himself as well as for his parents, his guests and all believers so that God might forgive their sins (71:28). Abraham too asked God's pardon for himself as well as for his parents and for believers in general (9:114; 14:41; 19:47; 26:86; 60:4). Jacob prayed to God for his sons to be forgiven their hostile attitude towards their younger brother, Joseph (12:98). Jesus interceded on behalf of his people (5:121), and so did Muhammad (4:64; 24:62; 48:11; 60:12).

Prophets are not the only ones to seek God's forgiveness for their people: angels do the same for us. Angels have received God's permission to pray on our behalf (21:28; 53:26). At the present time (before the Day of Judgment) they beg God's pardon for people in general (42:5) and for Muslims in particular:

> Those who bear up the Throne [of God] and those around it celebrate the praise of their Lord, and they believe in Him. They implore forgiveness for the believers: 'Our Lord! Your mercy and Your knowledge embrace all things. Forgive those that repent and follow Your way. Protect them from the punishment of Hell.'
> (40:7)

Now, is the prophets' intercession restricted to their mission on earth? Will the angels' intercession come to an end at the Day of Judgment? Or will God allow some to pray in favour of human creatures? The teaching of the Qur'an is ambivalent. On the one hand, it states that God will accept no intercession at all; on the other, it suggests that there might be some exceptions.

According to the Qur'an, the people of Israel were once God's chosen people. God made a 'covenant' (*mithaq*) with them. He sent them prophets and entrusted them with his word. Yet the Israelites did not respond to his kindness with gratitude. Instead, they often broke the covenant and disobeyed him (2:83–96; 4:154–156). Hence God's warning that they would have to give account to him on the Day of Judgment:

> O children of Israel! Remember the blessing which I bestowed upon you, [and remember that] I have favoured you over and against other

peoples. Dread the Day when everyone will stand alone: when neither
intercession nor ransom shall be accepted from anyone, nor any help be
given.
(2:47–48; cf. 2:123–124; 26:100; 36:23; 74:48)

The Israelites are called to recognize that on the Last Day God
will show them no favour. Polytheistic Arabs are also made aware
that their idols will be useless. They will have to stand before God
on their own:

> Instead of worshipping God, they worship [idols] that can neither harm
> them nor benefit them. They say: 'These will intercede for us with God.'
> Answer: 'Will you inform God of what He does not know either in
> heaven or in earth?' Glory to Him! He is exalted far above what they
> associate with Him.
> (10:18)

Polytheists will realize that they have no-one to help them (6:94;
7:53; 30:13; 39:43–44), neither 'guardian' (*waliyy*) nor 'intercessor'
(*shafi'*) (6:51–70; 32:4; 40:18). But what about Muslims, will they
also be helpless? The Qur'an suggests that God may give permission for intercession to be made on their behalf:

> Believers! Give [to Me] a part of what We have given you before that
> Day comes when there shall be neither trading nor friendship nor
> intercession. Truly the unbelievers are the evildoers. God, there is no
> god but Him, the Living, the Eternal. Neither slumber nor sleep
> overtake Him. To Him is everything in heaven and earth. Who shall
> intercede with Him except by His permission?
> (2:254–255a)

Most commentators understand this text to mean that intercession
will be denied to unbelievers, who are portrayed as evildoers
(2:254). In contrast, Muslims will benefit from the privilege of
intercession as a result of God's gracious permission (v. 255; cf.
34:23).[1] Intercession will be offered in favour of those who have
made a 'covenant' (*'ahd*) with God: 'None has the power to
intercede save him who made a covenant with the Ever-Merciful'

(19:87). Razi explains that making an exception in a negative statement about something (as is the case in this verse) means asserting it for some people.[2] He also explains that 'covenant' in this context means *shahada*; that is, the Islamic creed as regards God's 'oneness' (*tawhid*) and Muhammad's 'prophethood' (*nubuwwa*).[3] In other words, intercession will only profit Muslims. 'Evildoers' (*al-zalimun*) will be excluded: 'Warn them of the approaching Day, when people's heart will leap up to their throats and choke them; when the evildoers will have no close friend or intercessor who will be listened to' (40:18).

Intercession in the Hadith

Thus the doctrine of intercession is only hinted at in the Qur'an, which contains no explicit information as to who will intercede, whom they will intercede for and what they will intercede about. By contrast, the Hadith provides us with specific answers to these three points.

Who will intercede?

We have in the Hadith a few references to the Qur'an.[4] One hadith portrays the role of the Prophet as intercessor on the Day of Judgment. It ends with a quotation from the Qur'an made by Muhammad himself: '[O Muhammad!] Pray during the night an additional prayer for the fulfilment of which your Lord may raise you to a station of high honour' (17:79). The hadith concludes with a comment: this is 'the station of high honour' (*maqam mahmud*) that God promised your Prophet.[5] In another hadith the Prophet said, 'The station of high honour is the station where I will intercede for my Nation'.[6] Muhammad's intercession is also related to the Qur'anic promise that God will answer those who pray to him: 'Your Lord says: Invoke Me and I will hear you. Those who are too proud to serve Me shall enter Hell in utmost humiliation' (40:69). Muhammad made the following comment about this promise: 'Every prophet had an invocation which God always answered. I will keep my invocation so as to intercede for my Nation in the Hereafter.'[7]

Another hadith has it that Muhammad was given the choice either to have half of his community go to paradise or to be able to intercede for all of them. He preferred the latter option, because it would result in a greater number of Muslims being saved.[8] Muhammad's intercession is also seen as one of his five exclusive privileges:

> I have been given five favours which had not been given to anyone before me:
>
>   1. God made me triumph over my enemies by His frightening all of them that were at a one month distance from me.
>   2. The whole earth has been made a place for prayer as well as for ritual ablution for me. Anyone of my Nation can pray everywhere when the time for prayer is due.
>   3. The booty has been made lawful for me unlike those who came before me.
>   4. I have been given the right of intercession.
>   5. I have been sent to all nations whereas prophets before me were sent each to his own people.[9]

So, is Muhammad the only person with permission to intercede? According to one hadith, this privilege will also be granted to all prophets as well as to religious scholars and martyrs.[10] Another hadith says that prophets, angels and all believers will be given permission to intercede.[11] Those who have memorized the Qur'an will intercede for ten people in their household.[12] Martyrs will have, as part of their reward, the right to intercede for seventy of their relatives.[13] Muslims who cursed a lot in their life will be denied the privilege of interceding.[14] The multitude of people who will be granted the favour of interceding for others explains, according to another hadith, why Muhammad is seen as the first, but not the only intercessor on the Day of Judgment:

> I am the greatest of Adam's children – I say this without boasting;
> I will be the first to be raised from the dead on Resurrection Day when the earth will split to give back the dead – I say this without boasting;

I will be the first to be given the right to intercede – I say this without
  boasting;
I will lead men to praise God on Resurrection Day – I say this without
  boasting.[15]

Who will Muhammad intercede for?

One hadith says that Muhammad will intercede for all those who
sincerely confess that 'there is no god but God'.[16] In other words,
all Muslims will benefit from the Prophet's intercession, with the
exception of those who were deceitful towards the Arab people.[17]
Another hadith has it that Muhammad will intercede for those who
die in Medina.[18] Other accounts indicate that the Prophet will pray
especially in favour of 'sinful Muslims' (*al-khatta'un*) and the
'unclean' (*al-mutalawwithun*), who deserve to be sent to hell.[19] The
most disputed hadith is one in which Muhammad allegedly
declares that on the Day of Judgment his intercession will be for
a specific group of Muslims: 'My intercession will be for members
of my Nation that have committed major sins.'[20]

As result of Muhammad's intercession many Muslims will come
out of hell. They will enter paradise: 'Thanks to the intercession of
Muhammad some people will be taken out of Hell. They will be
called *al-juhannamiyyun* [i.e. the People of Hell].'[21]

Why will Muhammad have this privilege?

The Hadith reports an interesting story about Muhammad's role as
intercessor on the Day of Judgment. It tells us why he has been
granted the privilege of interceding for his community. People are
about to be judged. They are very anxious and try to find a way of
escaping God's condemnation:

On the Day of Resurrection the believers will be kept waiting so long
that they will become worried and say: 'Let us ask someone to intercede
for us with our Lord so that He may deliver us from our place.'

Then they will go to Adam and say: 'Adam! You are the father of
humankind. God created you with His own hand and made you dwell in
His Paradise. He ordered His angels to bow down before you, and He
taught you the names of all things. Will you intercede for us with your
Lord so that He may deliver us from this place of ours?' Adam will

reply: 'I am not fit for this task.' He will mention the disobedience he committed when he ate off the tree though he had been forbidden to do so. He will say to them: 'Go to Noah, the first prophet God sent to humankind.'

They will then go to Noah who will say: 'I am not fit for this task.' He will mention the disobedience he committed when he asked God a foolish question. He will say to them: 'Go to Abraham, the friend of God.'

They will then go to Abraham who will say: 'I am not fit for this task.' He will mention the three lies he made. He will say to them: 'Go to Moses, God's Servant who was entrusted with the Torah and with whom God spoke face to face.'

They will then go to Moses who will say: 'I am not fit for this task.' He will mention the murder he committed. He will say to them: 'Go to Jesus, God's Servant and Messenger, His Spirit and His Word.'

They will then go to Jesus who will say: 'I am not fit for this task. Go to Muhammad, God's Servant whose past and future sins have been forgiven.'

They will then come to me, and I will ask my Lord's permission to enter His house and I will be permitted. When I see Him I will fall down in prostration before Him. He will leave me on my knees as long as He will. He will then say to me: 'O Muhammad! Lift up your head and speak, for you will be listened to. Intercede, for your intercession will be accepted. Ask, for you will be granted.' I will raise my head and give praise and thanks to my Lord as He had taught me, I will then intercede. I will be shown a group of people to intercede for. I will go out and let them enter Paradise ... [For the third time] I will be shown a group of people to intercede for. I will go out and I will take them out of Hell and let them enter Paradise, till none remains in Hell except those whom the Qur'an has locked in, they will stay there for ever.

The Prophet then recited from the Qur'an this verse: 'Your Lord may raise you to a station of high honour' (17:79). This is 'the station of high honour' that God promised your Prophet.[22]

This rather lengthy hadith echoes Qur'anic teaching about Adam and the prophets, their respective privileges as well as their wrongdoing. Adam received many blessings from God, and yet he disobeyed (2:30–38; 7:19–25; 15:29–30; 20:115–123). Noah was God's first chosen prophet (4:163), but he was blamed for asking God to save his unbelieving son (11:41–49).[23] Abraham was God's friend (4:125), yet he told a lie three times: twice to his people (21:63; 37:89) and once to Pharaoh when he said Sarah was his sister.[24] As for Moses, God entrusted him with the Torah (6:154) and spoke with him face to face (4:164), but before that he had killed an Egyptian man who was fighting with a Jew (28:15). Not surprisingly, Jesus is described as God's servant (19:30), his 'Spirit' (*ruhuhu*) and his 'Word' (*kalimatuhu*) (4:171). Unlike Adam, Noah, Abraham and Moses, Jesus makes no mention of any sin of his own. This too is in line with the Qur'an which ascribes no sin to him. One version of this hadith specifies that 'Jesus had no sin to refer to'.[25] So why does he consider himself unworthy of interceding with God? Why does he point to Muhammad? We do not know. What we do know is that Muhammad's privilege is not that he did not commit sin; rather that, according to the Qur'an, God has already forgiven his sins (48:2). He also has the privilege of being the final prophet (33:40) according to another version of the same hadith.[26] Thus a qualified intercessor ought to have a special and unique position (e.g. being the last prophet) as well as to be in no need of God's forgiveness. Otherwise, he would need to beg God's pardon for himself.

Developments in Sunni theology

The Qur'an tells us that on the Day of Judgment people will proceed before God in three groups. One group will be sent to paradise, another to hell and a third group are described as the 'Nearest to God' (*al-muqarrabun*):

> When the Day which is coming suddenly comes, no-one shall then deny its coming. Some will be brought low, others exalted. When the earth profoundly shakes and the mountains crumble away and disintegrate into dust, you shall be sorted out into three multitudes: The Companions on the right – blessed shall be those on the right; the Companions on the left – miserable shall be those on the left; and the

Foremost – they shall be first [to enter paradise]. These are the Nearest to [God]: they shall dwell in gardens of bliss.

(56:1–12)

According to Baghdadi, this third group ('the Foremost' [al-sabiqun], who are the Nearest to God), will be the smallest. Their number will be seventy thousand.[27] They will go to paradise without even being judged. They include the prophets, the children of the believers (who died before reaching adulthood) and the 'miscarried foetuses' (siqt). Each member will intercede for seventy thousand Muslims. The second group, 'the Companions on the left', are the unbelievers who will receive eternal punishment. Finally, 'the Companions on the right' are Muslims who will go to paradise, although some will first have to atone for their sins in hell.[28]

Ash'ari considers that all Muslims will intercede for each other. He mentions in particular those people whose disadvantage qualifies them to intercede for other Muslims: the poor will pray for the rich, the oppressed for his oppressor and the miscarried foetus for its parents. The intercession of the Muslim community as a whole is the result of the honour granted by God to Muhammad, whose right to intercede comes first.[29] For Ash'ari, Muhammad will intercede for three categories of Muslims: sinful Muslims, so that God may disregard their sins; penitent Muslims, so that God may accept their acts of repentance (which they did while they were in this life); and charitable Muslims, so that God may increase their happiness. He indicates that Muhammad will intercede before people get to paradise so that God may shorten the time of their distress as they wait to be judged. He will also intercede after people enter paradise so that God may add to their blessedness. Finally, he will pray for Muslims who have already been sent to hell so that they may come out of it in fulfilment of this prophetic saying: 'Whoever has in his heart faith equal to the weight of an atom will be taken out of hell.'[30]

Sunni scholars refer to the hadith quoted in the previous section to back up their doctrine. They also base their argument on their understanding of Qur'anic teaching. They interpret 'the station of high honour' granted to Muhammad as his intercessory role on the

Last Day.[31] Muhammad prayed for Muslims in his lifetime (3:159; 4:67; 47:19) so that God might forgive their sins, these scholars remark. He thus anticipated the role he will have on the Day of Judgment. The fact that the Qur'an asserts that unbelievers will have no intercessors suggests that Muslims by contrast will enjoy this privilege.[32] God exhorts Muslims to forgive other Muslims (24:22). This exhortation is in a way perfectly fulfilled in Muhammad's intercessory role, which will aim at forgiving sinful Muslims (on behalf of God).[33]

Sunni theologians make use of rationalistic arguments as well. There is nothing unusual, they say, in a king accepting the pleading of one of his closest friends on behalf of a third person. Why then should Muhammad (and godly Muslims) be denied this faculty?[34] Juwayni claims that early Muslims all believed in Muhammad's role as intercessor and prayed to God to enable them to benefit from it. This belief was challenged by no-one until 'heresies' (bida') started to spread. In other words, the consensus of the Muslim community confirms the teaching of God's revelation.[35]

Developments in Mu'tazili theology

With a few exceptions, Mu'tazili theologians challenge the Sunni doctrine on eschatological intercession.[36] They consider that 'sinful Muslims' (fussaq) will undoubtedly go to hell (if they do not repent from their major sins), and their punishment will be eternal. In other words, Muslims will go either to paradise or to hell; there is no other alternative. Once there, they will stay there for ever. Muhammad's intercession, they say, will only be for believing and deserving Muslims, not for sinful ones.[37] For Mankdim, the idea of interceding for unrepentant sinful Muslims is unacceptable for two reasons. First, it seeks to obtain a reward for people who are unworthy of it, which is evil. Indeed, he says, man does not go to paradise undeservedly (tafaddul[an]). Second, God's word gives evidence that the punishment for sin is eternal. Therefore sinful Muslims will not escape God's punishment through Muhammad's intercession.[38]

Will Muhammad intercede at all on the Day of Judgment?

Mu'tazili theologians say yes. His intercession aims first of all at honouring him in the eyes of the community.[39] What will Muhammad pray for and for whom? The answer is that he will pray for repentant Muslims, but not so that God may accept their repentance. As we noted in the previous chapter, according to Mu'tazili theology God is under obligation to accept their repentance. Muhammad will intercede with God that he may increase his reward for deserving Muslims who have repented from their sins. Through their repentance they will have removed the punishment due for their sin, but they will still need God's additional reward to enable them to enter paradise. It is this extra reward and nothing else that God can grant undeservedly without denying his justice.

Mu'tazili scholars major on Qur'anic texts that seem to uphold their position. Their interpretation of these texts is very different, as one might expect, to that of the Sunni theologians. Four significant and controversial texts follow.

Sura 2 verse 48

Dread the Day when everyone will stand alone: when neither intercession nor ransom shall be accepted from anyone, nor any help given.
(2:48)

Mankdim quotes this verse to make the point that God's judgment will be based on the principle of individual responsibility. Therefore the Prophet's intercession in favour of sinful Muslims contradicts this principle. God, he says, has explicitly declared to Muhammad that he will not be able to rescue people who deserve eternal condemnation: '[O Muhammad!] Can you save from Hell those who have rightly earned the sentence of [eternal] punishment?' (39:19).[40] Razi refutes this argument by saying that if this text (2:48) were to be taken literally, it would deny intercession altogether. Mu'tazili theologians do not go that far (since they accept the intercession of Muhammad for righteous Muslims). Therefore this verse needs to be understood in specific rather than general terms ('ala al-takhsis). The context indicates that this warning is addressed to the people of Israel, who misleadingly believe that their forefathers will pray for them on the Day of Resurrection. This text has been revealed in order to remove any deceptive hope the Israelites may have had as to the attitude of their ancestors towards them.[41]

As for sura 39 verse 19, Razi agrees that Muhammad will not be able to save those who are lost. However, he explains that sinful Muslims are not among the lost. They still believe in God, and the Qur'an clearly declares that God's forgiveness covers all sins except polytheism (4:48; 39:53).[42]

Sura 40 verse 18

> The evildoers will have no close friend or intercessor who will be listened to.
> (40:18)

Mankdim quotes this verse, which clearly rules out the possibility that evildoers, including sinful Muslims, will benefit from intercession. If it were at all possible to pray for sinful Muslims, the Prophet would have been the most qualified person for the task. The fact is that not even Muhammad is allowed to intercede for them.[43] Ash'ari replies that the evildoers who have no-one to intercede for them are exclusively the polytheistic people in line with what the Qur'an declares: 'Polytheism is an abominable evil' [*zulm*] (31:13). Ash'ari puts forward another argument. If the Mu'tazilites believe that the word *zalimun* (evildoers) refers not just to polytheists but to sinful Muslims as well, then they should include the prophets among the sinful people, as Adam and Jonah admitted to being evildoers (7:23; 21:87).[44] The Mu'tazilites are certainly not prepared to accept the idea that God's prophets are evildoers. For them, prophets commit only minor sins.

Sura 21 verse 28

> They [angels] intercede for none save those whom He accepts, and they tremble for awe of Him.
> (21:28)

Mu'tazili scholars understand this text to mean that angels pray only for people who are accepted by God; that is, people who please him. Likewise, Muhammad will pray exclusively for godly people on the Day of Judgment. Sinful Muslims, they say, cannot be said to enjoy God's pleasure; hence no intercession will be offered on their behalf.[45] Ash'ari and Baqillani suggest two alternative ways of understanding this verse:

1. God will accept intercession for some people, not for all; in other words, he will grant permission for some people to be prayed for but will withhold it from others (i.e. non-Muslims).
2. God will accept intercession for those who please him. Sinful Muslims do please him, not of course because they are sinful but because of their monotheistic faith.

Baqillani comments that only unworthy Muslims need to be prayed for. Those who please God entirely through their good works have no such need.[46]

Sura 40 verse 7

[The angels] ... implore forgiveness for the believers: 'Our Lord! ... Forgive those that repent and follow Your way.'
(40:7)

Mu'tazili theologians point out that this text shows that angels pray for the believers (not for sinful Muslims) who have repented. This proves that, in a similar way, Muhammad will intercede only for believing and repentant Muslims. Nasafi (a Sunni Maturidite theologian) challenges this interpretation by asking why angels should seek God's forgiveness for repentant Muslims. According to Mu'tazili doctrine, God necessarily accepts people's repentance. Nasafi's interpretation consists in understanding repentance here in the sense of conversion to Islam. Hence angels ask God to forgive the sins people have committed since they became Muslims.[47] Before Nasafi, Ash'ari suggested a similar interpretation.[48]

A contested hadith

What do Mu'tazili theologians make of the hadith that clearly speaks about Muhammad's intercession for sinful Muslims? The hadith in which the Prophet said, 'My intercession will be for members of my Nation that have committed major sins' is hotly debated.[49] Mankdim contends that its authenticity (whether or not Muhammad really said what is attributed to him) is doubtful. Why? Because the chain of transmission through which it has been handed down is uncertain (it includes people whose trustworthiness remains unproven). Even if this chain turns out to be reliable, Mankdim comments, the authenticity of this hadith would still be debatable as it has been passed on through only one chain of transmission (*manqul bitariqi l-ahad*).[50] Mankdim argues that this hadith contradicts other hadiths; for instance this one: 'The slanderer, the wine-drinker and the rebel to his parents will not enter paradise.'[51] Therefore we should either reject these seemingly self-contradicting sayings altogether, or give them an interpretation compatible with the teaching of 'God's Book and the Sunna of his Prophet'. Hence, we need to understand the relevant hadith in this sense: 'My intercession will be for members of my Nation that have committed major sins *if they have repented.*' One might then object, the repentant Muslim does not need interceding for; why should Muhammad intercede for him? Mankdim answers as follows: the reward earned through one's obedience has been cancelled by the major sin he committed; he has no other reward than what he earned through his repentance (of the major sin he committed). Since this reward is insufficient, he needs God's favour to enable him to go to paradise. Mankdim quotes another objection: God has already promised that 'He will pay those that have faith and do good works their full wages, adding unto them of His favour' (4:173).[52] His reply envisages two options. It is quite possible that the additional favour (promised by God in this verse) is precisely what he will give in response to Muhammad's intercession. It is also possible that this promised favour is different from what he will grant repentant Muslims thanks to Muhammad's intercession.[53]

Nasafi criticizes the Mu'tazili understanding of Muhammad's intercession. They take God's favour to mean simply God's 'help' (*i'ana*), and since this help is not designed to save Muslims from the punishment of hell, they falsify the true meaning of the word 'favour'.[54] For Ash'ari, by contrast, God's favour will be demonstrated from the very moment Muhammad starts interceding. As a result, the time sinful Muslims will spend in hell will be shortened or their punishment will be less painful.[55]

A summary of the debate

In short, Muslim scholars are divided into two main groups as regards God's forgiveness in relation to Muhammad's intercession.

Sunni theologians	Mu'tazili and Khariji theologians
On the Day of Judgment Muhammad will intercede for *sinful Muslims*.	On the Day of Judgment Muhammad will intercede for *righteous Muslims*.
Sinful Muslims have the hope of being rescued from suffering eternal punishment. They will suffer temporary punishment before entering paradise.	Righteous Muslims will receive added blessing from God. Sinful Muslims will receive the punishment they deserve.

Table 10. Muhammad's intercession, according to Islamic theology

The first group believe that on the Day of Judgment God's mercy will be supremely demonstrated in his forgiving sinful Muslims. This disclosure of God's favour will take place in response to Muhammad's intercession and will make the difference between eternal punishment, on the one hand, and temporary punishment followed by eternal blessing, on the other. This group of theologians is called *al-Murji'a* (i.e. the Murji'ites). In this context their name means the derivation that the word suggests,[56] those who give hope to sinful Muslims by not condemning them to hell. They do not judge them but leave their judgment with God. This group includes mainly Sunni theologians from different schools (Ash'arites, Maturidites, Hanbalites).

The second group comprises Mu'tazili theologians and Kharijites. God's favour represents an added blessing given to deserving

Muslims thanks to Muhammad's intercession. People will basically be judged according to their deeds. The sinful, whether Muslims or not, will all suffer eternal punishment.[57]

What both groups have in common is their belief that Muhammad's intercession is a blessing destined to honour him as prophet and leader of the Muslim 'community' (*umma*). The doctrine of intercession demonstrates the solidarity that exists within the *umma*, in particular between its members and their leader. Like all humans, Muslims yearn to cross over the gap that separates the transcendent God and his humble creatures. The awareness of our unworthiness makes it impossible for us to fulfil this yearning. As God's final prophet, Muhammad is best qualified in the eyes of his community to mediate between the divine Judge and his creatures. Because his sins have already been forgiven, he is able to plead with God to look favourably upon his people.

Jesus as intercessor

On the Day of Judgment God will give permission for intercession to take place for the believers. This permission gives evidence that God is indeed a merciful God. Interceding on that day represents a great privilege for the intercessor. In Islamic tradition this privilege has been granted to Muhammad, and extended to other prophets and deserving Muslims (scholars, martyrs etc.). Muhammad's credentials as intercessor are twofold: God has already forgiven his sins (48:2) and he is the last prophet (33:40). These are worthy credentials, for it does not make sense to ask God's mercy for people if the person who is asking is himself under God's judgment. But how does the Islamic doctrine on intercession compare with the Bible's teaching?

Jesus is qualified to intercede for us – because he is sinless
One striking convergence between Christianity and Islam relates to the portrait of Jesus. Jesus is the only human being who has never committed a sin of any kind. His moral perfection makes him unique among God's prophets. Neither the Qur'an nor the Bible hides the fact that all the prophets fell short of God's highest

standards of holiness. Jesus is the only exception. His acts matched his words in such a way that even his opponents had no answer when he challenged them to find any sin in his life: 'Can any of you prove me guilty of sin?' (John 8:46). Jesus is the only person who had no need of God's forgiveness. In the prayer known as 'the Lord's Prayer' Christians ask God to forgive their sins ('Forgive us our sins, for we also forgive everyone who sins against us', Luke 11:4; this is a prayer Jesus taught his disciples. When they asked him to teach them how to pray, he replied, 'When *you* pray, say . . . ' (Luke 11:2; cf. Matt. 6:9; my italics). In fact, nowhere in the Bible or the Qur'an is Jesus depicted as doing something for which he later had to repent. He met God's highest standards of holiness in a way no other prophet did.

Jesus' holiness did not mean that he kept away from sinners: quite the opposite. He wanted to identify fully with them. He began his mission with a powerfully symbolic act. He went to John the Baptist, his cousin, and asked him to baptize him in the river Jordan. John was preaching 'a baptism of repentance for the forgiveness of sins' (Mark 1:4) so was astounded to see Jesus coming to him. Since Jesus had no sin to repent from, John tried to deter him, '*I* need to be baptised by *you*, and do *you* come to *me*?' (Matt. 3:14; my italics). Jesus insisted and John complied with his demand. Jesus' baptism, a meaningful act, prefigured the act that was the fulfilment of his mission on earth; namely his death on the cross.

Jesus is qualified to intercede for us – because he died for our sins

Jesus' violent death was no ordinary death. It was unique not only because it was a murder committed against God's sinless prophet. It was unique because Jesus, freely and voluntarily, chose to offer his life as a sacrifice for sin so as to accomplish our salvation. John the Baptist described him as 'the Lamb of God, who takes away the sin of the world' (John 1:29). Jesus knew that his mission would only be fulfilled after his death and resurrection. He taught his disciples about it, but they were completely unprepared to accept the idea that the Messiah had to die, let alone be put to death by his enemies (Matt. 16:21–23). When Jesus was about to be arrested, one of his disciples tried to defend him with a sword. Jesus said to him:

> Put the sword back in its place ... for all who draw the sword will die by the sword. Do you think I cannot call on my Father, and he will at once put at my disposal more than twelve legions of angels? But how then would the Scriptures be fulfilled that say it must happen in this way? (Matt. 26:52–54)

Jesus' response is highly significant. It provides three reasons that explain his amazing attitude. First, he was against reacting to violence with violence. Violence, he said, breeds violence, and he wanted to break the cycle of violence. Second, he was fully confident that God would rescue him if he wanted to be delivered from his enemies. But he didn't want to, because, third, he knew that his mission was precisely to fulfil what the prophets had said about him. Isaiah, for instance, described the Messiah as God's suffering servant who would offer his life as a sacrifice for the sin of many:

> But he was pierced for our transgressions,
>   he was crushed for our iniquities;
> The punishment that brought us peace was upon him,
>   and by his wounds we are healed ...
> Yet it was the LORD's will to crush him and cause him to suffer,
>   and though the LORD makes his life a guilt offering,
> he will see his offspring and prolong his days,
>   and the will of the LORD will prosper in his hand ...
> Therefore I [the LORD] will give him a portion among the great,
>   and he will divide the spoils with the strong,
> because he poured out his life unto death,
>   and was numbered with the transgressors.
> *For he bore the sin of many,*
>   *and made intercession for the transgressors.*
> (Is. 53:5, 10, 12 [my italics]; cf. Mark 10:45; Luke 22:37; 1 Peter 2:24)

Isaiah's prophecy, written hundreds of years before Jesus was born, links his sacrificial death with his role as an intercessor. In other words, Jesus is qualified to pray for sinners because he has

taken upon himself the punishment for their sins. The gospel
makes this point clear. God vindicated Jesus by raising him from
the dead. Then, having lifted him up to himself, he appointed him
as intercessor on our behalf. He is fit for that role for two reasons:
he was sinless and *he died for us*:

> I write this to you so that you will not sin. But if anybody does sin, we
> have one who speaks to the Father in our defence – Jesus Christ, the
> Righteous One. He is the atoning sacrifice for our sins, and not only for
> ours but also for the sins of the world.
>
> (1 John 2:1–2)

Jesus is qualified to intercede for us – because he is more than a prophet

We do not need to wait until the Day of Judgment to benefit from
Jesus' intercession. He is already pleading with God on our behalf.
The Greek word used in the above-quoted text, *paraklētos*, means
'advocate', 'defender'. Jesus defends our cause and asks God's
forgiveness for us. He is a perfect and compassionate intercessor.
He sympathizes with our weaknesses as he 'has been tempted in
every way, just as we are – yet was without sin' (Heb. 4:15; cf. 2:17–
18; 7:26; 9:14).

Jesus was fully human and yet, unlike any man or woman
(including the prophets), he did not commit any sin whatsoever.
The uniqueness of Jesus suggests that he was more than a prophet.
Jesus himself claimed that he was God's eternal Son (John 10:22–
39). This means that Jesus is a qualified intercessor not only
because of *what he did* (his atoning death) but also because of *who he
is*. He has a unique relationship with God, a relationship far above
the relationship enjoyed by God's most privileged creatures,
whether they be angels or prophets. The latter are still God's
servants, whereas Jesus is God's Son (Matt. 21:33–46). Thus Jesus'
intercession is based on his personal status as well as on his
mission. Those who believe in him as God's appointed intercessor
are entitled to enjoy peace with God – without having to await
God's verdict on the Day of Judgment. God himself, in response
to Jesus' intercession, has forgiven their sins once and for all, just
as Jesus died for their sins 'once for all':

If God is for us, who can be against us? He who did not spare his own Son, but gave him up for us all – how will he not also, along with him, graciously give us all things? Who will bring any charge against those whom God has chosen? It is God who justifies. Who is he that condemns? Christ Jesus, who died – more than that, who was raised to life – is at the right hand of God and is also interceding for us. (Rom. 8:31–34; cf. Heb. 7:23–28)

	Muhammad *(according to the Qur'an and Hadith)*	**Jesus** *(according to the Bible)*
When does he intercede?	On the Day of Judgment.	Now and on the Day of Judgment.
Why does he intercede?	*According to Sunni theologians:* To obtain forgiveness for sinful Muslims – so that they will enjoy paradise after they have been punished. *According to Mu'tazili theologians:* To obtain added reward and blessing for righteous Muslims.	To obtain forgiveness for his people – so that they can be sure now that they have peace with God and will not face punishment.
Why is he qualified to intercede?	Because: • his sins have already been forgiven • it is his honour as God's final prophet	Because: • he is sinless • he died for our sins • he is more than a prophet: he is God's eternal Son

Table 11. A comparison of the intercessory roles of Muhammad and Jesus

In brief, the Bible teaches that Jesus is the only person fit to intercede on our behalf. His intercession is a present reality, whereas in Islam Muhammad is seen as intercessor only on the Day of Judgment. Jesus' intercession aims primarily at obtaining God's forgiveness for his people. As regards the purpose of intercession, the Christian perspective is closer to Sunni doctrine than to Mu'tazili teaching. On the other hand, the Sunni belief in a temporary punishment in hell followed by admission to paradise is alien to the Bible's teaching (see Luke 16:26).[58]

Muslim theologians often raise serious objections against the Christian doctrine that salvation is founded on the atoning death of Jesus Christ. They consider it irreconcilable with Qur'anic teaching that 'no-one bears the burden of another' (6:164; 17:15; 38:18; 39:7; 53:38). Yet the Sunni teaching about Muhammad's intercession for sinful Muslims does indicate that God will grant his favour to these Muslims thanks to the Prophet's personal merits. Hence the Christian understanding of salvation, based on who Jesus is and what he did, should not be seen as antagonistic towards Sunni Islam.

Because Jesus' intercession is based on his atoning death, it fulfils God's mercy and his justice. In one sense, it solves the dilemma that divides Muslim scholars into two main groups: the Sunnites whose theology is underpinned by God's sovereign mercy, and the Mu'tazilites whose theology is determined by God's justice. In the next chapter we will take a more detailed look at God's forgiveness as understood by these two schools.

Notes

1. Razi on 2:254; III:6, pp. 174–176.
2. Razi on 2:48; II:3, p. 57. In Arabic: *al-istithna' 'ani l-nafi ithbat.*
3. Razi on 19:87; XI:21, p. 216.
4. Bukhari, *tawhid* 32: IX, bk 93, p. 426 quotes sura 2 verse 255 and sura 34 verse 23.
5. Bukhari, *tawhid* 24 [6886]:IX, bk 93, no. 532 (b), p. 395; Tirmidhi *tafsir* sura 17 verse 8 [3062].
6. Quoted by Razi on 17:79; XI:21, p. 26. Cf. Ibn Hanbal, *baqi musnad al-mukthirin* 3 [9307, 9358, 9810].

7. Bukhari, *daʻawat* 1 [5829]:VIII, bk 75, no. 317, p. 211; *tawhid* 31 [6920]:IX, bk 93, no. 566, p. 423; Muslim, *iman* 334–335 [293–300]:I, bk 1, no. 385–396, pp. 134–135; Tirmidhi, *daʻawat* 130 [3526].

8. Ibn Majah, *zuhd* 37 [4297]:V, bk 37, no. 4311, p. 528; Tirmidhi, *qiyama* 13 [2365]; Ibn Hanbal, *musnad al-mukthirin* 2 [5195].

9. Bukhari, *tayammum* 1 [323]:I, bk 7, no. 331, p. 199; *salat* 56 [419]:I, bk 8, no. 429, p. 256; Muslim, *masajid* 3 [810], 5 [812]:I, bk 4, no. 1058, p. 264; no. 1062, p. 265; Nasaʼi, *ghusl* 26 [429]; Darimi, *salat* 111 [1353].

10. Ibn Majah, *zuhd* 37 [4304]:V, bk 37, no. 4313, p. 532.

11. Bukhari, *tawhid* 24 [6886]:IX, bk 93, no. 532 (b), p. 395; Ibn Hanbal, *baqi musnad al-mukthirin* 5 [11463].

12. Ibn Hanbal, *musnad alʻashara* 4 [1203, 1213].

13. Abu Dawud, *jihad* 28 [2160]:II, bk 8, no. 2516, p. 699; Ibn Majah, *jihad* 16 [2789]:IV, bk 24, no. 2799, p. 159; Tirmidhi, *fadaʼil al-jihad* 25 [1586].

14. Muslim, *birr* 85 [4703]:IV, bk 32, nos. 6281–6283, p. 1371; Abu Dawud, *adab* 53 [4261]:III, bk 36, no. 4889, p. 1367.

15. Ibn Majah, *zuhd* 37 [4298]:V, bk 37, no. 4308, p. 526; cf. Muslim *iman* 332 [287]:I, bk 1, no. 381, p. 133; Abu Dawud, *sunna* 14 [4053]:III, bk 35, no. 4656, p. 1310; Tirmidhi, *qiyama* 9 [2358], *tafsir* sura 17 [3073], *manaqib* 1 [3546]; Darimi, *muqaddima* 8 [52].

16. Bukhari, *ʻilm* 33 [97]:I, bk 3, no. 98, p. 79.

17. Tirmidhi, *manaqib* 63 [3863].

18. Ibid. 61 [3852]; Ibn Hanbal, *musnad al-mukthirin* 2 [5180], 3 [5555].

19. Ibn Majah, *zuhd* 37 [4301]:V, bk 37, no. 4311, p. 528.

20. Abu Dawud, *sunna* 23 [4114]:III, bk 35, no. 4721, p. 1326; Ibn Majah, *zuhd* 37 [4300]:V, bk 37, no. 4311, p. 528; Tirmidhi, *qiyama* 11 [2359]; Ibn Hanbal, *musnad al-mukthirin* 7 [12745]. In Arabic: *inna shafaʻati li ahli l-kabaʼir min ummati*. It is worth noting that the English translation of this hadith in Ibn Majah's compilation is incorrect. It has nothing to do with the way Muslim theologians understand this narrative.

21. Bukhari, *riqaq* 51 [6081]:VIII, bk 76, no. 571, p. 371; *tawhid* 25 [6896]:IX, bk 93, no. 542, p. 408; Muslim, *iman* 304 [282], 306 [284]:I, bk 1, no. 355, p. 119; no. 357, p. 120; Abu Dawud, *sunna* 23 [4115]:III, bk 35, no. 4722, p. 1326; Ibn Majah, *zuhd* 37 [4306]:V, bk 37, no. 4315, p. 532; Tirmidhi, *juhannam* 10 [2525]; Darimi, *muqaddima* 8 [52].

22. Bukhari, *tawhid* 24 [6886]:IX, bk 93, no. 532 (b), p. 395; cf. Bukhari, *tafsir* sura 2 chapter 1 [4116]:VI, bk 60, no. 3, p. 3; *tafsir* sura 17 chapter 5 [4343]:VI, bk 60, no. 236, p. 198; *tawhid* 19 [6861]:IX, bk 93, no. 507,

p. 373; *tawhid* 36 [6955] [6956]:IX, bk 93, no. 600; no. 601, p. 442; Muslim, *iman* 331 [284]:I, bk 1, no. 378, p. 129; Ibn Majah, *zuhd* 37 [4302]:V, bk 37, no. 4312, p. 528 (Arabic) / p. 530 (English). Tirmidhi, *tafsir* sura 17 chapter 8 [3062]; *qiyama* 9 [2358].

23. Before Noah, Enoch (*Idris*) was a prophet (19:56). Adam was the first prophet according to the Qur'an (cf. 3:33; 19:58) and the Hadith (Bukhari, *tawhid* 37 [6963]:IX, bk 93, no. 608, p. 449). Therefore Noah is the first prophet sent to humanity *after* the flood.

24. The Hadith explains that Abraham was invited by his polytheistic people to take part in their idolatrous worship. Instead of telling them openly that he would not worship their idols, he excused himself and said, 'I am sick' (37:89). Taking advantage of their absence, he destroyed all their idols except one. When summoned by his people to tell the truth, he denied that he had destroyed the idols (21:51–67). See Bukhari, *anbiya'* 8 [3108]:IV, bk 55, no. 578, p. 368; *nikah* 13 [4694]:VII, bk 62, no. 21, p. 14; Muslim, *fada'il* 154 [4371]:IV, bk 30, no. 5848, p. 1262; Abu Dawud, *talaq* 16 [1891]:II, bk 6, no. 2206, p. 596; Tirmidhi, *tafsir* sura 21 [3090].

25. Bukhari, *tafsir* sura 17 chapter 5 [4343]:VI, bk 60, no. 236, p. 198. However, a version of this hadith found only in Ibn Hanbal has it that Jesus was not fit for intercession because some people believed he was God (Ibn Hanbal, *musnad bani hashim* 5 [2415, 2560]). This information is also in line with what the Qur'an says about Jesus (see 5:119–120). Jesus himself remains blameless; i.e. he never said he was God!

26. Muslim, *iman* 331 [284]:I, bk 1, no. 378, p. 129.

27. This statement is based on several narratives in the Hadith: 'Seventy thousand members of my nation will enter paradise without being judged; they are those who practise neither magic nor divination, but put their trust in their Lord.' Bukhari, *riqaq* 21 [5991]:VIII, bk 76, no. 479, p. 318; cf. Bukhari, *tibb* 17 [5270], 42 [5311]:VII, bk 71, no. 605, p. 406; no. 648, p. 434; *riqaq* 50 [6070]:VIII, bk 76, no. 551, p. 361; Ibn Majah, *zuhd* 34 [4275]: V, bk 37, no. 4286, p. 512 (Arabic) / p. 513 (English).

28. Baghdadi, *Usul*, pp. 242–243.

29. Ibn Furak, *Mujarrad*, p. 169.

30. Ibid., p. 167; cf. Baqillani, *Insaf*, p. 170; Bukhari, *iman* 33 [42]:I, bk 2, no. 42, p. 37. Ash'ari quotes three other traditions to back up his view about Muhammad's intercession for sinful Muslims.

31. Baghdadi, *Usul*, p. 244.
32. Sabuni, *Bidaya*, pp. 144–145.
33. Abu Ya'la, *Mu'tamad*, p. 206.
34. Juwayni, *Irshad*, p. 223; Sabuni, *Bidaya*, p. 144.
35. Juwayni, *Irshad*, p. 223.
36. Some Mu'tazili theologians (e.g. Abu Hashim) accept Muhammad's intercession in favour of sinful Muslims. See Mankdim, *Sharh*, p. 689; Baqillani, *Insaf*, p. 169; *Tamhid*, p. 374.
37. Mankdim, *Sharh*, p. 690.
38. Ibid., p. 689.
39. Ibid.
40. Ibid.
41. Razi on 2:48; II:3, p. 53.
42. Razi on 39:19; XIII:26, p. 229.
43. Mankdim, *Sharh*, p. 689.
44. Ibn Furak, *Mujarrad*, p. 169. Cf. Baqillani, *Tamhid*, p. 371; *Insaf*, p. 174; Nasafi, *Tabsira*, II, 794.
45. Mankdim, *Sharh*, p. 689.
46. Ibn Furak, *Mujarrad*, pp. 168–169; Baqillani, *Tamhid*, p. 371; *Insaf*, p. 173; Razi on 2:48; II:3, pp. 56–57.
47. Nasafi, *Tabsira*, II, p. 794.
48. Ibn Furak, *Mujarrad*, p. 168.
49. Razi on 2:48; II:3, pp. 59–60.
50. Mankdim, *Sharh*, p. 690. To appreciate Mankdim's argument fully, one needs to remember that for a saying attributed to the Prophet to be 'authentic' (*sahih*) it has to meet the criteria of *tawatur* (successive transmission). This means it has to be reported by several concordant and uninterrupted chains of transmission from Muhammad down to the compiler of the relevant hadith (e.g. Bukhari, Muslim etc.). In addition, all the people who were part of the chain of transmission must be known for their trustworthiness. It is a fact that this hadith, unlike others, is not found in the two most authoritative compilations of the Hadith; namely, Bukhari and Muslim, both of which are entitled *Sahih*.
51. Mankdim here combines two separate hadiths. One says that the wine-drinker, the rebel to his parents and the one who 'gives boastfully' (*mannan*) will not go to paradise (Nasa'i, *zakat* 69 [2515]; Darimi, *ashriba* 5 [2002]; cf. Qur'an 2:264; Muslim, *iman* 171 [154]:I, bk 1, no. 192, p. 60). The other states that 'the teller of false tales' or 'slanderer' (*nammam*) will

not go to paradise (Muslim, *iman* 168 [151]:I, bk 1, no. 189, p. 59; Tirmidhi, *birr* 78 [1949]).

Mankdim takes this hadith to mean any sinful person, Muslim or non-Muslim. For Sunni theologians, this hadith is not about the sinful Muslim but the 'irreligious Muslim' (*mustahill*); i.e. the Muslim who considers himself neither under the authority of God's law nor accountable to God. Practically this means he is no longer a Muslim.

52. Ibn Furak, *Mujarrad*, p. 167; Nasafi, *Tabsira*, II, p. 795.

53. Mankdim, *Sharh*, p. 691.

54. Nasafi, *Tabsira*, II, p. 795.

55. Ibn Furak, *Mujarrad*, p. 169; cf. Nasafi, *Tabsira*, II, p. 797.

56. The word *irja'* means both 'to give hope' and 'to defer'. In this context it is used with these two meanings. Sinful Muslims are given hope through deferring their judgment to the Resurrection Day; i.e. not prejudging in this life whether or not God will send them to hell (to receive a temporary punishment). Shahrastani, *Religions*, I, pp. 419–420.

57. See Ash'ari, *Maqalat*, II, pp. 166–167.

58. The Sunni teaching is akin to the Catholic doctrines on purgatory and the intercession of saints. Put in the simplest terms, these doctrines imply that God shortens the temporary punishment of those who are in purgatory in response to the saints' intercession (*Catechism*, paras. 1030–1031, p. 235, and paras. 1471–1479, pp. 331–333).

11. GOD'S FORGIVENESS: A REWARD OR A FAVOUR?

God made us for a purpose. He wanted us to serve and worship him: 'I have created the jinns and humans for no other end than they should worship Me' (51:56). To enable us to achieve this purpose God revealed his law and subjected us to its authority. According to Islam, therefore, we are 'people under a mandate' (*mukallafun*), our 'mandate' (*kulfa*) being to submit to our Creator and obey his law. This law has been revealed throughout history in the Scriptures: the Torah, the Zabur (Psalms), the Injil (gospel) and, finally and perfectly, the Qur'an. God's revelation, in turn, urges us to use our 'mind' (*'aql*) in order to think rightly, to live righteously and to believe truthfully.

Depending on how we fulfil our mandate, we deserve people's 'praise' (*madh*) or 'blame' (*dhamm*). Appraisal from others, however, is not what counts most. The Qur'an teaches that we are first and foremost accountable to God. On the 'Day of Reckoning' (*yawmu l-hisab*) our Judge will judge us according to his perfect justice: 'Whoever has done an atom's weight of good shall see it; whoever has done an atom's weight of evil shall see it too' (99:7–8).

God is not only just; he is also merciful, forgiving and sovereign (as we have seen in Part 1). How are these attributes going to affect his judgment? In the chapters on repentance and intercession we have already noted the importance of two concepts in Islamic theology: *istiḥqaq* (deservedness) and *faḍl* (favour). These are the key to how Muslim scholars have understood God's judgment on the Last Day. There is obviously a tension between these concepts, which are based on different but equally truthful attributes of God. The way God's justice and God's mercy relate to each other determines theological thinking in Islam. Put in simple terms, the dilemma is this: either God is just, and consequently has to punish those who have failed to carry out their mandate satisfactorily; or he is sovereign and merciful, and therefore has the right to save at least some of the people who deserve to be punished. In other words, if God acts according only to his justice by rewarding some and punishing others, where is his pardon? But if he forgives the guilty, will he not compromise and even deny his justice?

Attempting to reconcile the conflicting demands of God's justice, on the one hand, and his sovereign mercy, on the other, Muslims have developed four different schools:

1. God is just: he forgives no sin at all (the Kharijites).
2. God is forgiving: he will forgive the sins of all Muslims (a doctrine attributed to Muqatil bin Sulayman).
3. God is just: he will forgive only minor sins, and all sinful Muslims will go to hell for ever (the Muʿtazili school).
4. God is sovereign and merciful: he will decide whether to punish Muslims, and eventually all Muslims will go to paradise (the Murjiʾite school).

The first two of these schools are fairly marginal in Islamic theology, whereas the third and fourth represent major alternatives within mainstream Islam. All Muslim theologians agree that God's forgiveness concerns Muslims only, and that non-Muslims are excluded.[1] The problem is that they differ as to who is a Muslim and who is not. Below I examine these four views.

God is just: he forgives no sin at all

We have seen (in chapter 7) that for the Kharijites, all sins are major sins and Muslims who commit sin are no longer Muslims. People who do not comply with God's revelation are unbelievers (5:47). Therefore sinful Muslims (who in fact are nominal Muslims) will have exactly the same punishment as non-Muslims.[2] They argue that the Qur'an promises eternal punishment to those who disobey God and the Prophet (4:14), those who accuse God's messengers of falsehood (92:14–16), and, more generally, all unbelievers (3:131).

Central to God's law, according to the Kharijites, are the 'legal punishments' (hudud). These sentences are to be carried out against Muslims who transgress God's commands, and include the death penalty for adulterers, amputation of the hand for robbers and whipping for slanderers. Such legal punishments prefigure God's final judgment on the Last Day. The result of this rigid theology, based exclusively on God's uncompromising justice, is that it makes no room for God's forgiveness.

Other Muslim theologians challenge the Kharijite interpretation of the Qur'an. They offer an alternative understanding of sura 5 verse 47: 'Those that do not judge in accordance with God's revelation are unbelievers.' Baqillani considers that this text is not at all about lax Muslim leaders. It is about non-Muslim leaders, who are described as unbelievers because they do not govern their peoples on the basis of God's law.[3] Mankdim suggests a similar interpretation. This verse refers to those who are mustahillun: people who do not submit to the authority of God's law as revealed in Islamic law. The context clearly shows that it is directed at Jewish leaders.[4]

What about the enforcement of legal punishment? Baqillani contends that Muslims who are punished in this life because of their disobedience will not be punished in the hereafter. It is consistent, he says, for a father to punish his son for something wrong and to reward him for a commendable action. Moreover, Baqillani argues that legal punishments are imposed on sinful Muslims as a 'test' (mihna) for which they will be rewarded in the afterlife.[5] This belief is based on a well-known hadith that refers to sura 60 verse 12:[6]

We were with the Prophet in a gathering and he said: 'Take a pledge of allegiance to me that you will associate nothing with God, you will steal nothing, and you will commit no sexual immorality.' Then he recited sura 60 verse 12 in full and added: 'Whoever fulfils his pledge will receive his reward from God. Whoever does not keep his pledge in one way or another will be punished, and his punishment will be considered as an expiation for the sin he committed. Whoever does not keep his pledge and God does not uncover his sin, it will be up to God either to forgive him or to punish him.'[7]

Thus a Muslim who has been punished in this life for a sin he has committed will not be punished for the same sin in the hereafter. His sentence is more of a trial than a punishment. As he has already paid for his offence, he will not have to pay again in the life to come.

God is forgiving: he will forgive the sins of all Muslims

At the opposite end to the Kharijites, the second group considers that God will forgive all Muslims. As a result, no Muslim will ever go to hell; all will go to paradise without being punished, including those who committed major sins. This view is attributed to Muqatil bin Sulayman who is thought to have said, 'An act of disobedience will not affect adversely the person who does it if he is a believer; likewise an act of obedience will not profit the person who does it if he is an unbeliever.'[8]

This group of Muslims puts forward several arguments. First, God promises the believers that he will forgive all their sins without specifying any conditions; that is, repentance (39:53). Second, punishment will reach polytheists (16:27) and unbelievers (16:27; 34:17). As Muslims are all believers, including the sinful among them, they will not be punished. The Qur'an envisages no other groups than believers and unbelievers (3:106–107). Third, the Qur'an points out that God will not put the Prophet and the believers to shame (66:8), only the unbelievers (16:27). As going to hell means being put to shame (3:192), Muslims will not be sent to hell (3:194–195). Finally, they say, God's promises to the believers are worded in general terms; that is, no restrictions are made to exclude sinful Muslims. Muslims should therefore have no reason to fear, since salvation is promised to all of them without exception (2:5; 4:124).[9]

To the final argument of this school, Razi replies that God's punishment of the evildoers is promised in general terms as well; that is, Muslims are also included. These texts declare that God will send all sinful people to hell.[10] Mankdim refutes the view taken by this group of Muslims with a down-to-earth criticism: it represents nothing less than an incentive for Muslims to commit sin. If Muslims will not be punished whatever they do, what will stop them from sinning? It is as if they were told, do whatever you like, it won't do you any harm.[11]

God is just: he will forgive only minor sins; all sinful Muslims will go to hell for ever

For Mu'tazili theologians, God's justice means that on the Day of Judgment God will reward those who have complied with the difficult requirements of his law, and will punish those who have failed.[12] The way God's reward and punishment are understood by Mu'tazili scholars divides them into two groups: the Basrians and the Baghdadians.

Basrians	Baghdadians
God must reward those who deserve it: it is their right.	God will reward people because of his favour, rather than because it is their right. The reward is certain because God has promised it.
God does not have to punish those who deserve it – but he has decided to do so.	God has no choice but to punish those who deserve it.

Table 12. Reward and punishment, according to Mu'tazili theologians

The Ba$\underline{s}$rians believe that God's reward is mandatory (God has to grant it) because it is what people have earned through their obedience: it is their right. The Baghdadians disagree. They consider that people's obedience is their due response to God's blessings. God's reward is therefore not their due or right:[13] it is a favour, and this favour is certain because it has been promised.[14]

What about God's punishment? Is it as inescapable as his reward? Are we undoubtedly going to be punished if we disobey God's commands? The answer is a resounding yes. Mankdim substantiates this with two rational arguments and another based on the Qur'an. The scriptural evidence consists in asserting God's truthfulness. God promises that he will reward the obedient and punish the disobedient. If both reward and punishment were uncertain, it would not have been right for God to make such a double promise.[15] The first rational proof explains why God's precepts are compulsory. God's commands and prohibitions are obligatory precisely because we have been warned that failing to abide by them will unavoidably result in our loss.[16] The second proof is more surprising. God created in us 'the desire for what is wrong' (*shahwatu al-qabi$\underline{h}$*) and 'the dislike for what is good' (*nafratu al-$\underline{h}$asan*). The certainty of eternal punishment is indispensable for deterring us from following our natural inclination, and for prompting us towards obedience. Otherwise, we would be tempted to commit evil. Because God does not tempt us with evil, only the certainty of his punishment is able to offset our predisposition to evil.[17]

Thus God's punishment is as certain as his reward. But, as with God's reward, Mu'tazili theologians differ on whether or not punishment is mandatory for God: does he have to punish us? The Ba$\underline{s}$rian school considers that punishment is God's right because we have been created by him and we transgress his laws. But God is not bound to use his right. He is free to use or not to use it. If he decides to use it by punishing those who have transgressed his commands, he will display his justice. If he chooses not to use it, he will not deprive anyone of their right. Mankdim compares God to a moneylender who punishes for an unpaid debt. The creditor is totally free to claim his money back from his debtors, but he does not have to.[18] The Baghdadian school disagrees and their argument is rather paradoxical. God's punishment, they say, is mandatory: he cannot simply forgive us. The reason is that God's punishment is a blessing (*lutf*) in disguise, in the sense that knowing he has no other choice than to punish us represents a greater incentive for us to comply with his commands. God, they add, is under obligation to grant us this blessing to enable us to obey him fully.[19] The divergence between the two Mu'tazili schools remains purely theoretical, however. Whether or not God's punishment is mandatory, they all agree that he will indeed punish those who disobey him. He will claim his money back from everyone!

Balancing good and bad deeds

On the Day of Judgment God will judge each of us according to our deeds. Our destiny will depend on the balance of our good and bad deeds. If our evil deeds outnumber our good deeds, our good deeds will be cancelled: we will have no reward at all (25:23; 49:2). On the other hand, if our good deeds outnumber our evil deeds, they will atone for our evil deeds; and as a result of our evil deeds having been forgiven, we will receive the reward we deserve because of our good deeds. This is the theory of *al-iḥbat wa al-takfir* (cancellation and atonement) advocated by the Baghdadian school of Mu'tazilites, Abu 'Ali al-Jubba'i in particular.

God's judgment according to this theory is seen as unjust by the Baṣrian Mu'tazilites because it does not take into account the reward for good deeds or the punishment for evil deeds. The Qur'an, they say, promises that 'every atom's weight of good' will be rewarded and 'every atom's weight of evil' will be punished (99:7–8). Therefore they advocate an alternative theory, *al-muwazana* (compensation), developed by Abu Hashim in particular. According to this theory, if the evil deeds outnumber the good deeds, the punishment will be reduced in proportion to the reward for the good deeds. If the good deeds outnumber the evil deeds, the reward will be reduced in proportion to the punishment for the evil deeds.[20] In other words, eternal punishment will be more or less painful just as eternal bliss will be lesser or greater according to our merits.

Basrians The *al-muwazana* theory (compensation)	Baghdadians The *al-iḥbaṭ wa al-takfir* theory (cancellation and atonement)
If our evil deeds outnumber our good deeds: Our punishment will be reduced in proportion to the reward for our good deeds.	If our evil deeds outnumber our good deeds: Our good deeds will be cancelled. We will have no reward at all.
If our good deeds outnumber our evil deeds: Our reward will be reduced in proportion to the punishment for our evil deeds.	If our good deeds outnumber our evil deeds: Our good deeds will atone for our evil deeds. We will receive the reward we deserve because of our good deeds.

Table 13. Balancing good and bad deeds, according to Muʿtazili theologians

In both theories major sins play a decisive role in God's judgment. One major sin is enough to make the evil deeds outnumber the good ones, and consequently to deserve eternal punishment. God warned us that his pardon covers only minor sins: 'If you keep away from major [sins], We will pardon your [minor] sins' (4:31). In fact, God's forgiveness of minor sins is envisaged only in the cancellation theory. In the other, the reward is reduced in proportion to the punishment for the evil deeds. To the credit of the Baṣrian school, however, it must be said that (as we noted) God does not have to punish. It is his right either to punish or to forgive. Yet he has decided not to forgive!

Thus God's pardon plays a secondary role in Muʿtazilite theology. Based almost exclusively on God's justice, and on a very strict understanding of it, this theology maintains that sinful Muslims will be punished. To forgive them means to let them go

to paradise. Access to paradise, Mu'tazili scholars explain, can be
granted as either a reward or a favour. The first alternative is
unacceptable for a simple reason. To reward someone is to exalt
and honour that person. Hence rewarding undeserving people is
evil and God does not do evil. The second alternative is equally
unacceptable. To do a favour for people who are legally responsible for their actions is impossible. It amounts to treating them in a
similar way to children and mentally disabled people who are not
legally accountable. Thus on either account God cannot grant his
favour to sinful Muslims: they must be punished. In no way can
undeserving Muslims go to paradise.[21]

Qur'anic proofs for the Mu'tazili doctrine

What is the scriptural evidence that sinful Muslims will necessarily
be punished? The main argument is that many Qur'anic texts
promise eternal punishment to all people who have failed to
comply with God's law:

> He that disobeys God and His apostle and transgress His statutes, God
> will send them to hell where they will remain forever.
> (4:14; cf. 2:81; 4:33, 93, 123; 6:160; 8:16; 20:74, 75, 111; 25:68; 72:23;
> 79:37; 99:7–8)

> Those that sell the covenant of God and their own oaths for a small
> price shall have no share in the world to come.
> (3:77; cf. 4:10, 18, 97; 5:33; 9:34; 10:27; 83:2)

The debate raised by these texts (and others) is referred to as 'the
question of the general and the particular' (mas'alatu al-'umum wa al-
khusus). Mu'tazili theologians consider that these texts point to all
people who disobey God's commands; that is, non-Muslims as well
as sinful Muslims. Sunni theologians take the opposite view; for
them, these texts are aimed exclusively at non-Muslims. Mankdim
puts forward two arguments. The first is a hermeneutical principle.
God's message cannot have ambiguous or hidden meaning; otherwise God would be responsible for misleading us. Therefore texts
must be interpreted according to their plain meaning ('ala l-zahir).
The second argument is grammatical. Arab linguists agree that the

words *man* (he that), *alladhina* (those that), *kull* (all) and similar words have universal meaning unless an exception is made in the sentence or in the context.[22] As the Qur'anic texts that make use of these words make no restrictions, their meaning is general: they are aimed at all sinful people regardless of whether or not they are Muslims.[23] To restrict these texts to non-Muslims would be to deprive them of their main purpose, which is to deter Muslims from disobeying God's commands.[24] Likewise, Qur'anic texts about 'the wretched' (11:106–107; 92:14–16), 'the evildoers' (19:72), 'the wrongdoers' (43:74), 'the wicked' (82:14), 'the unjust' (83:1) and so on, include sinful Muslims as well as unbelievers.[25] Finally, the Mu'tazilis argue that the legal punishments carried out against sinful Muslims (adulterers, robbers, slanderers etc.) give evidence that they will be punished in the hereafter. These punishments represent mere tests for penitent Muslims, remarks Mankdim; yet for unrepentant Muslims they anticipate the eternal punishment they will receive on the Day of Judgment.[26]

God is sovereign and merciful: he will decide whether to punish Muslims; eventually all Muslims will go to paradise

The fourth school of Muslim theologians, the Murji'ites,[27] consider that God's pardon will reach every Muslim. Sinful Muslims will thus be saved from eternal punishment. So how do these theologians argue their case?

Razi

Razi's argument is threefold. First, he does not consider that the grammatical argument put forward by the Mu'tazilites is conclusive. The words 'he that', 'those that', 'all' and so on, do not necessarily have a universal sense. As a rich woman, the Queen of Sheba is described in the Qur'an as someone possessing 'all things' (27:23). Clearly, the expression 'all things' is not to be taken literally. The scope of these words is fairly flexible: it varies in the Qur'an as well as in ordinary speech. This implies that the 'evildoers', 'unjust' and so on, referred to in the Qur'an could be specifically the unbelievers or non-Muslims.

Second, Razi contends that the Qur'anic texts promising God's pardon to believers are specific, unlike the ones about the punishment of evildoers. What is specific takes precedence over what is general. Sinful Muslims must be seen as believers, since they do not cease to believe in God and the Prophet.

Third, because of the seeming contradiction between the texts about God's pardon, on the one hand, and those about his punishment, on the other, external considerations must be taken into account to tip the scales on one side or the other. Razi puts forward three arguments that favour God's granting his pardon to sinful Muslims:

1. Forgiving is more in line with God's generosity than punishing;
2. God's mercy is greater than his anger, as it is said in the Hadith;
3. God is more likely to give up his right to punish Muslims for their sin than to deny them their right to the reward they have deserved through their faith.[28]

Ash'ari

Ash'ari too acknowledges that there seems to be a contradiction between the promise God makes to believers and the one he makes to evildoers. For him, there is no compelling reason for one series of texts to prevail over the other. Second, he observes that the words used for believers and unbelievers ('he that', 'those that') sometimes have a general and sometimes a particular meaning.[29] Therefore the meaning of Qur'anic texts is determined by 'external evidence' (*qara'in*). This evidence includes the 'consensus' (*ijma'*) of the Muslim community, unequivocal texts and 'analogical reasoning' (*qiyas*).[30] Taking into account this threefold evidence, Ash'ari considers that the Qur'an clearly teaches that believers will go to paradise (5:9; 9:72; 48:29) and polytheists to hell (5:72). By contrast, the Qur'an does not have clear-cut teaching as regards sinful Muslims who die without having repented from their sins. God may forgive them and he may punish them for a time before admitting them into paradise. The Qur'an, he says, states that God will reward people for their good deeds (3:195; 18:30; 99:7–8). Sinful Muslims possess the greatest good deed, as they know God, acknowledge his oneness, love him and praise him. This means that their punishment cannot be eternal: they will assuredly come out of hell and get to paradise.[31]

Qur'anic proofs for temporary punishment

Are there any specific texts in the Qur'an supporting the doctrine of temporary punishment for sinful Muslims? Juwayni concedes that the plain meaning of the texts suggests that punishment in hell is eternal. However, he says, this eternity does not have to be understood literally. It could simply mean a very long time. We do, for instance, wish kings an everlasting reign.[32] Some Murji'ites point to a text which they think favours their view: 'Those that are wretched shall be in hell where, groaning and wailing, they shall abide as long as the heavens and the earth endure, unless your Lord decides otherwise: your Lord will do what He will' (11:106–107).

The Murji'ites claim that the duration of punishment is related in this text to the duration of the heavens and the earth, which are not eternal. Since God will put an end to the heavens and the earth, the punishment of sinful Muslims must be temporary. On the other hand, this punishment is described as subject to God's will; hence not necessarily eternal. In response to this argument Mankdim says that if the punishment of sinful Muslims is not eternal, neither should be that of unbelievers. The text makes no distinction between the two groups. The fact that the punishment of unbelievers is eternal, as Islam teaches, indicates that the punishment of sinful Muslims is also eternal. He adds that in the following verse the blessedness of the believers is described in exactly the same terms: 'As for the blessed, they shall dwell in Paradise as long as the heavens and the earth endure, unless your Lord decides otherwise. This is an endless gift' (11:108).

So should we conclude that God's reward (paradise) is also temporary? In fact, Mankdim says, the expression 'as long as' implies no time limit, but an endless time. Likewise, the Qur'an says that 'Those who accused Our revelations of falsehood ... will not enter Paradise until a camel will pass through the eye of a needle' (7:40). Clearly, this verse does not suggest that one day the unbelievers will get into paradise. What is meant is the opposite: unbelievers will never go to paradise.[33]

Murji'ite scholars claim that their belief that God will forgive sinful Muslims is based on specific and unambiguous Qur'anic verses. These verses depict God as the forgiving God. His willingness to forgive seems almost boundless. Let us consider the most significant of these verses.

Sura 4 verse 48

> God does not forgive that partners be associated with Him, but He forgives any other sin to whom He pleases.
>
> (4:48; cf. 18:58; 20:82; 40:3; 42:25, 30, 34)

This text clearly indicates that, except for polytheism, God's pardon knows no limits. Mankdim concedes that from a strictly rational point of view this verse suggests that God may forgive any sin apart from polytheism. Sura 4 verse 31, however, rules out this possibility, as it says God forgives only minor sins:[34] 'If you keep away from major [sins], We will pardon your [minor] sins and introduce you [to Paradise] through a gate of great honour' (4:31).

Baqillani interprets sura 4 verse 31 in the light of sura 4 verse 48. The major sins, he says, God will not forgive are sins related to polytheism.[35] The debate is therefore which verse of sura 4 must take precedence over the other, 31 or 48 (which is repeated in verse 116).

Sura 39 verse 53

> Say: 'O My servants who have transgressed against their souls! Despair not of God's mercy. God forgives all sins, for He is All-Forgiving, All-Merciful.'
>
> (39:53)

Mankdim comments that if taken literally, this verse would imply that God forgives all sins including polytheism. On the other hand, to claim that God forgives all sins amounts to encouraging people to commit evil. Therefore, he adds, this verse should be interpreted in the sense that if you repent, God will forgive you all your sins.[36] Abu 'Ali al-Jubba'i offers a similar interpretation to all Qur'anic texts relating to God's forgiveness. What they teach is that God forgives on the condition that people repent.[37] Juwayni replies to the Mu'tazilis who claim that God's pardon is conditional. According to their doctrine, he says, God has the obligation to accept people's repentance, and people's repentance removes the punishment for sin; therefore there is no need for God to forgive the sin people have repented from. In other words, forgiveness for the Mu'tazilis is a word without a meaning.[38]

In addition to those specific verses, Murji'ite theologians refer to the general teaching of the Qur'an on forgiveness. God glorifies himself because he is a merciful and forgiving God. This would be meaningless if God did not forgive those who indeed deserve his punishment.[39] Baqillani and Juwayni draw a parallel between God's commands for us to forgive (2:237; 3:134; 64:4) and his forgiving people. Baqillani asks the Mu'tazilites, 'How can we deny God the right to forgive our sins knowing that he commanded us to forgive our fellow human beings and he praised those who do forgive?'.[40] Juwayni reaches a similar conclusion but underlines the difference between God and ourselves:

> God's revelation encourages us to forgive although this is difficult for us because of our strong desire for revenge, our need to satisfy this desire and the harm resulting from our repressing our anger. If, nonetheless, forgiving is a commendable act for us, how much more is it for the Lord who has no need for taking revenge whatsoever and who is the only one to enjoy self-sufficiency.[41]

Juwayni makes use of rational arguments to confirm the teaching of God's revelation. Everyone knows from a strictly human perspective that forgiving is a good and advisable act.[42] Baqillani refers to Arab poetry to make the same point. He cites three quotations before concluding that, far from blaming them, we are to honour those who, instead of carrying out their threat, forgive others their wrongdoing.[43] The person who showed such a noble character to perfection was none other than the Prophet himself.[44]

Proofs from the Hadith

The Murji'ite doctrine is supported by several hadiths (some of which are quoted in chapter 10). One of them specifies that some people will come out of hell after having been burnt by its fire.[45]

Mankdim dismisses this tradition on the ground that it is historically unreliable. If its authenticity were to be proven, it must be understood allegorically in a way compatible with Islamic teaching in general. It would mean, when people come to faith they dissociate themselves from those who will go to hell after they have been harmed by what they have done as non-believers. Mankdim also refers to three other hadiths which indicate that hell is the final destiny of the evildoers; for example 'The slanderer, the wine-drinker and the rebel to his parents will not enter paradise.'[46]

Against the Mu'tazilite doctrine, Murji'ite theologians argue that the enforcement of legal punishments against sinful Muslims in this life does not imply at all that God is going to punish them in the hereafter as well. God punishes them for their sin now so that he may not hold it against them then.[47] The hadith specifies that because they have paid the penalty for their sin on earth they will not have to pay for it again on the Day of Judgment.[48] Juwayni comments that the Qur'an requires the death penalty for the Muslim who commits murder (2:178–179), but nowhere is he promised eternal punishment.[49]

A summary from Ash'ari

Among Murji'ite theologians who exalt God's sovereign will, Ash'ari is undoubtedly the most radical. For him, whether God punishes or forgives, it is on God's own initiative. In other words, God is not driven by any compelling 'cause' (sabab), be it unbelief or obedience. His punishment is 'an initiative of justice' (ibtida'u 'adl) and his pardon 'an initiative of favour' (ibtida'u fadl). He is entirely free to forgive unbelievers and let them go to paradise. This would be totally in line with his mercy and wisdom. He has the right to bestow his favour on those who have not obeyed him, and to grant them the same reward as those who have, and even more! God's reward to the believers is also an undeserved favour. Why? For their obedience is itself the result of God's favour and enabling. Having said that, Ash'ari claims that all unbelievers will receive eternal punishment and that all believers will in the end receive an eternal reward. This double certainty is based on God's 'revelation'; for example the Qur'an and the Hadith (khabar) as it has been unanimously ('ala l-ijma') interpreted by the Muslim community.[50] A Mu'tazili would probably endorse this statement with only one major proviso: sinful and unrepentant Muslims are not in fact believers.

Maturidite theologians do not go as far as the Ash'arites in affirming God's sovereignty. They rule out the possibility of unbelievers being forgiven, not only because of God's revelation, but also on rational grounds. Sabuni points out that there is a radical difference between believers and unbelievers (45:21; 55:60; 68:36). The divide between the two groups (unbelief) is the utmost crime (*nihaya fi al-jinaya*) for which there is no pardon or concession. Unbelievers seek no pardon for their sin and, because their unbelief is a never-ending sin, their punishment must be eternal.[51]

Ash'ari sums up the Murji'ite doctrine in describing the double status of sinful Muslims. On the one hand, they are believers; on the other, sinful. These qualifications are compatible and neither can remove nor even prevail over the other; hence the need to suspend our judgment about sinful Muslims. As Sunni Muslims say, he concludes, 'We do not claim they are destined to paradise nor do we claim they are destined to hell; we leave their judgment with God. He will punish them if he wants to punish them and he will forgive them if he wants to forgive them'.[52] This statement simply echoes many Qur'anic texts: 'He will forgive whom He will and He will punish whom He will. For God has supreme power over all things' (2:284; cf. 3:129; 5:20, 43; 48:14).

In his book reviewing Islamic sects and their beliefs Ash'ari gives a summary of what Muslims think about the possibility of sinful Muslims remaining in hell for ever. He divides Muslims into two main groups:

1. 'the Mu'tazilites and the Kharijites, who assert that sinful Muslims will remain in hell for ever. Whoever enters hell will never come out of it';
2. 'the Sunnites, who claim that God will bring out of hell monotheist Muslims. He will not leave them there for ever'.[53]

Thus, undoubtedly, for Sunni Muslims in particular and for Murji'ites in general, God's pardon is not a word devoid of meaning. But since God's pardon does not rule out his punishment, the word still lacks its full meaning.

| Kharijites | Mu'tazilites | | Sunnites |
	Basrians	Baghdadians	Murji'ites (Ash'arites and Maturidites)
Emphasize that God is uncompromisingly just: he forgives no sin at all.	Emphasize that God is just: he forgives only minor sins.	Emphasize that God is just: he forgives only minor sins.	Emphasize that God is sovereign and merciful.
God must reward those who deserve it: it is their right.	God must reward those who deserve it: it is their right.	God will reward people because of his favour, rather than because it is their right.	God will reward people because of his favour, rather than because it is their right.
God has no choice but to punish those who deserve it.	God does not have to punish those who deserve it – but he has decided to do so.	God has no choice but to punish those who deserve it.	God has the right to forgive or punish as he chooses.
Sinful Muslims will remain in hell for ever.			Sinful Muslims will suffer temporary punishment in hell before going to paradise.

Table 14. Reward and punishment across the theological schools

Unconditional and complete forgiveness

The Gospels show Jesus offering forgiveness of sins to several
people (Mark 2:1–12; Luke 7:36–50; John 8:1–11). In each case his
offer is *unconditional* (it does not depend on people's merits),
comprehensive (it covers all their sins) and *immediate* (people can
receive it on the spot).

What is the link between good deeds and forgiveness?
Jesus calls on his disciples to be the 'salt of the earth' and the 'light of
the world' (Matt. 5:13–15). The purpose of Christian living is not to
earn God's favour but to point people to the living God: 'let your
light shine before men, that they may see your good deeds and
praise your Father in heaven' (Matt. 5:16). Occasionally Jesus refers
to a heavenly reward his disciples will receive for helping the poor,
praying or fasting (Matt. 6:4, 6, 16). On the Day of Judgment people
who have shown mercy to the needy (e.g. the hungry, sick,
prisoners, strangers) will enter God's kingdom (Matt. 25:34–40).
Jesus says that on that day we will be judged according to our deeds:
'a time is coming when all who are in their graves will hear his voice
and come out – those who have done good will rise to live, and
those who have done evil will rise to be condemned' (John 5:28–
29). At first sight these words seem to suggest that people will be
saved (or not) according to the number of good deeds they have
produced in their lifetime. In fact, what Jesus actually means is that
people will be judged not on what they *claim* but on the *living evidence*
of their faith. In other words, no-one can claim to be Jesus' disciple
if that person's faith makes no difference to his or her life:

> Not everyone who says to me, 'Lord, Lord,' will enter the kingdom of
> heaven, but only he who does the will of my Father who is in heaven.
> Many will say to me on that day, 'Lord, Lord, did we not prophesy in
> your name, and in your name drive out demons and perform many
> miracles?' Then I will tell them plainly, 'I never knew you. Away from
> me, you evildoers!'
> (Matt. 7:21–23)

Thus obedience to God, resulting in godly living, represents a reliable test for our faith. A genuine believer is someone whose deeds match his words. This does not mean that we are saved by our good deeds. Jesus never presents God's forgiveness as a reward for our obedience. In the prayer he taught his disciples, the word used for 'sin' literally means 'debt': 'Forgive us our debts, / as we also have forgiven our debtors' (Matt. 6:12). In one of his parables Jesus compares our position before God to that of a servant who is unable to pay the debts he owes his master. His master first decides to get his money back by selling him and his household. However, in response to the servant's plea the merciful master cancels his debts and lets him go (Matt. 18:23–27; cf. Luke 7:40–42).

Jesus expects people to give an adequate response to the offer of forgiveness. This includes forgiving others (Matt. 18:28–35) and leading a new life. Thus he says to the woman who committed adultery, 'neither do I condemn you ... Go now and leave your life of sin' (John 8:11).

Why can't good deeds blot out evil ones?

Why does the gospel rule out the possibility of redeeming evil deeds with good deeds? The answer is that our acts of disobedience have deadly consequences. The Bible's account of Adam's disobedience is similar to the Qur'anic text in many ways. But there is one significant difference, which relates to the consequence of disobeying God's command. God's warning in Genesis, unlike the Qur'an, points out that Adam's disobedience would unavoidably result in his death: 'You are free to eat from any tree in the garden; but you must not eat from the tree of the knowledge of good and evil, for when you eat of it you will surely die' (Gen. 2:16–17; cf. Qur'an 2:35; 7:19).

As soon as Adam disobeyed, he became spiritually dead. He walked away from God, the source of life. God's warning became reality. Adam's spiritual death led to his physical death. God himself told him about the fatal consequences of his act:

> you [will] return to the ground,
>   since from it you were taken;
> for dust you are
>   and to dust you will return.
> (Gen. 3:19)

God expelled Adam and Eve from paradise to keep them away
from 'the tree of life' (Gen. 3:24). Moreover, from Adam's time
onwards, all human beings commit sin and, as a result, they all die.
Jesus also describes people who are outside God's kingdom as
spiritually dead (Luke 9:60).

In Christianity sin has far-reaching implications, for 'the wages
of sin is death' (Rom. 6:23; cf. Rom. 6:16; 8:2, 10; Eph. 2:6). This
means that it is not our evil deeds that need redeeming, but
ourselves. We need to be saved from sin and death. The climax of
Jesus' mission on earth was precisely to achieve our redemption.
On the evening of his arrest Jesus gathered his twelve disciples to
have a final meal with them. He then told them that his death was
imminent. Referring to the Old Covenant, which God had made
with Israel through Moses, he presented his death as the cornerstone for a New Covenant: 'This is my blood of the covenant,
which is poured out for many for the forgiveness of sins' (Matt.
26:28). The focus of the New Covenant is the forgiveness of sins
based on Jesus' death. This covenant reconciles God's mercy for
sinners with his justice that condemns their sins. Jesus died for us
so that God might forgive our sins without compromising his
justice.

Thus God's forgiveness by no means represents a reward in
Christianity. There is no way for us to earn God's favour by
obeying his commands: 'no-one will be declared righteous in his
sight by observing the law; rather, through the law we become
conscious of sin' (Rom. 3:20; cf. Gal. 2:16). In this respect Mu'tazili
theology and Bible teaching are at opposite ends of the spectrum.
What Christianity has in common with this theology is that God's
punishment is inescapable for everyone who commits sin. Such is
his justice that 'he does not leave the guilty unpunished', whatever
their sins (Exod. 34:7).

How can we receive forgiveness and be sure of it?
God's pardon is a free gift offered to everyone in spite of their sin
and regardless of their (non-existing) merits. This gift can be
offered without contradicting God's justice, because Jesus on the
cross took upon himself the punishment for sin. It is for all who
trust in what God did for them through Jesus Christ. We can be

assured of God's pardon because it does not depend on whether we deserve it or not. It is the expression of God's saving love. Our fitting response is to accept God's gift humbly and to commit ourselves to live according to his will for us:

> it is by grace you have been saved, through faith – and this not from yourselves, it is the gift of God – not by works, so that no-one can boast. For we are God's workmanship, created in Christ Jesus to do good works, which God prepared in advance for us to do.
> (Eph. 2:8–10)

Such teaching is certainly irreconcilable with Mu'tazili theology on more than one account. The thrust of their teaching is that 'the good deeds remove the evil ones' (11:114). The compensation theory reduces God's forgiveness to nothing, whereas in the cancellation theory it is limited to minor sins provided that evil deeds are outnumbered by good deeds.

The Christian understanding of God's pardon as an undeserved favour is undoubtedly more in tune with Sunni theology, but it goes far beyond it. Because of Jesus' atoning death, God's pardon covers *all* our sins. Those who believe in Jesus Christ enjoy God's favour to the full. They already have peace with God and have no reason to fear his verdict on the Day of Judgment (Rom. 8:1). God's perfect favour means eternal salvation for them, which rules out any idea of temporary punishment. The full scope and substance of God's forgiveness is disclosed in the gospel in a unique way.

In brief, salvation is God's greatest blessing for us. To receive this undeserved gift one needs to believe that Jesus is more than just a prophet. He is God's appointed Saviour. Forgiveness of sins comes through him. Acknowledging Jesus Christ as Saviour means repenting from sin and entering into a life-transforming relationship with God. Whoever experiences God's love and pardon will have no greater desire than to please his Lord by walking in Jesus' footsteps. But Jesus is not only 'the Saviour of the world' (John 4:42; 1 John 4:14). Having raised him from the dead, God appointed him as the one who is going to judge the world. These two roles, saviour and judge, are closely related: he who died to save the world is best qualified to be God's representative on the day when God will judge the world. If people do not respond to God's love, they will have to face his justice:

> In the past God overlooked such ignorance, but now he commands all people everywhere to repent. For he has set a day when he will judge the world with justice by the man he has appointed. He has given proof of this to all men by raising him from the dead.
> (Acts 17:30–31; cf. Matt. 7:21–23; 16:27; 25:31–33; John 5:27; Acts 10:42; Rom. 2:16)

Notes

1. There are a few exceptions to this consensus. Baqillani and other Sunni theologians do not completely rule out that some Jews, Christians and other non-Muslims may go to paradise. Although they are not Muslims, they cannot be simply identified as unbelievers (Baqillani, *Tamhid*, p. 353).

2. Some Kharijites take a different view. Najdah al-Ḥanafi, for instance, considers that sinful Muslims will go to hell to atone for their sins and that their punishment will be proportionate to their sins. After they have paid the penalty for their sins, they will go to paradise (Nasafi, *Tabsira*, II, p. 767).

3. Baqillani, *Tamhid*, p. 357.

4. Mankdim, *Sharḥ*, pp. 687, 722.

5. Baqillani, *Tamhid*, pp. 360–361.

6. 'O Prophet! When believing women come to you and pledge themselves to associate nothing with God, to commit neither theft, nor adultery, nor child-murder, nor to engage in any slander of their own making, nor to disobey you in any good thing, then accept their allegiance and seek for them the forgiveness of God. For God is All-Forgiving and All-Merciful' (60:12).

7. Bukhari, *tafsir* sura 60 chapter 3 [4515]:VI, bk 60, no. 417, p. 387; *ḥudud* 8 [6286], 14 [6303]:VIII, bk 81, no. 775, p. 509; no. 793, p. 518; *aḥkam* 49 [6673]:IX, bk 89, no. 320, p. 243; *tawḥid* 31 [6914]:IX, bk 93, no. 560, p. 420; Muslim, *ḥudud* 42 [3223]:III, bk 17, no. 4235, p. 924; Tirmidhi, *ḥudud* 12 [1359], *iman* 10 [2549].

8. Shahrastani, *Religions*, I, p. 187, n. 19, p. 427.

9. Razi on 2:81; II:3, pp. 141–142.

10. Ibid.

11. Mankdim, *Sharh*, p. 650. This view is also challenged by the arguments (explained later in this chapter) Mu'tazili theologians direct against the Murji'ite doctrine.

12. Ibid., p. 614.

13. Ibid., pp. 617–618.

14. Ibid., p. 645.

15. Ibid., p. 621.

16. Ibid., p. 619.

17. Ibid., p. 620.

18. Ibid., p. 645.

19. Ibid., pp. 646–647. This argument is based on the Mu'tazili understanding of the doctrine known as *al-aslah*. Because God has imposed on us to obey his law, he has the obligation to provide us with every help we need to meet the demands of this law. Otherwise, God would not be just when, on the Day of Judgment, he will call us to give account for how well we obeyed his law. The Sunni understanding of the same doctrine is very different (see chapter 9, n. 37).

20. Mankdim, *Sharh*, pp. 624–632.

21. Ibid., pp. 623–624, 650, 666–667, 689.

22. Ibid., p. 651.

23. Ibid., pp. 656–660. In fact, Mankdim should have said, 'As *nearly* all Qur'anic texts …' As noted earlier in this chapter, he interprets sura 5 verse 47 in a restrictive sense: it is directed at Jewish rulers (cf. *Sharh*, pp. 687, 722).

24. See Razi (on 2:81; II:3, pp. 132–148), who provides a comprehensive survey of 'the question of the general and the particular'.

25. Mankdim, *Sharh*, pp. 660–663.

26. Ibid., p. 649.

27. For the meaning of this word see chapter 8, n. 15, and chapter 10, n. 56.

28. Razi on 2:81; II:3, pp. 139–140.

29. Ibn Furak, *Mujarrad*, pp. 164–165. According to his disciple Ibn Furak, Ash'ari in his commentary on the Qur'an (*Tafsir*), which has been lost, took a different view, closer to the Mu'tazilites. He was of the opinion that the Qur'anic texts about God's punishment should be given a general sense in accordance with their plain meaning, except where there is evidence that they should be interpreted in a particular sense (Ibn Furak, *Mujarrad*, p. 165).

30. Ibid., p. 165.
31. Ibid., pp. 163–164.
32. Juwayni, *Irshad*, p. 220.
33. Mankdim, *Sharh*, pp. 674–675.
34. Ibid., p. 678.
35. Baqillani, *Tamhid*, p. 354.
36. Mankdim, *Sharh*, p. 683.
37. Gimaret, *Lecture*, 6:145 (p. 329); 13:6 (p. 504); 14:36 (p. 523); 40:3 (p. 717); 74:56 (p. 824).
38. Juwayni, *Irshad*, p. 220.
39. Nasafi, *Tabsira*, II, p. 775.
40. Baqillani, *Tamhid*, p. 352.
41. Juwayni, *Irshad*, p. 222.
42. Ibid.
43. Baqillani, *Tamhid*, pp. 351–352; cf. Nasafi, *Tabsira*, II, pp. 682, 781.
44. Nasafi, *Tabsira*, II, p. 782.
45. Bukhari, *riqaq* 51 [6081]:VIII, bk 76, no. 571, p. 371; *tawhid* 25 [6896]:IX, bk 93, no. 542, p. 408; Muslim, *iman* 304 [282], 306 [284]:I, bk 1, no. 355, p. 119; no. 357, p. 120; Abu Dawud, *sunna* 23 [4115]:III, bk 35, no. 4722, p. 1326; Ibn Majah, *zuhd* 37 [4306]:V, bk 37, no. 4315, p. 532; Tirmidhi, *juhannam* 10 [2525]; Darimi *muqaddima* 8 [52].
46. Mankdim, *Sharh*, pp. 772–774. For references to this hadith see chapter 10, n. 51.
47. Juwayni, *Irshad*, p. 222.
48. See n. 7 above for the text of this tradition and its reference.
49. Juwayni, *Irshad*, p. 222; cf. Nasafi, *Tabsira*, II, p. 777; Sabuni, *Bidaya*, p. 143; Baqillani, *Tamhid*, p. 355. Sura 4 verse 93 says, 'He that kills a believer deliberately, his reward will be hell where he will be eternally.' Juwayni (and others) seems to take this verse as referring to the unbelieving murderer, which is unlikely given the context (see preceding verse). Razi concedes that it is about a Muslim murderer. He also points out that a Muslim murderer will be forgiven if he repents (25:68; see Razi on 4:93; V:10, pp. 189–191). The Qur'an does not promise eternal punishment to robbers (5:41) or adulterers (24:2), but it does to unrepentant slanderers (24:23).
50. Ibn Furak, *Mujarrad*, p. 163. Baqillani takes a very similar view (*Tamhid*, pp. 351–353). Ash'ari knows that some Muslims do not believe that bliss in paradise and punishment in hell will be eternal. He probably considers

their opinion as marginal and non-representative of the Muslim community. Muslims who consider that God will put an end to both paradise and hell include Jahm bin Safwan and his disciples (see Ash'ari, *Maqalat*, II, p. 167; Shahrastani, *Religions*, I, p. 295).

51. Sabuni, *Bidaya*, p. 145.
52. Ibn Furak, *Mujarrad*, p. 164.
53. Ash'ari, *Maqalat*, II, p. 167.

12. DO THE PROPHETS NEED GOD'S PARDON?

Before we bring this part to a close we need to consider one more issue. In the chapter on intercession we noted that, although not so of Jesus, many prophets in the Qur'an are portrayed as having asked for God's pardon, for themselves as well as their people. In the same chapter we considered a few hadiths about the intercession of Muhammad on the Day of Judgment. In one of these traditions Adam, Noah, Abraham, Moses and Jesus consider themselves unworthy of intercession because (with the exception of Jesus) each disobeyed God in one way or another. By contrast, Muhammad was granted the right to intercede for his people, not because he was sinless, but because his 'past and future sins' had been forgiven (48:2). This suggests that the prophets, including Muhammad, are sinners and, like anyone else, need God's forgiveness.

Islamic theology, however, advocates 'the infallibility/sinlessness of the prophets' (al-'isma al-nabawiyya). Most Muslim theologians believe that the prophets are sinless in the sense that they may make 'a mistake' (khata'), as opposed to a sin, and that any mistake they make is done so 'inadvertently' (sahw^{an}). Sunni theologians, for whom all sins are major, consider that the prophets became protected from sin as soon as God called them to prophethood.[1] The Mu'tazilites and some Murji'ites, by contrast, believe that the prophets are preserved only from committing major sins.[2] Other Murji'ites do not rule out the possibility of prophets committing major sins, including murder and adultery.[3]

In this chapter we will examine the question of the prophets' sinlessness by looking first at some significant prayers the Hadith attributes to the Prophet. We will move on to look at the reasons behind the belief, focusing on the explanation given by Razi. Finally, we will review mainstream Islamic interpretation of Qur'anic texts that speak about the sins committed by some of the prophets including Muhammad himself.

Muhammad's prayers for forgiveness

The Hadith tells us that Muhammad frequently sought God's forgiveness. He often turned to God in repentance, asking God to cleanse him from sin: 'Lord! Accept my repentance and wipe out my sin. Answer my prayers and establish my argument. Make my speech persuasive and guide my heart.'[4]

The Prophet used to pray the following prayer persistently, which he also said on his deathbed: 'Lord! Forgive me and turn in mercy to me. For You are the Returning and the All-Forgiving God.'[5]

Muhammad had an acute awareness that God was both merciful and righteous. He appealed to God's mercy to save him from God's wrath:

I take refuge in Your good will to protect me from Your displeasure.
I take refuge in Your pardon against Your wrath.
I take refuge in You to be safe from You.
No-one can take away what You grant,
and no-one can give what You do not want to grant.[6]

Muslims see Muhammad as a man of prayer. He prayed day and night. Some of his prayers were profoundly inspired by Qur'anic

teaching about God's forgiveness. The following prayers reflect his
need to be assured as regards the forgiveness of his own sins:

> O God! Praise be to You!
> You are the Lord of heaven and earth.
> Praise be to You!
> You are the Sustainer of heaven and earth and whatever is in them.
> Praise be to You!
> You are the Light of heaven and earth.
> Your Word is true, Your Promise is true and the Meeting with You is
> true.
> Paradise is true, Hell is true, and the Hour of Judgment is true.
>
> O God! I surrender to You, I trust in You, I seek support in You. I turn
> in repentance to You.
> My quarrels are all about You and I make appeal to You.
> Forgive my past and future sins, and the sins I did in secret and in public.
> For You are my God, I have no other God.[7]
>
> O God! I seek refuge in You from the trial of Hell and the trial of the
> punishment of Hell, from the trial of the grave and the punishment
> of the grave, from the evil of the trial of affluence and the evil of the
> trial of poverty.
> I seek refuge in You from the evil of the trial of the Antichrist.
> O God! Wash away my sins with snow and hail water.
> Purify my heart from sin as the white garment is cleaned from dirt, and
> keep sin away from me as East is kept away from West.
> O God! I seek refuge in You from sloth, from senility, from evil and
> from debt.[8]
>
> O God! Forgive my fault, my ignorance, and my immoderation in my
> concerns. You are better aware of my affairs than I am.
> O God! Forgive me the sins I did seriously and jokingly, and the sins I
> did unwillingly and willingly. All these failings are mine.
> O God! Forgive my past and future sins, the sins I did in secret and in
> public. Forgive me the sins that You are better aware of than I am.
> You are the One who uncovers sin and who covers sin. You are
> powerful over everything.[9]

These moving and very personal prayers suggest that Muhammad was fully aware of his shortcomings. He was also aware of God's mercy and willingness to forgive his sins. The Prophet made no difference between himself and other Muslims in terms of his need of God's pardon:

> God's Messenger said:
> – There is none amongst you who will be saved because of his good deeds.
>   The Companions asked:
> – God's Messenger, not even you?
>   He replied:
> – Not even I, unless God wraps me in His mercy and grants me His pardon.[10]

Nowhere in the Hadith do we find any hint of the sinlessness of Muhammad or of any other prophet (apart from Jesus). This doctrine of the 'sinlessness of the prophets' has been developed on the basis of theological assumptions, which are allegedly based on the Qur'an, as we will see in the following section.

What the 'sinlessness of the prophets' means

Razi begins his discussion by clarifying what is meant by 'the sinlessness of the prophets'. He identifies four main areas in which the prophets could have been affected by sin:[11]

1. *Religious beliefs.* Is it possible for prophets to be misled in their beliefs? Most Muslims say no. It is impossible for prophets to wander away from the truth. Some Kharijites, however, accept the possibility of prophets having misperceptions in their faith. Prophets who were not immune from misguided ideas in their beliefs include Adam (7:189–190), Abraham (2:260; 6:77) and Muhammad (10:94).

2. *Delivery of God's message.* Is it possible for prophets to convey God's Word unfaithfully? Again the Muslim community agree that prophets are protected by God against any falsification of the message he entrusted to them. Otherwise, they would not be

reliable when they claim that their message is God's Word. Some Muslims, however, accept the idea that prophets can make some mistakes inadvertently in delivering God's message (22:52; 72:27–28; 87:6).

3. *Legal rulings*. Is it possible for prophets to give wrong interpretations of God's law? The answer is no, although some Muslims do not rule out the possibility of them erring unwillingly in their judgments about legal issues (8:67; 9:43; 21:78).

4. *Personal life*. Is it possible for prophets to commit acts of disobedience to God's commands? This is the most debated question and Muslims are divided into five groups:

- a. One group, labelled by Razi as *hashwiyya* (a derogatory word), believes that prophets are not immune from major sins, which they may commit even deliberately. Their main argument relates to the sin of Adam (2:37; 7:19–23; 20:121–122).
- b. The Mu'tazilites consider that it is possible for prophets to commit minor sins but certainly not major ones.
- c. Abu 'Ali al-Jubba'i (a Mu'tazili theologian) takes the view that prophets commit neither major nor minor sins deliberately. They only make mistakes due to wrong interpretations of God's law (*'ala jihati al-ta'wil*).
- d. Most Sunni Muslims are of the opinion that prophets make mistakes only 'inadvertently' (*sahw^{an}*) and 'unwillingly' (*khata^{an}*).
- e. Many Shi'i Muslims consider that prophets commit no sin or mistake, either willingly or unwillingly.

Now, what about the question concerning *when* the prophets became sinless? Again Muslims differ over this issue. For some (mainly Shi'is), the prophets were made sinless at birth. For others (the Mu'tazilites), they became sinless when they came of age and reached legal majority. But most Muslims (the Sunnites) believe that it is only when God called them to prophethood.

Why prophets are sinless

The arguments Razi (a Sunni Muslim) puts forward to make his case are many.[12] In fact, he lists no fewer than sixteen, most backed up with at least one Qur'anic text:

1. God honours people when he calls them to be his prophets. Because of his higher rank, a prophet would be more affected by sin. Sin is more serious for him than for average Muslims (33:30). It would bring a greater dishonour on him and would make his rank lower than ordinary Muslims, which is incompatible with God's calling.

2. The testimony of sinful Muslims is not valid in Islamic law (49:6). Prophets are God's witnesses (2:143). Their witness (their prophetic message) would not be reliable if they committed sinful acts.

3. If prophets were to commit major sins, they would be rebuked and they would have to be punished for their acts. God has forbidden anyone to do any harm to his prophets (33:57). On the contrary, they must be shown respect and honour.

4. Prophets represent role models to be followed by their people (20:90). If they were liable to sin, it would be impossible for their people to walk in their footsteps.

5. We know rationally that nothing is more evil than for a prophet to dismiss God's prohibitions and to enjoy what God has forbidden. He just cannot do that, having been honoured by God, entrusted with his revelation and appointed as his representative on earth.

6. People who disobey God deserve his punishment and curse (11:18; 72:23). The Muslim community agrees that none of the prophets will be cursed or punished.

7. Prophets call their people to obey God. If they failed to obey God, they would come under even sharper criticism than ordinary teachers and leaders (2:44; 11:88).

8. Prophets are keen to live good lives (21:90). This implies doing what they ought to do and avoiding what they must not do. In complying with this principle, prophets necessarily abstain from sin.

9. Prophets are described as God's elect and righteous people
    (38:47). God has chosen Adam, Noah, Abraham, Moses,
    Muhammad and so on (2:130; 3:33; 7:144). God's election
    means that they have been preserved from sin.
10. Satan has no power over God's faithful servants (38:82–83).
    Clearly, God's prophets are God's faithful servants (38:46;
    12:24).
11. The believers do not follow Satan (34:20); in other words,
    they do not commit sin. If prophets committed sin, they
    would bring dishonour upon themselves, and ordinary
    believers would be of greater honour than the prophets.
12. People belong either to God's party (58:22) or to Satan's
    party (58:19). If prophets committed sin, they would be
    members of Satan's party, the party of the 'losers'. Again,
    ordinary but faithful believers, 'the winners', would be better
    than them in God's sight.
13. God has favoured prophets even more than angels (2:34).
    Since angels are described as God's obedient servants (21:27;
    66:6), prophets necessarily enjoy a higher degree of
    obedience, which means they are without sin.
14. One of Muhammad's companions testified to the Prophet
    that his prayers were all excellent. If Muhammad (and more
    generally the prophets) were affected by sin, his prayers
    would not be perfect.
15. Like Abraham (2:124), prophets are *imams*; that is, leaders and
    models for their people. They must be obeyed and followed
    in whatever they do. If prophets were not blameless, people
    would have to follow their bad examples!
16. God says that 'the evildoers will not enjoy His covenant'
    (2:124). In this context God's covenant refers either to
    prophethood or to leadership. In the first case it means
    prophets are not 'evildoers'; therefore they are sinless. In the
    second case too the implication is that prophets are without
    sin because they are also leaders of their people.

In short, Razi considers that sin and the prophetic mission are at
opposite ends of the scale. Prophets are God's chosen instruments,
called to convey his Word and to lead his people. It is a great

honour, a priceless favour and an exclusive blessing to have been chosen to fulfil such a divine mission. Committing sin would bring disrepute upon their name, discredit them as God's messengers and disqualify them as leaders and role models for their people. Their deeds must be consistent with their words. Otherwise, they would be responding in a most disgraceful manner to God's calling and, more importantly, they would be undermining the truthfulness of God's revelation itself.

The sins of the prophets in the Qur'an

The Qur'an tells us about many prophets, with great details for some. Their failures are not concealed. Yet most Muslim exegetes and theologians maintain that the prophets are sinless. So how do they account for the shortcomings reported in the Qur'an? They use one of three arguments. The reported sins, they say, were committed before the call to prophethood (Adam, Moses); or these sins were, strictly speaking, mere 'mistakes' (Noah, Muhammad); or, when correctly interpreted, the relevant Qur'anic texts suggest that the prophets did not commit the sins mistakenly attributed to them (Abraham, Lot).

Adam and Eve

God commanded Adam and Eve not to eat from a certain tree in the garden: 'We said: "O Adam! Dwell with your wife in the Garden; and eat of the bountiful things therein as you will; but do not approach this tree, or you will run into harm and transgression"' (2:35; cf. 7:19).

Satan led them to another tree of the same kind, describing it as 'the tree of immortality and everlasting kingdom' (20:120–121). Adam and Eve disobeyed God's command and ate some of its fruit. So why did they fall into sin? The Qur'an says that Adam simply 'forgot' (20:115). What did he forget? Adam *forgot to think* about the real meaning of God's command. If he had not forgotten, he would have known that God had forbidden him to eat from any tree of that same species, not just from a specific tree (20:115). According to a second and similar interpretation, Adam *misinterpreted* God's prohibition. He thought that God had forbidden him to eat from one particular tree, whereas God's prohibition was about all the trees belonging to the same species.[13] Whether Adam's disobedience consisted in forgetting to interpret God's command (*nisyan^{an}*) or in failing to interpret it correctly (*ta'wil^{an}*), his sin was, according to Razi, a small mistake (*zalla saghira*).[14] Why then did Adam and Eve admit to being 'evildoers' (*zalimun*) just as God had warned them they would be if they disobeyed (7:23)? After a lengthy discussion, Razi is clearly at pains to provide a convincing explanation, so he concedes that, after all, it is quite possible that Adam committed his act of disobedience before God called him to prophethood.[15]

Noah's prayer for his son

Noah committed a mistake when he was in the ark immediately before God's judgment took place (11:41–47). He misjudged his son, thinking he was a believer; therefore he asked him to come on board the ark (v. 42). His son replied, 'I am going to take refuge on the peak of the mountain' (v. 43). He interpreted his son's answer as meaning that he believed God would rescue him on the mountain. So Noah prayed to God and asked him to save his son (v. 45). God revealed to Noah that his son was in fact an unbeliever (who wanted to save himself), and he rebuked him for having interceded on his behalf (v. 46), for God would not save the unrighteous. Noah then realized his mistake and begged God's pardon (v. 47).

Thus Noah's misjudgment was not a serious sin. It was just an oversight: if he had looked into the life of his son, he would have detected the marks of his unbelief; instead, he assumed that his son was a believer. He prayed for him and asked God to save him from the impending judgment. Had he known that his son was an unbeliever, he wouldn't have prayed for him. Noah's error in praying for his unbelieving son was a personal misjudgment (*khata' fi al-ijtihad*). It was probably due, comments Razi, to the indulgent and blind love of a father for his son.[16]

Lot and his guests

The angels came to visit Lot and stayed in his house. People in the city knew about their presence and wanted to abuse Lot's foreign

guests (the angels). Lot replied to them, literally, 'Here are my
daughters' (11:78). Muslim exegetes have suggested different interpretations of these words. Lot suggested that his people marry his
daughters. But how could a prophet let his daughters marry
unbelievers? The answer is either that Lot asked them first to
convert to his faith, or that it was then lawful for unbelieving men to
marry believing women, as was the case in the early days of Islam.

Razi puts forward three arguments against this interpretation.
First, giving one's daughters as spouses to wicked men is something honourable men are unlikely to do; how much more the
renowned prophets! Second, Lot had just two daughters: they
could not be given in marriage to the crowd. If Lot had had his
daughters in mind – the third argument – he would have used the
dual form ('here are my two daughters') instead of the plural. Razi
favours an alternative interpretation: Lot urged his people to marry
women from his (and their) people. He called them 'his' daughters
metaphorically because they were unmarried women and, as a
prophet, he was like a father to them. In a similar sense the Qur'an
describes the Prophet Muhammad's wives as mothers for Muslims
(33:6). In either interpretation Lot disapproved of his people's
wicked attitude towards his guests and suggested an honourable
alternative to prevent them doing what was evil.[17]

Abraham and his three lies

Abraham was a passionate monotheistic believer. One day he
secretly destroyed the idols of his people, except the biggest one.
When he was summoned to tell the truth, he told them that 'the
biggest [idol] did it' (21:63). Did Abraham tell a lie? Again Muslims
are divided into two groups. The first say that Abraham did not tell
a lie. They suggest several arguments, many of which are too subtle
to be convincing. The first and most plausible argument, suggested
by Razi, is that Abraham was being 'sarcastic' (*mustahzi'*). He gave
his people a sarcastic reply in order to expose the foolishness of
their idolatrous worship. If they answered, 'but an idol is unable to
do it', they would prove the point Abraham wanted to make.

The second group admits that Abraham told a lie, but it was a
justified lie. His people were very antagonistic to his faith and they
could have killed him. Lying, they say, is permitted in special

circumstances where one's intention is to achieve a commendable objective. This interpretation is based on traditions which claim that Abraham told three lies.[18] Razi vigorously rejects this interpretation. If it were possible for prophets to lie, their message would no longer be credible, and the laws they brought would be unreliable.

What does Razi make of the hadiths that mention Abraham's three lies? He considers that their reliability has not been proven. If these accounts were authentic as a whole, the words 'Abraham told a lie three times' are certainly not. Those who transmitted the sayings have made these words up. Those people, says Razi, are far more likely than the prophets to tell lies. When Abraham said to Pharaoh that Sarah was his sister, he did not lie: because they had the same faith, Abraham and Sarah were brother and sister in a religious sense. As for the third alleged lie, again Abraham was truthful. When he said, 'I am sick' (37:89), he was indeed slightly unwell.[19]

Moses' murder

A fellow Jew asked Moses for help when fighting an Egyptian man. Moses stepped in and killed the Egyptian (28:15), but a while later realized that what he had done was wrong (26:20). He asked God to forgive him and was forgiven (28:16). How should Moses' act be interpreted? Razi suggests that, although the Egyptian man was an unbeliever, killing him was either 'unlawful' (*haram*) or 'not commendable' (*ghayr mandub*). On the other hand, because Moses was a strong man, he could and should have rescued his fellow Jew without killing the Egyptian. Did Moses commit a sinful act? Yes, says Razi, but the murder took place before God called him to prophethood.[20]

Muhammad and the blind man

Razi explains the historical circumstances surrounding the incident, which is referred to in the beginning of sura 80. Muhammad was talking to a group of six well-known rich leaders of the Quraysh tribe, inviting them to convert to Islam. He was hoping that their conversion would bring many other Arabs to Islam. A blind man, 'Abdullah bin Shurayh, came to the Prophet and asked him, rather persistently, to teach him what God had taught him. Muhammad got annoyed. He rebuked the poor man and frowned upon him; hence, the title of the sura, 'He frowned' ('abasa). God revealed this sura to challenge the Prophet about his attitude to the man.

Did the poor man deserve to be reprimanded? He certainly did, according to Razi, for three reasons: (1) he should have been more courteous to the Prophet; (2) he was already a Muslim convert unlike the other men whose conversion was needed much more; and (3) he was distracting the Prophet from accomplishing his main mission. Therefore the Prophet was right when he rebuked him. But why then did God blame him for what he did? Razi indicates two reasons. This incident could wrongly suggest that the rich take precedence over the poor and that it is acceptable to despise the poor (6:52). Second, God reproached Muhammad not for his conduct but for the motive behind it. He ought not to have felt closer to the group of Meccan leaders than to the blind man. Unlike the poor man, they were from the same tribe as Muhammad and were from a prestigious social background. The conclusion Razi draws from this incident is that Muhammad committed no sin, for he was right in doing what he did with the blind man. However, he could have had a better and more appropriate attitude towards him. Thus he just failed to take the best course of action. In other words, God blamed him for a sin he committed only by omission (tarku al-afdal).[21]

Muhammad's 'past and future sins'
Muhammad will be granted the right to intercede for his community on the Day of Judgment because, according to the Hadith, God has forgiven his 'past and future sins'. In his prayers the Prophet asks God to forgive his 'past and future sins' (as we noted at the beginning of this chapter). This expression is directly linked to sura 48:

> We [God] achieved a glorious victory for you
> So that God may forgive your past and future sins,
> complete His goodness to you,
> and guide you in the right path.
> And that God may give you a great triumph.
> (48:1–3)

Most commentators consider that these verses are closely related to the Muslim conquest of Mecca in 630, 'the great triumph'. The question is, Why is the conquest of Mecca, which marked a turning point in Muhammad's mission and the advance of Islam, related to Muhammad's intercession and his sins being forgiven? Razi explains that the 'past sins' are the sins Muhammad committed before he was called to prophethood. The 'future sins' are either Muhammad's personal sins, in which case they are sins he committed by omission (e.g. his attitude to the blind man), or the sins committed by Muslims. Sins committed by Muslims are attributed to the Prophet because he is the leader of the Muslim community.[22]

The conquest of Mecca is also referred to in sura 110, the shortest sura in the Qur'an. According to Aisha, Muhammad's closest wife, the Prophet used to quote this sura when asking God's pardon. He often prayed this prayer after Mecca had been taken by the Muslims:[23]

> When God's triumph comes about, and victory,
> And you see people embrace God's religion in multitudes,
> Then give glory to your Lord, praise Him and ask pardon of Him.
> For He is the Most-Returning.
>
> (110:1–3)

Razi points out that this sura speaks of a threefold action God achieved in favour of his Prophet: he made his message conquer people's hearts; he made him victorious over the Meccans; and he drew people in large numbers to Islam (vv. 1–2). In response to God's action Muhammad is commanded to say a threefold prayer to celebrate God's glory, praise his name and seek his pardon (v. 3). Why should Muhammad beg God's forgiveness after multitudes of people (including Meccans) became Muslims? Razi makes two suggestions. First, in ordering Muhammad to pray for the Meccans (who for many years were his enemies), God is asking him to forgive them and not to take revenge against them. This is similar to what Joseph did with his brothers. Although they had hated and persecuted him, he proclaimed to them God's forgiveness (12:92). Second, the fact that the Muslim community had become very large meant that Muhammad's intercession for the forgiveness of their sins was more needed than ever.

Razi also envisages that Muhammad was to ask forgiveness not just for his community but for himself as well. God had previously ordered him to intercede for all Muslims, including himself: 'Ask forgiveness for your transgression and for the believers, men and women' (47:19). Why should Muhammad pray for himself? Was he not 'sinless'? Again Razi considers two cases that correspond to the two main schools in Islamic theology:

1. *Muhammad committed sin*: the Mu'tazilites do not rule out this possibility. In this case, his sins were minor ones. His prayer aimed at preserving him from any major sin; preventing him from the sin of persistence (committing the same sin repeatedly, where minor sins may add up to a major sin); and keeping the reward for his good deeds unaffected by his minor sins.

2. *Muhammad committed no sin at all*: as Sunni Muslims believe. His prayer was intended to glorify God as the forgiving God; to give Muslims an example to follow when they sin; and to ask God's pardon for 'sins' he committed by omission, or because of his insufficient obedience (compared with God's overflowing generosity) or imperfect submission to God.[24]

Thus Muhammad's prayer for himself does not point to his sin as much as to his full commitment to God, his law and his cause. People who ask God's pardon are not necessarily more sinful than others. In the case of the prophets in general and of Muhammad in particular, the contrary is true. Because they were closer to God than their people they were more aware of their shortcomings. This paradoxical truth is illustrated in a hadith that draws a contrast between the believer's attitude to sin and that of the unbeliever: 'The believer sees his sins as if he were sitting under a mountain which, he is afraid, may fall on him. The wicked considers his sins as flies passing his nose and he drives them away like this.'[25]

Razi's arguments – are they convincing?

The moral perfection of the prophets represents a belief not unanimously shared by Muslims. Some (a group of Murji'ites) believe that it is possible for prophets to commit major sins, while others (the majority of Mu'tazilites) claim that they can commit only minor sins. Most Muslims, however, take the view that prophets are faultless as regards their faith, their mission and their lives. The arguments put forward by Razi to explain this doctrine are certainly attractive and plausible, at least from a human point of view. Sins certainly dishonour those who commit them and damage their reputation, even more so in the case of religious leaders. Prophets undoubtedly belong to this category of people. If they sin they might discredit their message, if not God himself. Their responsibility is thus greatly increased.

If Razi's rational arguments carry considerable weight, his understanding of the sins attributed to prophets in the Qur'an is much less convincing. It does not account for Muhammad's prayers (in which he asks God to forgive his personal sins) or the Prophet's humble acknowledgment that, had it not been for God's mercy and forgiveness, he too would have deserved God's condemnation. Traditional Islamic interpretation of the Qur'anic texts is highly unlikely in the case of Adam, Lot and Abraham. Razi's exegesis of sura 80 verses 1–10 tends to minimize the seriousness of Muhammad's wrong attitude in relation to the Meccan leaders and the poor man. Why should the favouritism Muhammad showed to his tribesmen, which resulted in his uncharitable behaviour towards the blind man, be overlooked? His inner attitude may *explain* but not *excuse* the way he responded to this man.

Islamic teaching about the prophets' sinlessness understandably assumes that people whose mission is to speak God's word ought to be worthy of their calling. The messenger has to authenticate the message he has been commissioned to deliver. God enables his prophets to work 'miracles' (*bayyinat*) to accredit their mission. He also protects them from sin so that his honour, reflected in his special servants, remains unblemished. No-one would want to deny the rationality of Islamic teaching. Yet the Bible offers a different perspective.

A biblical perspective

Ideally, God's messengers should live up to God's message since they are role models for their people. This is true of religious leaders too. Jesus criticized the Jewish leaders of his time and blamed them for conducting their lives in a way that contradicted their teaching. He told his people to accept their teaching, but not to follow their example: 'you must obey them and do everything they tell you. But do not do what they do, for they do not practise what they preach' (Matt. 23:3). Jesus' followers noticed the difference between him and other Jewish leaders: 'The crowds were amazed at his teaching, because he taught as one who had authority, and not as their teachers of the law' (Matt. 7:28–29).

The sins of the prophets

However, the Bible narratives portray God's prophets as real human beings who lived in a real world. Because all human beings are sinful, God's messengers committed sin in one way or another. Only one prophet was sinless, but he was more than a prophet. He not only spoke God's word, but was himself God's Word according to both the Bible (John 1:1, 14) and the Qur'an (4:171).[26] We have seen (in chapter 10) that neither Scripture ascribes any sin to Jesus.

With regard to God's prophets in general, the Bible guarantees the truthfulness of their message (Matt. 5:17–19; John 10:35; Rom. 7:12). Yet, as for their life, they were not all blameless. In fact, some of them committed serious sins. Reference has already been made to Abraham telling a lie about his wife Sarah (Gen. 12:10–20). The Bible story about Lot shows clearly that he was prepared to let the people of Sodom abuse his two daughters instead of his guests. Eventually, it was his guests who managed to protect themselves as well as Lot and his daughters (Gen. 19:1–11).[27] As for Noah, although he was a man of God, his life was not spotless. After the flood he is said to have planted a vineyard and, on one occasion, 'he became drunk and lay uncovered inside his tent' (Gen. 9:21). Moses' act of murder is related in the Bible as a deliberate murder he tried to hide; but he was soon to run away and take refuge in Midian where God called him to be his prophet. Solomon is

another sad example of a man who was initially a wise, just and
God-fearing king (1 Kgs. 3:5–28). Yet in later years, 'his [many]
wives turned his heart after other gods, and his heart was not fully
devoted to the LORD his God, as the heart of David his father had
been' (1 Kgs. 11:4).

The example of David

The Torah describes David as God's chosen king, 'a man after his
own heart' (1 Sam. 13:14). At the same time, the Bible does not hide
the fact that David committed two sins for which the Torah
prescribed the death penalty: adultery (Lev. 20:10) and murder
(Gen. 9:6). One day David was attracted to a very beautiful woman,
Bathsheba. He abused his authority as king by having Bathsheba
brought to his palace. David slept with her and she became
pregnant. Since her husband Uriah was away, fighting with
Israel's army, David's adultery was likely to be uncovered. He tried
to conceal his sinful act by ordering that Uriah be sent back to
Jerusalem. Uriah declined David's offer to go home. David's various
attempts to cover up his sin failed. In a final and furious move to
save his honour he sent Uriah back to the battlefield with the view
of having him killed. Uriah was moved into the front line and died
while fighting the enemy. At last it seemed as though David had
managed to conceal his sin, and Bathsheba was brought back to the
palace and became David's wife. 'But the thing David had done
displeased the LORD' (2 Sam. 11:27). God himself decided to
uncover David's sin. He sent him a prophet, Nathan, who pointed
out David's sinful conduct by telling him the following story:

'There were two men in a certain town, one rich and the other poor. The
rich man had a very large number of sheep and cattle, but the poor man
had nothing except one little ewe lamb that he had bought. He raised it,
and it grew up with him and his children. It shared his food, drank from
his cup and even slept in his arms. It was like a daughter to him.

Now a traveller came to the rich man, but the rich man refrained
from taking one of his own sheep or cattle to prepare a meal for the
traveller who had come to him. Instead, he took the ewe lamb that
belonged to the poor man and prepared it for the one who had come
to him.'

David burned with anger against the man and said to Nathan, 'As surely as the LORD lives, the man who did this deserves to die! He must pay for that lamb four times over, because he did such a thing and had no pity.'

Then Nathan said to David, 'You are the man! ... Why did you despise the word of the LORD by doing what is evil in his eyes? You struck down Uriah the Hittite with the sword and took his wife to be your own ...'

Then David said to Nathan, 'I have sinned against the LORD.'
(2 Sam. 12:1–13)

It is remarkable that God himself should send a prophet to reveal the sins of his beloved servant David. Why did God take such an action? Did he want the name of one of his greatest prophets to be put to shame for ever? Why has this story been recorded in the Bible? God's initiative shows that he neither tolerates evil nor any covering up of evil, especially when such evil is committed by his prophets. God's honour would be at stake if he condoned the evildoing of his servants. On the other hand, God is merciful. David confessed his sins: he deeply regretted what he had done and expressed sincere repentance. His repentance was recorded in one of the most moving psalms ever written:

Have mercy on me, O God,
    according to your unfailing love;
according to your great compassion
    blot out my transgressions.
Wash away all my iniquity
    and cleanse me from my sin.
For I know my transgressions,
    and my sin is always before me.
Against you, you only, have I sinned
    and done what is evil in your sight,
so that you are proved right when you speak
    and justified when you judge.
Surely I was sinful at birth,
    sinful from the time my mother conceived me.

Surely you desire truth in the inner parts;
  you teach me wisdom in the inmost place.
Cleanse me with hyssop, and I shall be clean;
  wash me, and I shall be whiter than snow.
Let me hear joy and gladness;
  let the bones you have crushed rejoice.
Hide your face from my sins
  and blot out all my iniquity.
Create in me a pure heart, O God,
  and renew a steadfast spirit within me.
Do not cast me from your presence
  or take your Holy Spirit from me.
Restore to me the joy of your salvation
  and grant me a willing spirit, to sustain me.
Then I will teach transgressors your ways,
  and sinners will turn back to you.
(Ps. 51:1–13)

God accepted David's repentance and pardoned him. Nathan told him that he would remain king of Israel but that his sin would not go unpunished: 'The LORD has taken away your sin. You are not going to die. But because by doing this you have made the enemies of the LORD show utter contempt, the son born to you will die' (2 Sam. 12:13–14).

The fact that the prophets gave in to sin suggests that ordinary believers like us are unlikely to be spared temptation. We too will find it hard to resist sin. The Bible tells us these stories, not to put the names of the prophets to shame, but rather to encourage us to acknowledge our sins: no sin can be hidden from God. At the same time there is no sin God cannot forgive if we repent. Of course, God could have protected his prophets from sin. Yet since he chose not to do so, this is perhaps to teach us an important truth: sin is deeply ingrained in human nature. This is not to plunge us into despair, but rather to lead us, like David, to trust only in God's mercy and unfailing love for our salvation.

The story of David's sin is vaguely alluded to in the Qur'an (38:21–26).[28] It is presented as a test sent to him by God in a vision rather than in reality. The biblical story of David's fall is likely to upset the Muslim reader. Some Muslims may consider this story in particular (and those of other prophets in general) as clear evidence that the text of the Bible is unreliable. The question we need to ask is, why has this story been recorded in the Torah if it did not happen? After all, the Jewish writer would probably have preferred not to tell such a story, which does no good to the pride of the Jewish people or to the reputation of their greatest king. The fact that this story is recounted enhances the credibility of the writer. The refusal to cover up the truth about the sins committed by prophets, however shocking or dishonourable for the men involved, is a confirmation of the reliability of the Bible as God's inspired Word.

Notes

1. Ibn Furak, *Mujarrad*, p. 158.
2. Ash'ari, *Maqalat*, I, p. 297.
3. Ibid., p. 231.
4. Abu Dawud, *witr* 25 [1291]:I, bk 2, no. 1505, p. 394; Ibn Majah, *du'a'* 2 [3820]:V, bk 34, no. 3830, p. 200; Tirmidhi, *da'awat* 2 [3474].
5. Abu Dawud, *witr* 26 [1295]:I, bk 2, no. 1511, p. 395; Ibn Majah, *adab* 57[3804]:V, bk 33, no. 3814, p. 192; Tirmidhi, *da'awat* 38 [3356].
6. Nasa'i, *sahw* 85 [1329], *isti'adha* 62 [5439].
7. Bukhari, *tawhid* 8 [6837], 24 [6888], 35[6945]:IX, bk 93, no. 482, p. 358; no. 534, p. 402; no. 590, p. 436; cf. Bukhari, *da'awat* 9 [5919], 10 [5920]:VIII, bk 75, no. 327, p. 219; no. 329, p. 221; Muslim, *musafirin* 200 [1288]:I, bk 4, no. 1691, p. 372; Tirmidhi, *da'awat* 29 [3340]; Nasa'i, *qiyamu al-layl* 9 [1601].
8. Muslim, *dhikr* 49 [4877]:IV, bk 35, no. 6534, p. 1420; cf. Tirmidhi, *da'awat* 58 [3417], 63 [3470]; Nasa'i, *tahara* 48 [60], *miyah* 6 [331], *ghasl* 3 [399], 4 [400], *iftitah* 15 [885].
9. Muslim, *dhikr* 70 [4896]:IV, bk 35, no. 6569, p. 1425; cf. Muslim, *musafirin* 202 [1290]:I, bk 4, no. 1695, p. 373.
10. Muslim, *munafiqun* 73 [5036]:IV, bk 38, no. 6762, p. 1473; Bukhari, *marda* 19 [5241]:VII, bk 70, no. 577, p. 391; *riqaq* 18 [5986]:VIII, bk 76, no. 470, p. 313; Ibn Majah, *zuhd* 20 [4191]:V, bk 37, no. 4201, p. 462; Darimi, *riqaq* 23 [2617].
11. Razi on 2:36; II:3, pp. 7–12.

12. Razi on 2:36; II:3, pp. 8–10.

13. This interpretation and the previous one have been suggested by the Mu'tazili theologian Abu 'Ali. Other Muslims have suggested similar interpretations. See Gimaret, *Lecture*, sura 7 verse 19 (p. 339); sura 20 verse 115 (p. 607).

14. Razi on 2:36; II:3, p. 18.

15. Razi on 2:35–36; II:3, pp. 3–18; cf. Razi on 20:120–127; XI:22, pp. 109–114. Ash'ari takes the same view as Razi; i.e. Adam's disobedience was prior to his call to prophethood (Ibn Furak, *Mujarrad*, p. 158).

16. Razi on 11:45–47; IX:18, pp. 3–6.

17. Razi on 11:77–80; IX:18, pp. 27–29.

18. Bukhari, *anbiya'* 8 [3108]:IV, bk 55, no. 578, p. 368; *tafsir* sura 17 chapter 5 [4343]:VI, bk 60, no. 236, p. 198; *nikah* 13 [4694]:VII, bk 62, no. 21, p. 14; *tawhid* 24 [6886]:IX, bk 93, no. 532 (b), p. 395; Muslim, *fada'il* 154 [4371]:IV, bk 30, no. 5848, p. 1262.

19. Razi on 21:63; XI:22, pp. 160–162; cf. Razi on 37:89; XIII:26, pp. 127–129.

20. Razi on 28:14–17; XII:24, pp. 198–202.

21. Razi on 80:1–7; XVI:31, pp. 50–53.

22. Razi on 48:1–3; XIV:28, pp. 67–69.

23. Muslim, *salat* 220 [749]:I, bk 4, no. 984, p. 255; Bukhari, *tafsir* sura 48 chapter 1 [4458]:VI, bk 60, no. 359, p. 343.

24. Razi on 110:1–3; XVI:32, pp. 138–151.

25. Bukhari, *da'awat* 4 [5833]:VIII, bk 75, no. 320, p. 214; Ibn Hanbal, *musnad al-mukthirin* 1 [3446–3448].

26. Muslim scholars have suggested various interpretations with regard to the title 'Word of God' given to Jesus in the Qur'an. See Moucarry, *Faith to Faith*, p. 177.

27. Years later, when Lot was an old man, he was abused by his own daughters (Gen. 19:30–38).

28. The Qur'anic text is extremely obscure, to the point that any interpretation is bound to be highly speculative. The sins David committed, according to the Bible (adultery, murder), are not unknown to Muslim commentators. See Razi on 38:21–25; XIII:26, pp. 165–173.

PART THREE

FORGIVENESS
IN MYSTICISM

13. REPENTANCE AS CONVERSION TO GOD

Sufism, the mystical trend in Islam, takes a different approach to God. Sufis are God's seekers.[1] As Muslims they are dissatisfied with mainstream Islamic teaching and long for a relationship with God more personal than that of servant–Lord. They yearn for a close relationship with him, deeper than mere obedience to his commands. They want to know God not only rationally but with their whole being. They strive to engage with God himself, and to go beyond the dividing veil that separates the Creator and his creatures. Repentance is key to the Sufi's experiential approach to God and is at the heart of Sufi spirituality. It is also from the perspective of repentance that God's forgiveness is seen in Sufi tradition.

The Sufi path

Sufism is based on a spiritual reading of the Qur'an. God is often referred to as al-Ḥaqq (the Truth), a divine name found ten times in the Qur'an.[2] Muslim scholars have given this name three meanings:

1. God is the only 'true God' as opposed to idols, which are false gods.
2. God is 'a truthful God' and everything he says is trustworthy.
3. God is 'the truly existing One', since he is the only Being who does not derive his existence from someone else. Hence he is the Eternal God.[3]

The theologians' approach to God and the Sufis' approach to God are contrasted by Ghazali, who is both a theologian and a Sufi. Theologians, he says, reflect mainly on *God's actions*, whereas Sufis are concerned first and foremost with *God's being*:

> Among Sufi groups the name of God the most high which most often flows from their lips in their statements and during states of prayer is *al-Ḥaqq* [the Truth], in the measure that they attain to experience of self-annihilation with regard to their own essence, for they see the truly real essence to the exclusion of that which in itself is perishing. As for the practitioners of *Kalam* [i.e. theologians], the name which flows most frequently from their lips is *al-Bari'* [the Producer], which has the same meaning as *al-Khaliq* [the Creator], since they are still at the level of reasoning to God by way of His actions.[4]

Realizing that their real existence lies only with God, Sufis set out to return to their divine Origin, to the only One who 'is'. Their journey back to God is marked by a series of *maqam* (stages or stations). Each time a Sufi reaches a stage he acquires a *hal* (state). So for every stage there is a corresponding state. A stage is usually seen as a 'human achievement' (*maksiba*), whereas a state is considered a 'divine gift' (*mawhiba*). The number of stages and states varies from one author to another: seven (Sarraj), eight (Hujwiri), nine (Makki), fifty (Qushayri) or even a hundred (Kalabadhi, Ansari). These stages include 'repentance' (*tawba*), 'asceticism' (*zuhd*), 'patience' (*sabr*), 'fear' (*khawf*), 'thanksgiving' (*shukr*), 'hope' (*raja'*), 'trust' (*tawakkul*), 'contentedness' (*rida*), 'poverty' (*fakr*), 'remembrance' (*dhikr*), 'union' (*ittihad*) and so on. All Sufis, however, consider repentance as the first stage in the spiritual pilgrimage. It is impossible to start the journey to God without first getting through the experience of repentance. Repentance is not only the initial stage; it is also a decisive one, determining the subsequent steps. According to Abu Muḥammad Sahl, 'repentance is the best deed as no deed is acceptable (in God's sight) without it'.[5] The Sufi purpose is to know God. Achieving this purpose depends on how people start their journey. As Ḥallaj puts it, 'Spiritual knowledge (*ma'rifa*) is attained through repentance; the creatures that achieve their repentance best are those who will have the best knowledge of God.'[6]

Repentance: the gateway to God

Hujwiri comments on sura 2 verse 222, 'God loves those who turn to Him [in repentance] and those who purify themselves.' He draws a parallel between two levels of religious life, external and internal:

> He who would serve God must purify himself outwardly with water, and he who would come nigh unto God must purify himself inwardly with repentance ... Repentance (*tawbat*) is the first station of pilgrims on the way to the Truth, just as purification (*ṭaharat*) is the first step of those who desire to serve God.[7]

Purification by water is required before prayer but purification of the soul through repentance is necessary for those who want not only to fulfil their religious duties but to reach God. The duality between the physical realm and the spiritual realm is a recurrent theme in Sufi thought. Ḥallaj contrasts God's 'double provision' (*rizq*) as follows: 'In this life God's given means of sustenance are life and enjoyment, allowing us to desire and to subsist; in the hereafter they consist in us being forgiven and accepted by God.'[8]

For Suhrawardi, love is closely associated with repentance. It is the first state that pilgrims acquire when they repent. Just as repentance determines the subsequent stages, so love determines the subsequent states:

> The claims of those who say they enjoy a spiritual state should be tested by their ability to love. The claims of those who say they enjoy the state of love should be tested by the reality of their repentance, for *repentance is the mould which gives the spirit of love its shape.*[9]

Thus repentance and love are intertwined and spiritual progress is measured by these two criteria. In the spiritual realm, arrival cannot be guaranteed if the departure for the journey was not from the right place.

The experience of repentance is imperative for knowing God, whether people are Muslims or not. The degree of spirituality is assessed in relation to this experience. In Sufism, people are divided into two main groups: 'the Common' (al-'awamm), who have not experienced repentance, and 'the Élite' (al-khawass), who have started their spiritual journey. Among the pilgrims or itinerants are found the 'beginner' (mubtadi'), who is still in the early stages of spiritual pilgrimage, and the 'initiate' (muhaqqiq), who has been through repentance and consequently has acquired spiritual knowledge. Finally, there are those who have completed their journey. Their knowledge has reached perfection. 'Prophets' (anbiya') and 'saints' (awliya') belong to this highest class, called 'the Élite of the Élite' (khawass al-khawass).

Spiritual conversion

The concept of 'repentance' (tawba) is so important in Sufi teaching that it is best described as 'a spiritual conversion'. Through conversion, people return to God. As noted in chapter 6, the primary meaning of the word taba is 'to go back, to return'. In the Qur'an it is applied either to non-Muslims who convert to Islam (9:5) or to Muslims who regret an evil act they have committed. Sufism has developed a third meaning: tawba refers to what happens when someone, Muslim or non-Muslim, returns to God in order to find their real existence.

People convert to God in various ways. In Sufi literature we have many accounts describing how Muslims have been converted through dramatic experiences (see Appendix B). These conversions seem to have happened quite unexpectedly, and in some cases without human agency. While the details of these popular accounts cannot be guaranteed, the core fact they report (the conversion of the person) is likely to have a historical basis. Some converts were not particularly religious – indeed, their lifestyle was often in contradiction with Islamic moral values (e.g. Bishr bin al-Harith) – whereas others were practising Muslims (e.g. Malik bin

Dinar). Converts have come from different social backgrounds; there have been ordinary people as well as rich and influential people (e.g. Ibrahim bin Adham). It is also not limited to men; testimonies include both men and women. Most people seem to convert through the teaching of a Sufi 'leader' (*shaykh*) and in the context of a Sufi brotherhood. Conversion is an intense, sudden and life-changing experience. It opens new horizons, giving people a heavenly perspective on their life. Rumi compares it to a landslide: 'Repentance is a strange mountain – it jumps towards heaven in a single moment from the lowest place'.[10] The result of this experience is a God-focused life, where God becomes the only and unique centre. Repentance amounts to a U-turn in one's life. No longer does anything count, except God:

> An-Nuri said:
>> 'Repentance means, that you should turn from everything but God.'
> Ibrahim ad-Daqqaq said:
>> 'Repentance means, that you should be unto God a face without a back, even as you have formerly been unto Him a back without a face.'[11]

The convert lives 'in God's company' (*al-uns bi-llah*). In his commentary on sura 4 verse 1, which starts with the words 'O Humankind!' (*ya ayyuha al-nas*), Ibn 'Ata' explains that the Arabic word for human beings is *nas* 'because they enjoy God's company and feel estranged from everything except God'.[12] The Sufi is entirely engrossed with God's presence. His preoccupation is threefold according to Shah al-Kirmani: 'Contemplating God and enjoying his presence, counting his blessings and giving thanks to Him, and remembering one's sin, confessing it and returning to God fully repentant'.[13] Living in close fellowship with God transforms a person's character. Those who have genuinely repented become sensitive and gentle. They are characterized by 'the meekness of their hearts and the abundance of their tears'.[14] A hadith attributed to 'Umar, the second caliph, recommends their company to Muslims: 'Have close relationships with repentant people for they are meek in their heart.' Another narrative has it that 'there is nothing that God loves more than a youth who repents'.[15]

Conversion is a lifelong commitment to God. The convert is expected to lead a life that has nothing to do with sin. New converts are in danger of committing sin; they should watch their path. Yahya bin Mu'adh considers that 'one sin committed after repentance is more evil than seventy before'.[16] Is it possible for a convert to backslide? What should the attitude of his fellow Sufis be? Some converts did not keep up their commitment. But, in spite of the seriousness of their fall, they were encouraged to resume their journey, and many did. Abu 'Amr bin Nujayd tells his story:

> As a novice, I repented in the assembly-room of Abu 'Uthman Hiri and persevered in my repentance for some while. Then I fell into sin and left the society of that spiritual director, and whenever I saw him from afar my remorse caused me to flee from his sight. One day I met him unexpectedly. He said to me: 'O son, do not associate with your enemies unless you are sinless (ma'sum), for an enemy will see your faults and rejoice. If you must sin, come to us that we may bear your affliction'. On hearing his words, I felt surfeited with sin and my repentance was established.[17]

Conversion as the gateway to God is always open to everyone. People are invited to come in so that they might have a living relationship with God. This door will remain open as long as people are alive. Those who have been through it more than once need not despair. The lines written on Rumi's mausoleum in Konya invite everyone to repent: 'Come back, come back, even if you have broken your repentance a thousand times.'[18]

Repentance: God's favour and God's command

Sufi doctrine echoes Qur'anic teaching on repentance. This teaching is paradoxical in the sense that God commands people to repent, and yet repentance is a free gift from him. Sura 9 verse 118 states that 'God turned [with mercy] to them so that they may turn [with repentance] to Him.' People's repentance comes as a result of God's initiative. Abu Hafs al-Haddad puts it this way: 'Man has no part in repentance, because repentance is from God to man, not from man to God'.[19] Rabi'a was asked if God always accepted the repentance of his servants. She replied that the question did not make sense, for the very fact that people had repented indicated that God had already been at work in their lives:

- If a person commits many sins and repents, will God accept him?
- How can anyone repent unless his Lord gives him repentance and accepts him?[20]

Not only is repentance the fruit of God's undeserved favour, but every good deed reflects God's mercy. No good action can be done without God's decisive help. His grace extends to all aspects of our lives. Abu Sa'id bin al-A'rabi points out that God's action can be seen in every area of our existence:

God made his blessings the cause for people coming to know him; his enabling the cause for people obeying him; his protection the cause for people keeping away from sin; his mercy the cause for people repenting; and repentance the cause for people obtaining his pardon and drawing close to him.[21]

Thus God's power is displayed in every aspect of our lives. It starts by leading us to know him as the Creator God; then bringing us to obey him as the sovereign Lord; then moving us on to acknowledge him as the merciful and forgiving God; and finally, causing us to enjoy intimate fellowship with him.

On the other hand, we are called to repent in response to God's command. In sura 66 verse 8 God orders his servants to come to him: 'O believers! Turn to God with sincere repentance so that your Lord may absolve you of your evil doings.' Ansari refers to sura 24 verse 31 ('O Believers! Turn to God, all of you, so that you may attain success'), and goes on to explain why repentance is an imperative:

God the almighty made it necessary for everyone to repent. He disclosed to everyone how degrading sin is, and in so doing he made them all

guilty of negligence. Yet they are unable to pay what they owe him.
Although he owes them nothing, he forgave them.[22]

This insightful analysis points out the seriousness of sin in many
respects. It is *universal*; that is, it affects every human being. It is
profound, as it has a debasing effect on human nature. It is *irreparable*,
for no-one can compensate for evil deeds by good deeds. But
despite all this, God's favour is certain. He is under no obligation
to forgive, yet he does, freely and unconditionally. Thus repentance
is called for on two counts: the seriousness of sin and the mercy of
God. Such is the necessity for people to repent that Ansari divides
people into two groups: the repentant and the evildoers. He makes
this distinction on the basis of the Qur'anic text 'Those who do not
repent are the evildoers' (49:11).[23]

Ghazali explains why repentance is a command. His perspective is
quite different from that of Ansari. For him, good and evil are
kneaded together inextricably in human nature (lit. 'in Adam's clay').
Therefore it is impossible to purify the 'true essence of humankind'
(*jawhar al-insan*) except through fire: either the fire of regret or the
fire of hell. The fire of regret is required in this life if people want to
escape the much more painful fire of the afterlife.[24] Ghazali
considers that whether they are unbelievers or Muslims, when
people come of age they need to repent. For Muslims, repentance
implies understanding the message of Islam. The religion of their
parents is useless for them unless they commit themselves personally to it. Understanding Islam will necessarily lead people to
repentance.

Ghazali points out that repentance is not something people can
do once for all. It is an ongoing process because everyone sins in
one way or another. We commit sin with our 'limbs' (*jawarih*), just
as many prophets did, although they repented from their sins. If we
do not sin with our limbs, we sin when we decide in our heart to
commit sin. If we do not sin in our heart, we let the devil inflict
various thoughts upon us that distract us from remembering God.
If we do not commit this sin, we sin through heedlessness and
inadequate knowledge of God, his attributes and his actions. No-
one, concludes Ghazali, is immune from sin. We are all sinful to a
greater or lesser degree. Even the Prophet used to repent many

times a day: 'I ask God's pardon seventy times a day'.[25] If this was
the case with Muhammad, he asks, how much more should
ordinary people turn to God in repentance! Ghazali also teaches
that we should repent without delay. Otherwise, we will expose
ourselves to two fatal dangers. The first is a gradual hardening of
our heart. Evil is like a permanent stain and becomes so ingrained
that it is virtually impossible to get rid of. The second danger is
illness or death. In either case we would have no time to spend on
eradicating evil through repentance. Ghazali backs up his plea for
people not to put off their repentance by quoting a (non-canonical)
narrative: 'the regret of people in hell will mostly be motivated by
procrastination.'[26]

God commands us to repent, but not everyone complies with
this command. Those who do comply are not all the same. Their
repentance is genuine to varying degrees. Ghazali divides people
into four hierarchical groups according to the quality of their
repentance. He relates these groups to four Qur'anic attributes of
the human soul:[27]

1. People who repent sincerely (66:8). They persevere in their
    repentance and commit sin no more, except those sins
    associated with bad habits. The Qur'an describes the soul of
    such a person as 'peaceful' (*mutma'inna*), 'pleased with itself'
    (*radiya*) and 'pleasing' to God (*mardiyya*) (89:27–28).
2. People who repent sincerely and lead an obedient life. They
    still commit minor sins – not deliberately, but because evil is
    kneaded together with human nature. As soon as they
    commit sin, they blame themselves, which is why their souls
    are described as 'self-rebuking' (*lawwama*) (75:2).
3. People who repent, but their repentance does not last long.
    They are often overcome by their evil desires, which cause
    them to sin. Their life is a succession of disobedient acts
    often followed by delayed and short-lived repentance. Their
    souls are 'deceptive' (*musawwila*) (12:18, 83; 20:96).
4. People who sin often and rarely repent. They persist in their
    disobedience and when they repent, their repentance is not
    genuine. They do not really regret what they have done. Their
    souls are portrayed as 'prone to evil' (*ammara bi-l-su'*) (12:53).

Conditions for repentance

We noted earlier that repentance could be a sudden and unexpected experience. It can also take place after due preparation.
When repentance has been sought, there is usually a time during
which the novice receives a spiritual training. What does this
training imply? What prompts repentance? What are the conditions
required for true repentance to happen? And what is the evidence
for genuine repentance?

Spiritual awakening

Ansari's treatise *Manazil al-salikin* ('the stages of the itinerants')
starts with a chapter on spiritual awakening (*yaqaza*), followed by
one on repentance. In sura 34 verse 46 God gives this order to
Muhammad: 'Say: "I have just one thing to press upon you, that
you stand before God." ' To stand before God, explains Ansari, is
to wake up from the slumber of heedlessness and to rise from the
entanglement of slackness. He goes on to suggest a threefold
definition of what spiritual awakening means: to take notice of
God's innumerable blessings, to realize how serious our crimes are
and, finally, to make a critical evaluation of our life.[28] Thus spiritual
revival is a prerequisite for repentance. Dhu l-Nun sees no point in
embarking on repentance without starting from the preliminary
stage of awakening: 'I know no more ignorant physician than the
one who treats a man for addiction while he is still drunk; the
treatment will be useless until the man comes to his senses; once he
has recovered his consciousness, repentance is the appropriate
remedy for his disease'.[29] Makki believes that heedlessness is the
root of all acts of disobedience, which is why the Qur'an declares
that 'heedless people will surely be the losers in the Hereafter'
(16:108–109).[30] For Ibn 'Ata', heedlessness has a lethal effect on
people's spiritual predicament, but God is able to bring them back
to life: 'The hearts which were dead through heedlessness, We have
revived them through awakening (*yaqaza*), reflection (*i'tibar*) and
admonition (*maw'iza*).'[31]

For heedlessness to be overcome, Qushayri considers that the
heart needs to be made 'alert' (*intibah*). People will then realize how
bad their spiritual plight is. This can happen only when people

listen to God's 'reprimands' (*zawajir*) in their hearts. Indeed, the heart plays a key role in one's spiritual life, as shown by this narrative: 'There is a piece of flesh in the human body. If it is fit, the whole body is fit, but if it is not, then the whole body becomes ill. This piece is the heart.'[32]

Fear, hope and rational reflection

Provided that the heart is healthy enough to listen to God's voice, people will reflect on their evildoing. God will strengthen their resolve when they decide to repent. This will mean breaking with evildoers and seeking the company of those who have already repented. As a result, people will grow in fear of God's judgment and in hope of his mercy. This will lead them to repentance.[33]

For Suhrawardi too, fear and hope are closely associated with repentance. Without fear people will not be spurred on to repentance. On the other hand, they would not have fear if they did not have hope in God's mercy. In fact, comments Suhrawardi, fear and hope coexist in the believer's heart. They need to be in equal portions for repentance to be genuine:

> One Day the Prophet went to visit a man laying on his deathbed. He asked him:
> – How do you find yourself?
> – I am fearful because of my sins but I am hopeful too because of the mercy of my Lord.
> – When fear and hope are both found in a man's heart in this world, the Prophet commented, God will certainly grant him what he hopes for and reassure him with regard to what he is fearful of.[34]

Ghazali adds 'sensual desires' (*shahawat*) to heedlessness as another cause preventing repentance. He suggests a double remedy for these evils: 'science' (*'ilm*) as a cure for heedlessness, and 'endurance' (*sabr*) as a cure for sensual desire. The two medicines have very different tastes: 'Repentance is a mixture made of science, which is sweet, and endurance, which is bitter'.[35] He quotes a hadith showing that the way to paradise requires a determined struggle against one's natural inclinations: 'Paradise is surrounded by hardships (*makarih*) and hell by [evil] sensual desires (*shahawat*)'.[36]

Ghazali describes religious scholars as 'physicians of religion' (*atibba' al-din*). They are, according to another hadith, 'the heirs of the prophets'.[37] It is their responsibility to treat their patients with an adequate treatment (repentance). Provided they are not ill(!), it is their duty to administer two medicines that will bring about wholeness. The first, available in God's revelation, is represented by fear and hope. Fear should be administered to sinful Muslims who unduly put their hope in God's mercy. Hope should be given to Muslims fearful of God's judgment and who consequently impose upon themselves unnecessary burdens they are unable to carry.[38] The second medicine Ghazali suggests is 'rationality' (*fikr*). Religious teachers must also use rational arguments to respond to those who delay their repentance and carry on with their sinful life. They need to prove that battling against evil desires and resisting sin in this world make sense if one has a long-term perspective of eternal bliss and eternal punishment. But what if people deny the very idea of God, revelation, the prophets and eternity? Ghazali suggests that unbelieving people must be persuaded with rational counter-arguments. If there is no eternal judgment, the one who refuses to give in to his evil desires will suffer no damage. On the other hand, if there is life after death, the one who dismisses God's promise of eternal punishment will be irremediably lost.[39]

Self-examination

Thus spiritual alertness, endurance, fear and hope, reflection and so on all contribute to spiritual awakening, which in turn leads to repentance. Once repentance has taken place, people should not become complacent. They must watch their conduct. Sufi teaching indicates other stages that help new converts to stay on track, one of which is called *muhasaba*. In a secular context the word means 'accountancy'. In a religious sense it means 'examination of conscience'; in other words, keeping short accounts with God. Ansari's chapter on *muhasaba* immediately follows the one on repentance.[40] The Day of Judgment is also called *yawm al-hisab* (the Day of Reckoning or Accounts). Suhrawardi points out that repentance is inauthentic unless it leads to an 'examination of conscience'. A saying attributed to 'Ali, the fourth caliph, urges people to examine themselves thoroughly: 'Give account to

yourselves before you are requested to give account to God, weigh
out yourselves before you are weighed out by God and get
prepared for the Day of the great confrontation with God.'[41]

Evidence of genuine repentance

The new convert should also get involved in 'spiritual warfare'
(*mujahada*) in order to authenticate his repentance. Suhrawardi
explains what this means by quoting the following hadith: 'The
fighter is the one who fights against himself.' This fight, he
comments, can be won through endurance (*sabr*).[42] Makki points
out that examining oneself implies eradicating 'sensual desire'
(*shahwa*).[43] This is precisely the aim of spiritual warfare.[44] He
quotes a (non-canonical) narrative comparing military warfare with
spiritual warfare. The Prophet is believed to have said to Muslims
one day after they had fought a victorious battle against their
enemies, 'You have won the smaller *jihad* but you still have to win
the greater *jihad*, which is the fight against yourselves'.[45]

Qushayri's chapter on repentance is followed by one on spiritual
warfare where he points out the practical implications of genuine
repentance. The convert should be reconciled with his enemies. As
far as he can, he should meet their rightful demands, unless they
give up their rights and absolve him. If he is not in a position to do
so immediately, he should resolve to do it as soon as he can.
Meanwhile, he should sincerely pray for them and ask God to bless
them.[46]

'The repentant is God's beloved' (*al-ta'ib habibu llah*) according
to a (non-canonical) narrative. A Sufi was once asked in connection with this saying, 'When does the repentant become God's
beloved?' Abu Muhammad Sahl's answer suggests that God's love
is made perfect in a person whose life is fully consistent with God's
character: 'The [true] beloved does nothing which displeases his
lover.'[47]

Notes

1. The derivation of the Arabic word *sufiyya* or *tasawwuf* from which we
   have 'Sufism' is uncertain. It is likely that it comes from *suf*, 'wool', in
   reference to the woollen garment worn by the early Muslim mystics.

2. The name al-Ḥaqq is found alone in five texts (18:44; 22:6, 62; 24:25; 31:30). It is associated with other divine names in five other passages: Mawla (Helper) (6:62; 10:30), Rabb (Lord) (10:32) and Malik (King) (20:114; 23:116).

3. Gimaret, *Noms*, pp. 138–142.

4. Ghazali, *Names*, pp. 125–126.

5. Makki, *Qut*, II, p. 384.

6. Massignon, *Essai*, p. 394.

7. Hujwiri, *Kashf*, p. 294.

8. Massignon, *Essai*, p. 390.

9. Suhrawardi, *'Awarif*, p. 507 (italics mine; the Arabic words for *repentance is the mould which gives the spirit of love its shape* are: *al-tawba qalabu ruḫi l-ḫubb*).

10. Schimmel, *Dimensions*, p. 109.

11. Kalabadhi, *Doctrine*, p. 83; cf. Qushayri, *Risala*, p. 95; Sarraj, *Luma'*, p. 68.

12. Nwyia, *Nusus*, p. 45. This spiritual derivation is linguistically groundless. A reputable Arabic dictionary explains the derivation of this word according to the famous linguist Sibwayh. The word *nas* (originally *unas*) is the plural of *insan* (human being), which comes from *insiyan* (forgetful) and *nisyan* (forgetfulness). Ibn 'Abbas believes that man was called *insan* because he 'forgot', *nasiya*, the mission God had entrusted to him (Ibn Manẓur, *Lisan al-'arab*, VI, 'anisa'). We noted in chapter 12 that, according to Islamic tradition, Adam's sin consisted in forgetting God's command (20:115).

13. Sulami, *Ṭabaqat*, p. 184.

14. Makki, *Qut*, II, p. 370; Ghazali, *Ihya'*, IV, pp. 15, 34.

15. Hujwiri, *Kashf*, p. 294; Qushayri, *Risala*, p. 91. These two narratives, like many others in Sufi literature, are not found in the nine canonical collections of Hadith.

16. Qushayri, *Risala*, p. 97.

17. Hujwiri, *Kashf*, p. 298; cf. Qushayri, *Risala*, p. 93; Ghazali, *Ihya'*, IV, p. 15.

18. Schimmel, *Dimensions*, p. 110.

19. Hujwiri, *Kashf*, p. 299; Qushayri, *Risala*, p. 96.

20. Smith, *Rabi'a*, p. 55.

21. Sulami, *Ṭabaqat*, pp. 444–445.

22. Ansari, *Terrains*, p. 85.

23. Ibid.

24. Ghazali, *Ihya'*, IV, p. 3.

25. Ibid., pp. 9–10; Bukhari, *da'awat* 3 [5832]:VIII, bk 75, no. 319, p. 213.

26. Ghazali, *Ihya'*, IV, p. 12.

27. Ibid., pp. 43–46. As he often does, Ghazali draws a lot upon Makki (without giving him due credit), who groups people into exactly the same four categories (Makki, *Qut*, II, pp. 292–294). Muhammad al-Tirmidhi lists three kinds of repentance: 'agreeable' (*maqbula*), resulting in obeying God with enjoyment and feeling revulsion for sin; 'conditional' (*mawqufa*), characterized by painful obedience; and 'non-acceptable' (*marduda*), because it is associated with a sense of self-satisfaction and arrogance (*Kitab ma'rifat al-asrar*, in Nwyia, *Exégèse*, p. 288).

28. Ansari, *Manazil*, pp. 8–9; *Étapes*, pp. 158–159.

29. Sulami, *Tabaqat*, p. 26.

30. Makki, *Qut*, II, p. 382.

31. Nwyia, *Nusus*, p. 126.

32. Bukhari, *iman* 39 [50]:I, bk 2, no. 49, p. 44; Ibn Majah, *fitan* 14 [3974]:V, bk 36, no. 3984, p. 306; Darimi, *buyu'* 1 [2419].

33. Qushayri, *Risala* 92; cf. Suhrawardi, *'Awarif*, pp. 472, 476–477.

34. Suhrawardi, *'Awarif*, p. 482; cf. Ibn Majah, *zuhd* 31 [4251]:V, bk 37, no. 4261, p. 496.

35. Ghazali, *Ihya'*, IV, p. 50.

36. Ibid., p. 57; Muslim, *janna* 1 [5049]:IV, bk 40, no. 6778, p. 1476; Tirmidhi, *janna* 21 [2482]; Darimi, *riqaq* 117 [2720].

37. Ghazali, *Ihya'*, IV, p. 50; cf. Bukhari, *'ilm* 10:I, bk 3, p. 56, chapter 11; Abu Dawud, *'ilm* 1 [219]:III, bk 19, no. 3634, p. 1034; Tirmidhi, *'ilm* 38 [2606]; Darimi, *muqaddima* 32 [346].

38. Ghazali, *Ihya'*, IV, pp. 50–51.

39. Ibid., pp. 57–59.

40. Ansari, *Manazil*, p. 12; *Étapes*, p. 161.

41. Suhrawardi, *'Awarif*, p. 477. This narrative is attributed to 'Umar, the third caliph, in a hadith (Tirmidhi, *qiyama* 65 [2383]).

42. Suhrawardi, *'Awarif*, p. 480; Tirmidhi, *fada'il al-jihad* 2 [1546].

43. Makki, *Qut*, II, p. 373.

44. Ibid., p. 373.

45. Ibid., p. 381.

46. Qushayri, *Risala*, p. 94.

47. Makki, *Qut*, II, p. 384.

14. DEFINITIONS OF REPENTANCE

How do Sufis define repentance? And how do their definitions compare with those of the Muslim theologians? First, Sufi definitions of repentance tend to be *more radical*, in the sense that they have far-reaching implications. For them repentance is necessary for a person's whole attitude, not just for single acts of disobedience. Second, Sufi definitions are *hierarchical*: the meaning of repentance differs according to the person who repents, and repentance itself has various degrees of authenticity.

Radical definitions of repentance

Regret
Many Sufis suggest, in a way similar to theologians, threefold definitions of repentance, all based on the famous hadith 'to regret is to repent' (*al-nadamu tawba*).[1] Their definitions, however, are more demanding as they require from the repentant more radical changes. For Hujwiri, repentance has the following elements: 'remorse for disobedience, immediate abandonment of sin, and

determination not to sin again'.[2] All Sufis consider regret as essential to repentance, but in other ways their definitions vary. For Ansari, repentance means 'regretting in one's heart, making apologies with one's mouth and breaking with evil and evildoers'.[3] Junayd's definition is slightly different: 'Regret, resolve not to do again what God has forbidden and seeking to repair the wrong which has been done'.[4] Abu 'Ali al-Rudhabari puts 'confession [of sin]' (*i'tiraf*) first, then regret and abandonment of sin.[5]

Ghazali follows the same pattern but offers a more personal definition. Repentance for him is the meeting of three things: 'science' (*'ilm*), 'state' (*hal*) and 'act' (*fi'l*). The first element brings about the second and the second causes the third.

Science (*'ilm*) ⟶	State (*hal*) ⟶	Act (*fi'l*)
Knowing that sin sets up a veil between you and God.	The heart endures acute suffering and regret.	A new resolve to abandon sin, and to make up for the past.

Science consists in knowing that the damage caused by sin is tremendous, as it amounts to setting up a 'veil' (*hijab*) between the person and the One loved; that is, God. Feeling deeply the absence of the beloved, the heart endures acute suffering and this suffering is called regret. When suffering overwhelms the heart, it generates a determination to act accordingly as regards the present, the future and the past. This determination means, as regards the *present*, giving up sin; as regards the *future*, resolving to abandon for the rest of one's life what caused the absence of the beloved; as regards the *past*, making up for what has been done, if at all possible. Thus, concludes Ghazali, repentance is regret that is the result of science and that engenders a new resolve.[6]

Commitment

Repentance for the Sufis is an all-embracing commitment, not merely a quick fix for a particular act of disobedience. Sahl al-Tustari suggests that it means 'replacing all things reprehensible with all things commendable'.[7] Hujwiri makes a clear-cut distinction between an evil act and an evil desire. He explains why the evil

desire is far more serious: 'The actual sin is not as evil as the desire
of it, for the act is momentary, but the desire is perpetual.'[8]

Ghazali's own definition of repentance refers to spiritual
warfare: 'Repentance is to turn back from the path leading away
from God and closer to the devil.' This commitment, which is
supremely rational, requires fighting against and overcoming the
devil's soldiers ('sensual desires' [*shahawat*]) as well as renouncing
evil habits and striving wholeheartedly to bring oneself to comply
with religious observances.[9]

Humility

Repentance involves people's innermost being. It reminds them of
who they are and contributes to their self-humbling. Thus a
spiritual blessing may come out of an evil act: 'The most beneficial
disobedience is the one you keep in front of you, for which you cry
continuously until you depart from this life, and which causes you
to keep away from any similar sin.'[10]

Ahmad al-Antaki, the author of the above quote, is aware of the
danger of spiritual arrogance. He has an insightful comment about
the risks faced by an obedient person. Just as something wrong
may turn into good, something good may turn into wrong:

> The most damaging act of obedience is the one which makes you forget
> your fellow men, the one which you keep in front of you in order to
> show off and to be praised. In acting like that you prove that you are
> still fearful of the wrong you have done and which you try to hide.[11]

Dhu l-Nun goes further along these lines: 'He who takes pride
in his good deeds turns them into bad deeds.'[12] Ansari too points
out that humility should characterize the repentant in his relationship with God as well as with his fellow men: 'An act of obedience
which you feel complacent about will be held against you. An act of
disobedience for which you condemn your brother will be credited
to you.'[13]

Self-criticism

The Sufi critical perspective on good works includes repentance
itself. Ansari considers that one evidence for genuine repentance is

what he calls 'the charge brought against repentance' (*ittiham al-tawba*). This means that the repentant needs to realize that his repentance is inadequate and therefore he needs 'to repent from repentance' (*al-tawba min al-tawba*).[14] Before Ansari, Ruwaym suggested the following definition: 'The meaning of repentance is that you should repent of repentance'.[15] Kalabadhi relates this definition to what Rabi'a said about her prayer for forgiveness: 'I ask pardon of God for my little sincerity in saying, I ask pardon of God'.[16] Makki stresses that not only is the Sufi's repentance inadequate, but so are all the stages and the states he goes through during his pilgrimage. Therefore he will always need to repent. After all, Sufis are not greater than prophets and all prophets repented throughout their lives.[17] Self-critical assessment led Yahya bin Mu'adh to utter this humble prayer: 'My God! I cannot say, "I have repented and I will sin no more." I know myself only too well. Because I am aware of myself I cannot guarantee that I have abandoned sin once for all.'[18]

Thus, for Sufis, repentance is much more than regretting a transgression of God's command. It is the realization of who they are before God. Even their conversion to God is affected by sin. This suggests there is nothing wholly good in them. Ansari goes as far as to say, 'when one looks at his wrongdoing with sincerity and discernment, he realises that he is left without any good action to his credit whatsoever'.[19]

Hierarchical definitions of repentance

The meaning of repentance differs according to whether or not people have started their spiritual journey. Among the pilgrims some are still beginners, and others are closer to the final stage. Repentance means different things to different people. Dhu l-Nun suggested a threefold definition in relation to where people are in their pilgrimage:

> The repentance of the Common is from sin;
> The repentance of the Elect is from forgetfulness;
> The repentance of prophets is from seeing that they are unable to reach what others have attained.[20]

This definition suggests that sin does not have the same significance for all. Sufis who have already experienced repentance have
reached a higher degree of spirituality where sin is more subtle. It is
not as much committing an evil act as forgetting to do a good one.

The relative nature of sin is indicated by Dhu l-Nun in one of
his famous sentences: 'The sins of *those who are close to God*
(*al-muqarrabun*) are the good deeds of the righteous (*al-abrar*); the
hypocrisy of the initiates is the sincerity of the novices.'[21] Ansari
further expands the idea of specific repentance for specific people.
Everyone needs to repent, but not for the same reason:

> The obedient must repent from thinking that they have many acts of
> obedience to their credit; the disobedient must repent from thinking that
> they have just a few acts of disobedience to their debit; the initiate must
> repent from forgetting God's blessings.[22]

In another treatise, written many years later, Ansari develops the
same idea:[23]

1. The repentance of 'the common' (*al-'amma*) is for having
   considered that their acts of obedience have been many. This
   amounts to three things: denying God's grace manifested to
   us in covering and forbearing our sins; believing that our
   obedience earns us rights upon God; thinking that we do not
   really need God, which is the highest degree of arrogance
   and rebellion against him.
2. The repentance of 'the middle class' (*al-awsat*) is for having
   considered that their acts of disobedience are just a few. This
   represents the highest degree of insolence and defiance
   towards God. It means claiming mistakenly that we are under
   God's protection, which inevitably leads to breaking our
   relationship with him.
3. The repentance of 'the élite' (*al-khassa*) is for wasting time. The
   misuse of time is the cause of imperfection; it puts out the light of
   spiritual watchfulness and harms intimate fellowship with God.

This penetrating analysis of the dangers facing Muslims, or indeed
any believers, argues that the main problem in spiritual life lies not

so much with what people *do*, but rather with who they *are*. When good deeds are used, as happens only too often, to fuel a sense of self-righteousness, self-confidence and self-satisfaction, the human heart is revealed as it really is: sinful. Whether people are religious or not makes no difference. This distorted spirituality demonstrates that people need to be set free from their spiritual entanglement.

Ansari considers that unlike the problems that beset ordinary people, élite pilgrims strive with unachieved spiritual perfection: their repentance will be perfected only when they repent no more; in other words, when they return to God once and for all. Becoming one with God will necessarily bring to an end the need to repent. We will look again at the issue of the fulfilment of repentance later in this chapter.

Repentance and contrition

The first four chapters of Ansari's treatise are entitled 'awakening' (*yaqaza*), 'repentance' (*tawba*), 'examination of conscience' (*muhasaba*) and 'contrition' (*inaba*). This order suggests that contrition represents a higher degree of repentance. Just as awakening is a precondition for repentance to happen, so examination of conscience precedes contrition. In other words, contrition is the spiritual state of repentance that results after self-examination has been implemented in the life of the pilgrim. Ansari's first definition of contrition is quite simple: 'It is to return completely to God.' He explains what this definition means for prophets (11:75, 88; 31:15; 38:24), for non-Muslims (30:31; 39:54) and for the initiates (39:17).[24] In a later definition he expands the meaning of contrition:

> Returning to God through reforming oneself,
> as one has returned to him with one's apologies;
> Returning to God faithfully,
> as one has returned to him pledging one's loyalty to him;
> Returning to God in the fullness of one's being,
> as one has returned by responding to him.[25]

Ansari goes on to explain what each part of this definition means. Without making detailed comment, it is worth noting that the first part is about what needs to be done so that repentance becomes contrition. The second part is about renewing one's allegiance to God. The third is about staying in God's presence after drawing near to him.

Ansari is not the only Sufi to draw a distinction between repentance and contrition. Ibrahim bin Adham stated that 'when a person's repentance has been proved to be genuine, it becomes contrition; contrition is repentance at a higher level'.[26] Abu 'Uthman al-Maghribi explains that contrition is superior to repentance in that repentance can be partial, whereas contrition involves the totality of the person and rules out any form of disobedience.[27]

Comparing different kinds of repentance

Sufis are not always consistent in their teaching. Some refer to 'contrition' (*inaba*) as repentance motivated by fear. In this case, contrition is simply equivalent to repentance, and there are two kinds of repentance:

> Abu l-Husayn al-Maghazili, being asked concerning repentance, said:
> — Do you ask concerning the repentance of contrition, or the repentance of response?
> — What is the repentance of contrition?
> — That you should fear God because of the power He has over you.
> — What is the repentance of response?
> — That you should be ashamed before God because He is near you.[28]

The 'repentance of response' (*tawbat al-istijaba*) is motivated by being aware of God's presence wherever we go. This merciful presence, felt in our heart of hearts, prompts us to return to our God in response to his presence. This repentance is also related to a well-known Qur'anic text which underlines that God is not far from his servants:

> If My servants question you [Muhammad] concerning Me, [tell them that] *I am indeed near. I answer the call of the suppliant who cries to Me. So let them respond* to Me. Let them believe in Me so that they may walk in the right way.
> (2:186)

Ibn 'Aṭa' compares the repentance of contrition with the repentance of response in that the first is motivated by the fear of God's punishment, whereas the second is inspired by the shame due to God's generosity.[29] Dhu l-Nun contrasted the repentance of contrition with the repentance of shame. Hujwiri quotes him, making his own comment:

> 'There are two kinds of repentance, the repentance of contrition (*tawbat al-inabat*) and the repentance of shame (*tawbat al-istihya'*): the former is repentance through fear of Divine punishment, the latter is repentance through shame of Divine clemency.'
>   The repentance of fear is caused by revelation of God's majesty, while the repentance of shame is caused by vision of God's beauty. Those who feel shame are intoxicated, and those who feel fear are sober.[30]

Abu 'Ali al-Daqqaq compares three kinds of repentance using the three relevant verbs we find in the Qur'an. The use of these verbs is purely stylistic, for linguistically their meaning is virtually the same:

> Repentance has a start, a centre and an end:
> *Tawba* is motivated by fear of God's judgement,
> *Inaba* by an ambitious desire of God's reward,
> *Awba* by nothing else than the will to comply with God's command.[31]

This threefold definition of repentance seems to have been inspired by a prayer attributed to Rabi'a, a Sufi woman who lived long before Daqqaq. In this moving and daring prayer Rabi'a spells out the ultimate motivation for her worship: 'O God, if I worship Thee for fear of Hell, burn me in Hell, and if I worship Thee in hope of Paradise, exclude me from Paradise; but if I worship Thee for Thy own sake, grudge me not Thy everlasting beauty.'[32]

Qushayri, Daqqaq's disciple, comments that some Sufis consider that these three kinds of repentance correspond respectively to the repentance of believers (24:31), to that of the 'saints' (*awliya'*) (50:33) and to that of the prophets (38:44).[33] Hujwiri, who is a contemporary of Qushayri, follows this teaching. He makes an additional differentiation between the three kinds of repentance:

> *Tawba* is to return from great sins to obedience;
> *Inaba* is to return from minor sins to love;
> *Awba* is to return from one's self to God.[34]

Should the repentant forget his sin?

Does genuine repentance require forgetting one's sin so that the repentant may entirely concentrate on God? Or should he constantly remind himself of his sin so that he remains humble before God? Sufis disagree over this issue and belong to one of three groups, depending on how they answer these questions.

Sahl al-Tustari defines repentance in these terms: 'Repentance consists in not forgetting one's sin.'[35] Hujwiri explains the opinion of those who hold this view:

> Repentance consists in not forgetting your sins, but always regretting them, so that, although you have many good works to your credit, you will not be pleased with yourself on that account. Remorse for an evil action is superior to good works, and one who never forgets his sins will never become conceited.[36]

Sufis who take this view are concerned lest repentant people become complacent or even arrogant. Remembering one's sin is meant to enable a person to remain in the right position before God. Humility and putting one's trust in God alone is key to keeping an attitude in harmony with the spirit of repentance. Ibn 'Ata' comments on sura 12 verse 53 ('I do not want to justify myself') and says, 'I do not claim that I am innocent. I leave it to God to vindicate my innocence.'[37] This view seems in full accord with the warning against self-righteousness that the Prophet gave to Muslims:

> God's Messenger said:
> – There is none amongst you who will be saved because of his good deeds.

The Companions asked:

– God's Messenger, not even you?

He replied:

– Not even I, unless God wraps me in His mercy and grants me His pardon.[38]

Junayd, a contemporary of Sahl, challenged his view by advocating an opposite definition of what repentance means: 'Repentance consists of forgetting the sin.'[39] Junayd explains why one should forget his sin: 'To remember one's spiritual hardness (*jafa'*) in time of blessedness (*safa'*) is hardness.'[40] Abu Bakr al-Wasiti, Junayd's disciple, considers that 'sincere repentance is such that the repentant is no longer affected by his sin either inwardly or outwardly'.[41] Kalabadhi provides his own interpretation of Junayd's view: 'This saying of Junayd means, that the sweetness of such an act so entirely departs from the heart, that there remains in the conscience not a trace of it, and one is then as though one had never known it.'[42] Taking pleasure in remembering sin casts a doubt on the authenticity of one's repentance: 'When you feel no delight in remembering a sin,' says Abu l-Hasan Bushanji, 'that is repentance.'[43] For Ansari too, repentance implies two paradoxical attitudes: first, to consider one's transgression as tremendously serious (*ta'zim al-jinaya*); then, once it is repented from, to forget it altogether (*nisyan al-jinaya*).[44]

Hujwiri tells us how those who take Junayd's view argue their case. Their argument has to do, not just with sincere repentance, but with their spiritual life as a whole. Remembering one's sin takes the centre of the Sufi's life away from God: 'The penitent is a lover of God, and the lover of God is in contemplation of God, and in contemplation it is wrong to remember sin, for remembrance of sin is a veil between God and those who contemplate Him.'

Hujwiri goes on to add his own comment: 'Inasmuch as it behoves the penitent not to remember his own selfhood, how should he remember his sin?'[45]

Some Sufis consider that the views expressed by Sahl and Junayd are not necessarily incompatible. The way they seek to reconcile these seemingly conflicting opinions is based on the different classes of Sufis. Sahl's definition applies to the beginners who are still in their early stages of spiritual pilgrimage. They are not yet steadfast in their journey and need to be reminded of their sins.[46] Junayd's definition concerns the initiates who have reached a higher degree of spiritual achievement. They are preoccupied only with God and the completion of their journey. A beginner may object against this interpretation, why is the prophet David known for having wept abundantly over his sin if the initiates do not remember their sin?[47] Makki's response is that no-one should compare himself to the prophets. Occasionally, prophets may revert to the status of beginners to teach beginners the path to spiritual knowledge.[48] Ghazali endorses the opinion that remembering one's sin is justified for prophets but unfitting for initiates.[49]

Repentance and beyond

Repentance is a decisive stage on the spiritual pilgrimage, but it is only the first stage. Beginners need to go further to become initiates. These initiates, in turn, need to pursue their journey until they reach the final stage. Then the aim of repentance will be achieved. Ansari calls this ultimate stage *tawhid*. For theologians this word means 'oneness *of* God', but for Sufis it is 'oneness *with* God'. Many Sufis are aware that becoming one with God goes far beyond Islamic orthodoxy, which presents a person's relationship with God not in terms of union with God but of submission to him.

Repentance is fulfilled only when the itinerant reaches his final stage: God. Anything short of that means imperfection. Yahya bin Mu'adh compares pilgrims to four workmen. A radical difference exists between the fourth man and the other three: 'There are four workers: a repentant man (*ta'ib*), an ascetic man (*zahid*), a man longing for God (*mushtaq*) and a man united with God (*wasil*). God is hidden to all except the *wasil* for no veil stands between him and God.'[50]

Is such desire for oneness with God reasonable? Is it not crossing over the fence God has set up between himself and his creatures? The 'plain meaning' (*ma'na zahir*) of the Qur'an seems to prohibit such an audacious and possibly foolish endeavour. God created us so that we would serve and worship him (51:56). But the Qur'an also has a 'hidden meaning' (*ma'na batin*), which is accessible only to 'those who draw near God' (*al-muqarrabun*) (3:45; 56:11). Abu 'Abdillah al-Maghribi wonders why his yearning to merge with God should be condemned, as it is nothing but the expression of his love for God (2:165; 3:31; 5:57):

> You who counts union with You a sin
> How can I make apologies for my sins which are many?
> If my sin consists in loving You
> I will not repent from that sin.[51]

What do Sufis make of submission to God, which is taught by mainstream Islam as the only right relationship between God and human beings? Sufi Muslims understand submission in the sense of complete surrender to God. This surrender involves not only the will of man but his very self. The identity of the person yields to its maker. It becomes entirely possessed by the Lord and virtually absorbed in him. The end result of submission to God is then the same as union with God. A story from the life of Ibrahim bin Adham tells us metaphorically what servanthood means in the spiritual realm:

> 'Once I bought a slave,' Ibrahim recalled.
>   — What is your name? I asked.
>   — What you call me, he answered.
>   — What do you eat?
>   — What you give me.
>   — What do you wear?
>   — What you clothe me withal.
>   — What do you do?
>   — What you command.
>   — What do you desire? I asked.
>   — What has a servant to do with desire? He replied.
> 'Wretch that you are,' I said to myself, 'all your life you have been a servant of God. Well, now learn what it means to be a servant!'
> 'And I wept so long that I swooned away.'[52]

Thus sin is not only an evil act; it is ultimately our very existence as individuals and the claim that we have our own and separate identity. The truth according to Sufis is that we exist only in God. Our being is like a shade: it has no substance. Junayd expresses this truth in this significant statement:

> I have read many books, but I have never found anything so instructive as this verse:
>> When I say: 'What is my sin?'
>> She says in reply: 'Your existence is a sin with which no other sin can be compared.'[53]

Hallaj, Junayd's former disciple, taught this doctrine and lived it out throughout his life. He was convinced that he had accomplished his *tawba* and had returned to the divine Source, expressing this conviction by saying *ana al-Haqq*, 'I am the Truth (or God)'. He was to pay a high price for this claim, subsequently being condemned and hanged on a gibbet by the Muslim authorities as a blasphemer.[54] He had yearned for this death and said, 'I will die nailed (in heart and in body) according to the religion of the Cross.' The cross was for him the symbol, not of martyrdom, but of full 'annihilation' (*fana'*) of his humanity under God's supreme action, and the pure manifestation of God.[55] Commenting on sura 2 verse 54 ('Turn [in repentance] to your Maker and slay yourselves'), he explains the final purpose of repentance:

> Repentance is the effacement of humanity by the assertion of the divine. It is the annihilation of all things which are besides God and which are not God. They will thus return to their Origin which is non-existence. God will then exist as he was in pre-eternity [i.e. before he created the world].[56]

Not all Sufis are willing to go as far as Hallaj in their understanding of the fulfilment of repentance. In fact, some Sufis criticize him for his extremist views. Ghazali considers that Hallaj's statement is ambiguous and misleading:

> So the one who said: 'I am the truth' was wrong, unless it be taken according to one of two interpretations, the first of which being that he

means he exists by virtue of the Truth. But this interpretation is far-fetched because the statement does not communicate it, and because that would hardly be proper only to him, since everything besides the Truth exists by virtue of the Truth.

On the second interpretation, he is so absorbed in the Truth that he has no room for anything else. One may say of what takes over the totality of a thing and absorbs it that one *is* it, as the poet says: 'I am whom I desire, and he whom I desire is I,' and by that he means that he is absorbed in it [*istighraq*].[57]

Ansari has a slightly different perspective from that of Hallaj. Repentance does not lead to the destruction of selfhood but to its merging with God. It requires disassociating oneself from everything and reaching out to the only Being. Repentance itself will be done away with when its purpose is fulfilled; in other words, when one becomes entirely identified with God:

> The stage of *tawba* will be fully achieved only when the person has completed his return from all that is short of God to God, when he realises the deficiency of this return, and when he returns from realising this deficiency.[58]

Repentance has no *raison d'être* when the itinerant has reached the final stage of the journey; that is, union with God. It is worth noting that Ansari refers to repentance as being deficient and to the need for this penultimate obstacle to perfect union to be overcome. Why should the way leading to God be seen as inherently inadequate? Perfection is realized only after union with God is fulfilled. Anything short of that is stamped with inadequacy. While returning to God, the initiates still engage with God as if they exist in themselves. The reality is that they only exist in God. Apart from God nothing exists. It is God who returns to himself through them. He and only he is the *tawwab*, the One who causes everyone to return to him. This perspective is further developed by Ibn 'Arabi whose doctrine we will look at in the next chapter.

A new heart and a new spirit

In many ways Sufi teaching is consonant with Christian doctrine – much more than mainstream Islamic theology. The Sufi approach to Islam is spiritual compared to the rational approach of the theologians or the legal approach of the jurists. We have seen that repentance is a key Qur'anic concept. It refers either to the conversion of non-Muslims to Islam (5:36–37) or to a specific act of disobedience that Muslims need to regret and give up (66:8). For Sufis, repentance means, first and foremost, conversion to God for both Muslims and non-Muslims. This conversion is necessary and represents a divine command so that people may come to know God not just intellectually but at a deep and personal level. Conversion is a personal decision, yet not a merely human act: it is rather the outworking of God's generosity towards his servants.

The emphasis placed by Sufis on our inner being, or 'the heart', is very significant in their teaching. Their understanding of sin as being inherent in human nature, not just in human acts, reflects their insightful grasp of the human predicament. Like many Sufis, Ansari is fully aware that people are unable to redeem themselves. At the same time, he believes that God's merciful forgiveness is far greater than human misery and sin. For Suhrawardi, repentance results in what he calls 'a true spiritual birth', comparable to natural birth, which is necessary for entering 'the kingdom of God'.[59] These words echo what Jesus said about God's kingdom and how to enter it:

> no-one can enter the kingdom of God unless he is born of water and the Spirit. Flesh gives birth to flesh, but the Spirit gives birth to spirit ... The wind blows wherever it pleases. You hear its sound, but you cannot tell where it comes from or where it is going. So it is with everyone born of the Spirit.
> (John 3:5–8)

The promise of the Holy Spirit
The Sufi definition of repentance implies a U-turn in one's life, but this change remains a natural, human change. From a Christian

perspective, repentance is closely associated with the Holy Spirit; that is, God's Spirit. The Holy Spirit produces a supernatural, decisive and ongoing change in people's lives. They are cleansed from sin and are transformed into a new creation. Not only does God promise to work in our lives, but his Spirit also comes to dwell in our innermost being. The prophet Ezekiel described God's action in this way:

> I will sprinkle clean water on you, and you will be clean; I will cleanse
> you from all your impurities and from all your idols. I will give you a
> new heart and put a new spirit in you; I will remove from you your heart
> of stone and give you a heart of flesh. And I will put my Spirit in you
> and move you to follow my decrees and be careful to keep my laws.
> (Ezek. 36:25–27)

The fulfilment of this promise took place with the coming of Jesus. John the Baptist (*Yahya* in the Qur'an) was sent to prepare the way. He called his people to repent, and those who responded to his call were baptized in the river Jordan. John's mission pointed to Jesus. The water in which he baptized repentant people prefigured God's Spirit, who would be poured out on those who believe in Jesus: 'I baptise you with water for repentance. But after me will come one who is more powerful than I, whose sandals I am not fit to carry. He will baptise you with the Holy Spirit and with fire' (Matt. 3:11).

Jesus died on the cross 'for the forgiveness of sins' (Matt. 26:28). On the third day God raised him from the dead. His resurrection gives evidence that his death achieved its purpose in God's eyes (Rom. 4:25). Before he ascended to heaven Jesus appeared to his disciples over a period of forty days. They were given over-whelming evidence that he was not only crucified, but also raised from the dead. They also received Jesus' final instructions about the kingdom of God (Acts 1:1–3). He told them that they would not be left alone, but promised them the Holy Spirit: 'Do not leave Jerusalem, but wait for the gift my Father promised, which you have heard me speak about. For John baptised with water, but in a few days you will be baptised with the Holy Spirit' (Acts 1:4–5).

Having completed his mission on earth, Jesus returned to God
as king of the universe (Phil. 2:6–11). Ten days later, just as he had
promised, he sent the Holy Spirit upon his disciples (2:1–4). That
same day, known as Pentecost, the gospel was preached to a large
crowd gathered in Jerusalem. When many accepted the truth about
Jesus, they were summoned to express their faith by taking two
actions to receive God's twofold promise:

> Repent and be baptised, every one of you, in the name of Jesus Christ
> for the forgiveness of your sins. And you will receive the gift of the
> Holy Spirit. The promise is for you and your children and for all who
> are far off – for all whom the Lord our God will call.
> (Acts 2:38–39; cf. 3:19; 20:21)

Thus faith and repentance, expressed in baptism, represent our
due response to the gospel. Forgiveness of sins and the gift of the
Holy Spirit are the gospel's promise to us. Precious as it is, God's
pardon is associated with God himself dwelling in our lives
through his Spirit.

The purpose of God

God's purpose for our lives is to save us from eternal punishment,
by declaring us righteous because of Jesus' atoning death. But
salvation also includes sanctifying us and enabling us to be
conformed to the likeness of Christ, the perfect man, reconciling
us with God and making us his adopted children. Ultimately,
salvation will result in our sharing God's glory. Will not a well-off
and generous father share his wealth with the children he loves so
much? God's supreme purpose is to create a new humanity who
will display his majesty, love and power:

> we know that in all things God works for the good of those who love
> him, who have been called according to his purpose. For those God
> foreknew he also predestined to be conformed to the likeness of his
> Son, that he might be the firstborn among many brothers. And those he
> predestined, he also called; those he called, he also justified; those he
> justified, he also glorified.
> (Rom. 8:28–30)

Thus, unlike Islam in general and Sufism in particular, Christianity considers that believing men and women are not just God's servants. They are God's adopted children. Their calling is not simply to submit to the Sovereign Lord, but to love their heavenly Father. Christians see themselves not as having to renounce their selfhood, as Sufis do, but as having to give up their selfishness in order to enjoy closer fellowship with the loving and saving God. Such fellowship with God will reach its climax in the life to come. This will not entail, as in Sufism, merging with God, but living in perfect harmony with him.

Jesus Christ is the model of what human creatures are to become. Just as he is in perfect unity with the Father, so we are called to be, but with one major difference: he is God's eternal Son; we are God's adopted sons and daughters. To put it in Sufi terms, we do not seek to return to our past non-existence in God. Instead, we look forward to the time when we will live to the full potential of our human existence. As God's most privileged creatures we will then enjoy God's eternal and immediate presence. The source of our present alienation from God is not our existence as such but our self-centred, sinful existence without him.

The dangers of mysticism

Many Christian and Muslim mystics have run the risk of confusing selfhood with sin. They have considered annihilation in God, instead of perfect peace with God, as their final goal. Muslim mystics have been more exposed to this danger because in Islam God is not the One-in-Three God (i.e. the Father, the Son and the Holy Spirit). Christians have in the trinitarian God a perfect model of oneness and otherness: the three persons of the Holy Trinity are united in the one divine Essence.

Élitism represents another risk in Sufism. Believers are grouped according to their spiritual achievements. Although humility is highly regarded by Sufis, they differentiate between the Common, the Élite and the Saints (or the prophets). With this hierarchy comes the danger of spiritual pride. The Prophet himself acknowledged in a hadith (quoted above) that, like all Muslims, he needed God's mercy and forgiveness. Otherwise, he would be lost. The Prophet's example should keep all Muslims (including Sufis) aware that human beings, whatever their spiritual experiences, remain sinners in need of constant humility before God. As we noted in chapter 12, prophets are not seen in the Bible as sinless. David is the most significant prophet in this respect, but he is not the only prophet who disobeyed God. Christians know both through their own experience and through Jesus' teaching that they need God's forgiveness and his protection: 'Forgive us our sins ... and lead us not into temptation' (Luke 11:4; cf. 1 Cor. 10:12–13).

Should we remember our sins?

We have seen that Sufis are divided over the issue as to whether or not we should forget our sins. Is it possible to focus on God without losing sight of our true position before him? Is it possible to remember our sins without feeling guilty about them and dwelling on them? The Bible offers a realistic perspective. We are all sinful creatures living in a fallen world. As long as we live in this world we are bound to commit sin, to a greater or lesser degree. The Holy Spirit renews us and sanctifies our lives, but his ongoing work will not finish until Jesus comes back to establish God's kingdom in all its fullness. Only then will sin, suffering and death disappear for ever:

> Now the dwelling of God is with men, and he will live with them. They will be his people, and God himself will be with them and be their God. He will wipe every tear from their eyes. There will be no more death, or mourning or crying or pain, for the old order of things has passed away. (Rev. 21:3–4)

Until that day, Christians will always have to confess their sins and ask God's forgiveness. As we do so, we will praise him – the forgiving and saving God. What we do need to remember is that, although we are sinners, we are *forgiven sinners*, and that God is holy, but also merciful.

Notes

1. Ibn Majah, *zuhd* 30 [4242]:V, bk 37, no. 4252, p. 491.
2. Hujwiri, *Kashf*, p. 294; cf. Qushayri, *Risala*, p. 92.
3. Ansari, *Terrains*, p. 86; cf. Ansari, *Manazil*, p. 10; *Étapes*, p. 160.

4. Qushayri, *Risala*, p. 95.

5. Sulami, *Tabaqat*, p. 366.

6. Ghazali, *Ihya'*, IV, pp. 3–4.

7. Ibid., p. 4. Similar definitions have been suggested by several Sufis: Qushayri (*Risala*, p. 91), Ibn 'Ata' (Nwyia, *Nusus*, pp. 104–105), Yusuf bin Hamdan al-Susi (Sarraj, *Luma'*, p. 68; Suhrawardi, *'Awarif*, p. 488).

8. Hujwiri, *Kashf*, p. 299.

9. Ghazali, *Ihya'*, IV, p. 9.

10. Massignon, *Recueil*, p. 12.

11. Ibid.

12. Sulami, *Tabaqat*, p. 29.

13. Ansari, *Manazil*, p. 12; *Étapes*, p. 162.

14. Ansari, *Manazil*, p. 10; *Étapes*, p. 160.

15. Kalabadhi, *Doctrine*, p. 83; *Ta'arruf*, p. 93; Sarraj, *Luma'*, p. 68; Suhrawardi, *'Awarif*, p. 487; Ibn 'Arabi, *Futuhat*, II, p. 143.

16. Kalabadhi, *Doctrine*, p. 83; *Ta'arruf*, p. 93; Makki, *Qut*, II, p. 385; Suhrawardi, *'Awarif*, p. 487.

17. Makki, *Qut*, II, p. 389.

18. Qushayri, *Risala*, p. 95.

19. Ansari, *Manazil*, p. 11; *Étapes*, p. 160.

20. Kalabadhi, *Doctrine*, p. 83; *Ta'arruf*, p. 93; cf. Hujwiri, *Kashf*, p. 298; Sarraj, *Luma'*, p. 68; Qushayri, *Risala*, p. 95.

21. Sarraj, *Luma'*, pp. 68–69.

22. Ansari, *Terrains*, p. 86.

23. Ansari, *Manazil*, p. 11; *Étapes*, p. 161.

24. Ansari, *Terrains*, pp. 87–88.

25. Ansari, *Manazil*, p. 12; *Étapes*, p. 162.

26. Suhrawardi, *'Awarif*, p. 479.

27. Nwyia, *Exégèse*, pp. 301–302.

28. Kalabadhi, *Doctrine*, p. 83; *Ta'arruf*, p. 93; Suhrawardi, *'Awarif*, p. 487.

29. Qushayri, *Risala*, p. 96.

30. Hujwiri, *Kashf*, p. 299. I have slightly changed Nicholson's translation in this quote: 'repentance of return' has been replaced with 'repentance of contrition'.

31. Qushayri, *Risala*, p. 94; Ibn 'Arabi, *Futuhat*, II, p. 143.

32. 'Attar, *Saints*, p. 51.

33. Qushayri, *Risala*, p. 94.

34. Hujwiri, *Kashf*, p. 295.

35. Kalabadhi, *Doctrine*, pp. 82–83; *Ta'arruf*, p. 92; Sarraj, *Luma'*, p. 68; Qushayri, *Risala*, p. 95.

36. Hujwiri, *Kashf*, p. 296.

37. Nwyia, *Nusus*, p. 63.

38. Muslim, *munafiqun* 73 [5036]:IV, bk 38, no. 6762, p. 1473; Bukhari, *marda* 19 [5241]:VII, bk 70, no. 577, p. 391; *riqaq* 18 [5986]:VIII, bk 76, no. 470, p. 313; Ibn Majah, *zuhd* 20 [4191]:V, bk 37, no. 4201, p. 462; Darimi, *riqaq* 23 [2617].

39. Hujwiri, *Kashf*, p. 296; Kalabadhi, *Doctrine*, p. 82; *Ta'arruf*, p. 92; Sarraj, *Luma'*, p. 68; Qushayri, *Risala*, p. 95; Makki, *Qut*, II, p. 371.

40. Qushayri, *Risala*, p. 95.

41. Ibid.

42. Kalabadhi, *Doctrine*, p. 83; *Ta'arruf*, p. 92.

43. Hujwiri, *Kashf*, p. 299; Qushayri, *Risala*, p. 96.

44. Ansari, *Manazil*, p. 10; *Étapes*, p. 160.

45. Hujwiri, *Kashf*, p. 296.

46. Sarraj, *Luma'*, p. 68; Qushayri, *Risala*, p. 95.

47. Although David is reputed for his repentance and tears, he is by no means the only prophet to have wept over his sin. According to a (non-canonical) narrative, David's tears outweighed the tears of all human beings put together. But Noah's tears outweighed the tears of David, and Adam's tears outweighed Noah's (Razi on sura 2 verse 37; II:3, p. 25).

48. Makki, *Qut*, II, p. 371.

49. Ghazali, *Ihya'*, IV, p. 42.

49. Ghazali, *Ihya'*, IV, p. 42.

50. Suhrawardi, *'Awarif*, p. 516.

51. Sulami, *Tabaqat*, p. 241.

52. 'Attar, *Saints*, p. 75.

53. Hujwiri, *Kashf*, p. 297; Suhrawardi, *'Awarif*, p. 487.

54. See Massignon, *Hallaj*, pp. 64–71.

55. Ibid., pp. 273–275. The Arabic words for 'I will die nailed according to the religion of the Cross' are *'ala dini al-salib yakunu mawti*.

56. Massignon, *Essai*, p. 360.

57. Ghazali, *Names*, p. 125. Cf. Suhrawardi, *'Awarif*, p. 508.

58. Ansari, *Manazil*, p. 11; *Étapes*, p. 161.

59. Suhrawardi, *'Awarif*, p. 476. The Arabic words for 'a true spiritual birth' are *wilada ma'nawiyya haqiqiyya*; for 'the kingdom of heaven', *malakut al-samawat*.

15. IBN 'ARABI: MERCY, FORGIVENESS AND REPENTANCE

Mercy, being one of God's main attributes, is key to the way Sufis perceive God. Ibn 'Arabi, arguably the most influential figure in Sufism, considers mercy to be God's overarching attribute, a defining attribute that tells us who God is.

God's universal mercy

Consider the first sura in the Qur'an, *al-Fatiḥa*:

> In the name of God, the Ever-Merciful, the All-Merciful.
> Praise be to God, Lord of the Worlds;
> The Ever-Merciful, the All-Merciful;
> The Master of the Day of Judgment.
> You alone we worship, and You alone we ask for help.
> Show us the straight way,
> The way of those upon whom You have bestowed Your grace,
> those whose portion is not wrath, and who do not go astray.
> (1:1–7)

Ibn 'Arabi explains that this sura is known as *ummu l-Kitab* (the mother of the book).[1] It serves as a hermeneutical paradigm for the whole Qur'an; that is, it determines the way the whole Qur'an should be interpreted. No verse in this sura is about God's wrath. It is all about God's mercy, in line with the hadith which says that 'God's mercy prevails over His anger'.[2] For Ibn 'Arabi, the entire universe is moving towards divine pardon and mercy. Sooner or later God's mercy will embrace everyone. It falls into two categories:

1. *God's universal mercy (rahma 'amma)*, represented by the divine name Rahman. It is a completely free and undeserved 'gift' (*minna*) and is bestowed on all people. Muslims are shown this mercy in this world; it enables them to believe in God and obey his commands. Sinful Muslims and non-Muslims will benefit from it only in the afterlife, when God will put an end to their punishment in hell.

2. *God's specific mercy (rahma khassa)*, referred to by the divine name Rahim. It is a deserved mercy in the sense that it will be granted to obedient Muslims in the hereafter as a reward for their faith and obedience. Unlike God's universal mercy, this mercy is 'mandatory' (*wajiba*), because it represents a 'recompense' (*thawab*) granted to deserving people for their compliance with God's commands (6:54; 7:156).[3]

Thus God's mercy extends to all human beings. Everyone will enjoy it, if not in this world, then certainly in the next. All people will eventually benefit from God's overwhelming blessing. The extent of this mercy fills Ibn 'Arabi with wonder:

> How great God's mercy is, even towards those who are unaware of its width! ... I know people who discuss God's mercy and its scope ... They believe that it is limited to a certain group of people. In doing so they restrict what God has made most comprehensive. If God were to deprive someone of his mercy, he would start with those people.

But God is determined, comments Ibn 'Arabi, to bestow his mercy on all (i.e. on committed Muslims as well as disobedient Muslims and non-Muslims).[4]

In this life	In the life to come
Universal mercy Obedient Muslims are enabled to believe in God and obey his commands.	**Universal mercy** Punishment will come to an end for sinful Muslims and non-Muslims. **Specific mercy** Obedient Muslims receive a reward from God.

Table 15. Universal and specific mercy in this life and the next, according to Ibn ʿArabi

God is the best of those who show mercy

The Qurʾan describes God as 'the most merciful of those who are merciful (*arḥamu al-raḥimin*)' (7:151). Ibn ʿArabi explains that if God granted his mercy only to those who deserve it, he would not be described as 'the Most Merciful One'. In the Hadith God has promised that 'He will show His mercy to those who are merciful';[5] but he will also show his mercy to those who are not. Being surrounded by God's mercy wherever we turn, concludes Ibn ʿArabi, we will certainly not be disappointed.[6] The Qurʾan also portrays God as 'the best of those who show mercy (*khayru al-raḥimin*)' (23:109). For Ibn ʿArabi, God's mercy is superior because unlike human mercy it is 'pure' (*khaliṣa*). People show mercy in order to alleviate their own suffering and their mercy is based on 'sorrow' (*shafaqa*), whereas God's mercy is 'absolute' (*muṭlaqa*) since God knows no such emotion. God's mercy is pure mercy, whereas his judgment is always mixed with mercy. His mercy reached its climax when 'He struck' humankind by bringing them into existence from nothingness.[7] Since people were created out of God's mercy, they will be judged mercifully. When a human being punishes his servant, his punishment is always mixed with mercy because between them there is a 'servant–master relationship' (*nisbat ʿubudiyya*). The same applies to God's judgment because all human beings are his servants. Ibn ʿArabi points out that the

Qur'an says that God is 'the best of those who show mercy', but never the best of those who punish or take revenge. This indicates that there is no symmetry between God's mercy and his judgment. His mercy and pardon take precedence over his judgment. His punishment is not his preference.[8]

Ibn 'Arabi quotes sura 9 verse 67: 'They [the hypocrites] have forgotten God; so He has forgotten them.' Then he offers a rather unexpected interpretation. People have forgotten God, he says, by ignoring his right over them (*taraqu ḫaqqa allah*); that is, his right to be acknowledged as God. In return, God has forgotten them by ignoring 'the right' they have earned through their disobedience; that is, to be punished by him as their Judge. In other words, God has renounced his right to deal with them according to what they deserve; instead, he has decided to show them mercy and to forgive them. Muslims are summoned 'not to be like those who have forgotten God' (59:19) lest God forgets them.[9]

God punishes a little and pardons a lot

Ibn 'Arabi devotes a whole chapter to God's name al-'Afuww (pardoning) (4:43, 99, 149; 22:60; 58:2).[10] He relates this name to the Qur'anic texts which say that 'God pardons a lot' (42:30, 34). He remarks that to forgive is meaningless without the reality of punishment. On the other hand, if punishment is carried out, there would be no forgiveness. Forgiveness therefore requires that punishment be applied, but only a little (*la budda mina l-mu'akhadha wa lakin fi qilla*). Practically, this means that divine punishment and forgiveness will be expressed in two different ways:

1. With regard to *Muslims*, God's punishment will be reduced either in time or in the degree of pain. The first amounts to shortening the time during which sinful Muslims are punished; the second to lessening the severity of their suffering. In either case these Muslims will eventually go to paradise.

2. With regard to *polytheists*, God's punishment will be expressed in the shortening of the time of their punishment in hell. In other words, their punishment will not be eternal. However, at the end of this time they will not go to paradise. They will be placed under the rule of their fate, which is endless.[11]

Thus God is pardoning in that he punishes only a little and 'pardons a lot'. If God has commanded us to forgive our fellow human beings who sin against us, argues Ibn 'Arabi, how much more will he forgive his servants. Indeed, God says to his servants who have wronged themselves not to despair of his mercy, for he forgives all transgressions: 'Say, "O My servants who have transgressed against their souls! Despair not of God's mercy. God forgives all sins, for He is the All-Forgiving, the All-Merciful"' (39:53).

Ibn 'Arabi comments that God's forgiveness, as shown in this text, is limitless and unconditional. It depends neither on our repentance nor on our good works. It covers all our wrongdoing and embraces this world as well as the next. God's mercy and forgiveness, he concludes, necessarily includes all those who have wronged themselves.

Mercy and predestination

Ibn 'Arabi strongly believes in predestination as a result of God's sovereignty. He has a deterministic conception of the future, which he bases on Qur'anic teaching. A clear-cut division separates humankind into two groups, each moving towards the destination it is fit for. God is fully involved in bringing everyone to their final destiny:

> None of us in this life can achieve what we were not destined for, nor can we fulfil more than the potential we have gained through our education. Likewise, in the hereafter, people will only be able to go to the 'habitat' (*mawṭin*) that has been assigned to them. Those who have been created for eternal happiness, God will make ready their way to ease; [as the Qur'an says] 'Whoever gives [in charity], fears [God] and trusts in what is good, We will indeed make ready their way to ease' (92:5–7). And those who have been created for hell, God will make ready their way to hardship (cf. 92:8–10).[12]

The result of this double predestination is that people in each group will go to their natural 'home' (*dar*) in the hereafter: paradise for 'monotheists, whatever their monotheism is' (*al-muwaḥḥidun* *bi'ayyi wajh^{in} wahhadu*) and hell for non-monotheists. The second group will be disappointed not because they are unhappy in their own home, but because they compare their home with the other.[13]

Thus Ibn 'Arabi considers that all of us are predetermined in such a way that we can be happy only if we stay where we belong. Some of us are fit for paradise, and others for hell. Eternal happiness consists in remaining in our proper habitat:

> Some people will go to hell on their way to paradise. They will feel
> discontent in hell. They will be there until they have received the
> punishment they deserved because of their evil deeds. Then they will
> come out of hell thanks to the intercession of the intercessors and the
> solicitude of the Most Merciful One.
>
> As for the people of hell they will endure extreme suffering at the
> beginning and will ask to be allowed to get out of hell. But when their
> punishment will have come to an end, they will remain in hell, 'not to be
> punished any longer, but to be where they belong' (*bi-l-ahliyya la bi-l-jaza'*).
> Hell will then become bliss for them so much so that, should they go to
> paradise, they would feel a terrible pain.[14]

God wants all people to enjoy eternal happiness, explains Ibn 'Arabi, despite what they endure in this life. God's forgiveness has been ordained to this end and it unfolds in successive stages: in this life, in the grave, on the Day of Judgment and in hell. As a result of God showing his mercy to people in hell, some will come out of hell but others will remain. Those who stay in hell will experience 'a punishment without suffering' (*'adhab bila alam*).

In short, people are inherently and fundamentally different. This difference is not only religious, depending on whether or not we believe in God and obey his commands. Our very nature is different, for we have not been created the same way:

> God's forgiveness will not benefit all those who will go to hell, but his
> generosity will eventually be shown to everyone. Those who have been
> created from fire will remain in hell which is their 'natural habitat'
> (*mawtin*). Should they be taken out of hell in the end, they would suffer a
> tremendous harm. Indeed it is only in hell that they can enjoy
> 'permanent bliss' (*na'im muqim*).[15]

Ibn 'Arabi and Muhammad

Ibn 'Arabi believes that he has a key role in the dispensation of God's mercy. He is a special witness to that mercy and a trustee of it. He relates his mission to Muhammad and to Jesus, seeing himself as the spiritual heir of both: 'I am, without any doubt, the Seal of Sainthood, appointed to inherit the Prophet and the Christ.'[16]

According to the Qur'an, Muhammad is 'the Seal of the prophets' (33:40). Ibn 'Arabi uses similar language to describe himself and Jesus. He points to himself as 'the Seal of sainthood' (*khatm al-walaya*) especially of the Muhammadan sainthood, which is linked with legislative prophecy (i.e. Muhammad's prophetic ministry included bringing a law). Jesus is seen as 'the Seal of the saints', his sainthood being a universal sainthood. Unlike Muhammad, Jesus did not bring a law, and so his sainthood is linked with general prophecy, which characterizes the higher rank of saints known as *afrad* (the solitary ones).[17]

Ibn 'Arabi considers that his own mission is to highlight God's mercy, and that this is reflected in the way he was created by the Most Merciful One. As the Seal of Sainthood, he is aware that his character is in the likeness of God and his Prophet, and gives thanks for such a privilege:

> I praise God that I am not a revengeful person who likes to vent his anger against people. God created me [as a token of his] mercy and he made me heir of mercy to the one [i.e. Muhammad] whose mission is portrayed in these words, 'We have sent you as a mercy to the worlds'.
>
> (21:107)[18]

Muhammad as mediator of God's mercy

For Ibn 'Arabi, the Prophet Muhammad plays a unique role in the unfolding of God's mercy.[19] He is the mediator of divine mercy and his mission is to bestow that mercy upon humankind. He refers to the hadith in which Muhammad declares, 'I will be the chief of all the people on the Day of Resurrection'.[20] As prophets are human beings, Muhammad is also their 'leader' (*sayyid*). His rank is above theirs as he is before them. Muhammad's existence predates Adam's creation. According to a tradition, Muhammad was already a prophet when Adam was still 'in the form of water and clay'.[21] In his pre-existence Muhammad was commissioned by God to be his agent in conveying his pardon to humankind. He personally fulfilled this mission 'during the time of his physical appearance' (*fi zamani zuhuri jasadihi*). Before that, all prophets throughout history carried out his mission. As Muhammad's 'deputies' (*nuwwab*), the prophets were sent each to his own people. In the hereafter they will realize that their specific mission was part of Muhammad's universal mission. On Resurrection Day Muhammad will be the first to intercede. After him people will intercede for one another. The prophets will be granted God's specific pardon on behalf of their peoples. Muhammad will be awarded God's general pardon on behalf of his nation.

Muhammad's mission is universal: 'We have sent you to all people' (34:28). Therefore, according to Ibn 'Arabi, his nation is not restricted to the Muslim community. Everyone, from Adam's day until the end of time, is a member of his nation. God will grant his pardon to everyone, for he told Muhammad that he has forgiven 'his past and future sins' (48:2). Muhammad's sins are not his own, for he is sinless. These sins are attributed to him because he is their representative. In a similar way, the Qur'an refers to Muhammad's doubts concerning God's revelation (10:94) and God's warning to him that his good deeds would be reduced to nothing if he associated anything with God (39:65). Certainly, Muhammad did not have doubts about what was revealed to him, remarks Ibn 'Arabi, nor was he tempted to associate anything with God. The deeds of his community have been ascribed to him as their leader. His past sins are the sins of the people from Adam to his own time, and his future sins are the sins of the people from then to the Day of Resurrection. Thus through Muhammad God will grant his pardon to everyone and everyone will rejoice in God's future happiness.

Thus Muhammad conveys God's pardon to humankind. This universal forgiveness is worthy of God's mercy, which is all-embracing (7:156), and of God's favour, which is immeasurable (2:105).

Repentance and love

One highly significant characteristic of Ibn 'Arabi's thought is his understanding of repentance and sin. He opens his chapter on repentance with two Qur'anic texts. In sura 24 verse 31 God calls people to turn penitently to him so that they may attain success. At the same time the Qur'an declares that 'God turned [with mercy] to them so that they may turn [with repentance] to Him' (9:118). This proves that it is God who makes people turn to him. Ibn 'Arabi explains why the same verb *taba* is used for both God and man but with two different prepositions. The word *'ala* (above/over) is used for God because one of God's names is al-'Aly (the Most High). For people the word *ila* (towards) is used 'because it is God who is sought through their repentance and he is thus its destination' (*li'annahu al-matlub bi-l-tawba fahuwa ghayatuha*).

Ibn 'Arabi draws a parallel between God's *return to us* (and our return to him) and God's *love for us* (and our love for him) (5:57). He considers that love is the driving force behind God's return and ours. God's return to us is based on his eternal love for us. When we return to him, he rewards us with another love (sura 2 verse 222: 'God loves those who turn to Him [in repentance]'). On our side, we love God with two kinds of love. We love him in response to his blessings and we love him just because of who he is. In other words, God and man have reciprocal relationships based on love and aiming at reaching out to one another. This type of relationship is referred to by the hadith which says that 'God created Adam in his own image'.[22] It means that all divine attributes are applicable to people, whoever they are. Repentance is designed to achieve the goal of God and humans sharing in the same divine attributes.[23]

The meaning of repentance

Having highlighted the motivation and the aim of repentance, Ibn 'Arabi goes on to quote a threefold definition: 'The meaning of repentance is to abandon sin immediately, to regret what has been done and to resolve not to commit this sin again.' He interprets this fairly common definition of repentance in the most unexpected

way, for, as we will see, he categorically rejects the third part
of it.

Abandon sin

The first step in repenting is to abandon sin on the spot (*fi l-ḥal*).
What motivates this step is simply *ḥaya'* (shame/shyness). Ibn
'Arabi starts by talking not about people's shame, but about God's
shame. He refers to a hadith that describes God as 'ashamed': 'God
is *ḥayyi'* and generous. When someone lifts up his hands to Him [in
prayer], He is ashamed to send him away empty-handed.'[24]

Another (non-canonical) narrative has it that 'On Resurrection
Day, God will be ashamed in front of an old man with white hair.'
God's shame, comments Ibn 'Arabi, is such that on the Day of
Judgment he will not punish a person who stands distressed before
him (because he did not repent) if this person recites sura 9 verse
118 ('God turned to them so that they may turn to Him'). The
implication is that this person did not return to God because God
did not first return to him. The repentant person expresses his
sense of shame by being well mannered with God. He will attribute
his sin to himself although he knows God is the author of his act.
Indeed, the Qur'an says God causes people to be wicked or
righteous (91:8), remarks Ibn 'Arabi. However, inasmuch as his act
is reprehensible, the repentant person gives it up by stopping
attributing it to God. Instead, he takes responsibility for it.[25]

The word for sin that Ibn 'Arabi uses in this context is *zalla*,
which literally means 'to slip', 'to slide off' or 'to glide'. He explains
what sin is when he explains what giving up sin means for 'spiritual
leaders' (*'ulama'*). What they say, he adds, is exactly how God
defines sin. For them to give up sin means denying it is sin, seeing it
instead as a mere 'slip'. Initially, it represents God's act and as such
'it is extremely beautiful and wonderful'. It becomes sin when it
slips away from being God's act to being a human act deemed
reprehensible by God. Other spiritual leaders believe that to give
up sin is simply to consider sin as an act that has 'slid off' from
God to man, regardless of whether this act is commendable or
reprehensible. In fact, all acts produced in the universe, commendable and reprehensible, are 'downgraded acts'; that is, they are
divine acts that have been attributed to creatures. Sin is therefore

the downgrading of an act prior to its moral qualification as being bad or good.[26]

Ibn 'Arabi considers it possible for the same act to be either good or bad. Indeed, God has promised that he will turn evil deeds into good deeds: 'Those who repent, believe and do what is right, God will change their evil deeds into good deeds, for God is All-Forgiving and All-Merciful' (25:70). There is a fundamental difference between good and evil in every act. The goodness in an act is 'essential' (*dhati*), it is part of it, whereas the evil is 'accidental' ('*arid*). What is essential is 'permanent' (*baq^{in}*), unlike the accidental, which is 'passing' (*za'il*). The goodness of an evil act that has been transformed into a good act is two times greater than that of a good act. It is good because, like all acts, it is a divine act and because God has turned its evil into good. Ibn 'Arabi uses a parable to illustrate the added value of such an act. It is like two people who are equally good-looking. Both are naked, yet while the first remained clean, the second got dirty. This second man was washed from his temporary dirt and recovered his initial beauty. He was then given decent clothes to put on, and became much more attractive than the first man.

Regret what has been done

The second element in the definition of sin is regret. Ibn 'Arabi understands regret in a way no less unexpected than the first. The repentant person regrets his act in the sense that he did not realize its true implications. He did not grasp that it would lead to greater blessedness. Once he understands the far-reaching implications of his sin, his sadness gives way to an endless joy. The repentant is compared to a lover who is sorrowful because of his failure towards his beloved. When he meets his beloved, he is deeply embarrassed and ashamed. He suspects that his beloved will have a very negative reaction. In fact, the response is amazingly reassuring. The failure of the lover is met by an even greater love on behalf of the beloved. The lover, then, regrets the false ideas he had about his beloved.[27]

Resolve not to commit the sin again

The third part of the definition of sin is to resolve not to commit sin any more. Ibn 'Arabi considers that it is completely inappropriate to

THE SEARCH FOR FORGIVENESS

make such resolve. To resolve not to sin amounts to 'being offensive to God' (*su'u adab ma'a allah*). There can be only three possibilities:

1. The repentant knows (because God has told him) that he is not going to commit sin again; in this case resolving not to sin is meaningless.
2. The repentant does not know, in which case, if God has decided that he will sin again, he would break the commitment he made with God.
3. The repentant knows (because God has told him) that he is going to commit sin again; in this case resolving not to sin amounts to being defiant and presumptuous.

In any case it is unfitting for the repentant to resolve not to commit the same sin. In fact, adds Ibn 'Arabi, such commitment shows complete ignorance. When one sins again, he does not commit the same sin, but a similar one, for God [*sic*] never repeats the same thing. If the repentant ought to resolve to do one thing, he should resolve that he would never attribute to himself an act that is not his own but God's. Thus repentance consists simply in (confessing) one's sin and (asking) God's forgiveness (*i'tiraf wa du'a'*). Ibn 'Arabi makes his point by quoting a hadith about a repentant person who commits sin for the third time. Knowing that God is a forgiving God as well as a just God, he confesses his sin and asks God's pardon. God forgives him each time, but after the third time he says to him, 'I have forgiven My servant [his sin], let him do whatever he likes'.[28] Ibn 'Arabi draws a parallel between these words and Qur'anic texts that give permission to Muslims to eat unlawful food (e.g. a dead animal) if they are compelled to do so by the lack of other food (5:3; 6:146; 16:115). He concludes that no evidence is found in God's 'revelation' (*shar'*) that repentance requires resolving not to sin any longer.[29]

What a blessed sin!

In order to support his understanding of repentance and sin Ibn 'Arabi refers to Adam. He says that the repentant is in the same position as Adam, and interprets Adam's thoughts after he disobeyed God's command with this line:

O my obedience, had you existed I would have been sorrowful!
O my disobedience, had you not existed I would not have been chosen!

Following his disobedience, all Adam did was to speak the words he received from God (2:37). These words represent a mere confession of sin: 'Our Lord! We [Adam and Eve] have wronged our own souls. If You do not forgive us and bestow Your mercy upon us, surely we shall be among the lost ones' (7:23; cf. 11:47; 23:109). Adam and Eve exposed their souls to 'ruin' (*talaf*) through their disobedience. In disobeying God's command not to eat from the tree, they failed to preserve their wholeness. God's response to their confession was to show them mercy and forgiveness: 'Subsequently his Lord chose him. He turned [in mercy] to him and guided him' (20:122). God's forgiveness of Adam's sin was part of Adam's election by God. God then guided Adam 'in showing him the right measure of what his act meant, the right measure of the reward he deserved [*sic*] and the right measure of the grace of his election'. It was God who turned to Adam; the Qur'an never says that Adam turned to God. Having turned mercifully to Adam, God commanded him to get down (20:123). This command did not amount to banishing him from paradise but to commissioning and appointing him as his representative (*hubut walaya wa istikhlaf la hubut tard*). So when Adam was moved from paradise to earth it was a 'change in location rather than a change in rank' (*hubut makan la hubut rutba*).[30]

Thus when we repent in response to God's call, we need only confess our sin and ask God to turn in mercy to us. It is right for us to do exactly what Adam did and not to commit ourselves with regard to the future. If we make any decision without knowing what God has in store for us, we expose ourselves to great danger. Far from undermining God's purpose for us, our disobedience fulfils this purpose. In fact, God has ordained our disobedience, which is nothing more than his own act accomplished through his servants. In this perspective sin cannot be thought of as sin, but only as a slip. It is only sin when it is falsely attributed, but even then what a blessed sin![31]

Repenting from repentance

In his long chapter on 'repentance' (*tawba*),[32] Ibn 'Arabi begins by
explaining that the repentance of 'ordinary people' (*al-'amma*)
consists in returning from what is in contradiction with God's law
to what is in accordance with it. As far as Sufis are concerned, their
repentance is one of three kinds: the beginners return to God from
themselves, the 'initiates' (*'arifun*) return to God from God, and the
spiritual leaders return to God from their return to God. Ibn
'Arabi's chapter concludes with a quotation of Ruwaym's celebrated
statement about repentance: 'The meaning of repentance is that you
should repent from repentance.'[33]

Ibn 'Arabi gives his own interpretation of this statement in the
subsequent chapter entitled 'Giving up repentance' (*tark al-tawba*).
He begins by referring to three Qur'anic texts. The first is about
God's presence being all around us: 'He is with you wherever you
go' (57:4). In the second, God reveals how close he is to his human
creatures: 'We are closer to him than his jugular vein' (50:16). In the
third, God declares that he is nearer the dying person than those
who are next to him: 'We are nearer to him than you are' (56:85).
Giving up repentance, he says, is giving up returning to God. But
first we must repent; we must return to God.

To repent is to return to God in order to receive his light. God
calls those who live in the darkness of their universe to seek his
light:

> A Day is coming when you will see believers, men and women, their
> light gleaming before them ... it is a Day when the hypocrites, men and
> women, say to the believers: 'Wait for us, and let us take from your
> light!' It will be said to them: *Go back yourselves and seek out your own light.*
> (57:12–13)[34]

To go back is to return to 'the One who caused people to exist'
(*al-mujid*). He is the Light that brings everything from darkness into
the light. When people see the Light, it will be disclosed to them
that God is closer to them than themselves (56:85). Once they
acquire spiritual knowledge through their encounter with the Light,
they realize that in fact it is God who returns to them. People are

just the place where 'the attribute of repenting manifests itself' (*mahall zuhur al-sifa*). Ibn 'Arabi points out that the divine name Tawwab (Most-Returning) is an intensive form, meaning that God is the author of the first return ('He turned to them') as well as the second return ('So that they may turn to Him'; cf. 9:118). He quotes a Qur'anic verse in support of this view. It reminds Muslims that their victory is actually God's victory because God was behind them when they fought their enemies: 'It was not you who slew them: it was God who slew them. When you made your throw, it was not yours but God's' (8:17).[35]

Thus, concludes Ibn 'Arabi, 'the one who returns does not return, but it is God who returns'. The Sufi community considers that 'the meaning of repentance is to give up repenting and to repent from repenting'. In a paradoxical way, to deny oneself the reality of returning is to assert it for God and to assert it for God is to deny it for oneself. To give up repenting for the Sufi means to disclaim repentance, and to repent from repentance is to claim that 'it is God who returns from Himself to Himself through Himself' (*al-ruju' minhu ilayhi bihi*). The completion of this return results in total 'transparency' (*khashf*) between God and the Sufi. No 'veil' (*hijab*) exists any longer between them. Ibn 'Arabi compares those who have completed their return to those who have returned to the 'home' (*mawtin*) where they were born. They are no longer exiled. The one who keeps returning home is not yet back home. He is still 'away' (*gha'ib*) and remains a 'stranger' (*gharib*). God loves them though as one loves those of his family when they come home, and he shares in their joy. In loving them, God loves himself, as is the case with the lover and his beloved. If the return aims at achieving union, the one who has returned home is already 'one with God' (*muttasil*). He does not seek this union. His 'love' (*mahabba*) and 'pleasure' (*ladhdha*) have reached a climax. This is what giving up repentance means, concludes Ibn 'Arabi.[36]

The return of the universe to God

What is the ultimate purpose of the universe? And what is its relationship to God? Ibn 'Arabi argues that the whole universe is in

the process of returning to God. All things go back to God, as the
Qur'an says: 'To God belong the secret things of the heavens and
the earth, the Great Act will entirely return to Him' (11:123). 'The
Great Act' (al-amr) is God moving forward throughout the
universe. The amr is exiled in 'those who are still veiled' (mahjubun).
They attribute to themselves what is God's. If they contemplated
the reality of things, they would realize that it is God who is
moving, not them. Will this universal process reach an end one
day? Ibn 'Arabi believes not. The Great Act will always be moving
on ever more because the 'Self-Existing One' (Wajib al-Wujud) is
boundless. He is by his very nature ever 'creating' (khallaq).
Therefore there is no end for the 'potential realities in God'
(mumkinat) to come into existence.[37]

God's self-revelation is available in his word. But the revelation
of his very self is through the emanation of the universe from
himself and its return to himself. Thus the universe is more than a
mirror in which God is reflected. It partakes of the divine essence.
Ibn 'Arabi quotes a (non-canonical) hadith in which the Prophet
says, 'He that knows his self knows his Lord.' It is worth noting
that the starting point for knowing God is within oneself, not in
God's revelation. God is immanent; he is not to be sought outside
ourselves:

> We are 'evidence for God' (dalil^{un} 'alayhi). We should not seek to know
> ourselves except in order to know God. If we forget this knowledge, we
> forget the knowledge about ourselves, and the knowledge about
> ourselves is the only way for us to know God ... *for He created us in the
> divine image* (khalaqana 'ala al-sura al-ilahiyya).[38]

Ibn 'Arabi quotes the same narrative in the chapter about *tajalli*
(theophany/God's self-manifestation). He relates it to a hadith and
to a Qur'anic text. The hadith is actually a prayer of the Prophet,
which ends with this request: 'O God! Let me be light'.[39] The
Qur'anic text is what is known as *ayat al-nur* (the verse about the
light):

> God is the Light of heavens and earth. The likeness of this light is a
> lamp set in a niche. The lamp is encased in glass; the glass, as it were, is

a glistening star. It is lighted from a blessed tree; the olive tree is
confined neither to the east nor to the west. Its oil is almost luminous
without the touch of fire. It is light upon light. God guides to this
light whom He will. God sets forth parables to people, for God knows
all things.

(24:35)

Ibn 'Arabi's comment on this much celebrated verse among the
Sufis is very significant. He highlights the likeness between God
and man. This likeness reflects a deeper reality: God and human
beings are of the same essence. The divine light radiates throughout the entire universe. Man is a microcosm of God, illuminated by
him as the cosmos is illuminated by the sun:

> You are in yourself both the reality and the parable of that reality. You
> witness the lights pouring out from within you so as to illuminate the
> universe of your heavens and earth. You do not need to use an alien
> light, for you are the lamp and the wick and the niche and the glass. If
> you know that, you know the oil – which is the divine sap – and the
> tree. If the glass is like the glistening star, which is the sun, what should
> be the lamp if not your very self. Hence, my brother, in your prayer you
> should always ask God to let you be light.[40]

The purpose of *tawba* is ultimately for people to return to God in
order to rescue their true identity. This identity is not different
from God's identity. The human self is the emanation of the divine
self. There is only one Being: God. He is 'the Truth' (al-Ḥaqq),
manifested in and through 'the plain reality' (*al-ẓahir*) and concealed
in 'the hidden reality' (*al-batin*). For Ibn 'Arabi, the fact that God is
immanent means that when he refers to the hadith which says that
'God created Adam in His own image', the emphasis is on the
noun 'image', rather than the verb, 'created'.[41] However, Ibn 'Arabi
does quote the Qur'anic text 'there is nothing whatever like unto
God' (42:11). He maintains, at least in theory, God's transcendence
as well as his immanence. He asserts that God revealed himself
in the Qur'an and the Sunna (Prophetic Tradition) in 'two conflicting ways' (*bil-naqidayn*). The first (his immanence) is *tashbih*
(anthropomorphism/assimilation); that is, ascribing to God what

characterizes his creatures. The second (his transcendence) is *tanzih*, which consists precisely in dissociating God from any attributes that apply to his creatures.[42]

Ibn 'Arabi is known by his disciples as *al-shaykh al-akbar*, 'the great spiritual master'. He is undoubtedly more than a great Sufi. In his doctrines, mysticism and philosophy blend to form what might be called 'a mystical philosophy'. At the heart of this thinking is the belief known as *wahdat al-wujud* (the oneness of being) or monism (God and the universe partake in the same reality). So does this belief represent a radical shift from monotheism (God is one) towards pantheism (God and the universe are identical)? Or does God's transcendence and his being a personal God still have real meaning in Ibn 'Arabi teaching? In the latter case, his doctrine would be best described, as Corbin puts it, as 'theomonism' (God and the universe are one) or 'panentheism' (God is in everything in the universe):

> The pair Creator-created (*haqq-khalq*) is repeated at all levels of theophany and at all stages of the 'descent of being'. This is neither monism nor pantheism; rather, it can be called theomonism and panentheism. Theomonism is no more than the philosophical expression of interdependence of Creator and created – interdependence, that is, on the level of theophany.[43]

Notes

1. According to the Hadith, the first sura, *al-Fatiha*, is the greatest sura in the Qur'an (Bukhari, *fada'il al-qur'an* 9 [4622]:VI, bk 61, no. 528, p. 489).

2. Ibn 'Arabi, *Futuhat*, III, p. 551. Cf. Muslim, *tawba* 14 [4039]:IV, bk 37, no. 6626, p. 1437; Bukhari, *tawhid* 15 [6855]:IX, bk 93, no. 501, p. 369. One may remark that sura 1 verse 7 refers to people who are under God's wrath. However, Muslims ask God to lead them on the path of those who have been blessed, *not* of those who are the object of God's displeasure.

3. Ibn 'Arabi, *Futuhat*, III, pp. 550–551.

4. Ibid., IV, p. 163 (cf. III, p. 552). In Arabic: *aba allah illa shumul al-rahma*.

5. Bukhari, *tawhid* 2 [6829], 25 [6894]:IX, bk 93, no. 474, p. 351; no. 540, p. 407; Muslim, *jana'iz* 11 [1531]: II, bk 4, no. 2008, p. 438; Abu Dawud,

jana'iz 28 [2718]:II, bk 14, no. 3119, p. 890; Ibn Majah, *jana'iz* 53 [1577]:II, bk 6, no. 1588, p. 406; Tirmidhi, *birr* 16 [1847].

6. Ibn 'Arabi, *Futuhat*, III, pp. 551–552.

7. To appreciate Ibn 'Arabi's argument fully, one needs to know that the Arabic verb *batasha*, 'to hit' or 'to strike', could also mean 'to attack', 'to aggress', 'to punish', and (as it is the case here) 'to create'.

8. Ibn 'Arabi, *Futuhat*, III, p. 553.

9. Ibid., p. 552.

10. Ibid., IV, pp. 303–304.

11. In Arabic: *baqiya 'alayhim hukmu al-zaman alladhi la nihayata li-abadihi*. What Ibn 'Arabi means by this expression is explained later.

12. Ibn 'Arabi, *Futuhat*, IV, p. 119.

13. Ibid.

14. Ibid., p. 120.

15. Ibid., p. 137.

16. Ibid., I, p. 244. In this quote the Arabic word for 'the Prophet' is 'the Hashimite', as Muhammad was from the clan of Banu Hashim of the Quraysh tribe. Cf. Chodkiewicz, *Seal*, ch. 9, 'The seal of Muhammadan sainthood', pp. 128–146.

17. Ibn 'Arabi, *Futuhat*, II, p. 49; cf. I, pp. 151, 185; cf. Chodkiewicz, *Seal*, ch. 8, 'The three seals', pp. 116–127.

18. Ibn 'Arabi, *Futuhat*, IV, p. 163.

19. The remaining part of this section is based on *Futuhat*, II, pp. 138–139.

20. Bukhari, *anbiya'* 1 [3092]:IV, bk 55, no. 556, p. 350; Abu Dawud, *sunna* 14 [4053]:III, bk 35, no. 4656, p. 1310; Tirmidhi, *qiyama* 9 [2358], *tafsir* sura 17 [3073], *manaqib* 1 [3548].

21. Ibn 'Arabi's version of this hadith has it that Muhammad was asked, 'When did you become prophet?' He replied, 'I was made prophet when Adam was still *in the form of water and clay*', *bayna l-ma'i wa-l-tini* (see *Futuhat*, I, pp. 151, 243; III, p. 497). The canonical version of this hadith is slightly different. It does not refer explicitly to Muhammad's pre-existence but to his appointment as prophet. He was asked, 'When was prophethood assigned to you?' He answered, 'When Adam was still *in the form of spirit and body*', *bayna l-ruhi wa-l-jasadi* (Tirmidhi, *manaqib* 1 [3542]). Muhammad's primordial existence is known as *al-haqiqa al-muhammadiyya*, 'the Muhammadan truth' (see Chodkiewicz, *Seal*, ch. 4, 'The Muhammadan reality', pp. 60–73; Schimmel, *Messenger*, ch. 7, 'The light of Muhammad', pp. 123–143).

22. Bukhari, *isti'dhan* 1 [5759]:VIII, bk 74, no. 246, p. 160; Muslim, *birr* 115 [4731]:IV, bk 32, no. 6325, p. 1378; *janna* 28 [5075]:IV, bk 40, no. 6809, p. 1421.

23. Ibn 'Arabi, *Futuhat*, II, p. 139.

24. Abu Dawud, *witr* 23 [1273]:I, bk 2, no. 1483, p. 389; Ibn Majah, *du'a'* 13 [3855]:V, bk 34, no. 3865, p. 227; Tirmidhi, *da'awat* 104 [3479].

25. Ibn 'Arabi, *Futuhat*, II, pp. 139–140.

26. Ibid., p. 140; cf. p. 342.

27. Ibid., p. 141.

28. Bukhari, *tawhid* 35 [6953]:IX, bk 93, no. 598, p. 440; Muslim, *tawba* 29 [4953]:IV, bk 37, no. 6642, p. 1439. This hadith is reproduced in full in chapter 2, p. 40.

29. Ibn 'Arabi, *Futuhat*, II, p. 142. Ibn Hanbal reports the following definition of sin given by the Prophet: 'Repentance is to repent from sin and not to commit it again' (Ibn Hanbal, *musnad al-mukthirin* 1 [4043]). It is true, however, that this saying does not specify that the repentant must *resolve* not to commit the sin he repented from.

30. Ibn 'Arabi, *Futuhat*, II, p. 141.

31. Ibid., p. 142.

32. Ibid., pp. 139–143.

33. Kalabadhi, *Doctrine*, p. 83; *Ta'arruf*, p. 93; Sarraj, *Luma'*, p. 68; Suhrawardi, *'Awarif*, p. 487.

34. The text is reminiscent of the parable of the ten virgins in the Gospel of Matthew (Matt. 25:1–13).

35. Ibn 'Arabi, *Futuhat*, II, p. 144; cf. p. 142.

36. Ibid., p. 144.

37. Ibid.

38. Ibid., III, p. 553; my italics.

39. The canonical version of this prayer is, 'O God! Place light in my heart, light in my hearing, light in my sight, light on my right, light on my left, light in the front of me, light behind me, light above me, light below me, make light for me'; or he said, 'Make me light!' (Muslim, *musafirin* 191 [1279]:I, bk 4, no. 1677, p. 370). Whether the Prophet really said 'Make me light!' is a debated issue. One variant of the same hadith has it that he said 'Make me light!' *beyond any doubt* (no. 1678), but according to another variant *he made no mention of* 'Make me light!' (no. 1679). See also Bukhari, *da'awat* 10 [5841]:VIII, bk 75, no. 328, p. 220; Tirmidhi, *da'awat* 30 [3341]; Nasa'i, *tatbiq* 63 [1109].

40. Ibn 'Arabi, *Futuḥat*, II, p. 448.
41. Ibid., I, p. 107; II, p. 139.
42. Ibid., I, p. 290; II, p. 3.
43. Corbin, *History*, pp. 294–295.

16. IBN 'ARABI: A CHRISTIAN PERSPECTIVE

Divine mercy is the cornerstone of Ibn 'Arabi's thought. It is much more than a divine attribute. For him, it is the divine essence, defining the reality of the cosmos. It determines God's relationships with the universe as a whole and with individual beings in particular. It is also the core message God commissioned his servants to convey to humankind. According to Ibn 'Arabi, the people who manifest the most divine mercy are the Prophet Muhammad (21:107), and Jesus Christ, 'the Seal of sainthood'. Ibn 'Arabi sees himself as the spiritual heir of both the Prophet and the Christ. Moreover, he interprets mercy as a paradigm of the ultimate reality:

> Allah, then, is neither merciful in the usual sense of a personal benevolence, nor is His mercy simply a manifestation of a personal emotion. It seems, rather, that His mercy here is a metaphysical entity the main purpose of which is to impart various kinds of existence to the variety of existing things; it constitutes a more basic and integral part of His nature than His wrath, not because He is more kind than cruel – this formulation would be within the boundaries of the conventional

meanings which now have been transcended – but because His mercy has the highest ontological status as existence-giver to all things, His wrath included.[1]

In the context of God's mercy Ibn 'Arabi often refers to God's boundless favour (2:105), his love, his generosity and his pardon. God's mercy is the all-embracing reality, manifesting itself in all these forms. It is the divine light overflowing into the world and breaking up into the colours of the rainbow. In chapter 1 I suggested that love is the Christian equivalent to God's mercy in Islam: 'God is love. Whoever lives in love lives in God, and God in him' (1 John 4:16). One of Ibn 'Arabi's expert and loyal disciples goes a step further by suggesting an alternative translation of the Arabic word:

> *Rahma* should be translated, in the context of *Futuhat*, by 'love' rather than 'mercy' as it is usually done. The universe is born out of *rahma*; it is formed in 'the Breath of the *Rahman*'; it is sustained by it and it returns to it. Hence Ibn 'Arabi's rejection of punishment as an endless punishment.[2]

Mercy and grace

Mercy in Ibn 'Arabi's doctrine includes both *universal mercy* and *specific mercy*. These two categories of mercy are paralleled in Christian theology by what is known as *general grace* (or common grace) and *special grace* (or saving grace). The meanings of these two words, mercy and grace, are similar. Perhaps mercy points more to God's goodness towards us, whereas grace speaks more of his sovereignty in dealing with us. Both refer to God's initiative in meeting our needs. The blessings we receive from him represent free and undeserved gifts.

Universal mercy (as defined by Ibn 'Arabi) and general grace (in Christian teaching) have in common that God's favour is bestowed upon all of us regardless of who we are and irrespective of our religious beliefs. There are, however, major differences between the two concepts. Universal mercy is a saving mercy. It enables

Muslims to live up to their faith in this world. It will also put an end
to the punishment of sinful Muslims and non-Muslims in the world
to come. General grace, by contrast, is not a saving grace. It is
displayed through temporal goods (both material and spiritual)
granted by God to humankind (e.g. his ongoing care for his
creation, sustaining it, upholding it and preserving it from chaos)
and the awareness he has given us of many of his moral standards:

	In this life	In the life to come
Ibn 'Arabi	**Universal mercy** Obedient Muslims are enabled to believe in God and obey his commands.	**Universal mercy** Punishment will come to an end for sinful Muslims and non-Muslims. Some will go to paradise. Others will remain in hell, which will become a place of happiness. **Specific mercy** Obedient Muslims receive a reward from God.
Christian teaching	**General grace** All people (both Christians and non-Christians) receive blessings from God. **Special grace** God leads people to turn to him in faith, assures them of his forgiveness, and enables them to live for him.	**Special grace** Believers enjoy eternal life in God's presence.

Table 16. Categories of mercy and grace according to Ibn 'Arabi and
Christian teaching

> God has not left himself without testimony: He has shown kindness by giving them rain from heaven and crops in their seasons; he provides them with plenty of food and fills their heart with joy.
> (Acts 14:17)

> He causes his sun to rise on the evil and the good, and sends rain on the righteous and the unrighteous.
> (Matt. 5:45)

Special grace is all about God's saving action, leading his people to have faith in him and empowering them 'to do [the] good works, which God prepared in advance for us to do' (Eph. 2:10). As a result of their faith, believers will go to heaven, unlike non-believers who will endure eternal punishment. To a certain degree this grace corresponds to God's mercy towards Muslims in this life (universal mercy) as well as in the hereafter (specific mercy). Table 16 compares Ibn ʿArabi's understanding of God's mercy with Christian teaching as regards the recipients of this mercy.

Temporary punishment

Ibn ʿArabi's doctrine of temporary punishment in hell for sinful Muslims and non-Muslims does not represent mainstream Islamic teaching. We have seen that Muʿtazili theologians believe in the eternity of hell (for sinful Muslims and non-Muslims) and the eternity of paradise (for righteous Muslims). Sunni theologians, however, teach that hell is temporary for sinful Muslims only, and that all Muslims will eventually go to paradise. Thus all Muslim theologians agree that non-Muslims will be in hell for ever. Traditional Christian teaching is more in line with mainline Islamic doctrine. It is true that some Christians in the past and many Christians today adhere to 'universalism',[3] a belief according to which all people from all religions (or none) will eventually be saved.[4] Nevertheless, the doctrine of eternal punishment is still part of the official teaching of the church and is accepted by most Christians. The majority understand this punishment in the sense of an unending suffering in hell, while some interpret it as the final destruction of the unrighteous that will end their pain in hell.[5]

Ibn 'Arabi	Mu'tazili	Sunni	Christian
Temporary punishment for both sinful Muslims and non-Muslims.	Eternal punishment for both sinful Muslims and non-Muslims.	Temporary punishment for sinful Muslims, before entering paradise.	Eternal punishment for unbelievers.
Monotheists will eventually go to paradise.		Eternal punishment for non-Muslims.	
Non-monotheists will remain in hell – but it will become a place of happiness.			

Table 17. Different views on eternal and temporary punishment

It has already been noted that Ibn 'Arabi's doctrine on temporary punishment is based on his understanding of divine mercy, which rules out the possibility of eternal punishment. Jesus, whose teaching and life were a powerful demonstration of God's love, speaks clearly about eternal punishment. He describes 'the blasphemy against the Holy Spirit' (see chapter 7) as 'an eternal sin'. Anyone who commits this sin, he says, 'will not be forgiven, either in this age or in the age to come' (Matt. 12:32; cf. Mark 3:29). Jesus compares 'eternal punishment' with 'eternal life' (Matt. 25:46). He uses metaphors to illustrate the endless duration of punishment: 'eternal fire' (Matt. 18:8; 25:41), 'unquenchable fire' (Matt. 3:12) and undying worm (Mark 9:48). In doing so he alludes to the prophet

Isaiah and his vision of God's new creation. God's people will enjoy eternal life in God's presence; they will also witness the dreadful punishment of the unrighteous:

> 'As the new heavens and the new earth that I make will endure before me,' declares the LORD, 'so will your name and descendants endure.
> From one New Moon to another and from one Sabbath to another, all mankind will come and bow down before me,' says the LORD. 'And they will go out and look upon the dead bodies of those who rebelled against me; their worm will not die, nor will their fire be quenched, and they will be loathsome to all mankind.'
> (Is. 66:22–24)

Ibn ʿArabi's eschatology appears to be at odds with the teaching of the Bible as well as the Qur'an, not only because he considers punishment to be limited in duration. His doctrine is unconventional on other grounds. For him punishment in hell is temporary, yet hell is eternal. Hell will not be destroyed but will cease to be a place of damnation. It will become a place of enduring happiness, separate from paradise and having a different form of happiness. People in hell will be different in nature from those in paradise. Since they have been created from 'fire', hell will be their 'home'.

God's sovereign purpose

Thus Ibn ʿArabi's personal eschatology is based on his peculiar anthropology, which in turn is rooted in his distinctive theology. God's sovereignty means that it is God who 'produces' everything in the world. He creates people as well as their acts. Hence, Ibn ʿArabi's belief in 'double predestination': God formed monotheistic people to send them to paradise just as he did non-monotheistic people to send them to hell (92:5–10). This deterministic vision of the cosmos is consistent with Ibn ʿArabi's theory of sin and repentance. For him, sin is just 'a slip'; that is, an act that derives from God and is falsely attributed to man. It is therefore not an evil act. To repent is to give up sin, which means denying that sin is an evil act. To repent is also to regret one's misconception about the real consequence of sin. Sin does not lead away from God (as one may mistakenly think); it leads back to God.

More importantly, Ibn 'Arabi's interpretation of God's oneness, combined with God's sovereignty, results in seeing the world as proceeding from God rather than created by him. From this perspective repentance is understood as people coming back home from their exile in the cosmos to their divine origin. Their spiritual journey is completed when they become who they are: God's servants. This implies the annihilation of self, not just total submission to God as in traditional Islam:

> In Ibn 'Arabi's eyes the state of *'ubudiyya* [servitude] surpasses all others. It is the state every disciple must aspire to and the goal of spiritual realisation, because it represents the return to the original state: to the ontological nothingness of the creature or created being. Whoever has realised *'ubudiyya* or servitude has stripped himself of *rububiyya*, of the 'Lordship' which really belongs to God alone but which ordinary men in their arrogance claim for themselves.[6]

God: transcendent or immanent?

Although Ibn 'Arabi wants to maintain the tension between God's transcendence and immanence, his cosmology clearly portrays God as an immanent God, perhaps in reaction to the exclusively transcendent God in Islamic theology. By contrast, in the Bible God is depicted as both transcendent and immanent. The first verse declares that 'In the beginning God created the heavens and the earth' (Gen. 1:1). Thus, right from the start, the emphasis is laid on God as the Creator (and therefore the transcendent) God. Diversity, hence 'otherness' within God's creation, is stressed by the fact that every creature was made according to its own kind (Gen. 1:11, 12, 20, 24, 25). Every creature is unique.

The creation of humankind comes as God's final and crowning act:

> God created man
>   in his own image,

in the image of God
   he created him;
male and female
   he created them.
(Gen. 1:27)

The emphasis in this verse is twofold: on the one hand, we have the verb 'create' three times, which underlines God's otherness vis-à-vis his human creatures; on the other hand, the repetition of the word 'image' highlights that, although God and his human creatures are radically different in nature, we do reflect his character.[7] Moreover, there is a unique and special relationship between us and God. Thus, while the verb 'create' points to God's transcendence, the noun 'image' indicates his immanence; that is, his likeness to us, or our resemblance to him. The fact that only human beings have been created in God's image establishes the uniqueness, the privilege and the dignity of humankind. The distinct identity of man and woman as human creatures (both created in God's image) is also worth noting. Sexual differentiation is part of human identity. In this sense sexual distinctiveness is far more fundamental to our identity than any other human attribute, including ethnic and cultural characteristics.

It is significant that the Qurʾan does not refer to the creation of humankind in God's image. We do find in the Hadith, however, a narrative reporting that 'God created Adam in his image'.[8] Ibn ʿArabi's spiritual interpretation of this saying highlights God's immanence in a way opposite to what Muslim theologians have suggested.[9] Islamic theology understands God's transcendence in terms that rule out the possibility of his being immanent as well as transcendent (42:11). For Ibn ʿArabi, the cosmos represents more the disclosure of God than his creation.

Sin: a blessing in disguise?
The implications of Ibn ʿArabi's 'theomonism' are considerable, especially with regard to his understanding of sin as essentially a divine act. Sin is neither a transgression of God's law (as in the Qurʾan and the Bible) nor a morally evil act. Such a concept of sin seriously undermines its gravity and the moral responsibility of the

sinner. The very concept of good and evil is blurred. God's holiness and condemnation of evil become inconsistent.

Ibn 'Arabi's interpretation of Adam's banishment from paradise as a commissioning act whereby God appointed him as his representative on earth contradicts the plain meaning of the Qur'anic text (2:38; 20:123). The biblical text also leaves us with no doubt as to the consequence of Adam's disobedience and the punishment he deserved. God had warned Adam that he would certainly die if he disobeyed God (Gen. 2:15–17). Adam did disobey and God confirmed to him that he would indeed die (3:19). Death is both the result of and the penalty for his sin. His physical death points to his spiritual death; that is, his spiritual separation from God. Yet, at the same time, God promised Adam and Eve that he would one day send a Saviour who would defeat evil, though not without being personally wounded (Gen. 3:15). Jesus' atoning death on the cross represents his costly victory over sin and evil. Through his triumphant resurrection he conquered death and liberated humankind from its tyranny. Jesus' mission demonstrates God's sovereign power over evil, but in no way does God's sovereignty excuse us or diminish our responsibility: 'where sin increased, grace increased all the more, so that, just as sin reigned in death, so also grace might reign through righteousness to bring eternal life through Jesus Christ our Lord' (Rom. 5:20–21).

The words Ibn 'Arabi puts in Adam's mouth implies that Adam's disobedience, and sin in general, is an integral part of God's generous purpose for humankind. In this perspective sin is associated not with guilt but with thankfulness for what God has achieved for us in dealing with sin. Ibn 'Arabi's understanding of sin as the means by which God fulfils his grand plan is not without parallel in Christian theology. In fact, a Christian scholar contemporary to Ibn 'Arabi, expressed a similar thought:

But *why did God not prevent man from sinning*? [...] St Thomas Aquinas wrote, 'There is nothing to prevent human nature's being raised up to something greater, even after sin; God permits evil in order to draw forth some greater good. Thus St Paul says, "Where sin increased, grace abounded all the more"; and the *Exsultet* sings, "O happy fault ... which gained for us so great a Redeemer!"'[10]

The teaching of the Bible does not go that far. Sin does not represent a blessing in disguise. The sovereign God overcame sin and became our Saviour, but this is no excuse for us. Sin provides no reason for rejoicing whatsoever. Otherwise, sin would be justified and its outrageous character minimized. Just because Adam was free, it does not explain why he made the wrong choice in disobeying his loving Creator. He could and he should have remained in trusting fellowship with his Lord. The rise of evil in a world God declared 'good' (Gen. 1:25) will always defy our understanding. It is an intractable enigma that finds no satisfactory answer. It is precisely because evil is rationally inexplicable that it is morally unjustifiable. It ought to raise our deepest indignation and call for our radical opposition (Rom. 12:9) as it does for God (Hab. 1:13). The fact that God in his great wisdom and power defeated evil, and in doing so brought us a greater blessing, does not make evil less evil or more acceptable (Is. 5:20).[11]

Jesus and Muhammad

Muhammad is described in the Qur'an as 'the Seal of the prophets' (33:40), but for Ibn 'Arabi he is much more than that:

1. Muhammad is, in a sense, *God's only messenger*. All other prophets are Muhammad's deputies or representatives.
2. Muhammad is *God's universal messenger* whose mission, characterized by mercy (21:107), is to convey God's pardon to humankind.
3. Muhammad is the *head of humanity*; his existence predates that of Adam, although his historical 'incarnation' took place in the sixth century AD.

Jesus too has a very high and special status in Ibn 'Arabi's thought. He is 'the Seal of universal sainthood' just as Ibn 'Arabi himself is 'the Seal of the Muhammadan sainthood'. Ibn 'Arabi declares that he was converted to God through Jesus. Ever since his *tawba* (conversion) he was under the care of his first spiritual master: '[He is] our first *shaykh* who converted us, keeps

caring for us and does not neglect us not even an hour.'[12] Ibn
'Arabi describes Jesus as God's faithful servant who is alive in
heaven and continues to be involved in the lives of those who seek
God:

> [While on earth] Jesus was an ascetic apostle and a traveller. He was
> faithful to what God entrusted to him and he delivered his message
> truthfully. Yet the Jews made him their enemy, but never was he blamed
> by God. I had many encounters with him in my visions; it is he who
> converted me and he prayed for me that I may persevere in religion in
> this world and the next. He called me 'the beloved one' (al-habib) and
> he commanded me to practise asceticism (zuhd) and deprivation
> (tajrid).[13]

Ibn 'Arabi is fascinated by what the Qur'an says about Jesus. In
his book *Fusus al-hikam*, the chapter devoted to Jesus points out
his Qur'anic title 'Word of God' (4:171).[14] He starts the chapter
with a poem, highlighting Jesus' extraordinary birth from the
Virgin Mary (21:91). The poem also describes Jesus as 'the Spirit
of God', another title the Qur'an reserves for Jesus (4:171).
Finally, the poem depicts Jesus as having such a relationship with
God that he is a life-giver, like God, when he raises the dead (3:49;
5:110).[15]

Ibn 'Arabi's rich and admirable meditation on the Qur'anic
portrait of Jesus emphasizes Jesus' uniqueness. Yet this portrait of
'Isa bin Maryam falls short of the one we find in the Gospels. In fact,
it remains typically Islamic; for example Jesus was rescued by God
when his life was threatened by his opponents, he was lifted up by
God and will come back at the end time to enforce Islamic law on
earth.[16] There is nothing in Ibn 'Arabi's writings which suggests
that he knew first hand what the Bible says about Jesus. We find no
quote from the Gospels or any specific reference to Jesus' teaching.

More than a prophet
In more than one respect Ibn 'Arabi's portrait of Muhammad is
reminiscent of what the Gospels say about Jesus. The Gospel of
John depicts Jesus as the Logos, 'the Word [of God]', whose
existence predates the creation of the world, and who was God's

agent in creating the universe. The pre-existent Word of God was manifested historically in the person of Jesus Christ:

> In the beginning was the Word, and the Word was with God, and the Word was God. He was with God in the beginning.
>
>   Through him all things were made; without him nothing was made that has been made. In him was life, and that life was the light of men. The light shines in the darkness, but the darkness has not understood it ...
>
>   The Word became flesh and made his dwelling among us. We have seen his glory, the glory of the One and Only, who came from the Father, full of grace and truth.
>
> (John 1:1–5, 14)

As God's Word, Jesus is more than God's *messenger*; he is God's *message*. Whereas in Ibn ʿArabi's thought God manifests himself *in the world*, in the Bible Jesus Christ is the incarnation of God *in one unique person*. He is the full revelation of God's love and God's qualified agent in granting pardon to humankind. His credentials are not only his sinlessness, but also the fact that he offered his life as a sacrifice for sin to save the world: 'God made him who had no sin to be a sin offering for us, so that in him we might become the righteousness of God' (2 Cor. 5:21).

Jesus represents God's self-disclosure. Ibn ʿArabi's teaching on Muhammad is based on his non-conventional interpretation of the Qur'an and the Hadith, which assumes that the text has a 'hidden meaning' (*maʿna batin*). The Christian doctrine about Jesus is founded on the plain meaning of Scriptures. In the Gospels Jesus makes claims that no other prophet, including Muhammad, ever dared to make. One of these claims is that he and God are perfectly united: 'Anyone who has seen me has seen the Father ... believe me when I say that I am in the Father and the Father is in me; or at least believe on the evidence of the miracles themselves' (John 14:9–11).

Love, lordship and humble service

God's love is a key motive in Sufism in general and in Ibn ʿArabi's thought in particular. ʿAbdullah al-Qurayshi defines love in these terms: 'Genuine love is that you give yourself entirely to the one you love and that you keep nothing for yourself'.[17] Jesus Christ demonstrated God's love for us in this way. Because we were created in God's image, it was possible for God to reveal himself in human form; and having become a man, to give his life for us through his death. God's incarnation in Christ does not undermine his transcendence. Because God in Christianity is the Trinitarian God, it was the *Father* who sent Jesus to the world. The *Son* took upon himself our humanity without giving up or compromising his divinity. Likewise, the *Holy Spirit* unites believers to God in a way that neither deifies man nor humanizes God.

God's self-disclosure in Christ reveals the transcendent God as the loving and forgiving God. We now know him in a way that no human being would ever have imagined. The Lord of lords and King of kings became the servant of his human creatures. He humbled himself and became one of us. In doing so he taught us what divine, true lordship means: serving one's people. Ibn 'Arabi quotes a hadith that perfectly illustrates God's mission through Jesus: 'The leader of a people is their servant.'[18] God's self-humbling in Jesus Christ did not result in the Father stripping Jesus of his lordship once and for all. On the contrary, Jesus' lordship as the Creator was reinforced when he became the Redeemer of humankind. Because of his humble and costly service, he was exalted by God the Father who made him the Lord and Saviour of the world:

[Jesus Christ], being in very nature God,
    did not consider equality with God something to be grasped,
but made himself nothing,
    taking the very nature of a servant,
    being made in human likeness.
And being found in appearance as a man,
    he humbled himself
    and became obedient to death – even death on a cross!
Therefore God exalted him to the highest place
    and gave him the name that is above every name,
that at the name of Jesus every knee should bow,
    in heaven and on earth and under the earth,

and every tongue confess that Jesus Christ is Lord,
  to the glory of God the Father.
(Phil. 2:6–11; my italics)

It is not God's purpose for his servants to return to 'the ontological nothingness of the creature' (see p. 260). He wants to honour us and to share his glory with us. He loves us, calls us to himself, and adopts us as his most loved sons and daughters.

Notes

1. Nettler, 'Notion', p. 224.
2. Chodkiewicz, *Illuminations*, p. 72 (my translation). *Futuḥat* refers to Ibn ʿArabi's major work *al-Futuḥat al-makkiyya*.
3. In the early church Christians who professed the doctrine of *apokatastasis*, or 'universal restoration', include Clement of Alexandria (150–215), his disciple Origen (185–254) and Gregory of Nyssa (330–95).
4. Throughout history the Christian church has never accepted the belief about universal salvation of humankind. Today, however, there is a growing number of Christian theologians (Catholic, Orthodox and Protestant) who distance themselves from the teaching of the church and advocate this view. The main texts commonly used to support this belief are John 12:32; Romans 5:18; 11:32; 1 Corinthians 15:22, 28; Ephesians 1:9–10; Philippians 2:10; Colossians 1:20; 1 Timothy 2:4; 4:10; Titus 2:11; 2 Peter 3:9.
5. See Evangelical Alliance Commission, *Nature of Hell*. This document sums up the current debate among evangelical Christians about the meaning of eternal punishment. While evangelical Christians do not adhere to universalism, they differ on 'whether hell is eternal in *duration* or *effect* – i.e. whether an individual's punishment in hell will literally go on "for ever", as a ceaseless conscious experience, or whether it will end in a destruction which will be "for ever", in the sense of being final and irreversible' (p. 132).
6. Addas, *Quest*, pp. 61–62. Ibn ʿArabi believed that he achieved this state of servitude better than anyone else: 'There is in fact no-one who to my knowledge has realised the station of servitude (*maqam al-ʿubudiyya*) better than I have, and if such a being exists he can scarcely be more than my

equal because I have attained to the plenitude of servitude. I am the Pure and Authentic Servant; I have not the slightest aspiration to sovereignty (*rububiyya*).' Ibn 'Arabi, *Futuhat*, III, p. 41, cited in Addas, *Quest*, p. 120.

7. The Hebrew text actually has two different words for 'image', but their meaning is very similar.

8. Bukhari, *isti'dhan* 1 [5759]:VIII, bk 74, no. 246, p. 160; Muslim, *janna* 28 [5075]:IV, bk 40, no. 6809, p. 1421; *birr* 115 [4731]:IV, bk 32, no. 6325, p. 1378.

9. See Moucarry, *Faith to Faith*, pp. 84–88.

10. *Catechism*, p. 93, para. 412 (italics original). St Thomas is one of the leading Christian theologians (1225–1274). His *Summa theologiae* develops a Christian theology based on Aristotelian philosophy. In Christian liturgy the *Exsultet* is a song of praise, sung on the Saturday before Easter, that exalts Christ as the Saviour.

11. See Blocher, *Evil and the Cross*, pp. 128–133.

12. Ibn 'Arabi, *Futuhat*, III, p. 341; cf. p. 49, IV, p. 77.

13. Ibid., II, p. 49.

14. Ibn 'Arabi, *Fusus al-hikam*. The chapter on Jesus, 'Isa, is entitled *Fass hikma nabawiyya fi kalima 'isawiyya*, 'The bezel of wisdom of the prophecy in Jesus' word'.

15. See D'Souza, 'Jesus'; Singh, 'Jesus'.

16. Ibn 'Arabi, *Futuhat*, I, p. 150; III, p. 341.

17. Suhrawardi, *'Awarif*, p. 507.

18. *Sayyidu l-qawmi khadimuhum*. This non-canonical hadith is quoted by Ibn 'Arabi as follows: 'The servant of a people is their leader. The person who through his service demonstrates his lordship is indeed a perfectly dedicated servant' (Ibn 'Arabi, *Futuhat*, I, p. 244).

PART FOUR

FORGIVENESS
IN ETHICS

17. FORGIVENESS AND PENAL LAW

God's law governs the Muslim community. It is all embracing, regulating not only the relationship between God and humankind, but also the relationships common to every society. Thus Islamic law is as much a religious and moral law as a social, political and criminal law. This chapter will examine the issue of forgiveness and penal law. Is it possible to reconcile pardon and punishment in the area of criminal justice? Because God is both merciful and just, his law is expected to reflect these attributes. So how does his mercy impinge on his justice in the case of a criminal offence? Muslims too are expected to show mercy to each other. How can they act mercifully when a crime has been committed against them? This chapter will address these questions by looking at five transgressions of God's law: apostasy, murder, adultery, theft and slander. For each of these crimes Islamic law requires a 'legal punishment' (*hadd*). But what happens if those who have committed these offences repent? Should they still be punished or should their punishment be lifted?

Apostasy

We noted in the chapter on sin that 'unbelief' (*kufr*) is seen by all Muslims as the most serious sin people can ever commit. Unbelief takes many forms: polytheism, not acknowledging Muhammad as God's prophet, committing an act of idolatry, or blasphemy. The Qur'an relates how the Israelites committed an incredible act of disobedience just after God delivered them from Pharaoh's oppression. While Moses was away on the mountain receiving God's law, they made an idol in the form of a golden calf. This idolatry provoked God's anger. Moses too was outraged by the conduct of his people. God's response was twofold: pardon and punishment. According to the Qur'an, he commissioned Moses to call his people to repent *and* to kill each other:

> We had Moses with us [on the mountain] for forty nights. In his absence you took up the calf and worshipped it, thus committing evil. Yet after that We pardoned you so that you will give thanks.
>
> Moses said to his people: 'You have wronged yourselves, my people, in worshipping the calf. Turn [in repentance] to your Maker and slay yourselves. That will be best for you in His sight'. And He turned to you [in mercy], for He is Most-Returning and All-Merciful.
> (2:51, 52, 54; cf. 7:149–151)

Razi explains that God showed his favour to the Israelites (2:47) by forgiving their idolatrous act. He told them how to escape its consequences (eternal punishment): they must repent and slay themselves. Why did God command them to kill each other? Paradoxical as it may sound, the answer is this: to show that their repentance was genuine they had to accept the punishment they deserved; that is, the death penalty. God also bestowed his favour on the Israelites by letting them survive as a nation. According to some accounts, the number killed was seventy thousand. Therefore all the survivors, who were spared God's judgment, experienced his mercy.[1]

This episode demonstrates that unbelief is so great a sin that only death can be an adequate punishment. When a Muslim turns his back on Islam, he commits 'apostasy' (*radda*), which is arguably the most abhorrent form of unbelief in Islamic law. The penalty for the 'apostate' (*murtadd*) is capital punishment. The Qur'an tells us that God will not forgive those who, having embraced Islam, revert to unbelief (4:137; cf. 2:217; 3:86; 5:57). On the Day of Judgment they will receive eternal punishment. The legal penalty for apostasy is found not in the Qur'an but in the Hadith. Several sayings attributed to the Prophet require the death penalty for Muslim renegades: 'He that leaves Islam for another religion, let him be killed.'[2]

Thus God shows no mercy to Muslims who have given up their religion (or replaced it with another religion), neither in this life nor in the hereafter. Conversion to Islam is a one-way move. Once people have become Muslims they are expected to remain Muslims for the rest of their lives. Renouncing Islam is seen in terms of being unfaithful to God and disloyal to the Muslim community. The *umma* represents not only a religious community but also a national, political and cultural community based on God's final revelation to the Prophet.

The severity of Islamic law appears to have a dual purpose: preventing Muslims from abandoning Islam and deterring non-Muslims from converting to Islam without seriously considering the full implications of their decision. During Muhammad's lifetime many Arabs converted superficially and hastily to Islam, but several tribes reverted to polytheism shortly after his death. This led to what are known as *ḥurub al-radda* (the wars against apostasy), which marked the reign of Abu Bakr, the first caliph (632–4). There were also those who converted to Islam only for a while, with the clear intention of discrediting the new religion by reverting to their former beliefs.

Murder

Murder is another crime for which the death penalty is required. As with idolatry the Qur'an refers to the Mosaic Law, which is based on the principle of justice. But unlike the Jewish law, Islamic law does not rule out the possibility for the murderer to be forgiven and escape the death penalty:

Believers! Retaliation is prescribed for you in cases of murder: a free
man for a free man, a slave for a slave, and a woman for a woman. He
who is pardoned by his aggrieved brother must pay a reasonable
compensation with grateful attitude. This is an alleviation from your
Lord and a mercy. He who transgresses afterwards will receive a painful
retribution. In the law of retaliation there is life for you – you who are
endowed with intelligence – so that you may fear [God].
(2:178–179)

Razi argues that Islamic law concerning murder is different and
superior to all pre-existing laws. He explains that the Jewish law
prescribes only the death penalty for murder and that the Christian
law requires forgiveness for the murderer. Arabs used either to
apply the Jewish law or require blood money for the victim's
family. In both cases miscarriage of justice was rife. Vengeance
instead of just retaliation was the rule and the amount of blood
money varied according to the victim's social status. The basic
principle of Islamic law is perfect justice with the possibility of the
murderer being forgiven. Thus Islamic law, Razi explains, is a good
compromise between Jewish law (which is too strict) and Christian
law (which is too lenient). This compromise represents an 'alleviation' or a 'softening' (*takhfif*) of the retaliation law and 'a mercy',
since it is intended to benefit both parties. The murderer can hope
to be forgiven and consequently escape the death penalty. The
aggrieved party has the possibility of getting financial compensation that could be much needed in certain circumstances. Thus 'the
blood owner' (the victim's family) is encouraged to forgive the
murderer. In doing so, the family comply with Qur'anic teaching:
'Forgiving is closer to righteousness [than claiming one's rights]'
(2:237). If the family do, the murderer must pay 'blood money'
(*diya*) to the aggrieved party promptly and willingly. Once the blood
money is paid, the murderer's life is safe and no-one should
attempt to kill him. The aggrieved party may forgive the murderer
even without claiming blood money. But what if they do not want
to forgive the murderer, or if the murderer refuses to pay the blood
money? In either case, the sentence must be carried out and the
murderer be put to death.[3]

In short, Razi's exegesis is based on the teaching of the Hadith according to which the aggrieved party has the choice between three alternatives: retaliation, forgiveness with blood money or forgiveness with no blood money.[4] Some accounts rule out the right to retaliation if the murder is committed against a non-Muslim. The only option is the payment of blood money, and the blood money for a Jew or a Christian is half what it is for a Muslim.[5]

Thus Islamic law shows some leniency towards the murderer. Whether he will be put to death or forgiven depends entirely on the aggrieved party and their decision. If they decide to forgive the murderer, it will be credited to them as a good work: 'If a man forgoes charitably his right to retaliation, his act will be an act of atonement for him' (5:48). Forgiving is such a noble attitude that God will in return forgive people their wrongdoing. One of the Prophet's sayings underlines that people who have been wounded (and perhaps mutilated) will be rewarded by God if they show a forgiving attitude: 'Those who have been injured and forego charitably their right to retaliation will be honoured by God who will forgive them an evil deed.'[6]

Adultery

The punishment for adultery in the Qur'an is one hundred lashes (24:2). However, Muslim commentators consider that this text has been abrogated by what is known as 'the verse about stoning' (*ayat al-rajm*). This verse is not found in the Qur'an but in the Hadith. For some reason, it went missing when the Qur'an was put together into one volume under the caliph 'Uthman. According to the verse, the punishment for adultery is not the same for married and single people. For married people it is 'one hundred lashes and stoning to death'; for unmarried people 'one hundred lashes and exile for one year'. However, the sentence cannot be carried out unless the evidence has been well established. This requires either four witnesses, the adulterers' confession or the woman being found pregnant.[7]

We are told in the Hadith that the Prophet and his close companions passed sentences against adulterers (some from Jewish background).[8] We have several detailed accounts of the stoning of three people in particular: a man called Ma'iz[9] and two women, one from the tribe of Ghamid,[10] the other from the tribe of Juhayna. These people were praised for having asked the Prophet to carry out the sentence for adultery against them. Their request is seen as the fruit of a genuine and perfect repentance. As the two women were pregnant the sentence was executed after they had given birth. Not only did the Prophet praise them for their exemplary repentance, but he also prayed over them before they were buried:

> A woman from the tribe of Juhayna came to God's Apostle. She was pregnant because of adultery. She said:
> – God's Apostle! I have done something for which legal punishment must be imposed upon me, so impose that punishment.
> God's Apostle called her master and said:
> – Treat her well, and when she delivers bring her to me.
> He did accordingly. Then God's Apostle pronounced judgement on her and her clothes were tied around her and then he commanded she be stoned to death. He then prayed over her. Thereupon 'Umar said to him:
> – God's Apostle! You offer prayer for her, whereas she had committed adultery!
> Thereupon the Prophet said:
> – She has repented in such a way that if it were to be divided among seventy men of Medina, it would be enough. Have you found any repentance better than this that she sacrificed her life for God, the most Exalted.[11]

The three offences reviewed so far are the only ones for which the death penalty is required by Islamic law. In a well-known narrative the Prophet states that a Muslim will not be put to death except in one of three cases:

> The blood of a Muslim who confesses that none has the right to be worshipped but God and that I am His Apostle cannot be shed except in three cases: In *qisas* (retaliation) for murder, a married person who commits illegal sexual intercourse, and the one who reverts from Islam and leaves the Muslim community.[12]

Theft

According to Islamic law the punishment for robbery is the amputation of the robber's hand. This sanction is based on the following Qur'anic text:

> As for the man or the woman who is guilty of theft, cut off their hands as a punishment for their crimes and a deterrent enjoined by God. God is Almighty and Wise.
>
> But whoever repents after his evil deed and makes amends, God turns to him [in mercy]. For God is All-Forgiving, All-Merciful.
> (5:41–42)

Sentence against people who committed theft was pronounced by the Prophet and his companions. The Prophet declared that he would not hesitate to cut off the hand of his own daughter if she were found guilty of theft.[13] He also said that those who have been punished for their crime on earth will not have to pay for it on the Day of Judgment.[14] After people were punished they were invited to repent.[15] Those who did repent were fully reintegrated into the community. The evidence of their rehabilitation was given by the fact that they recovered their status as legal witnesses. Hence, their testimony was valid in court: 'If a thief repents after his hand has been cut off, then his witness will be accepted. Similarly, if any person, upon whom any legal punishment has been inflicted, repents, his witness will be accepted.'[16]

Thus God's pardon is granted to the thief who repents *after* he has been punished. Muslims too are invited to forgive him and to treat him as if he had never committed a theft.

Slander

The Qur'an prescribes flogging for those who accuse married Muslim women of adultery without producing sufficient evidence for their allegations:

> Those who defame honourable women and fail to present four witnesses
> shall be flogged with eighty lashes. Never again accept witness from them.
> Such people are utterly sinful except those of them who subsequently
> repent and make amends. For God is All-Forgiving, All-Merciful.
> (24:4–5)

This sentence against people who brought false charges against
'believing married women' (*muḥsanat*) was enforced by the leaders
of the early Muslim community.[17] Slanderers who did not repent
from their crime were deprived of their legal capacity as trustworthy witnesses. Like those who committed theft, repentance was
the required condition for them to be forgiven.

Thus God's mercy is shown by the fact that applying legal
punishments on offenders does not rule out the possibility of them
repenting. If they do, God will forgive them. In the case of murder,
God's law prescribes either retaliation or, that which is a better
option for both the victim's family and the murderer, forgiveness
and payment of blood money.

Does repentance prevent legal punishment?

So far we have considered the teaching of the Qur'an and the way
the Prophet (and the first Muslim community) enforced legal
punishments on people who committed serious offences against
God's law. How do Muslim scholars interpret these punishments?
Do Muslim jurists think they are to be implemented in the same
way as in the Prophet's time? This issue is obviously of primary
importance for the Muslim community everywhere.

Before answering this question we need first to understand how
Islamic law looks at 'legal punishments' (*ḥudud*). These punishments
are conceived in Islam as 'legal rights' (*ḥuquq*). Since all crimes
represent transgressions against God's law, it is God who owns
these rights. However, Islamic penal law considers murder, theft and
slander as crimes committed against people as well. Hence, unlike
apostasy and adultery, the penalty for these offences represents 'a
right' owned not only by God, but also by the people who have been
wronged. The aggrieved party are entitled to use their right in one of

two ways: they can ask for justice to be done through the punishing of the criminal, or they can forgive the offender.

The enforcement of legal punishments on repentant Muslims divides Muslim scholars into three groups (see table 18).

Kharijites (seen as the most radical school)	Mu'tazilites and most Sunni theologians	Shafi'ite school (seen as the most liberal Sunni school of jurisprudence)
Legal punishments must be carried out whether or not the transgressors have repented.	Repentance does not prevent legal punishment. However, these punishments are no longer to be seen as punishments but as tests or trials.	Repentance removes the legal punishments for apostasy and adultery. Legal punishments for murder, theft and slander are lifted if the aggrieved party forgives the offender.

Table 18. How legal punishments should be enforced if the offender repents

The Kharijites adopt a literal interpretation of Qur'anic texts and the Hadith narratives. They claim that legal punishments must be carried out whether or not the transgressors have repented. They argue that this is what the Prophet himself did with people who transgressed God's commands. The Qur'an explicitly orders that unbelievers who fought against God and his Prophet be executed. If they repent (convert to Islam) after they have been defeated, they will not escape God's punishment (5:36–37). Ibn 'Abbas is believed to have said that even if they repented before they were defeated, the polytheists could still be put to death.[18]

For the Mu'tazilites, and most Sunni theologians too, repentance does not prevent legal punishment. However, strictly speaking, these punishments are no longer to be seen as punishments but as

God putting his people to the test (*ibtila'^{an} wa imtihan^{an}*). These tests (or trials) are in a sense similar to what believers experience through illness.[19]

How are Jews and Christians to be treated with regard to legal punishments? Although they are unbelievers according to Islamic law, they have the right (according to Islamic law) to live alongside the Muslim community without having to convert to Islam. Razi justifies this exception by the honour due to Moses and Jesus, to the Scriptures they brought (respectively the Torah and the Gospel), and to early Jews and Christians whose religion had not yet been corrupted. Because of this 'honour' (*ta'zim*), Jews and Christians do not have to face the same dilemma as other unbelievers; that is, either to convert to Islam or to be fought against by Muslims. They are offered a third alternative; namely, to submit to Islamic rule and to pay a special tax, the *jizya*. Razi adds that this tolerance shown to them, combined with their lower status, is designed to lead them eventually to acknowledge Muhammad as God's prophet and Islam as God's religion.[20]

A third group of Muslim scholars consider that repentance removes the legal punishments that represent only God's right (apostasy, adultery). Shafi'i, the founder of the Shafi'ite school of Islamic jurisprudence,[21] is one of the scholars who advocates this view.[22] Ash'ari takes a similar view to Shafi'i.[23] Thus a Muslim who returns to Islam after he converted to another religion should not be put to death, nor an adulterer who has repented. As for the punishment that represents people's rights, it depends on whether or not the aggrieved party is willing to forgive the offender. Thus if the murderer is forgiven by the victim's family, or the robber or the slanderer by the people whom they wronged, then they will escape the legal punishment they deserve. If offenders do not repent, all Muslim jurists and theologians agree that they have to be punished, whether the punishment represents God's right or people's rights.

Contemporary understanding of Islamic penal law

Today most Muslims take similar views to those represented by the Shafi'ite school. Lodi, a distinguished Pakistani lawyer, offers a

FORGIVENESS AND PENAL LAW

fresh and orthodox perspective on Islamic law. In an article entitled 'Modernity of penal justice of Islam', he puts forward the following arguments to make his case:

1. Qur'anic texts about legal punishments include the possibility for all criminals to repent (5:36–37; 5:41–42; 4:15–17; 24:4–5). This suggests that Qur'anic teaching aims primarily at bringing transgressors to repentance.
2. The Qur'an takes into account not only the act of transgression, but also the intention of the person (33:5). Thus the death penalty is prescribed not for homicide (4:92–93), but for murder (2:178; 5:36). He says: 'the modernity of Islamic penal system lies in the fact, among others, that it subordinates the criminal conduct to the attitude of the malefactor's mind, inasmuch as, if there is inconsistency between the two, the judgment is in accordance with the former. By "conduct" is meant human acts adjusted to the consequences intended.'[24] Applying this principle is likely to result in implementing penal justice in a humane manner.
3. The main objective of Islamic criminal law is not to punish offenders, but rather to change people and reform them:

> The antithesis of retaliation is reformation. Islamic penology does not take it for granted that each and every wrongdoer is irredeemable and beyond rehabilitation in the Islamic society. The chief object of punishment with us is reformation in the first instance. Elimination from society of the offender is to be used as a last resort. This finding is in accord with the Qur'anic concept of human nature which is said to be basically righteous (cf. 30:30; 45:4).[25]

4. Public enforcement of legal punishment, prescribed by Islamic law, is intended as a deterrent for weaker Muslims who might be tempted to commit criminal acts: 'Al-Qur'an clearly indicates that physical punishment has indeed a deterrent effect for the potential offenders; that is, those who are like-minded with the offender (cf. 24:2)'.[26] Thus law-abiding Muslims have nothing to fear from Islamic criminal law.

The conclusion Lodi draws from Qur'anic texts (see his first point) is that legal punishments should be carried out only against non-repentant criminals. Even in their case the enforcement of the sentence could be suspended in order to give the criminals the chance to make amends. If they reoffend, then they will have to bear the consequences of their acts. The modernity of Islamic law, he contends, lies precisely in the fact that it gives offenders a second chance designed to urge them to reform:

> Sentence follows conviction. If the law so provides that after conviction no sentence may be passed or it may be authorised to be suspended by the court passing it, then the offender can thereby be allowed a *locus poenitentiae* [a place for repentance] to reconstruct and rehabilitate himself in society under the threat of severe sentence if he repeated his misconduct. In this way the Islamic Law is perhaps ahead of the present time.[27]

Thus Lodi does not challenge Islamic criminal law. He only suggests a flexible and lenient way of implementing it.

Other Muslims, however, take a more radical view. For them, the Islamic legal system represented a major step forward in ethics both when it was set up and for later generations. But Muslim societies (and indeed all human societies) in the twenty-first century are very different from seventh-century Arabia. Muslims today face many new challenges. Islamic 'legal punishments' (*ḥudud*), they observe, are nowhere fully enforced in the Muslim world. This fact demonstrates that an update of the judicial system in Islam is one of the major challenges that needs to be taken up by Muslims worldwide. Those Muslims advocating such changes are not many and their voice is not easily heard. Their publications are often censured in Islamic countries by the religious and political establishment. Deemed as 'unbelievers' by radical Muslims, they are under considerable pressure.

In Egypt this movement has developed in response to the growing influence of Islamic fundamentalism. Its promoters include Faraj Fudat, who was assassinated in 1992; Naṣr Abu Zayd, who was forced to leave his country and seek asylum in the Netherlands; Aḥmad S. Manṣur, who was dismissed from his teaching post at al-Azhar University; and Saad Eddin Ibrahim, head of Ibn Khaldoun Centre for Development Studies, who was put in jail having been accused of carrying out activities that allegedly undermined public order. In Sudan, Mahmoud Mohamed Taha advocated the concept of 'abrogation in reverse', by which he meant that earlier and prophetic Islam in Mecca takes precedence over later and political Islam in Medina. Taha was the leader of the Republican Brothers. His opposition to the Islamic regime in his country led to his arrest and execution in 1985.[28]

Jesus' kingdom

Like many Muslims, Razi misunderstands Christian teaching. The fact that the gospel offers no penal code similar to Islamic criminal law does not mean that Christianity is too lenient with evildoers or that it has no adequate answer to the problem of evil in society. We have seen (in chapter 3 in particular) that justice is one of God's main attributes in the Bible. The gospel, which is a message of salvation, presupposes that all human beings are guilty because we do not live up to God's law, for 'all have sinned and fall short of the glory of God' (Rom. 3:23).

A different kind of kingdom

The difference between Islam and Christianity lies in the way God's justice is administered. In his teaching Jesus made a clear distinction between God's kingdom and the presiding political government: 'Give to Caesar what is Caesar's, and to God what is God's' (Matt. 22:21). God's kingdom is both superior to and separate from any political power. In fact, Jesus claimed to be God's appointed king as he stood before Pontius Pilate, the Roman governor, as well as the Jewish authorities of his time. However, Jesus' kingship was totally different from what people thought (John 6:15):

> Jesus said, 'My kingdom is not of this world. If it were, my servants would fight to prevent my arrest by the Jews. But now my kingdom is from another place.'

'You are a king, then!' said Pilate.

Jesus answered, 'You are right in saying I am a king. In fact, for this reason I was born, and for this I came into the world, to testify to the truth. Everyone on the side of truth listens to me.'
(John 18:36–37)

Jesus' kingdom is *spiritual* (not an earthly one), *universal* (not restricted to a specific nation) and *non-violent* (not to be established by force).

The subject of the Crusades is sometimes raised in this context. In spite of its claims, the crusading movement was in fact a most outrageous distortion of Jesus' kingdom. The crusaders sought to establish an earthly kingdom in the 'Holy Land'. They resorted to violence to achieve their purpose and were driven by an anti-Muslim feeling in flagrant contradiction with Jesus' teaching (Matt. 5:43–48).

A kingdom characterized by forgiveness

The truth Jesus came to proclaim is that 'God our Saviour ... desires all people to be saved' (1 Tim. 2:3–4, ESV). God does not want to judge us according to his justice. If he were to judge us on the basis of his moral standards, we would all deserve the death penalty; that is, eternal punishment. Like Islamic law, the law God revealed to Moses prescribes the capital punishment for blasphemy (Lev. 24:15–16), adultery (Lev. 20:10) and murder (Deut. 19:21). This does not mean, however, that those who have not committed these sins are blameless. Jesus declares to all of us, 'unless you repent, you too will all perish' (Luke 13:3, 5). But he also claims that his mission is precisely to offer God's salvation to everyone: 'the Son of Man came to seek and to save what was lost' (Luke 19:10).

God's forgiveness is at the heart of the gospel. The good news of the gospel is that God suspends his judgment until the Day of Judgment comes. Instead, he shows his mercy and calls people to accept his forgiveness. The contrast between Jesus' message and Muhammad's message is best reflected in the way they dealt with the women who were convicted of adultery. We noticed above that Muhammad sentenced to death the woman who came to him, despite her genuine repentance. The woman brought to Jesus stood silent before him. We do not know whether she was repentant or not. Nevertheless, Jesus' words revealed at the same time his own compassion and the sinfulness of those who accused the woman:

> The teachers of the law and the Pharisees brought in a woman caught in adultery. They made her stand before the group and said to Jesus, 'Teacher, this woman was caught in the act of adultery. In the Law Moses commanded us to stone such women. Now what do you say?' They were using this question as a trap, in order to have a basis for accusing him.
>
> But Jesus bent down and started to write on the ground with his finger. When they kept on questioning him, he straightened up and said to them, 'If any one of you is without sin, let him be the first to throw a stone at her.' Again he stooped down and wrote on the ground.
>
> At this, those who heard began to go away one at a time, the older ones first, until only Jesus was left, with the woman still standing there. Jesus straightened up and asked her, 'Woman, where are they? Has no-one condemned you?'
>
> 'No-one, sir,' she said.
>
> 'Then neither do I condemn you,' Jesus declared. 'Go now and leave your life of sin.'
>
> (John 8:3–11)

Jesus did not challenge the fact that this woman was liable to the death penalty as prescribed by the Jewish law for adultery. Yet his mission was to offer God's forgiveness to those who would otherwise remain under God's condemnation.

A kingdom that grows and influences society

Unlike the *umma*, the Christian community does not coincide with society at large. Its agenda is not to take over political power in order to enforce 'a Christian law' in society. Its mission is rather to offer an alternative to the way society is ruled. This alternative consists in letting God's kingdom grow and develop among and beyond God's people. Civil society is governed by a law based on justice. Christians do recognize the legitimacy of civil and judicial authorities and their role in restraining social evil. They support the responsibility of the state in promoting justice and punishing criminals (Rom. 13:1–5; 1 Pet. 2:13–14). Yet Christians have to keep a critical distance from their government. Their specific mission is to emphasize God's universal mercy, for believers and unbelievers, for law-abiding people and for criminals, for the righteous and the unrighteous.

Christians know that they are not better than others. Knowing this, they need to tell their people, as Jesus did with his own people, that we are all sinful. Above all, Christians have the responsibility to proclaim not only God's justice, but also his unconditional love. Forgiveness, reconciliation and peace are the distinctive marks of the gospel. They represent the foundational law of God's kingdom. Christians are called to implement this law peacefully in all aspects of social life. This involves, for instance, respecting the human rights of all people regardless of their criminal records, their religious or ethnic background, their social status, their gender or their age. This also implies that Christians will always strive to forgive people who have wronged them – without denying the judicial authority the right to judge them. Finally, the fact that the gospel advocates justice and forgiveness, instead of establishing a detailed penal code, means that Christians will seek to improve the penal code in their society to keep it in pace with the ever changing circumstances in which it has to be enforced. They will bring a critical contribution to ensure that both justice and mercy are reflected in the criminal law of their nation.[29]

Notes

1. Razi on 2:54; II:3, pp. 74–77. The number of Israelites put to death was significantly lower according to the Bible narrative: 'The Levites did as Moses commanded, and that day about three thousand of the people died' (Exod. 32:28).

2. Bukhari, *jihad* 149 [2794]:IV, bk 52, no. 260, p. 160; *istitaba* 2 [6411]:IX, bk 84, no. 57, p. 45; *i'tisam* 28:IX, bk 92, p. 341; Abu Dawud, *hudud* 1 [3787]:III, bk 33, no. 4337, p. 1212; Ibn Majah, *hudud* 2 [2526]:IV, bk 20, no. 2535, p. 2; Tirmidhi, *hudud* 25 [1378]; Nasa'i, *tahrim* 14 [3991]. In Arabic: *man ghayyara* (or *baddala*) *dinahu fa'qtuluhu*.

3. Razi on 2:178–179; III:5; pp. 40–48.

4. Bukhari, *tafsir* sura 2 chapter 23 [4138]:VI, bk 60, no. 25, p. 22; *diyat* 8 [372]:IX, bk 83, no. 19, p. 12; Abu Dawud, *diyat* 3 [3898]:III, bk 34, no. 4481, p. 1258; Ibn Majah, *diyat* 3 [2613]:IV, bk 21, no. 2623, p. 52; Tirmidhi, *diyat* 1 [1308]; Darimi, *diyat* 1 [2245].

5. Ibn Majah, *diyat* 21 [2648]:IV, bk 21, no. 2658, p. 72; Tirmidhi, *diyat* 16 [1333]; Nasa'i, *qasama* 8 [4653].

6. Ibn Majah, *diyat* 35 [2679]:IV, bk 21, no. 2693, p. 90; Tirmidhi, *diyat* 5 [1313].

7. Bukhari, *hudud* 30 [6327], 31 [6328], 47 [6353]:VIII, bk 81, no. 816, p. 536; no. 817, p. 537; no. 842, p. 562; Muslim, *hudud* 15 [3201]:III, bk 17, no. 4194, p. 912; Abu Dawud, *hudud* 23 [3835]:III, bk 33, no. 4401, p. 1231; Ibn Majah, *hudud* 7 [2543]:IV, bk 21, no. 2550, p. 11; Tirmidhi, *hudud* 8 [1351]; Darimi, *hudud* 19 [2219].

8. Bukhari, *manaqib* 25 [3363]:IV, bk 56, no. 829, p. 532; *hudud* 38 [6336]:VIII, bk 81, no. 825, p. 550; Muslim, *hudud* 26 [3211], 28 [3212]:III, bk 17, no. 4211, p. 918; no. 4214, p. 919.

9. Muslim, *hudud* 16–22 [3202–3207]:III, bk 17, nos. 4196–4204, pp. 913–915; Abu Dawud, *hudud* 23 [3805]:III, bk 17, no. 4405, p. 1232; Tirmidhi, *hudud* 5 [1347–1349].

10. Muslim, *hudud* 23 [3208]:III, bk 17, no. 4206, p. 916; Abu Dawud, *hudud* 24 [3853]:III, bk 33, no. 4428, p. 1238; Darimi, *hudud* 17 [2221].

11. Muslim, *hudud* 24 [3209]:III, bk 17, no. 4207, p. 917; Abu Dawud, *hudud* 24 [3852]:III, bk 33, no. 4426, p. 1237; Tirmidhi, *hudud* 9 [1355]; Nasa'i, *jana'iz* 64 [1931]; Darimi, *hudud* 18 [2222].

12. Bukhari, *diyat* 6 [6370]:IX, bk 83, no. 17, p. 10; Abu Dawud, *hudud* 2 [3788]:III, bk 33, no. 4338, p. 1212; Ibn Majah, *hudud* 1 [2524]:IV, bk 20, no. 2533, p. 1; Tirmidhi, *hudud* 15 [1364]; Nasa'i, *tahrim* 5 [3951]; Darimi, *hudud* 2 [2190].

13. Bukhari, *hudud* 11 [6300], 12 [6301], 13:VIII, bk 81, no. 778, p. 512; no. 779, p. 512; ch. 14, p. 513; Muslim, *hudud* 9 [3196]:III, bk 17, no. 4187, p. 909; Tirmidhi, *hudud* 6 [1350]; Nasa'i, *qat' al-sariq* 6 [4810].

14. Bukhari, *hudud* 14 [6303]:VIII, bk 81, no. 793, p. 518; Ibn Majah, *hudud* 33 [2593]:IV, bk 20, no. 2604, p. 38; Tirmidhi, *hudud* 12 [1359].

15. Ibn Majah, *hudud* 29 [2587]:IV, bk 20, no. 2597, p. 34; Darimi, *hudud* 6 [2201].

16. Bukhari, *hudud* 14 [6303]:VIII, bk 81, no. 793, p. 518.

17. Bukhari, *shahadat* 8:III, bk 48, ch. 8, p. 495.

18. Abu Dawud, *hudud* 3 [3801]:III, bk 33, no. 4359, p.1217; Nasa'i, *tahrim* 9 [3978].
19. Mankdim, *Sharh*, p. 649; Baqillani, *Tamhid*, pp. 362–363; cf. Ibn Furak, *Mujarrad*, p. 167.
20. Razi on 9:29–30; VIII:16, pp. 23–30.
21. Among the four schools of Islamic jurisprudence (*fiqh*) the Shafi'ite school is traditionally seen as the most liberal.
22. Mankdim, *Sharh*, p. 648; 'Abd al-Jabbar, *Mughni*, XIV, p. 437.
23. Ibn Furak, *Mujarrad*, p. 167.
24. Lodi, 'Modernity', p. 155.
25. Ibid., p. 170.
26. Ibid., p. 167.
27. Ibid., p. 171.
28. See M. M. Taha, 'The second message of Islam', in Kurzman, *Liberal Islam*, pp. 270–283. See also in the same book, pp. 222–238, 'Shari'a and basic human rights concerns' by 'A. A. An-Na'im, who is a disciple of Taha.
29. See Moucarry, *Faith to Faith*, pp. 233–237, 258–260.

18. FORGIVENESS IN HUMAN RELATIONSHIPS

In the previous chapter we looked at the way Muslims may forgive people who have committed criminal offences. Islamic law prescribes legal punishments for offences such as apostasy, murder, adultery, theft and slander. But God's pardon is promised to all those who repent, whether or not legal punishments are carried out against them. At the same time, Muslims who have been wronged through murder, theft or slander have the right to demand that justice be done.

Now what about people who do harm to Muslims in a way that does not represent a legal offence (e.g. telling a lie, insulting someone, engaging in deceitful, hostile or arrogant conduct)? Do Muslims have to forgive them or can they hold their wrongs against them? Are Muslims expected to overlook such wrongdoing or are they allowed to retaliate? To what extent do Muslims have to forgive their fellow Muslims in particular and non-Muslims in general? We will consider these questions in this chapter as we look at the issue of forgiveness in human relationships.

In chapter 12 we noted that Razi sees leaders in general and prophets in particular as role models for their peoples. Muhammad is described as an excellent model for all Muslims (33:21). His conduct serves as an example for all believers. We will therefore focus on his attitude, which personifies Islamic teaching about the need for Muslims to forgive their Muslim brothers and their fellow human beings.[1]

Forgiving fellow Muslims

The Qur'an tells us that just as God is merciful, so his people must be. Indeed, Muslims are portrayed as merciful people (48:29). The mercy people show each other is very small compared to the extent of God's mercy. All creatures, from the least significant to the most privileged, know something of his mercy:

> There are one hundred parts of mercy for God and He has sent down out of these one part of mercy upon *jinns* and humans and [even] insects. It is because of this one part that they love one another and show kindness to one another. Even the beasts treat their young ones with affection. God has reserved ninety-nine parts of mercy with which He would treat His servants on the Day of Resurrection.[2]

Muslims have experienced God's mercy in a very special way. The mission of Muhammad, 'the Prophet of mercy',[3] revealed God as the 'the Most-Merciful One' (7:151; 23:109) and 'the Most-Forgiving One' (7:155). As a community they are expected to demonstrate in their relationships a deep concern for one another. The Prophet describes his community as forming one body made up of many parts deeply united to one another: 'The believers show mercy, affection and compassion with one another like one body. If any of its members is unwell, then the whole body shares in its sleeplessness and fever.'[4]

The Prophet also called his people to mould their character upon God's: 'Be in the likeness of God in your moral dispositions.' Razi comments that people will not reach moral perfection until they have acquired God's character.[5] The implications of imitating God's character are that Muslims should be prepared to forgive. The Prophet is believed to have said, 'The highest moral attribute that characterises Muslims is their willingness to forgive'.[6] Muslims need to forgive relentlessly. Forgiving must become part of their daily and natural behaviour. One day a Muslim came to the Prophet. He said to him that he had a servant who kept wronging him. Should he smack or forgive him? The Prophet replied, 'Forgive him seventy times every day.'[7]

Forgiving others may be seen by some as a demeaning attitude, but in God's sight it is not. In fact, God will honour such people for their noble conduct: 'Charity does not in any way decrease the wealth, and God adds respect to the servant who forgives. The one who shows humility God elevates in the eyes of the people.'[8]

People who forgive have a stronger character. The Qur'an underlines the courage of those who do not let their anger determine their conduct: 'Those who endure patiently and forgive demonstrate a stern resolve [to doing what is good]' (42:43; cf. 16:126). God will grant his blessings to forgiving Muslims in this life and in the hereafter. He will reward compassionate Muslims but he will be unmerciful to the resentful ones:

If you are merciful with others, God will be merciful with you. If you forgive them, God will forgive you.[9]

God will not be merciful with those who are not merciful, and He will not forgive those who do not forgive.[10]

Thus forgiving others is a condition of obtaining God's forgiveness. It is also a good deed that God will greatly reward on the Day of Judgment:

On the Day of Resurrection, a herald will call: 'Let those to whom God owes recompense come forth.' No-one will come forth except those who practised forgiveness. The herald will then recite: *'Let evil be rewarded with like evil. The retribution for an evil action is one equivalent action. God does not love the evildoers.'*
(42:40)[11]

The Qur'an urges Muslims to forgive other Muslims so that God will forgive their sins. On the Last Day people will come

before his throne to give account for what they have done in this
life, and will be rewarded according to their deeds:

> Do not let those of you who have been favoured by God and those who
> are rich set themselves against helping their kinsmen, the poor, and
> those who have emigrated for the cause of God. Rather let them
> pardon and forgive. Do you not yearn that God will forgive you? God
> is All-Forgiving and All-Merciful.
>
> (24:22)

Muslim commentators explain the historical context in which this
text was revealed.[12] Three Muslims accused Aisha, Muhammad's
favourite wife, of adultery. Mistah, one of these men, belonged to
the group of Muslims who emigrated with the Prophet from
Mecca to Medina. He was the cousin of Aisha's father, Abu Bakr,
who supported his family, since he was a poor orphan. When
Aisha's innocence was established by divine revelation (24:23),
her father decided to punish Mistah by stopping his assistance
to him. As Abu Bakr was a wealthy man and one of the leaders
of the Muslim community, God disapproved of his decision.
He therefore revealed sura 24 verse 22 to make him change his
mind and forgive Mistah. Razi points out in connection with this
verse that forgiving the evildoer is highly commendable and
sometimes required. In this case God made his forgiveness of
Abu Bakr's sins depend on his pardon of his cousin. Razi also
explains that 'forgiveness and righteousness (*taqwa*) are intertwined; the one who is strong in righteousness is also strong in
forgiveness'.[13]

The Qur'an reminds Muslims that 'forgiving is closer to righteousness [than claiming one's rights]' (2:237). Muslims are therefore urged to forgive their fellow Muslims, especially their relatives
(64:4). If Muslims want to be forgiven on the Day of Judgment,
they need not only to give to the poor, but also to be willing to
pardon those who do them harm:

> Press on towards forgiveness from your Lord and a Paradise as wide as
> heavens and earth, prepared for those who fear God, who give alms in
> prosperity as well as in adversity, who control their anger and pardon

their fellow men. God loves those who do good ... Their reward is
forgiveness from their Lord and Paradise with running rivers where they
shall dwell for ever. How great is the reward of those who do so!
(3: 133, 134, 136)

Thus God's pardon is promised to those who strive to curb
their anger and forgive. Razi remarks that controlling one's anger
requires patience and forbearance. He quotes several narratives to
illustrate the reward in store for Muslims 'who forgive [others] after
they have been made angry' (42:37). According to one narrative,
God will appoint them as leaders over his creation in the hereafter:
'If anyone suppresses anger when he is in a position to give vent to
it, God will call him on the Day of Resurrection over the heads of
all creatures, and ask him to choose any of the bright and large-
eyed maidens he wishes.'[14]

A slightly different version of this narrative promises the same
people that 'God will fill their heart with peace and faith'.[15] Razi
rarely refers to the gospel in his commentary. But in his exegesis of
sura 3 verses 133–136 he explains the meaning of this text by
quoting one of Jesus' sayings: 'Goodness (*ihsan*) does not consist in
doing good to those who do good to you – this is pure recompense
(*mukafa'a*); goodness consists in doing good to those who do evil to
you'.[16] Muslims who forgive others, concludes Razi, will enjoy a
double blessing: God's forgiveness, which will protect them from
eternal punishment; and God's reward, which means eternal bliss
in paradise.[17]

Forgiving non-Muslims

Muslims should forgive their fellow Muslims. But should they
forgive non-Muslims? As we have seen, neither Qur'anic texts nor
the Hadith narratives are specific. The exhortation to forgive is
expressed in general terms: 'A kindly word and a forgiving attitude
are better than a charitable deed followed by a harmful act, for God
is Self-Sufficient and Patient' (2:263). The underlying theological
principle is that God himself is a forgiving God: 'Whether you do
good openly or you keep it hidden or you forgive an evil deed, God

is Pardoning and All-Powerful' (4:149). There is, however, one text that encourages Muslims to forgive unbelievers:

> Tell those who believe to pardon those who ignore God's Days when God will reward people according to their deeds. He that does what is right does it to his own advantage; and he that commits evil does it to his detriment. To your Lord you shall all be brought back.
> (45:14–15)

For Razi 'God's Days' are the historical days either in the past (e.g. Israel) or in the future (e.g. the end time). In these days God deals with peoples of the earth in spectacular ways. His mighty acts are designed to judge the peoples or to rescue them.[18] Those who ignore (lit. 'who do not set their hope on') God's days are the unbelievers who are indifferent to God's reward and punishment. The purpose of this text, according to Razi, is to call Muslims to overlook the evil deeds of the unbelievers and to ignore their provocations. A day will come when God will reward Muslims for their noble attitude. Razi mentions that some commentators understand 'people' in verse 14 to mean the unbelievers who will be rewarded (punished) for their (bad) deeds. He also recognizes that most exegetes consider this text as having been abrogated by those texts that order Muslims to fight the unbelievers. He does not endorse this opinion.[19]

The example of the Prophet

What about the Prophet? How did he respond to God's revelation about forgiving evildoers? How did he enact the teaching he was commissioned to convey to his community?

Muhammad's attitude towards fellow Muslims

The Qur'an portrays Muhammad in these terms: 'There has now come to you an Apostle of your own, one who grieves at your pain, who cares for you, who is lenient and merciful with the believers' (9:128).

This verse ascribes to the Prophet two names among God's

most beautiful names: *ra'uf* (lenient) and *raḥim* (all-merciful). These names are applied to God in eight verses (2:143; 9:117; 16:7, 47; 22:65; 24:20; 57:9; 59:10). Leniency and mercy also characterize Jesus' disciples, according to sura 57 verse 27. Razi points out that Muhammad's leniency and mercy embrace believers (Muslims) as opposed to unbelievers.[20] The Hadith gives us a similar portrait of Muhammad, based on what the Torah is believed to have said about him long before he was born:

> [Muhammad] is described in the Torah with some of the qualities attributed to him in the Qur'an as follows:
>
> O Prophet! We have sent you as a witness and a giver of good tidings and a warner and guardian of 'the nations'. You are My slave and My messenger. I have named you *al-Mutawakkil* (he who depends upon God). *You are neither discourteous, harsh nor one who makes noise in the markets, and you do not do evil to those who do evil to you, but you deal with them with forgiveness and pardon.* God will not let him die until he makes straight the crooked people by making them say: 'No-one has the right to be worshipped but God,' which will open blind eyes and deaf ears and enveloped hearts.[21]

Muhammad's leadership over the Muslim community was at times challenged by fellow Muslims. Razi remarks that circumstances such as these revealed Muhammad as a skilful and caring leader, and that thanks to his divinely inspired wisdom and God-given compassion, Muslims remained united and committed to God's cause:

> [O Muhammad!] It was thanks to God's mercy that you dealt gently with them. Had you been harsh or cruel, they would have surely deserted you. Therefore pardon them and seek forgiveness for them. Take counsel with them in any situation. When you have reached a decision, put your trust in God. God loves those who put their trust in Him.
> (3:159)

Razi explains the historical context of this verse. In 625 the battle of Uḥud saw the Muslim army opposed to the Meccan polytheists. Many Muslims, up to a third of the army and including leaders such as 'Umar and 'Uthman, deserted the battle. The Muslim army was routed. The unity of the Muslim community was threatened. Then God stepped in, reasserting his sovereignty over recent events, promising his pardon to those who were on the battlefield and, last but not least, forgiving those who had deserted. God ordered Muhammad to do the same; that is, to forgive, pray for and keep consulting them in the future. Muhammad complied with God's command. He forgave his people and in so doing attained the virtue of moulding his moral character upon God's.[22]

Muhammad's attitude towards unbelievers

Muhammad treated his fellow Muslims kindly. But what about unbelievers? He had a markedly different attitude towards non-Muslims. In fact, his policy towards them evolved significantly according to God's instructions. The Qur'anic texts suggest that his relationships with polytheists and Jews were lenient at the beginning. Later, however, God commanded the Prophet and the Muslim community as a whole to adopt a rather stern attitude towards them. At first God ordered Muhammad to turn away from the hostile unbelievers: 'Show forgiveness, command what is right and turn away from the ignorant' (7:199).[23]

In his exegesis of this text Razi quotes a tradition which tells us that when Gabriel revealed this verse to Muhammad, the Prophet asked him to clarify its meaning. Gabriel answered, 'Your Lord says, "it entails that you seek reconciliation with those who made you their enemy, that you give to those who deprived you of your rights and that you forgive those who did evil to you." '[24] Razi suggests how this threefold explanation applies to the above verse. Reconciliation requires forgiving people, giving means doing what is right, and forgiving implies turning away from the ignorant; that is, the unbelievers. Turning away from the ignorant, adds Razi, consists in not repaying them for their bad behaviour. This, he notes, does not rule out the possibility of fighting them.[25]

The Prophet had to be patient with those who showed contempt for his message. Before him many prophets had been ill-treated by their people. A day would come when God would avenge his Prophet as he did his forerunners: 'The Hour is surely coming;

therefore forgive them with gracious forgiveness' (15:85). Muhammad was certainly discouraged by the persistence of the Meccans in their rejection of his mission. So was he tempted to give up? Did he think that his opponents would never accept his message unless they were forced to? The Prophet needed God's reassurance:

> [The Prophet] says: 'O my Lord! These men are not going to believe!'
> [God replied]: 'Bear with them and say "Peace!" Before long they shall know.'
> (43:88–89)

Razi suggests here that God is encouraging the Prophet to put up with the unbelief of his people. This meant that he was not allowed to call God's judgment down on them. However, adds Razi, this conciliatory approach was not to last for ever. God's response to Muhammad also contained 'a threat' (*tahdid*). The unbelievers would soon realize that they could not indefinitely reject God's message with impunity. They would have to face up to the consequences of their unbelief.[26]

Muhammad had been preaching the Qur'an for twelve years. 'With wisdom and kindly exhortation' he called his people to God's way. He argued with them 'in the best possible way' (16:125). Yet the result was disappointing; he met with little success. Very few Meccans converted to Islam. In 622 he left Mecca, his hometown, with seventy converts and emigrated to Yathrib where he settled for the rest of his life. Ever since the *hijrah* (emigration) this town has been known as *Madina*, 'the City' (of the Prophet). The people in Medina were much more responsive to his mission. Many converted to Islam and gave him their allegiance. They came to be known as *al-ansar* ('the supporters' of the Prophet). Gradually Muhammad became their acclaimed leader.

The Jewish community in Medina was fairly large and had the upper hand. The rapid growth of the Muslim community challenged their position. In 623 Muhammad issued what is known as 'the Constitution of Medina', a declaration allowing every citizen in the city to live on an equal footing with the Muslim community regardless of their beliefs. The only condition was their recognition of Islamic supremacy. This declaration did not put an end to the

growing rivalry and hostility between the Jewish and the Muslim
communities. The conflict was political, a struggle to win power and
control over the city. The religious disagreements were secondary.
The Muslim community prayed towards Jerusalem, like the Jewish
community. There was, however, one dividing issue. The Jews did
not accept Muhammad as a prophet. To acknowledge him as God's
messenger would have meant accepting his political leadership as
well. They argued that, despite what Muslims claimed (7:157), there
was no prediction of his coming in the Torah. The Jews were then
charged with breaking the covenant God made with them, falsifying
their Scripture and 'forgetting' much of its content. Many were also
blamed for devising deceitful schemes to get rid of Muhammad: 'All
but a few of them [the Jews] have constantly engaged in treachery.
Pardon and forgive. God loves those who do good' (5:13).

The Jews in Medina were accused of conspiring with the
polytheists in Mecca against the Prophet. According to the Hadith
some of the Jews attempted to poison him, but their plot was
discovered. When they were brought before the Prophet, they
sought to justify their action: 'We wanted to know if you were a liar
in which case we would get rid of you, or a prophet in which case the
poison would not harm you'.[27] On another occasion a Jew cast a
spell on Muhammad. He was bewitched for a while and began to
imagine he had done things that he had not.[28] In both cases
Muhammad did not take revenge against those who did evil to
him. In refusing to retaliate he complied with God's command and
showed himself worthy of his love. Thus the Prophet was called to
bear with the unbelievers and not to pay them back for their evil
actions. Razi reports that, according to an alternative interpretation,
sura 5 verse 13 was abrogated by 'the verse about the sword' (*ayat al-
sayf*) that was revealed later (see below). Consequently, unbelievers
were no longer to be forgiven either by Muhammad or by Muslims.[29]

Forgiveness or the sword?

Sura 2 verse 109 urges Muhammad in particular and Muslims in
general to forgive 'the People of the Book'. The context indicates
that this verse is about hostile Jews:

Many of the People of the Book desire to make you revert from faith to
unbelief. They do so out of envy within themselves, after the truth has
been made plain to them. Forgive them and bear with them until God
brings about His Directive. God has power over all things.
(2:109)

Razi relates this text to a group of Jews who came to see two
Muslims after the Muslim army had been defeated at Uhud. They
tried to persuade them to renounce their faith and convert to
Judaism. Their argument was that if Islam were the true religion,
Muslims would not have been overcome. The Muslim men
remained loyal to Islam and the Prophet. When they reported the
incident, Muhammad praised them for their loyalty and soon
afterwards was given the above revelation (2:109). God ordered
Muhammad to forgive the Jews as he had commanded him earlier
to forgive the polytheists (14:46; 73:10). Razi explains that this text
commands Muhammad to forgive unbelievers 'until God brings
about His Directive (amr)'. In other words, one day Muhammad's
patience with unbelievers will have to come to an end. When will
this happen? Razi suggests three answers. Some people believe that
Muslims should forgive non-Muslims as long as the Day of
Judgment has not come. Others think that Muslims will no longer
forgive when Muhammad is powerful enough to challenge his
enemies and when the Muslim community is very large. According
to a third interpretation, which Razi attributes to most of
Muhammad's companions and second generation Muslims,
Muslims will need to forgive no longer when God calls Muslims
to warfare. People will then have to convert to Islam or pay the
jizya tax. This call came with the revelation of 'the verse about
the sword'.

The verse about the sword

When Muslim exegetes refer to 'the verse about the sword' they do
not specify which verse they are talking about. It seems that they
take it to mean any Qur'anic texts about jihad (understood as holy
war), which are many (e.g. 2:216; 3:167; 4:76; 8:65; 9:36; 22:39). The
texts most often quoted in connection with the obligation to fight
unbelievers are sura 9 verses 5 and 29:

When the sacred months [of truce] are over, then slay the polytheists wherever you find them. Capture them, besiege them, and lie in ambush everywhere. If they repent, perform the prayer-rite (*salat*) and pay the alms-tax (*zakat*) let them go their way. God is All-Forgiving and All-Merciful.

(9:5)

Fight against those who believe neither in God nor in the Last Day, who do not forbid what God and His Apostle have forbidden, who do not embrace the religion of truth, from among those to whom the Book was given. Do so until they pay the *jizya* tax personally, having been utterly subdued.

(9:29)

'God's Directive' was therefore that Muslims should fight polytheists until they convert to Islam (9:5) and fight 'the People of the Book' (Jews and Christians) until they submit to Islamic rule and pay the *jizya* tax (9:29). Razi endorses this interpretation which is by far the most representative among Muslim scholars. This means that sura 2 verse 109, and others that urge Muslims to forgive non-Muslims, have been abrogated. Having explained this, Razi mentions briefly the alternative and marginal opinion which considers that this text has not been abrogated. In other words, Muslims are still called upon to forgive, since this is a praiseworthy attitude in any case.[30]

Is it possible to fight unbelievers and at the same time show leniency to them? Yes, says Razi, in the sense that if they repent (convert to Islam), they will not be put to death. Once they have been defeated, any prisoners should be released either freely or with a ransom (47:4). The Hadith tells us that the turning point in Muhammad's career took place at the battle of Badr in 624 when the Muslim army waged war against the unbelievers. From that year on the Prophet became a successful army leader:

God's Apostle and his companions used to forgive the polytheists and the People of the Book and to overlook their wrongdoing as God ordered them. The Qur'an says, *You shall certainly suffer much harm from those who have been given the Scripture before you and the polytheists; but if you endure patiently and act righteously, you will demonstrate a stern resolve [to doing what is good]* (3:186). It also declares, *Many of the People of the Book desire to make you revert from faith to unbelief . . . Forgive them and bear with them until God brings about His Directive . . .* (2:109). God's Apostle used to comply with God's command by forgiving them until God allowed him to fight against them. It was when God's Apostle fought the battle of Badr that God killed a number of leaders of the unbelievers and of Quraysh tribe chiefs. God's Apostle and his companions came back from this battle triumphant and with booty. As they brought with them some captives, Ubayy b. Salul and the polytheists who used to worship idols with him said, 'Now things have become clear.' They pledged their allegiance to God's Apostle, committed themselves to Islam and became Muslims.[31]

As far as the conflict between the Muslim community and the Jewish community is concerned, we have already noted that it started when Muhammad and his companions emigrated to Medina, which had a large Jewish population. 'The Constitution of Medina' was short-lived and the confrontation between the two communities reached a climax in 624. It turned to the advantage of the Muslim community. All Jews were subsequently killed or expelled from Medina. Muslims stopped praying towards Jerusalem. The *qibla* (the direction for prayer) became Mecca and its temple al-Ka'ba (which was allegedly built by Abraham and Ishmael; 2:127). In 627 the Jews were banished from the whole Arabian Peninsula:

We were in the mosque when the Prophet came out and said, 'Let us go to the Jews.' We went out with him till we reached their school. He said to them, 'If you embrace Islam, you will be safe. You should know that the land belongs to God and His Apostle, and that I want to expel you from this land. So, if anyone among you owns a property, let him sell it; otherwise you should know that the land belongs to God and His Apostle.'[32]

The conflict between Muslims and Meccans was halted provisionally in 628 when 'the Treaty of Hudaybiyya' was signed between the two parties. Two years later, having accused Meccans of breaking the truce, the Muslims marched towards Mecca.

Realizing that they were not in a position to win a war against a highly motivated army, the Meccans surrendered. The Prophet entered the city peacefully, cleansed the Kaʿba of its idols and proclaimed a general amnesty (48:1–3). The fact that he did not take revenge on his long-standing enemies is indicative of his shrewd mind as a leader and, for Muslims, of his noble character as well.

Contrasting attitudes

In short, Muhammad's policy towards unbelievers was at first non-confrontational. But when 'the verse about the sword' was revealed, a radical change in his policy took place starting with the battle of Badr in 624.[33] This policy brought about the supremacy of Islam over all religions in Arabia and the victory of Muslims over non-Muslims. This achievement was seen as God's vindication of his Prophet.

Thus the Prophet in particular and Muslims in general demonstrated contrasting attitudes with regard to forgiving others. Just as they were compassionate and forgiving towards each other, they were merciless towards non-Muslims: 'Muhammad is God's Apostle. Those who are with him are ruthless to the unbelievers but merciful to one another' (48:29; cf. 5:57; 9:73; 66:9).

From an Islamic perspective this double conduct is possible, appropriate and even necessary as the Muslim community is not just a religious society. It is a political nation, ruled by God's civil, social and penal law. Like any other nation, at times it has to deal with the hostility of other nations. *Jihad* then becomes not only permissible, but obligatory: 'Going to war is prescribed for you, though it is to you a hateful thing' (2:216; cf. 4:74–76; 5:33; 8:65; 9:111; 61:4). In addition to this, Muslims consider themselves as having been entrusted with God's final message. They have to take this message outside the boundaries of the *umma*. If they are prevented from carrying out their *daʿwah* (mission) this would create a situation where *jihad* becomes mandatory. If there is one noble cause for which the use of force is legitimate, it is certainly, from an Islamic perspective, God's cause. Muhammad's calling was to preach the Qur'an and, where necessary, to fight unbelievers until they accepted the Qur'anic message:

I have been commanded to wage war against men as long as they do not say: 'There is no god but God'. As soon as they make this confession, I have no rights over their lives and possessions – unless they commit an offence against God's law. They are accountable only to God.[34]

Thus forgiveness in human relationships plays a far more important part within the Muslim community than between Muslims and non-Muslims. As individuals, Muslims are exhorted to show a forgiving attitude to non-Muslims, but certainly not as a community dealing with potentially hostile and threatening nations.

Love your enemies

We noted in Razi's exegesis of sura 3 verse 134 that he refers to Jesus' teaching to explain what 'goodness' (*iḥsan*) means. Indeed, many Muslims believe that Jesus' message was characterized by love, mercy and forgiveness. Yet these Muslims do not realize that the fulfilment of his preaching was found in his death and resurrection. The words Razi attributes to Jesus are best understood in their original context. They are found in what is known as 'the Sermon on the Mount', where Jesus' definition of goodness is part of his command about loving our enemies:

Love your enemies, do good to those who hate you, bless those who curse you, pray for those who ill-treat you. If someone strikes you on one cheek, turn to him the other also ... Do to others as you would have them do to you.

If you love those who love you, what credit is that to you? Even 'sinners' love those who love them. And if you do good to those who are good to you, what credit is that to you? Even 'sinners' do that ... But love your enemies, do good to them, and lend to them without expecting to get anything back. Then your reward will be great, and you will be sons of the Most High, because he is kind to the ungrateful and wicked. Be merciful, just as your Father is merciful.

(Luke 6:27–36; cf. Matt. 5:38–48)

It is worth noting that Jesus relates his teaching to God himself. Christians must love their enemies because God loves everyone, including those who do not deserve his love. The words 'Be merciful, just as your Father is merciful' represent a striking parallel to the above-quoted hadith 'Be in the likeness of God in your moral dispositions'. Christianity and Islam exalt God as a merciful God. But despite this theological agreement about who God is, Christian and Islamic ethics differ as to the outworking of divine mercy in human relationships. We will look at this variance, first as regards the mission of Jesus and of Muhammad, then as regards the way Christians and Muslims are to reflect God's mercy in their lives.

Muhammad

As noted above, Muhammad's career developed significantly after the *hijrah*. In Mecca he was simply God's prophet. He met with opposition from his own people and had a relatively small following. His main resource was his deep-rooted conviction that God had called him to be his prophet. During this time of hardship, God upheld and provided him with the resolve to face his opponents with a remarkably forgiving attitude. His emigration to Medina in 622 certainly marked a turning point in his career. The Arabs in Medina were much more attracted by the Qur'anic message than those in Mecca. They joined Muhammad en masse. This success led in 624 to a decisive stage in the development of Islam. The revelation of 'the verse about the sword' conveyed the divine justification needed to overcome God's enemies by force. The Prophet was no longer just a prophet, but a political leader and a chief commander as well. The obligation of *jihad* (understood as holy war) against unbelievers abrogated previous revelations. It reduced dramatically the scope of forgiveness in Muhammad's dealings with his opponents.

David

From Mecca to Medina the Prophet's mission evolved in a way quite contrary to what we find in the Bible. Under the covenant God made with Israel, the use of force for establishing or maintaining God's rule was justified. It was through holy war that the Israelites conquered the land of Canaan under the leadership of Moses and his successor Joshua (Deut. 20:10–20; Josh. 6:20–21). King David is acclaimed in the Torah for his faith as well as for his military achievements (1 Sam. 18:5–7). He conquered Jerusalem and made it the capital of his kingdom (2 Sam. 5:6–12). Yet when David wanted to build a temple for God, he was not allowed to do so. The reason God gave him represents a sharp criticism of his military career in particular and religious violence in general:

> You have shed much blood and have fought many wars. You are not to build a house for my Name, because you have shed much blood on the earth in my sight. But you will have a son who will be a man of peace and rest ... He is the one who will build a house for my Name.
> (1 Chr. 22:8–10; cf. 1 Chr. 28:3)

Thus because of his military career, David, God's beloved prophet (1 Sam. 13:14) and Israel's greatest king, was denied the privilege of being known as the one who built God's temple in Jerusalem. The God of peace did not want his name to be compromised by the violence that characterized the life of his servant.

Jesus

The coming of Jesus marked a new era in God's dealings with humankind. The New Testament clearly shows that neither Jesus nor his disciples ever used any force when preaching the gospel. When Jesus was about to be arrested, one of his disciples tried to rescue him. He reached for his sword but Jesus stepped in immediately and told him, 'Put your sword back in its place, for all who draw the sword will die by the sword. Do you think I cannot call on my Father, and he will at once put at my disposal more than twelve legions of angels?' (Matt. 26:52–53). Jesus' response is a clear indication that God's kingdom is not to be established or spread by force. This kingdom is based on love, mercy and forgiveness as demonstrated in his life as well as in his sacrificial death. Hence it is inconsistent to use coercion, be it military, political or legal, to bring people into the kingdom. Jesus remained faithful to God to the end of his life. He was arrested, tried, sentenced to death and crucified. Before he died he uttered a few short sentences, one of which was a prayer for his enemies: 'Father, forgive them, for they do not know what they are doing' (Luke 23:34). Thus not only did Jesus preach forgiveness; he also asked God's forgiveness for his enemies. Loving one's enemies is fulfilled by forgiving them their extreme wrongdoing. Stephen, the first Christian martyr, showed the same loving attitude towards his enemies. As he was being stoned, he uttered this prayer just before he died: 'Lord, do not hold this sin against them' (Acts 7:60).

Forgive as God forgave you

Just as Muhammad's example is normative for Muslims, so is Jesus' life for Christians. Jesus' disciples are expected to walk in his footsteps, to follow his example and to obey his commands. In the prayer he taught his disciples he made a close link between God's forgiveness and our willingness to forgive others: 'Forgive us our sins,/for we also forgive everyone who sins against us' (Luke 11:4; cf. Matt. 6:12). So what is the nature of this link? Is God's forgiveness conditioned by our forgiveness? Does God reward us by forgiving our sins when we forgive others, as in the above-quoted Qur'anic text (3:136) and Hadith narratives?

Following the prayer he taught his disciples, Jesus seems to suggest that God's forgiveness depends on ours: 'if you forgive men when they sin against you, your heavenly Father will also forgive you. But if you do not forgive men their sins, your Father will not forgive your sins' (Matt. 6:14–15). In fact, these words simply point out that receiving God's forgiveness and forgiving others are inseparable. They represent two sides of the same reality.

The parable of the unmerciful servant

Jesus tells a story known as 'the parable of the unmerciful servant'. Here he compares God's kingdom to a merciful king who cancels the enormous debt his servant owes him. Later this same servant refuses to cancel the small amount of money a fellow-servant owes him. His harsh attitude is reported to the king who is so outraged that he decides to punish him until he pays back all his debts (Matt.

18:23–35). This parable shows that it is God who first forgives our sins. He also expects us to respond to his mercy by forgiving those who have wronged us. For it is not consistent to ask God to forgive our sins if we are unwilling to forgive others. In the same way as God's love precedes ours, so does his forgiveness. Our response to his forgiveness should be the same as to his love: 'We love because he first loved us. If anyone says, "I love God," yet hates his brother, he is a liar' (1 John 4:19–20). Only when we forgive others do we give an adequate response to God's forgiveness.

Is there any limit to forgiving others? Do we always have to forgive? This question, which was put to Muhammad (see above), was also put to Jesus by one of his disciples:

> Then Peter came to Jesus and asked, 'Lord, how many times shall I forgive my brother when he sins against me? Up to seven times?'
>
> Jesus answered, 'I tell you, not seven times, but seventy-seven times.' (Matt. 18:21–22)

The parable of 'the unmerciful servant' comes immediately after this answer. Jesus is saying, in other words, that we should always be willing to forgive. The sins God has forgiven us by far outnumber the sins we have to forgive. The mercy we must have for others will never match God's mercy for us. If we are immensely grateful to God, as we ought to be, we need to prove it in our relationships with others. Failing to do that would mean that we have not really grasped the extent of God's mercy for us.

A command or an exhortation?

Another important aspect of Jesus' teaching relates, as we have seen, to the fact that Christians are commanded to love everyone, including their enemies (Luke 6:27–36). Loving our enemies implies forgiving them. Unlike the Muslim community, the Christian community is not a political community. Christians can and should have the same loving and forgiving attitude towards believers as well as unbelievers. All have been created in God's image and all are loved by God (Gen. 1:27; John 3:16). The command about loving our neighbour as ourselves embraces everyone, whatever their religious, political or ethnic background (Luke 10:25–37). The way

Christians should look at non-Christians, as first and foremost fellow human beings, differs from the way Muslims relate to non-Muslims, who are perceived primarily as unbelievers (48:29).

In an article entitled 'The concept of forgiveness in the Qur'an' the Egyptian scholar M. Allam points out that the Qur'an does not require Muslims to forgive others. Muslims are encouraged to forgive but are not commanded to do so. Why does the Qur'an fall short of making forgiving others an obligation? Allam explains:

> pardon, if applied indiscriminately, is a most dangerous thing. There are undoubtedly some offences, some circumstances, in regard to which resort to forgiveness would be a gross mistake, since it would then defeat its own end. That is why the Qur'an, as we shall see, has given man an absolute right to protect his interests against the aggressor. Moreover, it is in the very nature of man to defend himself and protect his interests; nor is it in his nature to be too willing to forgive. It is in recognition of these facts that the suggestion to forgive is not given in the form of a command. And yet the suggestion is to be found in the Qur'an so frequently and is invariably interlocked with so many aspects of moral and social life, that no one could fail to realise the *force* of the suggestion notwithstanding what seems to me to be a *deliberate avoidance of a command.*[35]

The author groups Qur'anic texts about forgiveness in particular and leniency in general into three categories. The first refers to God as a forgiving God (2:52; 3:152, 155; 42:25, 30); the second relates to the Prophet (3:159; 5:13, 15; 7:199; 15:85; 23:96; 43:89); the third concerns 'the most pious and ardent believers' (25:63; 41:34; 42:43). The first caliph, Abu Bakr, falls into this category of believers (24:22). These texts, Allam remarks, represent three degrees of the *ideal* set before Muslims. The *command* about forgiving others, which is found in the second and the third groups, is not addressed to Muslims in general. Texts that relate to ordinary Muslims are not many (2:237; 3:133–134; 16:126; 42:37): 'The teaching [in these texts] does not assume the form of a command expressed in the *imperative*, but rather it takes the form of an *exhortation* expressed in the most inviting terms.'[36]

From an Islamic perspective, the law, based on the Qur'an and the Hadith, regulates the social and religious life within the *umma*. On the one hand there is the criminal code; on the other, the exhortation to forgive and to try to reach, as far as possible, the ideal of forgiveness set by God and the Prophet. The combination of these two is the best guarantee for a just and equitable society. Allam argues that by following the God-given law, the Muslim community will be a balanced society, avoiding the two opposite dangers of cruelty and anarchy: 'If punishment alone were advocated, a spirit of vengeance would prevail; and if, on the other hand, forgiveness alone were enjoined, chaos might reign, and in any case people would be apt to reject it.'[37]

In the previous chapter we noted that Christians do acknowledge the role of civil authorities to administer justice and to punish evildoers. However, unlike Islam, Christianity is not meant to be a state religion. Consequently, God's mercy is fully revealed in the gospel, without any hindrance or confusion due to the collusion between religion and state. The gospel *commands* Christians to love and forgive their fellow human beings as well as their fellow Christians. This command is designed to give evidence that God indeed loves *all* human creatures and offers them the forgiveness of their sins.

Through his life, death and resurrection, Jesus demonstrated in a unique and powerful way God's character as the saving God. Christians are to carry on this mission. They are called to share the good news with non-Christians, not just by words but through their relationships. Their witness will only be credible if they can provide the living proof that the saving God is at work in their own lives. Allam is certainly right in pointing out that 'forgiveness is not the most natural emotion which man would feel towards his aggressor. Actually forgiveness is a form of injustice – injustice to oneself.'[38] The gospel is precisely about God's kingdom ruling over and within God's people. Its power transforms believers into the likeness of the Creator so that they become merciful just as he is merciful. In this sense, unlike Islam, Christianity is not a 'natural religion' (*din al-fiṭra*) (30:30). Christians' spiritual life is not based on their natural ability to comply with God's character. Their main resource is God himself empowering them, by his Holy Spirit, to live up to his perfect commands:

As God's chosen people, holy and dearly loved, clothe yourselves with
compassion, kindness, humility, gentleness and patience. Bear with each
other and forgive whatever grievances you may have against one
another. Forgive as the Lord forgave you.
(Col. 3:12–13; cf. Eph. 4:32)

Notes

1. Three verbs are used in the Qur'an in the context of Muslims forgiving
   those who do harm to them: (a) The verb *ghafara*, the strongest and most
   common for God's pardon, is found five times (2:263; 42:37, 43; 45:14;
   64:14); (b) The verb *'afa* is used eleven times (2:109, 237; 3:134, 159; 4:99,
   149; 5:13; 7:199; 24:22; 42:40; 64:14); (c) The verb *safaha* (never used for
   God) literally means 'to turn away', 'to ignore', hence 'to forget' or 'to
   forgive'. It is used six times, once with *ghafara* (64:14) and three times
   with *'afa* (2:109; 5:13; 24:22).
   The three verbs are used in sura 64 verse 14. Thus there are in total
   eighteen verses about forgiveness in human relationships. A few other
   texts invite Muslims to be patient with hostile people (*sabara*), to ignore
   them (*a'rada*) or to keep away from them (*hajara*).

2. Muslim, *tawba* 19 [4944]:IV, bk 37, no. 6631, p. 1437; Bukhari, *adab* 19
   [5541]:VIII, bk 73, no. 29, p. 20; Ibn Majah, *zuhd* 35 [4284]:V, no. 4293,
   p. 516.

3. Ibn Majah, *iqamat al-salat* 189 [1375]:II, bk 5, no. 1385, p. 298.

4. Bukhari, *adab* 27 [5552]:VIII, bk 73, no. 40, p. 26.

5. In Arabic: *takhallaqu bi-akhlaqi allah*. This (non-canonical) hadith is
   quoted by Razi in his exegesis of sura 3 verse 159 (V:9, p. 53). It is often
   quoted in Sufi literature (e.g. Ghazali, *Names*, p. 149; Suhrawardi, *'Awarif*,
   p. 508). Schimmel translates it as follows: 'Qualify yourself with the
   qualities of God' (*Dimensions*, p. 142). Burrell's translation is slightly
   different: 'You should be characterised by the characteristics of God'
   (Ghazali, *Names*, p. 149). This saying represents a remote echo of a
   command found in the Bible: 'Be holy because I, the LORD your God,
   am holy' (Lev. 19:2; cf. Lev. 11:45; 1 Pet. 1:16). It is also reminiscent of
   Socrates' words 'We ought to try to escape from earth to the dwelling of
   the gods as quickly as we can ... To escape is to become like God, so far
   as this is possible; and to become like God is to become righteous and
   holy and wise' (Plato, *Theaetetus*, 176 a-b; tr. Harold North Fowler).

6. In Arabic: *afdalu akhlaqi al-muslimin al-'afw*. This (non-canonical) saying is quoted by Razi in his exegesis of sura 24 verse 22; XII:23, p. 166.

7. Abu Dawud, *adab* 124 [4496]:III, bk 36, no. 5145, p. 1427; Tirmidhi, *birr* 31 [1872]; Ibn Hanbal, *musnad al-mukthirin* 3 [5377].

8. Muslim, *birr* 69 [4689]:IV, bk 32, no. 6264, p. 1369; Tirmidhi, *birr* 81 [1948]; Darimi, *zakat* 35 [1614].

9. Ibn Hanbal, *musnad al-mukthirin* 4 [6255, 6744]; Bukhari, *tawhid* 2 [6829], 25 [6894]:IX, bk 93, no. 474, p. 351; no. 540, p. 407; Muslim, *jana'iz* 11 [1531]:II, bk 4, no. 2008, p. 438; Abu Dawud, *jana'iz* 28 [2718]:II, bk 14, no. 3119, p. 890; Ibn Majah, *jana'iz* 53 [1577]:II, bk 6, no. 1588, p. 406; Tirmidhi, *birr* 16 [1847].

10. Ibn Hanbal, *musnad al-kufiyyin* 146 [18447]; Bukhari, *adab* 18 [5538], 27 [5554]:VIII, bk 73, no. 26, p. 18; no. 42, p. 26; *tawhid* 2 [6828]:IX, bk 93, no. 473, p. 351; Muslim, *fada'il* 65 [4282], 66 [4283]:IV, bk 30, no. 5736; no. 5737, p. 1244; Abu Dawud, *adab* 156 [4541]:III, bk 36, no. 5199, p. 1440.

11. This (non-canonical) hadith is quoted by Razi in his exegesis of sura 24 verse 22; XII:23, pp. 166–167.

12. Muslim, *tawba* 56 [4974]:IV, bk 37, no. 6673, p. 1450.

13. Razi on 24:22; XII:23, pp. 162–167.

14. Abu Dawud, *adab* 3 [4147]:III, bk 36, no. 4759, p. 1339; Ibn Majah, *zuhd* 18 [4176]:V, bk 37, no. 4186, p. 455; Tirmidhi, *birr* 74 [1944], *qiyama* 48 [2417]. Cf. Qur'an 44:54; 52:20; 56:22.

15. Abu Dawud, *adab* 3 [4147]:III, bk 36, no. 4760, p. 1339.

16. This verse is a non-literal quote from the Gospel (Luke 6:33).

17. Razi on 3:133–136; V:9, pp. 7–10.

18. Razi on 14:5; X:19, pp. 66–67.

19. Razi on 45:14–15; XIV:27, pp. 225–226.

20. Razi on 9:128; VIII:16, pp. 186–188.

21. Bukhari, *buyu'* 50 [1981]:III, bk 34, no. 335, p. 189 (my italics); cf. Bukhari, *tafsir* sura 48 chapter 3 [4461]:VI, bk 60, no. 362, p. 345; Tirmidhi, *birr* 68 [1939]. This narrative clearly refers to Isaiah's prophecy known as the first 'Servant Song' (Is. 42:1–9). The Gospel of Matthew applies this prophecy to Jesus' mission (Matt. 12:15–21). The Arabic word for 'the nations' is *al-ummiyyun* (from *umma*, 'nation'). An alternative translation would be 'the illiterates' (from *ummiyya*, 'illiteracy'). As this hadith echoes Isaiah's prophecy, which speaks in verses 1 and 6 of 'the nations' (Heb. *gôyîm*), it seems more appropriate to choose the first option.

22. Razi on 3:159; V:9, pp. 50–56.

23. The words *khudhi l-ʿafw* have been translated by 'show forgiveness' in line with the most usual meaning of the word *ʿafw* (Bukhari, *tafsir* sura 7 chapter 5 [4277]:VI, bk 60, no. 167, p. 133; Abu Dawud, *adab* 5 [4155]:III, bk 36, no. 4769, p. 1341). An alternative translation would be 'take the surplus' as the word *ʿafw* could mean 'surplus' (Bukhari, *nafaqat* 1:VII, bk 64, ch. 1, p. 201). In this case God asked Muhammad through this verse to collect taxes from Muslims at the time when the regulations about *zakat*, 'almsgiving', were not yet given.

24. Ibn Hanbal, *musnad al-shamiyyin* 51 [16696, 16810].

25. Razi on 7:199; VIII:15, pp. 78–79. One narrative explains that ʿUmar became extremely angry when a polytheist criticized his leadership. ʿUmar was about to beat the polytheist up when a Muslim reminded the angry man of sura 7 verse 199. This calmed him down, as 'he was respectful of God's Book' (Bukhari, *tafsir* sura 7 chapter 5 [4276]:VI, bk 60, no. 166, p. 132).

26. Razi on XIV:27, pp. 200–201.

27. Bukhari, *jizya* 7 [2934]:IV, bk 53, no. 394, p. 261.

28. Bukhari, *jizya* 14 [2940]:IV, bk 53, ch. 34, p. 266, and no. 400, p. 267.

29. Razi on 5:14; VI:11, pp. 147–149.

30. Razi on 2:109; II:3, pp. 213–221.

31. Bukhari, *adab* 115 [5739]:VIII, bk 73, no. 226, p. 145; cf. Bukhari *tafsir* sura 3 chapter 15 [4200]:VI, bk 60, no. 89, p. 70.

32. Bukhari, *jizya* 6 [2931]:IV, bk 53, no. 392, p. 259. The Arabic word for 'land', *ard*, can also mean 'the earth'.

33. The texts most often quoted in connection with the obligation to fight unbelievers are sura 9 verses 5 and 29. As sura 9 (revealed probably in 630) is six years later than the battle of Badr referred to in the above-quoted hadith (see n. 31), it seems that these verses are quoted for their theological significance, which overrides their historical context.

34. Ibid., pp. 797–798. Bukhari, *iman* 16 [24]: I, bk 2, no. 24, p. 25; *iʿtisam* 28:IX, bk 92, p. 339; Muslim, *iman* 15 [31]:I, bk 1, no. 29, p. 15; Ibn Majah, *fitan* 1 [3917]:V, bk 36, no. 3927, p. 267; Tirmidhi, *tafsir* sura 88 [3264]; Nasaʾi, *jihad* 1 [3042].

35. Allam, 'Concept', p. 139 (italics original).

36. Ibid., p. 143 (italics original). The author admits that three Qurʾanic verses seem to contradict his argument (2:109; 3:200; 16:90). However, he observes that sura 3 verse 200 and sura 16 verse 90 'do not, in fact,

explicitly order forgiveness as such' (p. 144). The only exception is sura 2 verse 109, which points out 'the fact that the Qur'an can at least once address the average man on the subject of forgiveness in such an emphatic manner as would, when considered in the light of the other verses, show that the Qur'anic view of forgiveness is that it is very strongly recommended, though not absolutely enforced' (p. 145).

37. Ibid., p. 141.
38. Ibid.

CONCLUSION:
SOVEREIGNTY, JUSTICE, MERCY

Forgiveness is not an occasional act; it is a permanent attitude.
Martin Luther King, *The Lion Christian Quotation Collection*

We have seen that the Qur'an and the Hadith portray God as the forgiving God. Having the right to forgive his creatures is one of his exclusive prerogatives and being willing to forgive indicates his merciful character. Within Islam, however, the scope of God's forgiveness varies in as much as the Muslim community is diverse. Theologians and Sufis do not share the same understanding of God, and even the theologians themselves tend to emphasize different aspects of God's character.

Why does God forgive?

The subtle secrets of repentance
Ansari, the famous Sufi of Herat (in today's Afghanistan), meditates extensively on repentance in the second chapter of his treatise *Manazil al-salikin* ('The stages of the itinerants'). He sees it as the key to knowing God, referring to what he calls 'The Subtle Secrets of Repentance' (*lata'if sara'ir al-tawba*).[1] These three secrets

point to the main motives for God's forgiveness in Islamic thought. The first deals with the theological motives. Anṣari explains that it is God who has ordained sin, in order to give us a fuller revelation of himself:[2]

> The *First Secret* consists in considering how [your] sin relates to [God's] Order so that you may come to appreciate God's purpose in letting you commit sin. Indeed, God does not prevent his servant from sinning for either reason.
>
> First, to make known his sovereignty through his Order with regard to sin,
>
> and his goodness in covering it,
>
> his forbearance in giving respite to the sinner,
>
> his generosity in accepting his apologies,
>
> and his favour in forgiving him.
>
> Second, to make the case for his justice against his servant so that he may punish him for his sin on the basis of this case.

This secret has two parts. The first explains that God forgives so that his *sovereignty* and his *mercy* might be made known. These are precisely the key motives in Sunni theology. Sunni theologians hold that Muslims will go to paradise either immediately after the Day of Judgment or after they have paid for their sins in hell. The second part refers to God's *justice*, which is the overarching principle in Mu'tazili theology. Mu'tazili theologians hold that God can forgive only minor sins; sinful Muslims will be sent to hell together with non-Muslims where they will be eternally punished.[3]

The second and third secrets describe God's motives for forgiving according to Sufi tradition:

> The *Second Secret* consists in knowing that any discerning and honest person, who seeks to identify his evil deeds, is bound to realise that he is left without any good deed whatsoever. Such a person will find himself walking between the sight of God's free gift on one side, and the inspection of the deficiency which characterises [his] soul and action on the other side.
>
> The *Third Secret* is that, when the servant ponders upon the [Divine] Decree, he no longer considers good any good action or evil any evil

deed, for he has reached beyond all concepts to the very concept of [Divine] Decree.[4]

The Second Secret encapsulates important aspects of Sufi teaching. As spiritually minded Muslims, Sufis have a penetrating assessment of human life and deeds. Their understanding of sin is much deeper than in Islamic theology, which defines sin merely as transgression of God's law. For them sin affects almost all our actions, including those that are apparently good. Likewise, Sufi doctrine is concerned with our 'heart' as much as with our conduct. Sin is present deep within us, and not only in our wrongdoing. And yet, in Sufism God is seen as generous and his blessings are overwhelming. Genuine repentance means returning to God, not to gain his reward nor to escape his judgment, but simply because he is the Source of our true being.

The Third Secret is revealed when the traveller reaches his destination; that is, God. He then realizes that the very concept of good and evil has been superseded by God's ultimate Decree (or Act). Since God has decreed evil and has used it to reveal himself to us and to bring us back to him, evil is not really evil. If anything, it is a blessing in disguise.

The primary motive of love

The motives for God's forgiveness in Christianity are akin to those in Islam, with some noticeable differences. His love, and not only his mercy, is the primary motive in his dealings with us. God is also just and his justice requires that we all should be punished because of our sins. Yet, instead of condemning us, God has acted in sovereign power to forgive us. He has demonstrated his love for us without compromising his justice.

In Christianity God's forgiveness is found in Jesus' mission. Jesus Christ revealed who God is in a unique way. His message, the gospel, is all about God's love, justice and sovereignty. As a prophet, his mission was to promise God's forgiveness. He gave his life in fulfilment of this promise, which is why he is more than a prophet: he is the Saviour. Through his death and resurrection he enacted the message he preached. Thus the major difference between Christianity and Islam lies in the fact that in Christianity

	What motivates God to forgive?	Key texts
Sunni Muslims	**Sovereignty** Mercy Justice	'God does not forgive that partners be associated with Him, but He forgives any other sin to whom He pleases. Those who associate partners with God commit a great sin' (4:48). He will forgive whom He will and He will punish whom He will. For God has supreme power over all things' (2:284).
Mu'tazili Muslims	**Justice** Mercy Sovereignty	'If you keep away from major [sins], We will pardon your [minor] sins and introduce you [to paradise] through a gate of great honour' (4:31). On that Day men will proceed in companies sorted out, to be shown the deeds that they have done. Whoever has done an atom's weight of good shall see it, and whoever has done an atom's weight of evil shall see it too' (99:6–8).
Ibn 'Arabi (a Sufi Muslim)	**Mercy** Sovereignty Justice	'Say, "O My servants who have transgressed against their souls! Despair not of God's mercy. God forgives all sins, for He is the All-Forgiving, the All-Merciful"' (39:53).
Christians	**Love** Sovereignty and Justice	'For God so loved the world that he gave his one and only Son, that whoever believes in him shall not perish but have eternal life' (John 3:16).

Table 19. God's motives in forgiving, according to Islam and Christianity

God's attributes have been historically displayed in the unique person of Jesus. He reconciled God's mercy, sovereignty and justice, three attributes over which Islamic theology is divided.

The outworking of God's attributes in Islam is eschatological (they will be revealed on the Day of Judgment), whereas in Christianity it is historical: they have been demonstrated in the saving ministry of Jesus. This difference can be accounted for on two grounds. First, *God is the loving God* in Christianity. He is willing to commit himself to humanity to a far greater degree than in Islam. His engagement with his people reached a climax through his coming to our world to live personally among us. Second, *sin is far more serious* in Christianity than in Islam. Christian teaching about sin is much closer to Sufism than to Islamic theology. Because we are sinful, we need to be redeemed, not just forgiven. Because we are alienated from God, we need to be reconciled with him. Because we are spiritually dead, we need to be given new life. This is why God sent Jesus Christ to die for our sins, and the Holy Spirit to recreate us and to restore our relationship with our heavenly Father.

In Islam God is the merciful but not the loving God. He is the forgiving but not the saving God. Hence the paradigm of Islamic faith is creation–submission–judgment, where the focus is on God's judgment. On the last day God will condemn those who have not acknowledged their Creator as the one and only God: 'God does not forgive that partners be associated with Him, but He forgives any other sin to whom He pleases' (4:48, 116). By contrast, the paradigm of Christian faith is creation–sin–redemption, where the focus is on God's salvation. Forgiveness of sins is granted to those who believe in Jesus Christ as God's appointed Saviour: 'God our Saviour ... desires all people to be saved and to come to the knowledge of the truth' (1 Tim. 2:3–4, ESV).[5]

The demonstration of God's sovereignty

In his reflection on repentance, Ansari praises God for his sovereignty. He contends that God has shown his sovereignty in determining humankind's sin. This statement, which is in line with Sufi doctrine and Sunni teaching, amounts to explaining away 'the problem of evil'. Attributing sin to God's sovereignty is likely to lead, as it has done for many Muslims, to fatalism and moral laxity.

The Bible too praises God for his sovereignty. Some texts appear to suggest that God is the creator of both good and evil (Is. 45:7; Lam. 3:38; Prov. 16:4; Rom. 9:19–23). What they really mean is that God remains in full control of evil. His sovereignty is displayed, not in his decision to let us commit sin, but in his spectacular victory over evil. Because God is a holy God, evil is totally unjustifiable. The fact that God in his sovereignty uses his triumph over evil to give us a fuller revelation of himself does not mean that evil can be tolerated or that we are excused for committing sin.

Take Joseph's brothers, for example. When they sold Joseph into slavery, what they did was completely wrong. Just because God used the consequences of their crime to provide deliverance in Egypt for their household did not lessen the guilt of their behaviour (Gen. 50:20; Qur'an 12:21, 91–22). God proves his sovereignty not by allowing evil to exist, but by defeating it. Similarly, he will show his justice by judging evildoers.

Above all, however, God's justice and sovereignty are best demonstrated in forgiveness. But how does he forgive *and* demonstrate his justice and sovereignty at the same time? Through forgiving sinners on the basis of Jesus' atoning death: 'God presented him as a sacrifice of atonement ... He did it to demonstrate his justice at the present time, *so as to be just and the one who justifies* those who have faith in Jesus' (Rom. 3:26; my italics).

How can a God of mercy send people to hell?

What if we do not heed the prophetic warning about the Day of Judgment? The Qur'an promises eternal punishment to those who do not repent and believe in God. Eternal punishment is the object of God's 'threat' (*wa'id*) just as much as paradise is the object of his 'promise' (*wa'd*). Punishment and recompense are part of the same divine 'promise'. The Qur'anic message is as emphatic about hell as it is about paradise.[6] So, is eternal punishment compatible with divine mercy? We have seen that for Ibn 'Arabi the answer is no. He believes that because God is first and foremost a merciful and forgiving God, his punishment will necessarily be limited in duration. Suffering in hell will come to an end. Non-Muslims will eventually enjoy eternal bliss, although their happiness will not be the same as that for Muslims.

Whether God's punishment is consistent with his mercy is undoubtedly one of the most challenging issues for believers. The Hadith tells us that this question was put to the Prophet by an ordinary Muslim mother who had heard him saying that 'God is more merciful towards His servants than a woman is to her child':[7]

> We were in the company of God's Apostle in some of his military expeditions. He happened to pass by a people and asked, 'Which people are you?' They replied, 'We are Muslims.' A woman was throwing firewood in her oven and her son was with her. When the oven blazed, she moved him away. Then she came to the Prophet and said,
>
> — Are you God's Apostle?
> — Yes.
> — Is God most merciful of the merciful?
> — Yes.
> — Is God not more merciful to His servants than a mother is to her child?
> — Yes.
> — Then a mother does not throw her child into the fire?
>
> On this, God's Apostle threw himself prostrate weeping. Then he raised his head towards her and said:
> — Verily, God does not torment anyone of His servants except the defiant who rebels against God and refuses to confess, 'There is no god but God.'[8]

Muhammad's reaction to the woman's blunt questioning is remarkable. He was deeply moved by the prospect of people suffering, yet he did not let his emotions dictate his answer. His response appears to be that of a man who was concerned first of all with conveying God's message faithfully. His reply also suggests that God's judgment will be fair. Only people who have rejected the truth about God, deliberately and knowingly, will be condemned.

This incident is in a way parallel to Jesus' attitude towards his people. Jesus was sent to Israel in fulfilment of the promises God made through many prophets. His miracles proved that he was indeed the Messiah (Is. 35:5–6; 61:1; Matt. 11:1–6). Yet, despite his relentless appeals, the Jewish people refused to believe in him. When he realized that they were determined to go their own way, he was deeply moved and wept. He knew, however, that he must declare God's impending judgment on them:

> As he [Jesus] approached Jerusalem and saw the city, he wept over it and said, 'If you, even you, had only known on this day what would bring you peace – but now it is hidden from your eyes. The days will come upon you when your enemies will build an embankment against you and encircle you and hem you in on every side. They will dash you to the ground, you and the children within your walls. They will not leave one stone on another, *because you did not recognise the time of God's coming to you.*'
> (Luke 19:41–45; my italics; cf. Luke 21:20–24; 23:28–31)

Jesus' prophecy was fulfilled in AD 70 when Jerusalem was invaded by the Roman army. The temple was destroyed, many people were killed and others had to flee the city. Jesus presented the judgment of Jerusalem as a historical and local foreshadowing of the last days and the universal judgment (Luke 21:20–27). Jesus was full of compassion for the people of Israel in particular and for humanity in general. His love for Jerusalem and for the world led him to give his life as a sacrifice so that people from every nation would escape punishment on the Day of Judgment. Yet it is this same Jesus who was unambiguous about the reality of God's judgment. He used graphic images to describe the torment of hell where, he says, 'there will be weeping and gnashing of teeth' (Matt. 8:12; 13:42, 50; 24:51; 25:30).

While recognizing the difficulty of reconciling God's love with eternal punishment, the teaching of both the Bible and the Qur'an remind us that God is a just God. His justice would be undermined if unrepentant people were allowed to go unpunished. Would we not be outraged if we knew that criminals who have caused so much suffering in this world would be punished neither in this life nor in the hereafter? If we, though we are sinners, have such an acute sense of justice, how much more has God, whose justice and holiness are perfect? Moral accountability is a distinctive mark of our humanity and dignity. We are responsible for our actions. The implication of this is that we must be prepared to face the consequences of our conduct. Punishment is a fitting response to evil when the evildoer remains unrepentant: 'Do not be deceived: God cannot be mocked. A man reaps what he sows. The one who sows to please his sinful nature, from that nature will reap destruction; the one who sows to please the Spirit, from the Spirit will reap eternal life' (Gal. 6:7–8). Thus eternal punishment is the consequence of both God's justice and our moral responsibility. His judgment will be fair, and his punishment will be proportionate to people's sin (Luke 12:47–48).

The Bible describes eternal punishment as 'the second death' (Rev. 2:11; 20:6, 14; 21:8) in contrast to our physical death. This second death is the result of spiritual alienation from God. It means 'a conscious experience of rejection and torment'.[9] In the parable of 'the rich man and Lazarus' (Luke 16:19–31) Jesus suggests that hell and paradise are eternal; there will be no chance for people in hell to go to paradise (v. 26). Torment in hell consists of regretting the selfish way of life one has conducted while on earth. Yet such regret will be fruitless, for it will come too late. God's offer of salvation will have come to an end on the Day of Judgment. Regret without the prospect of forgiveness leads to remorse, the full awareness of one's irretrievable failure. Remorse without the possibility of repentance produces despair, pain and rage. Repentant people, by contrast, are aware of their sin. Their regret, which is met by God's forgiveness, leads them to faith, hope and peace: 'Godly sorrow brings repentance that leads to salvation and leaves no regret, but worldly sorrow brings death' (2 Cor. 7:10).

The difference between regret and remorse is personified respectively in the lives of Peter and Judas. Both disciples betrayed Jesus. Judas handed over his master for thirty silver coins (Matt. 27:3–5) and Peter denied that he had ever known him (Matt. 26:69–75). Although both acknowledged their evil action, one wept bitterly, whereas the other was full of guilt and committed suicide. After his resurrection Jesus met with Peter, reassured him and restored his relationship with him (John 21:15–19). Death was the end product of Judas's remorse. Eternal life, though not without suffering in this life, was promised to Peter by his loving and forgiving Lord.

Forgiveness of sins makes no sense without the reality of eternal punishment (Dan. 12:2; Matt. 25:46). Whether eternal punishment means eventual annihilation (as suggested by some Christians) or conscious and endless pain (according to traditional Christian and Islamic teaching) this punishment shows us how much we need God's forgiveness. It highlights the incredible promise of God's pardon, a promise that will only become effective when we repent: 'Forgiveness needs to be accepted, as well as given, before it is complete' (C. S. Lewis).[10]

From a Christian perspective the promise of forgiveness is the gateway to eternal life. Eternal life is to be fully enjoyed when Jesus comes back to establish God's kingdom on earth. Yet we can experience it as soon as we respond to God's love, powerfully demonstrated in the life, death and resurrection of Jesus Christ. To possess eternal life is to take part in God's decisive victory that Jesus won two thousand years ago. It is to work towards God's final triumph when Jesus comes back: the triumph of life over death, good over evil, joy over sorrow, hope over despair, justice over injustice, peace over conflict and love over hatred. To be forgiven is to enjoy life to the full and to know God's supreme blessing *here and now*:

> Blessed is he
>> whose transgressions are forgiven,
>> whose sins are covered.
> Blessed is the man
>> whose sin the LORD does not count against him
>> and in whose spirit is no deceit.
> (Ps. 32:1–2)

Knowing the reality of forgiveness

The gospel is perceived by Muslims as a message of love and forgiveness, which it truly is. While admiring this message, they often think of it as idealistic, far beyond people's reach. Christian teaching reflects God's character, whereas Islamic law represents a compromise between God's character and human weakness. It is true that because of our sinfulness it is not only difficult but impossible to live up to God's standards. Yet as Christians we do not rely on our own resources but on God's power. Through his Spirit, he is at work in our lives, transforming our hearts and enabling us to walk in the footsteps of Jesus Christ.

The following prayer is a testimony of the reality of God's work in the life of one of his people. It was written by H. B. Dehqani-Tafti, the Anglican bishop in Iran during the Iranian Revolution. His only son, Bahram, was murdered in May 1980, aged twenty-four. Anger, hatred and revenge is our natural reaction to violence. Instead, we see here that God inspired peace, love and forgiveness to a suffering father in response to the murder of his son.

O God,
We remember not only Bahram but also his murderers;
Not because they killed him in the prime of his youth and made our
    hearts bleed and our tears flow,
Not because with this savage act they have brought further disgrace
    on the name of our country among the civilized nations of the
    world;
But because through their crime we now follow thy footsteps more
    closely in the way of sacrifice.
The terrible fire of this calamity burns up all selfishness and
    possessiveness in us;
Its flame reveals the depth of depravity and meanness and suspicion,
    the dimension of hatred and the measure of sinfulness in human
    nature;
It makes obvious as never before our need to trust in God's love as
    shown in the cross of Jesus and his resurrection;
Love which makes us free from hate towards our persecutors;
Love which brings patience, forbearance, courage, loyalty, humility,
    generosity, greatness of heart;
Love which more than ever deepens our trust in God's final victory and
    his eternal designs for the Church and for the world;
Love which teaches us how to prepare ourselves to face our own day of
    death.

O God,

Bahram's blood has multiplied the fruit of the Spirit in the soil of our
    souls;

So when his murderers stand before thee on the day of judgment

Remember the fruit of the Spirit by which they have enriched our lives,

And forgive.[11]

A final word

Islam is no longer an Eastern and exotic religion. The Muslim
community is well established in many Western countries. But
there remains much ignorance and misunderstanding about Islam
and Muslims. September 11 has been followed by an ongoing
debate about what Islam is (a religion of peace?) and what it is not.
I hope that this book provides a useful contribution to this debate.
It has provided first-hand information on Islam based on how
Muslims understand their own Scriptures. Like other religious
traditions, Islam is not a monolithic religion, and Muslims do not
form a homogenous community. Sufism, or Islamic mysticism,
undoubtedly represents an attractive spiritual interpretation. But
even within mainstream Islam, Islamic faith has been understood
in significantly different ways by different Muslims.

Up to a third of the Muslim population worldwide live in non-
Muslim countries. Many live in the West in pluralistic and secular
societies. As they interact with these societies, Muslims are
developing new expressions of Islam based on Islamic traditions
that have historically coexisted within the Muslim community.
God's mercy, patience and forgiveness, so emphatically proclaimed
in the Qur'an, will have to be interpreted as key to understanding
Islam if Muslims want their religion to be perceived by non-
Muslims as a religion of peace and tolerance. The full implications
of these concepts also need to be enhanced in relationships within
the Muslim community as well as between Muslims and non-
Muslims.

Christian readers of this book will, I trust, have gained new
insights into Islam. Christians do not usually realize how much they
have in common with Muslims in many areas and particularly
in terms of who God is. Christians and Muslims disagree not so
much about who God is, but rather about the outworking of his

attributes in history. It is important for Christians to realize *why* Islam denies Christian truths. It is often to affirm other truths about God that are also part of the Christian message. Thus Muslims think they have to reject the Christian doctrine of the Trinity in order to protect God's oneness. They think they have to reject Jesus' death on the cross in order to protect God's power and his faithfulness to one of his greatest prophets. The Qur'an declares that Jesus was not crucified, because God rescued his servant from the hands of those who wanted to kill him (3:54–55; 4:157–159). In other words, God powerfully vindicated Jesus and foiled the murderous plan of his enemies. Sunni Muslims think they have to reject the Christian teaching that it is possible to be sure of God's forgiveness, because they see it to be irreconcilable with God's sovereignty on the Day of Judgment.

Christians need to learn how to relate the gospel to Islamic teaching. This book has been an attempt to present the message of Jesus Christ in terms familiar to Muslims. My hope is that many Christian readers will have found its approach to Islam an example for their relationship with their Muslim friends.

Finally, it is my prayer that this book, when read by Muslims, will contribute to their understanding of the gospel. I believe that God's character in Islam (that he is one, sovereign, merciful, forgiving and just) is by no means undermined in the gospel. In fact, these divine attributes are perfectly displayed in Jesus Christ. Paradoxically, the cross demonstrates God's triumph over evil, and Jesus' resurrection proclaims God's victory over death. Not only did Jesus reveal God through his message; God's character is also fulfilled in Jesus' life, death and resurrection. Jesus showed that Allah is indeed *akbar*: God is greater than our understanding of his greatness. He is powerful, merciful and just, far beyond our expectations.

The unique way in which Jesus revealed God and his glory proves that Jesus himself is a unique prophet. His uniqueness is summed up in the divine prerogative he claimed for himself to have authority to forgive people's sins (Mark 2:1–12) and in his unparalleled resurrection from the dead, followed by his ascension to heaven.

The great news of the gospel is that we do not have to wait until the Day of Judgment to know whether or not God will grant us his forgiveness. Because of Jesus Christ, we can receive God's forgiveness *here and now*. This is literally a life-changing experience. For this fantastic good news to become a reality, we need to acknowledge God's oneness, which is at the heart of Islamic faith, and Jesus' uniqueness. The Qur'an points to Jesus' uniqueness through his virgin birth, his sinlessness, his being God's word and spirit and his bodily elevation to heaven. But only the Bible speaks plainly about this uniqueness. Jesus is the only mediator between God and humankind. I invite the Muslim reader to consider a Christian equivalent to the *shahada* and to re-examine, before God, his or her belief as to who Jesus truly is: 'There is one God, and there is one mediator between God and men, the man Jesus Christ, who gave himself as a ransom for all' (1 Tim. 2:5, ESV).

Notes

1. The word *sarira* (pl. *sara'ir*) means secret, intimate or hidden thought, intention. The word *latifa* (pl. *lata'if*) refers to something subtle, soft, refined. It can be a story, a joke, an expression etc. Alternative translations of the Arabic expression could be 'the subtleties of the secrets of repentance', 'the hidden meanings of repentance', 'the spiritual mysteries of repentance'.

2. This view is in line with Ansari's personal background as a Hanbalite Muslim and with Sunni theology in general.

3. However, Mu'tazili theologians teach that people's disobedience is the outcome, not of God's determination, but of their own free will. They argue that God's justice precludes divine predestination; otherwise people cannot be held fully accountable for their actions.

4. Ansari, *Manazil*, pp. 10–11. Ansari spells out these secrets in a literary style that can be fully appreciated only in the original Arabic. The first secret speaks of God's 'Order' (*qadiyya*); the third secret refers to his 'Decree' (*hukm*).

5. God is described as Saviour eight times in the New Testament (Luke 1:47; 1 Tim. 1:1; 2:3; 4:10; Titus 1:3; 2:10; 3:4; Jude 25), and Jesus Christ is called Saviour sixteen times (Luke 2:11; John 4:42; Acts 5:31; 13:23; Eph. 5:23; Phil. 3:20; 2 Tim. 1:10; Titus 1:4; 2:13; 3:6; 2 Pet. 1:1, 11; 2:20; 3:2, 18; 1 John 4:14). Jesus revealed God as Saviour in fulfilling, through his

death and resurrection, his Father's merciful purpose to save humanity. In doing so he became 'the Saviour of the world' (John 4:42). This is what singles out Jesus' mission among all God's prophets: 'the Father has sent his Son to be the Saviour of the world' (1 John 4:14).

6. The Qur'anic vocabulary for hell is very rich. No fewer than eight words are used in connection with 'punishment' ('adhab) in the hereafter: nar (fire), jahannam (Gehenna), jahim (furnace), sa'ir (flame), saqar (Hades), laza (blaze), hutamat (devouring fire), and hawiya (pit).

7. Muslim, tawba 22 [4947]:IV, bk 37, no. 6635, p. 1438; Bukhari, adab 18 [5540]:VIII, bk 73, no. 28, p. 19.

8. Ibn Majah, zuhd 35 [4287]:V, bk 37, no. 4297, p. 518.

9. Nature of Hell, p. 132.

10. Ward and Wild, Lion Christian Quotation Collection, p. 278.

11. Dehqani-Tafti, Hard Awakening, pp. 113–114.

APPENDIX A | ARABIC WORDS

Divine names

al-'adl, al-'adil	The Just
al-'afuww	The Pardoning
al-'alim	The All-Knowing
al-'aly	The Most-High
al-'aziz	The Almighty
al-bari'	The Producer, the Maker
al-ghaffar	The Ever-Forgiving
al-ghafir	The Forgiving
al-ghafur	The All-Forgiving
al-ghani	The Self-Sufficient, the Rich
al-hakim	The All-Wise
al-halim	The Patient, the Forbearing
al-hannan	The Full of Pity
al-hayyi	The Bashful
al-haqq	The Truth
al-khaliq	The Creator
al-malik	The King, the Master
al-mawla	The Helper, the Master, the Protector
al-qadi	The Judge
al-qadir	The All-Powerful
al-qahir	The Sovereign, the Dominator
al-quddus	The Flawless
al-ra'uf	The Lenient
al-rabb	The Lord
al-rahim	The All-Merciful
al-rahman	The Ever-Merciful
al-salam	The Perfect
al-shakur	The Grateful
al-tahir	The Pure

al-tawwab   The Most-Returning
al-wadud   The Loving-Kind
al-wahid   The One

Life and obedience

da'wah	mission
hajj	pilgrimage
hasana	good deed
i'tibar	reflection
i'tiraf	confession
ihsan	goodness, kindness
iman	faith
inaba	contrition
islam	submission
istislam	surrender
jihad	struggle, fight
khawf	fear
kulfa	mandate
ma'rifa	spiritual knowledge
muhasaba	examination of conscience
mujahada	spiritual warfare
nawafil	supererogatory acts (sing. *nafila*)
qibla	direction for prayer
raja'	hope
rida	contentedness
sabr	patience, endurance
salat	ritual prayer
sawm	fasting
shahada	confession of faith
shukr	thanksgiving
taba	to return, to come back
tasdiq	trusting
tawakkul	trusting, relying
tawba	repentance
thawab	recompense
yaqaza	awakening

zakat	almsgiving
zuhd	asceticism

Sin

dhanb	sin
'isyan, ma'siya	disobedience
fasiq	sinful Muslim, guilty of *fisq*
fisq	wickedness, sinfulness
haram	unlawful
ibahiyya	permissiveness
ithm	crime
jinaya	transgression, offence
kaba'ir	major sins (sing. *kabira*)
kafir	unbeliever (pl. *kafirun* or *kuffar*)
khata'	mistake, misjudgment
kufr	unbelief
lamam	small, minor sins
munafiq	hypocritical (pl. *munafiqun*), guilty of *nifaq* (hypocrisy)
murtadd	apostate (pl. *murtaddun*), guilty of *radda* (apostasy)
mushrik	polytheist, 'a person who associates', guilty of *shirk*
nisyan	forgetfulness
sagha'ir	minor sins (sing. *saghira*)
sayyi'a	evil deed
shirk	polytheism, the sin of associating partners with God
zalim	evildoer, unjust (pl. *zalimun*), guilty of *zulm*
zalla	false step, mistake

Pardon and punishment

'adhab	punishment
'afw	pardon (from *'afa*, to erase, forgive)

fadl	undeserved favour
ghafara	to hide, forgive
ghufran, maghfira	forgiveness
hadd	legal punishment (pl. *hudud*)
haqq	legal right (pl. *huquq*)
istihqaq	deservedness
jaza'	retribution
karam, jud	generosity
lutf	divine grace, undeserved blessing
mithaq, 'ahd	covenant
ni'ma, minna	divine grace, gift
rahma	mercy
shafa'a	intercession
shafi'	intercessor
takfir	atonement (from *kaffara*, to atone, forgive)
tawhid	monotheism, oneness of God
wa'd	promise
wa'id	threat, punishment

Community and theology

al-'amma	common, ordinary people
al-khassa	élite
anbiya'	prophets
awliya'	saints
fiqh	jurisprudence
ijma'	consensus
kalam	theology
shari'a	law
shaykh	Sufi leader
sufiyya	Sufism
tafsir	commentary
tanzih	transcendence
tashbih	anthropomorphism, the act of ascribing to God a human form
'ulama'	scholars
umma	community, nation

The following are testimonies about the dramatic conversion to God of four Muslims, resulting in their commitment to the Sufi path. The Arabic spelling of names of people, places and so on is slightly different from the way these names are written in Persian. These testimonies have been compiled by Farid al-Din al-'Attar in his *Tadhkirat al-awliya'*, and are here reproduced by permission of Penguin Books Ltd.

Malik bin Dinar (130/748)

Now his conversion came about as follows. He was a very handsome man and fond of wordly [*sic*] things, and he possessed great wealth. He lived in Damascus, where Mo'awiya had built the cathedral mosque, endowing it liberally. Malek was very eager to be appointed in charge of that mosque. So he went and threw his prayer rug down in the corner of the mosque, and there for a whole year continued in devotion, hoping that whoever saw him would find him at prayer.

'What a hypocrite for you!' he would say to himself.

A year passed in this way. By night he would leave the mosque and take his amusement. One night he was enjoying music, and all his companions had fallen asleep. Suddenly a voice came from the lute he was playing.

'Malek, what ails thee that thou repentest not?'

Hearing these words, Malek dropped the instrument and ran to the mosque in great confusion.

'For a whole year I have worshipped God hypocritically,' he communed with himself. 'Is it not better that I should worship God in sincerity? Yet I am ashamed. What am I to do? Even if they offer me this appointment, I will not accept it.'

So he resolved, and he put his conscience right with God. That night he worshipped with a truthful heart. Next day people assembled as usual before the mosque.

'Why, there are cracks in the mosque,' they exclaimed. 'A superintendent ought to be appointed to keep it in order.'

They reached the unanimous view that no one was better fitted for the post than Malek. So they came to him. He was at prayer, so they waited patiently until he was finished.

'We have come to plead with you to accept this appointment,' they said.

'O God,' cried Malek, 'I served Thee hypocritically for a whole year, and no one looked at me. Now that I have given my heart to Thee and firmly resolved that I do not want the appointment, Thou hast sent twenty men to me to place this task on my neck. By Thy glory, I do not want it.'

And he ran out of the mosque and applied himself to the Lord's work, taking up the life of austerity and discipline. So respected did he become, and of such excellence of life, that when a certain citizen of Basra died, leaving a lovely daughter, the latter approached Thabet-e Bonani.

'I wish to become the wife of Malek,' she announced, 'so that he may help me in the labour of obedience to God.'

Thabet informed Malek.

'I have divorced the world,' Malek replied. 'This woman belongs to the world I have divorced. I cannot marry her.'[1]

Al-Fudayl bin 'Iyad (187/803)

At the beginning of his career, Fozail-e Iyaz pitched his tent in the heart of the desert between Merv and Bavard. He wore sackcloth and a woollen cap, and hung a rosary around his neck. He had many companions who were all of them thieves and highwaymen. Night and day they robbed and pillaged, and always brought the proceeds to Fozail since he was the senior of them. He would divide the loot among the bandits, keeping for himself what he fancied. He kept an inventory of everything, and never absented himself from the meetings of the gang. Any apprentice who failed to attend a meeting he expelled from the gang.

One day a great caravan was passing that way, and Fozail's confederates were on the alert for it. A certain man was travelling in the convoy who had heard rumour of the brigands. Sighting them, he took counsel with himself how he might conceal his bag of gold.

'I will hide this bag,' he said to himself. 'Then if they waylay the caravan, I will have this capital to fall back on.'

Going aside from the road, he saw Fozail's tent and Fozail himself close by it, an ascetic by his looks and the clothes he wore. So he entrusted the bag of gold to him.

'Go and put it in the corner of the tent,' Fozail told him.

The man did as he was bidden, and returned to the caravan halt, to find that it had been pillaged. All the luggage had been carried off, and the travellers bound hand and foot. The man released them, and collecting the little that remained they took their departure. The man returned to Fozail to recover his bag of gold. He saw him squatting with the robbers, as they divided up the spoil.

'Ah, I gave my bag of gold to a thief!' the man exclaimed.

Seeing him afar off, Fozail hailed the man, who came to him.

'What do you want?' he asked.

'Take it from where you deposited it,' Fozail bade him. 'Then go.'

The man ran into the tent, picked up his bag, and departed.

'Why,' cried Fozail's companions, 'in the whole caravan we did not find so much as one dirham in cash, and you give back ten thousand dirhams!'

'The man had a good opinion of me, and I have always had a good opinion of God, that He will grant me repentance,' Fozail replied. 'I justified his good opinion, so that God may justify my good opinion.'

One day later they waylaid another caravan and carried off the baggage. As they sat eating, a traveller from the caravan approached them.

'Who is your chief?' he asked.

'He is not with us,' the brigands replied. 'He is the other side of the tree by the river bank, praying.'

'But it is not the hour of prayer,' the man exclaimed.

'He is performing a work of supererogation,' one of the thieves explained.

'And he is not eating with you,' the man went on.

'He is fasting,' the thief replied.

'But it is not Ramazan.'

'Supererogation again,' the thief retorted.

Greatly astonished, the traveller drew near Fozail who was praying with great humility. He waited until he had finished, then he remarked, 'Opposites do not mingle, they say. How can one fast and rob, pray and at the same time murder Muslims?'

'Do you know the Koran?' Fozail asked the man.

'I know it,' the man replied.

'Well then, does not the Almighty God say *And others have confessed their sins; they have mixed a righteous deed with another evil?*' [9:102]

The man was speechless with astonishment.

It is said that by nature he was chivalrous and high-minded, so that if a woman was travelling in a caravan he never took her goods; in the same way, he would not pillage the property of anyone with slender capital. He always left each victim with a due proportion of his belongings. All his inclination was towards right doing.

At the beginning of his exploits Fozail was passionately in love with a certain woman, and he always brought her the proceeds of his brigandage. In season and out of season he climbed walls in the infatuation of his passion for the woman, weeping all the while.

One night a caravan was passing, and in the midst of the caravan a man was chanting the Koran. The following verse reached Fozail's ears: *Is it not time that the heart of those who believe should be humbled to the remembrance of God?* [57:16] It was as though an arrow pierced his soul, as though that verse had come out to challenge Fozail and say, 'O Fozail, how long will you waylay travellers? The time has come when We shall waylay you!'

Fozail fell from the wall, crying, 'It is high time indeed, and past high time!'

Bewildered and shamefaced, he fled headlong to a ruin. There a party of travellers were encamped. They said, 'Let us go!' One of them interjected, 'We cannot go. Fozail is on the road.'

'Good tidings!' Fozail cried. 'He has repented.'

With that he set out and all day went on his way weeping, satisfying his adversaries.[2]

Ibrahim bin Adham (165/782)

Ebrahim ibn Adham's saintly career began in the following manner. He was king of Balkh, and a whole world was under his command; forty gold swords and forty gold maces were carried before and behind him. One night he was asleep on his royal couch. At midnight the roof of the apartment vibrated, as if someone was walking on the roof.

'Who is there?' he shouted.

'A friend,' came the reply. 'I have lost a camel, and am searching for it on this roof.'

'Fool, do you look for the camel on the roof?' cried Ebrahim.

'Heedless one,' answered the voice, 'do you seek for God in silken clothes, asleep on a golden couch?'

These words filled his heart with terror. A fire blazed within him, and he could not sleep any more. When day came he returned to the dais and sat on his throne, thoughtful, bewildered and full of care. The ministers of state stood each in his place; his slaves were drawn up in serried ranks. General audience was proclaimed.

Suddenly a man with aweful (*sic*) mien entered the chamber, so terrible to look upon that none of the royal retinue and servants dared ask him his name; the tongues of all clove to their throats. He advanced solemnly till he stood before the throne.

'What do you want?' demanded Ebrahim.

'I have just alighted at this caravanserai,' said the man.

'This is not a caravanserai. This is my palace. You are mad,' shouted Ebrahim.

'Who owned this palace before you?' asked the man.

'My father,' Ebrahim replied.

'And before him?'

'My grandfather.'

'And before him?'

'So-and-so.'

THE SEARCH FOR FORGIVENESS

'And before him?'

'The father of so-and-so.'

'Where have they all departed?' asked the man.

'They have gone. They are dead,' Ebrahim replied.

'Then is this not a caravanserai which one man enters and another leaves?'

With these words the stranger vanished. He was Khezr,[3] upon whom be peace. The fire blazed more fiercely still in Ebrahim's soul, and the anguish within him augmented momently. Visions by day followed the hearing of voices by night, equally mysterious and incomprehensible.

'Saddle my horse,' Ebrahim cried at last. 'I will go to the hunt. I know not what this thing is that has come upon me today. Lord God, how will this affair end?'

His horse was saddled and he proceeded to the chase. Headlong he galloped across the desert; it was as if he knew not what he was doing. In that state of bewilderment he became separated from his troops. On the way he suddenly heard a voice.

'Awake!'

He pretended not to have heard, and rode on. A second time the voice came, but he heeded it not. A third time he heard the voice. And hurled himself farther away. Then the voice sounded a fourth time.

'Awake, before you are stricken awake!'

He now lost all self-control. At that instant a deer started up, and Ebrahim prepared to give chase. The deer spoke to him.

'I have been sent to hunt you. You cannot catch me. Was it for this that you were created, or is this what you were commanded?'

'Ah, what is this that has come upon me?' Ebrahim cried.

And he turned his face from the deer. He thereupon heard the same words issuing from the pommel of his saddle. Terror and fear possessed him. The revelation became clearer yet, for Almighty God willed to complete the transaction. A third time the selfsame voice proceeded from the collar of his cloak. The revelation was thus consummated, and the heavens were opened unto him.

Sure faith was now established in him. He dismounted; all his garments, and the horse itself, were dripping with his tears. He made true and sincere repentance. Turning aside from the road, he saw a shepherd wearing felt clothes and a hat of felt, driving his sheep before him. Looking closely, he saw that he was a slave of his. He bestowed on him his gold-embroidered cloak and bejewelled cap, together with the sheep, and took from him his clothes and hat of felt. These he donned himself. All the angelic hosts stood gazing on Ebrahim.

'What a kingdom has come to the son of Adham,' they cried. 'He has cast away the filthy garments of the world, and has donned the glorious robes of poverty.'[4]

Bishr bin al-Ḥarith (150/767)

Bishr the Barefoot was born in Merv and settled at Baghdad. The beginning of his conversion happened as follows. He had lived a life of dissipation, and one day as he was staggering along the road drunk he found a piece of paper on which was written, 'In the Name of God, the Merciful, the Compassionate.' He bought some attar of roses and perfumed the paper with it, and deposited it reverently in his house. That night a certain holy man had a dream in which he was bidden to tell Beshr:

'Thou hast perfumed my Name, so I have perfumed thee. Thou hast exalted my Name, so I have exalted thee. By my Majesty, I will surely perfume thy name in this world and the world to come.'

'He is a dissolute fellow,' thought the saint. 'Perhaps I am seeing erroneously.'

So he made ablution, prayed and returned to sleep. He saw the selfsame dream a second and a third time. In the morning he arose and went in search of Beshr.

'He is at a wine-party,' he was told.

He went to the house where Beshr was.

'Was Beshr here?' he enquired.

'He was,' they said. 'But he is drunk and incapable.'

'Tell him I have a message for him,' said the saint.

'A message from whom?' demanded Bishr when he was told.

'A message from God,' replied the saint.

'Alas!' cried Beshr, bursting into tears. 'Is it a message of chiding or of chastisement? Wait, till I tell my friends. Friends,' he addressed his drinking-companions, 'I have had a call. I am going. I bid you farewell. You will never see me again at this business.'

And from that day onward he lived so saintly, that none heard his name mentioned without heavenly peace invaded his heart. He took to the way of self-denial, and so overwhelmed was he by the vision of God that he never put shoes on his feet. For that reason he was called Beshr the Barefoot.

'Why do you not wear shoes?' he was asked.

'I was barefooted the day when I made my peace with God,' he said, 'and ever since I am ashamed to wear shoes. Moreover God Almighty says, 'I have made the earth a carpet for you.' It is not seemly to tread with shoes on the carpet of kings.'

Ahmad-e Hanbal visited Beshr frequently, having a complete faith in him to such a point that his pupils protested.

'Today you are without rival as a scholar of Traditions, the law, theology and every manner of science, yet every moment you go after a dissolute fellow. Is that seemly?'

'Indeed, in all the sciences you have enumerated I have better knowledge than he,' Ahmad-e Hanbal replied. 'But he knows God better than I.'

So he would pursue Beshr, saying, 'Tell me about my Lord.'[5]

Notes

1. 'Attar, *Saints*, pp. 27–28.
2. Ibid., pp. 53–55.
3. Al-Khadr (or *al-Khidr*) is a legendary and popular figure in Islamic tradition and literature, especially in Sufism. He is associated with Qur'an 18:60–82, although the enigmatic character in this passage is nameless. This allegedly immortal and supernatural creature has been associated with numerous historical figures (e.g. Enoch, Elijah, Jesus).
4. 'Attar, *Saints*, pp. 63–65.
5. Ibid., pp. 81–82.

APPENDIX C | Muslim Theologians AND Mystics

The following short biographical notes concern those Muslim theologians and mystics quoted more than once in the book. Their names, listed alphabetically, are followed by the year of their death according to the Islamic and Christian calendars.

Theologians

'Abd al-Jabbar, al-Qadi (415/1025)

This prominent Mu'tazili theologian was born and lived in Baghdad. In 367/978 he moved to Rayy (near modern-day Teheran) where he was appointed chief *Qadi* (judge) of the province, hence his surname.

'Abd al-Jabbar belongs to the later generation of Mu'tazili theologians (as opposed to that of Abu 'Ali and Abu Hashim al-Jubba'i). His major work, *Kitab al-Mughni fi usul al-din*, is an enormous theological treatise. He authored other important theological writings that had a lasting impact on Islamic thought. One of them, *Sharh al-usul al-khamsa*, 'Explanation of the Five Fundamentals', is a (lost) commentary on his own (extant) treatise *al-Usul al-khamsa*, 'The Five Fundamentals'. Thus the *Sharh al-usul al-khamsa*, which we have, is wrongly attributed to him. Recent studies have established that it is in fact the work of Ahmad bin Abi Hashim al-Husayni, a Zaydite Persian theologian more commonly known as Mankdim Sheshdiv (425/1034). The real title of this key Mu'tazili treatise is actually *Ta'liq* [Commentary] *Sharh al-usul al-khamsa*, which has been written as a commentary on 'Abd al-Jabbar's *Sharh*.[1]

The 'Five Fundamentals' of Mu'tazili theology are as follows:

1. *al-Tawhid*: God's (absolute) oneness.
2. *al-'Adl*: God's (paramount) justice.
3. *al-Wa'd wa l-wa'id*: God's Promise (of eternal paradise) and Threat (of eternal hell) – made respectively to believers and unbelievers.
4. *al-Manzila bayn al-manzilatayn*: the intermediate status of disobedient Muslims who are neither believers nor unbelievers.
5. *al-Amr bi l-ma'ruf wa l-nahyi 'ani l-munkar*: the obligation of doing good and the prohibition of doing evil.

Abu 'Ali al-Jubba'i (303/915)

Born in Jubba (Iran) Abu 'Ali moved to Basra (Iraq) where he spent the rest of his life. He joined the group of Mu'tazili theologians and contributed greatly to the development of Mu'tazili theology. He is a contemporary of Nazzam (221/836), an important Mu'tazili theologian with whom he took issue on several points.

Jubba'i, or Abu 'Ali as he is commonly called, had many disciples. Two of the most famous are his son Abu Hashim, who eventually joined the Baghdadian school of Mu'tazilism, and Ash'ari, who departed from Mu'tazilism altogether and founded a rival theological school. Although Ash'ari often criticizes Abu 'Ali, his theology remains significantly influenced by his former mentor.

Abu 'Ali produced many theological and polemical works, but none has survived. His teaching has been transmitted by other theologians; namely, Ash'ari in his *Maqalat*. He is the author of an important commentary on the Qur'an, which is quoted by many Muslim exegetes (e.g. Razi, Tusi, Tabarsi, Jushami). Part of this commentary has been collated and published in French.[2]

Abu Hashim al-Jubba'i (321/933)

Son of Abu 'Ali, Abu Hashim is a prominent figure in Mu'tazili theology, particularly of the Baghdadian school. He promoted a theology markedly more radical than his father's. His rational views stand in sharper contrast to Ash'ari theology with regard, for instance, to God's justice and transcendence. Yet in terms of 'God's attributes' (*al-sifat*) Abu Hashim is known for his theory of *ahwal*, 'modes of being'. According to him, the divine attributes (God's will, word, power, science, and life) are more than mere words (as for Basrian Mu'tazilites). They refer to the 'modes of being' of the divine essence; hence they have a certain degree of reality. This theory was later taken up and developed, in their own perspective, by Ash'arite theologians (Baqillani, Juwayni).

Abu Hashim's writings have not been preserved. His teaching has been passed on by other Muslim scholars.

Abu l-Hudhayl, Muhammad al-'Allaf (226/840)

Abu l-Hudhayl is a founder of Mu'tazili theology; hence his title *Shaykh al-mu'tazila*, 'the Master of Mu'tazilites'. He was born in Basra but moved to Baghdad, where he died. He was regularly invited by the 'Abbasid caliph al-Ma'mun (813–33) to hold theological debates in the palace.

In his career Abu l-Hudhayl engaged with two groups of opponents. The first comprised those Muslims who held beliefs deemed non-orthodox (e.g. anthropomorphism, determinism, divinization of imam 'Ali). The second included non-Muslims whose doctrines (e.g. Zoroastrianism, Manichaeism, Greek philosophy) threatened the very core of Islamic teaching. Abu l-Hudhayl asserted the oneness of God and his transcendence. He taught that God's attributes are identical to his essence. God is invisible in the other world. People will only see him 'with their hearts'. God does not do evil and people have a free will, which enables them to choose between good and evil. Therefore they are the authors of their actions and are entirely responsible for their acts and their consequences.

Abu l-Hudhayl had many disciples, of whom the most famous is Nazzam. He produced a lot of writings but none has survived. His teaching has been transmitted by other theologians and historians.

Abu Ya'la, al-Qadi (458/1066)

Born in Baghdad in 380/990, Abu Ya'la's actual name is Muhammad Ibn al-Farra'. He exercised the office of judge in the caliph's palace, hence his surname (*Qadi*).

Abu Ya'la was a reputed Hanbali scholar. He taught *hadith* and *fiqh* (jurisprudence). He often engaged in debate with Ash'ari theologians who accused him of having anthropomorphic views about God. He is the author of several writings; his major work is *al-Mu'tamad fi usul al-din*, 'Reliable exposition of the Fundamentals in religion'. He criticized Muslim theologians (Mu'tazilites as well as Ash'arites) for their rationalistic understanding of the Islamic faith. He had many disciples, including his son Abu l-Husayn (525/1131) who wrote a survey on Hanbali scholars and their teachings (*Tabaqat al-hanabila*).

Ash'ari, Abu l-Hasan (324/935)

Born in Basra in 260/873, Ash'ari died in Baghdad. For many years he was the disciple of Abu 'Ali al-Jubba'i, the leader of the Mu'tazili school in Basra. He later departed from Mu'tazilism and produced an alternative school of theology, which is named after him. This school has become the most representative in Sunni Islam. Its prominent theologians include Ghazali, Razi and, before them, Baqillani and Juwayni.

For the sake of consistency and clarity, Ash'ari is in many ways a radical thinker. He founded his teaching on the Qur'an as well as the Hadith, interpreting them in a highly rational, yet not rationalistic way. For him, God's key attribute, apart from his oneness, is his sovereignty. Divine attributes are entities that exist *in* God but they are distinct from his essence: 'they are neither identical to God (against the Mu'tazilites) nor other than God (against anthropomorphic views)' (*laysat hiya huwa wa la ghayruhu*). He taught that God is the author of human acts, good and evil. Good and evil have no moral value in themselves, but depend entirely on God's judgment. God predestines some people to paradise and others to hell.

Ash'ari produced a large number of works of a dogmatic and polemical nature. His writings present us with a comprehensive, systematic and coherent body of teaching. Only a few have been preserved, including the famous *al-Luma'*, 'Shafts of lights', edited as *The Theology of al-Ash'ari* (by R. J. McCarthy). In his *Ibana 'an usul al-diyana*, 'Exposition of the Fundamentals in religion' he presents his teaching in such a way as to win the favour of Hanbalite scholars. Ash'ari is also the author of a famous survey on Islamic sects and beliefs called *Maqalat al-islamiyyin*, 'The Doctrines of Muslims'.

Baghdadi, 'Abu Mansur (429/1037)

His surname suggests that 'Abu Mansur was from Baghdad. His father took him to Nishapur (Iran) for his religious education. He stayed in the city for most of his life. He became a renowned scholar and had many pupils.

Baghdadi wrote many books on different subjects (including one on arithmetic). His *Usul al-din*, 'The Fundamentals in religion', is a comprehensive theological treatise written from a Sunni perspective. The book is divided into fifteen chapters (each chapter addressing fifteen questions) dealing with issues such as the nature of knowledge, creation, God's attributes, his names, his justice and wisdom, prophecy, miracles and eschatology. The author adopts a fair approach when discussing views not his own. This is not the case in Baghdadi's other famous treatise *al-Farq bayn al-firaq*, 'The Discrimination between different sects'. His treatment of what he considers as non-orthodox beliefs is not only biased but also polemical.

Baqillani, Abu Bakr (403/1013)

Baqillani (the 'greengrocer') was born in Basra and lived in Baghdad where he exercised the office of *Qadi*. He is credited with more than twenty works of which only a few are extant.

As a speaker and writer, Baqillani engaged in polemics to defend Islamic orthodoxy. His aim was to refute non-Muslim beliefs and what he saw as heretical ideas. He is one of the few Muslim authors to use Arabic quotes from the Old and the New Testament when he discusses Christian doctrine. In *I'jaz al-qur'an*, 'The Qur'anic miracle', he looks at the evidence for the divine origin of Islamic Holy Scripture. The *Tamhid*, 'Prolegomena', is a comprehensive précis of Ash'ari theology. The *Insaf fima yajibu 'tiqaduhu*, 'A just treatment of what we ought to believe', is an apologetic treatise dealing with controversial issues. Baqillani's contribution to Islamic theology consists in providing and promoting a systematic presentation of Sunni theology based on Ash'ari's seminal work.

Ibn Furak, Abu Bakr (406/1015)

Born in Isfahan (Iran) in 330/941, Ibn Furak was a contemporary of Baqillani and, like him, was a prominent representative and promoter of Ash'ari theology. He spent many years in Basra, Baghdad, and later in Rayy and Nishapur, where he died.

Ibn Furak produced a few important works. His *Mushkil al-hadith* is concerned with controversial Hadith narratives, especially those that depict God in human form (e.g. God's hands, eyes). His interpretation of these anthropomorphic narratives consists in accepting their plain meaning and admitting not to know how they apply to God. This typically Ash'arite exegesis is called *bila kayfa*, 'without (knowing) how'. It is seen by Ash'ari theologians as a sound alternative to both literal (anthropomorphic) and allegorical (Mu'tazili) exegesis. The other major work of Ibn Furak is his *Mujarrad maqalat al-Ash'ari*, which is a methodical exposition of the teaching of the master. This treatise, written some sixty years after the death of Ash'ari, represents an invaluable source of information on the thought of one of Islam's greatest theologians.

Juwayni, Abu l-Ma'ali (478/1085)
This great figure of the Ash'arism was born in 419/1028 at Juwayn, a small village near Nishapur. He is known as *Imam al-haramayn*, 'the Imam of the two holy sites', because he taught at Mecca and Medina for four years (450–4). After he returned to Nishapur he taught at the Nizamiyya *madrasa* (school) until he died.

Juwayni authored several works. These include two key theological writings: *al-Shamil fi usul al-din*, a précis of an elaborated Ash'ari theology, and *al-Irshad*, 'Instruction'. With Juwayni's contribution the development of Ash'ari theology reached its maturity. The author adopts a highly rational approach in his apologetic study of Islamic doctrine. Unlike other Ash'ari theologians, he favours a metaphorical interpretation of Qur'anic texts that depict God in human form (3:73; 7:54). When he responds to Mu'tazili theologians, he often uses many of their concepts and arguments.

Razi, Fakhr al-Din (606/1209)
One of the greatest Muslim scholars, Razi was born at Rayy. He became a popular preacher and an independent Ash'ari theologian, and spent many years in central Asia refuting Mu'tazilite doctrine. He eventually settled and died in Herat (in present-day Afghanistan).

This hagiography reaches a climax in the last chapter, which is about Hallaj. Some manuscripts have up to twenty more biographies than others. Very early the book was translated into other languages, including Turkish and Uighur. 'Attar is credited with many other writings, but it is very unlikely that he wrote all of them.

Dhu l-Nun al-Misri (246/861)

The son of a Nubian man, Dhu l-Nun was born in Ikhmin (Upper Egypt) about 180/796. He went on pilgrimage to Mecca several times while travelling in Syria and Iraq. He returned to Egypt and died in Giza (near Cairo).

Before he committed himself to Sufism, Dhu l-Nun is said to have written books on medicine, magic and alchemy, but none has survived. He developed the theory of 'mystical stages' (maqamat) and 'mystical states' (ahwal), and taught the true nature of 'spiritual knowledge' (ma'rifa). 'Mystical love' (hubb) and joy play an important part in his teaching. He promoted 'music and dancing' (sama') in spiritual experience and was the first to use the symbol 'wine of love' to describe the relationship between the mystic and God, comparing intoxication by drinking wine to intoxication by falling in love with God.

Ghazali, Abu Hamid (505/1111)

Known in Europe as Algazel, Ghazali was born and died in Tus (Iran). He moved to Nishapur where he became one of Juwayni's disciples. Some years later he went to Baghdad and taught at the Nizamiyya madrasa. He wrote a famous pamphlet against the philosophers, Tahafut al-falasifa, 'The inconsistency of the philosophers'. Having experienced a personal and dramatic conversion he eventually turned to Sufism.

Ghazali's greatest work is Ihya' 'ulum al-din, 'The Revival of religious sciences', parts of which have been translated into many languages. He also wrote a spiritual treatise on God's names, al-Maqsad, translated as The Ninety-Nine Beautiful Names of God (see bibliography). Ghazali's concern throughout his writings is to reconcile Islamic theology with Sufism. His thought represents a kind of spiritual theology or orthodox mysticism.

Hallaj, al-Husayn bin Mansur (309/922)

Hallaj, whose name means 'the wool-carder', was born at Tus. He moved with his father to Wasit (Iraq). His first spiritual master was Sahl al-Tustari. In Basra he met another famous Sufi, 'Amr al-Makki, and became a Sufi through experiencing a personal *tawba* (conversion). In 264/878 he moved to Baghdad and became the disciple of Junayd.

Hallaj spent many years preaching the Sufi path. He called people to find God in their own hearts, a call earning him the title *Hallaj al-asrar*, 'the carder of consciences'. His preaching took him beyond the Muslim community as far as the Indian subcontinent and Turkistan. He attracted a large following and many enemies. In 301/913 he was arrested in Baghdad and put in prison. Eight years later he was condemned to death, exposed on a cross and beheaded. Before he died, he is said to have asked God to be merciful and to forgive his enemies.

The mystical experience proposed and modelled by Hallaj was that of union with God. His teaching has been put into writing by his son Hamd. The life and doctrine of Hallaj has been made accessible thanks to the highly academic work of the French scholar Louis Massignon (1883–1962).

Hujwiri, 'Ali bin 'Uthman (c. 469/1072)

Born at Hujwir, near Ghazni (Afghanistan), Hujwiri travelled extensively before he settled in Lahore where he died. Among his writings the only extant manuscript is *Kashf al-mahjub*, 'The Unveiling of what is hidden'. It is the oldest Persian treatise on Sufism, probably written during the author's last years. The book (see bibliography) has a similar pattern to other classical manuals on Sufism. The author gives a personal touch to what he says, sharing his own views and experiences as he discusses Sufi doctrines and practices.

Ibn 'Arabi, Muhyi l-Din (638/1240)

Ibn 'Arabi was born at Murcia in Andalusia (southern Spain) in 560/1165. He grew up in an Arab home of Sufi tradition. He travelled extensively throughout North Africa and the Middle East, eventually settling in Damascus, where he died.

Ibn 'Arabi was a prolific writer. His greatest work is *al-Futuhat al-makkiyya*, 'The Meccan Revelations'. He is said to have received these revelations over three years while he was living in Mecca. The book is a complete system of mystical knowledge laid out in 560 chapters, of which the penultimate chapter gives a summary of the whole. In a work he wrote a year before he died, *Fusus al-hikam*, 'Bezels of Wisdom', he explains that God's multifaceted wisdom is displayed in each of his prophets: for example, transcendence in Noah, light in Joseph, love in Abraham, truth in Isaac, grandeur in Ishmael, mercy in Solomon, prophecy in Jesus, and unity in Muhammad.

Ibn 'Arabi was seen as heretical by many Muslims who tried to assassinate him. But he also had (and still has) a large and devout following. He is known to his disciples as *al-Shaykh al-akbar*, 'the greatest Master'.

Ibn 'Ata', Abu l-'Abbas Ahmad (309/922)

Ibn 'Ata' was a Sufi whose mystical experience was deeply rooted in his spiritual understanding of the Qur'an and the Hadith. He is said to have memorized the whole Qur'an, which he used to recite every day.

Ibn 'Ata' was a personal friend to Hallaj throughout his life. Like him, he was a disciple of Junayd. When Hallaj was put in prison, he left his manuscripts with him. In terms of their spiritual experience and teaching the two men were very close. For them suffering has a redemptive virtue in the sense that it cleans the self from what hinders achieving complete union with God. However, unlike Hallaj, Ibn 'Ata' asked God to vindicate him and to avenge him by punishing his persecutors. He publicly supported Hallaj and his teaching at the cost of his own life. He was tortured by his enemies and died a week later. Hallaj was executed the same year.

Junayd, Abu l-Qasim (298/910)

Junayd was born in Baghdad and died in the same place. He is one of the greatest Sufis and many Muslim mystics have been influenced by his teaching. He was given prestigious titles such as *Shaykh al-mashayikh*, 'the Master of masters'.

He is the first to have developed the doctrine of *fana'*, 'passing away' of the self as a result of achieving perfect union with God. He taught that all things originate in God and ultimately return to him. Junayd was associated with another famous Sufi, Harith al-Muhasibi. His teaching has survived through his *Rasa'il*, 'Epistles', in which he elaborates on mystical themes and Qur'anic texts.

Kalabadhi, Abu Bakr (384/994)

Kalabadhi's family name suggests that he was from Kalabadh, near Bukhara (present-day Uzbekistan) where he died. He is mostly known for his famous Sufi manual *al-Ta'arruf li-madhahib ahl al-tasawwuf*, 'The Doctrine of the Sufis' (see bibliography). The treatise is divided into three parts. The first lists the main Sufis in the first three centuries of the Islamic era. The second aims at demonstrating the harmony between Sufism and Islamic orthodoxy. The final part focuses on the mystical path and its stages. Like other Sufi manuals, the *Ta'arruf* frequently uses quotations from previous Sufis and comments on them.

Makki, Abu Talib (386/998)

Makki lived in Basra as well as in Baghdad where he died. His writings often refer to Hadith narratives. His main work is *Qut al-qulub*, 'Food for the hearts', which is a précis on Sufism. In his *Ihya'*, Ghazali quotes this treatise extensively (without giving due credit to the author).

Qushayri, Abu l-Qasim 'Abd al-Karim (465/1072)

Qushayri was born at Ustuwa (Iran) in 376/986 to parents of Arab descent. As a young man in Nishapur, he met Abu 'Ali al-Daqqaq who became his first Sufi master and (some years later) his father-in-law. He also studied *kalam* (theology), *fiqh* (jurisprudence) with Ash'ari scholars such as Ibn Furak. When al-Daqqaq died he succeeded him and his *madrasa* came to be known as *al-madrasa al-qushayriyya* (the Qushayri School). He visited Baghdad and taught at the caliph al-Qa'im's palace. He then spent a few years in Tus before returning to Nishapur where he died. Qushayri was both a theologian and a Sufi. His writings attempt to reconcile Islamic mysticism with traditional Islamic teaching. His famous *Risala*,

'Epistle', sums up his doctrine and represents a key reference for the study of Sufism.

Rabi'a al-'Adawiyya (185/801)

One of not-so-many mystic women in Islam, Rabi'a was born to a humble home in the last decade of the first Islamic century. The story has it that she was stolen as a child and sold as a slave. Thanks to her spirituality, she recovered her freedom. She then retired to a life of seclusion and celibacy. She lived in Iraq and died in Basra.[5]

Rabi'a's disciples included Malik bin Dinar and Shaqiq al-Balkhi, two famous Sufis. She is credited with many miracles. The focus of her teaching is divine, pure and ardent love (*mahabba*) that unites the lover and the beloved (God). Rabi'a is such a prestigious mystic that her spiritual experience has been embellished throughout the years with many legends. She wrote no book; all her sayings have been recorded by people who admired her spirituality.

Rumi, Jalal al-Din (672/1273)

Son of a famous Sufi preacher, Jalal al-Din was born in Balkh in 604/1207. He died in Konya (Turkey) where his family had settled. Konya was then at the border of the Byzantine Empire; hence his surname.[6] He was renowned for his mystical poetry and was given the title *Mawlana*, 'our Master', by his disciples. The order of whirling dervishes, founded by him, is known as *Mawlawiyya*. Listening to 'religious music and sacred dancing' (*sama'*) plays a key role in the religious practices of the order.

Rumi's main works (written in Persian) include his voluminous *Diwan* (a collection of poems) and his *Mathnawi*, a six-tome-long poem in double verses.[7] His mysticism is influenced by Greek thought and other Sufis, especially Ibn 'Arabi. As a Sufi poet, Rumi celebrates the passionate and consuming love of God. His poetical writings stand in sharp contrast with both Islamic theology and Islamic philosophy.

Sahl al-Tustari (283/896)

Sahl was born in Tustar (Iran). He was forty when he emigrated to Basra where he spent the rest of his life. Among his disciples were

Hallaj, who stayed two years with him, and Junayd. Sahl led an ascetic life before he committed himself to Sufism. He claimed to be _Hijjat Allah_, 'the proof of God'. This led him to engage in controversy with a number of theologians.

Sahl was a Hanbalite Sufi. His rigorist teaching is reflected in his works. Two of his writings have been preserved; namely, a Qur'an commentary and a collection of sayings, both compiled by his disciples. He developed the mystical method known as _dhikr_, 'remembrance', designed to achieve union with God. It consists in remembering God by repeating a short prayer. Sahl's prayer was _Allah shahidi_, 'God is my witness'. His Qur'anic exegesis is based on the Qur'an's double meaning: 'plain' (_zahir_) and 'hidden' (_batin_). He conceives God primarily as the Light (see Qur'an 24:35); 'the Light of Muhammad' refers to the primal man who conveys the divine Light to humanity.

Sarraj, Abu Nasr (378/988)
Originally from Tus, Sarraj travelled a lot and lived for a while in Iraq, Syria and Egypt. He returned to his birthplace where he died.

Sarraj's only known work is _Kitab al-Luma'_, 'Book of Shafts of Lights'. This treatise represents one of the main sources of information on Sufism in the first Islamic centuries. It includes a detailed exposition with key quotes of the great Sufi masters. Sarraj's own teaching, moderate but firm, gave much credit to Sufism as a genuinely Islamic spirituality. Among his disciples was Abu 'Abd al-Rahman al-Sulami, the author of a survey on Muslim mystics entitled _Tabaqat al-sufiyya_.

Suhrawardi, 'Abd al-Qahir bin 'Abd Allah (632/1234)
Also known as Shihab al-Din Abu Hafs 'Umar al-Suhrawardi,[8] 'Abd al-Qahir was born at Suhraward (north-west Iran) in 539/1145. He moved to Baghdad when he was still very young, and eventually died there. There he followed the teaching of his uncle Abu l-Najib, himself a Sufi master. He became a brilliant preacher, whose sermons were able to put his audience into ecstasies.

Suhrawardi enjoyed the support of the 'Abbasid caliph al-Nasir who wanted his rule to have a mystical dimension. In return the _Shaykh_ ascribed to the caliphate a spiritual role and became the caliph's representative. He was sent on diplomatic missions to several political leaders as the caliph's special emissary.

Among Suhrawardi's numerous writings (in Arabic and Persian), his book *'Awarif al-ma'arif*, 'On spiritual knowledge', represents a classical treatise in Sufism. A contemporary of Ibn 'Arabi (although twenty years older), he criticized the Spanish-born Sufi for his pantheistic mysticism, deeming it to be too much influenced by Greek philosophy. Yet in his polemical work (e.g. *Rashf al-nasa'ih*) he reveals his own leanings towards a mystical philosophy far from being purely Islamic.

Suhrawardi had a large following from the Middle East to India. His disciples founded the *suhrawardiyya*, a famous Sufi order named after their master. After his death his son 'Imad al-Din (655/1257) became the custodian of his spiritual legacy in Baghdad.

Sulami, Abu 'Abd al-Rahman (412/1021)

Sulami was born in Nishapur in 325/937 and died in the same city. He travelled a lot in Khurasan and Iraq, but spent most of his life in his hometown. He had studied Hadith and theology when he committed his life to Sufism.

Sulami produced many writings: hagiographies, commentaries on the Qur'an and Sufi manuals. Many of his extant writings have been published. His *Tabaqat al-sufiyya* lists short biographies of more than a hundred Sufis, with selections of their sayings. He is also the author of an important commentary on the Qur'an, *Haqa'iq al-tafsir*. His works have been incorporated, to a lesser or greater degree, into later writings by other Sufis. His disciples included the famous Sufi and theologian Abu l-Qasim al-Qushayri.

Notes

1. Gimaret, *Usul*, pp. 9–96. The second part of the article is in fact a critical edition of 'Abd al-Jabbar's *al-Usul al-khamsa* (pp. 79–96).

2. Gimaret, *Lecture*. Gimaret considers that Jubba'i is 'the greatest Mu'tazili theologian' (p. 13).

3. The first edition of this book was published by W. Cureton, 2 vols. (London, 1842–6). In 1986–93 it was published in French as *Livre des Religions et des Sectes* (see bibliography).

4. This treatise has been edited and translated into French by S. de
   Beaurecueil (see bibliography).
5. The name *Rabi'a* means 'the fourth (daughter)'. This Rabi'a (from Basra)
   is not to be confused with another Sufi woman who had the same name,
   Rabi'a al-Shamiyya (from Syria) who was married to Ibn Abi l-Hawwari.
   M. Smith, though an expert on Rabi'a al-'adawiyya, makes such an error.
6. The word *rum* means 'Byzantine'. In the Qur'an sura 30 is entitled *al-rum*.
7. This work has been translated by R. A. Nicholson *The Mathnawi of
   Jelalu'ddin Rumi*, edited from the oldest manuscripts available; with
   critical notes, translations and commentary, E. J. W. Gibb Memorial
   Series, new series, VI, 1–8 (London, 1924–40).
8. This Sufi is not to be confused with his contemporary, the great Sufi
   philosopher Shihab al-Din Yahya al-Suhrawardi, who is also known as
   al-Maqtul (the slain one) because he was put to death in Aleppo (Syria) in
   587/1191, at the age of thirty-six.

BIBLIOGRAPHY

The following is a select bibliography. Only titles (books or articles) quoted in the present book are included.

'ABD AL-JABBAR, al-Qadi, *al-Mughni*, 16 vols. (Cairo: 1960–5).

ABU DAWUD, *Sunan*, tr. A. Hasan, 3 vols. (Lahore: Ashraf Publishers, 1984, repr. 1988).

ABU YA'LA, al-Qadi, *al-Mu'tamad fi usul al-din*, ed. W. Z. Haddad (Beirut: 1974).

ADDAS, Claude, *Quest for the Red Sulphur: The Life of Ibn 'Arabi* (Cambridge: Islamic Texts Society, 1993).

AJURRI, Abu Bakr, *al-Shari'a*, ed. M. H. al-Fiqi (Cairo: 1950).

ALI, Abdullah Yusuf, *The Holy Qur'an: Translation and Commentary*, 6th ed. (Beltsville, Md.: Amana, 1989).

ALLAM, Mahdi, 'The Concept of Forgiveness in the Qur'an', *Islamic Culture* 41.3 (July 1967), pp. 139–153.

ANSARI, 'Abd Allah, *Manazil al-sa'irin*, ed. and tr. S. de Beaurecueil, with introduction, notes and commentary, as *Les étapes des itinérants vers Dieu* (Cairo: Institut français d'archéologie orientale, Arabic–French ed., 1962).

— *Chemin de Dieu. Trois Traités Spirituels: les Cent Terrains; les Étapes des Itinérants vers Dieu; les Déficiences des Demeures*, tr. S. de Beaurecueil (Paris: Actes Sud, 1997).

ASH'ARI, Abu l-Hasan, *Maqalat al-islamiyyin*, 2 vols., ed. M. M. 'Abd al-Hamid (Beirut: al-Maktaba al-'asriyya, 1995).

'ATTAR, Farid al-Din, *Tadhkirat al-awliya'*, ed. and tr. A. J. Arberry as *Muslim Saints and Mystics* (London: Routledge & Kegan Paul, 1966; repr. London: Arkana, 1990).

BAGHDADI, Abu Mansur, *Usul al-din* (Istanbul: 1928).

BAQILLANI, Abu Bakr, *al-Tamhid*, ed. R. J. McCarthy (Beirut: Dar el-Machreq, 1957).

— *al-Insaf*, ed. M. Z. al-Kawthari, 2nd ed. (Cairo: 1963).

BLOCHER, Henri, *Evil and the Cross: Christian Thought and the Problem of Evil* (Leicester: Apollos, 1994).

BUKHARI, *Sahih*, tr. M. M. Khan, 9 vols. (Beirut: Dar al-arabia, Arabic– English ed., 1985).

CASTLE, Tony (comp.), *The Hodder Book of Christian Quotations* (London: Hodder & Stoughton, 1982).

Catechism of the Catholic Church (London: Geoffrey Chapman, 1994).

CHODKIEWICZ, Michel, *Seal of the Saints: Prophethood and Sainthood in the Doctrine of Ibn 'Arabi* (Cambridge: Islamic Texts Society, 1986).

— (ed. and tr.), *Les Illuminations de la Mecque*. Abridged edition of Ibn 'Arabi's *al-Futuhat al-makkiyya* (Paris: Sindbad, 1988).

CORBIN, Henry, *History of Islamic Philosophy* (London: Kegan Paul International, 1993).

CRAGG, Kenneth, *Readings in the Qur'an* (London: Collins, 1988).

D'SOUZA, Andreas, 'Jesus in Ibn 'Arabi's *Fusus al-hikam*', *Bulletin of Christian Institutes of Islamic Studies* 6.1–2 (January–June 1983), pp. 28–54.

DARIMI, *Sunan*.

DEHQANI-TAFTI, H. B., *The Hard Awakening: The Bishop in Iran* (London: SPCK/Triangle, 1981).

Encyclopaedia Judaica, 16 vols. (Jerusalem: Keter, 1972).

Encyclopaedia of the Hadith (Mawsu'at al-Hadith al-sharif) (Cairo: Sakhr Software, 1995).

Encyclopaedia of Islam, 11 vols., 2nd ed. (Leiden: Brill, 1960–2002).

Evangelical Alliance Commission, *The Nature of Hell*. A Report by the Evangelical Alliance Commission on Unity and Truth among Evangelicals (ACUTE) (Carlisle: ACUTE, 2000).

GHAZALI, Abu Hamid, *Ihya' 'ulum al-din*, 4 vols. (Beirut: 1933).

— *al-Maqsad al-asna fi sharh ma'ani asma' allah al-husna*, tr. D. Burrell and N. Dahar as *The Ninety-Nine Beautiful Names of God* (Cambridge: Islamic Texts Society, 1995).

GIMARET, Daniel, 'Les *Usul al-hamsa* du Qadi 'Abd al-Gabbar et leurs commentaires' in *Annales Islamologiques* (Cairo: Institut français d'archéologie orientale, 1979), XV, pp. 9–96.

— *Les Noms divins en Islam*, coll. 'Patrimoines' (Paris: Cerf, 1988).

— *La Doctrine d'al-Ash'ari*, coll. 'Patrimoines' (Paris: Cerf, 1990).

— (ed.), *Une Lecture Mu'tazilite du Coran. Le Tafsir* d'Abu 'Ali al-Djubba'i (m. 303/915) partiellement reconstitué à partir de ses citateurs (Paris: Peeters, 1994).

BIBLIOGRAPHY

359

HUJWIRI, 'Ali bin 'Uthman, *The Kashf al-mahjub*, tr. R. A. Nicholson, E. J. W. Gibb Memorial Series, vol. 17, 2nd ed. (London, 1936; repr. Delhi: Taj, 1997).

HURAYFISH, Shu'ayb 'Abd Allah, *al-Rawd al-jamil*, 2 vols. (Bulaq, Egypt: 1872).

IBN 'ARABI, Muhyi l-Din, *al-Futuhat al-makkiyya*, 4 vols. (Beirut: Dar Sader, 1911, repr. 1980).

— *Fusus al-hikam*, ed. Abu l-'Ala 'Afifi (Beirut: Dar al Kitab al-'arabi, 1980, 2nd ed.) tr. R. J. W. Austin as *Bezels of Wisdom* (Ramsey, N.J.: Paulist, 1981).

IBN FURAK, Abu Bakr, *Mujarrad maqalat al-Ash'ari*, ed. D. Gimaret (Beirut: Dar el-mashreq, 1987).

IBN HANBAL, *Musnad*.

IBN MAJAH, *Sunan*, tr. M. T. Ansari, 5 vols. (New Delhi: Kitab Bhavan, Arabic–English ed., 1994).

IBN MANZUR, *Lisan al-'arab*, 15 vols. (Beirut: 1955–6).

JUWAYNI, Abu l-Ma'ali, *al-Irshad*, ed. J. D. Luciani (Paris: Leroux, 1938).

KALABADHI, Abu Bakr, *al-Ta'arruf li-madhahib ahl al-tasawwuf*, ed. A. J. Arberry (Cairo: 1933, repr. 1960).

— *The Doctrine of the Sufis*, tr. A. J. Arberry (Cambridge: Cambridge University Press, 1935, repr. 1977).

KURZMAN, Charles (ed.), *Liberal Islam: A Sourcebook* (Oxford: Oxford University Press, 1998).

LODI, Zakaur Rahman Khan, 'Modernity of Penal Justice in Islam', *Islamic Culture* 41.3 (July 1967), pp. 139–153.

MAKKI, Abu Talib, *Qut al-qulub*, 2 vols. (Cairo: 1961).

MANKDIM, Sheshdiv, *[Ta'liq] Sharh al-usul al-khamsa*, ed. 'A. K. 'Uthman, 3rd ed. (Cairo: 1996).

MASSIGNON, Louis, *Recueil de textes inédits concernant l'histoire de la mystique en pays d'Islam* (Paris: Geuthner, 1929).

— *Essai sur les origines du lexique technique de la mystique musulmane* (Paris: Vrin, 1968).

— *Hallaj: Mystic and Martyr*, ed. and tr. H. Mason (Princeton, N.J.: Princeton University Press, abridged ed., 1994).

MOUCARRY, Chawkat, *Faith to Faith: Christianity and Islam in Dialogue* (Leicester: Inter-Varsity Press, 2001). Published in the USA as *The Prophet and the Messiah: An Arab Christian's Perspective on Islam and Christianity* (Downers Grove, Ill.: InterVarsity Press, 2001).

MUSLIM, *Sahih*, tr. A. H. Siddiqi, 4 vols. (New Delhi: Kitab Bhavan, 1977, repr. 1982).

Nasai'i, *Sunan*.

Nasafi, Abu l-Mu'min, *Tabsirat al-adilla fi usul al-din*, ed. C. Salamé, 2 vols. (Damascus: Institut français de Damas, 1993).

Nettler, Ronald, 'Ibn 'Arabi's Notion of Allah's Mercy', *Israel Oriental Studies*, 8 (1978), pp. 219–229.

Nwyia, Paul, *Exégèse Coranique et Langage Mystique*, coll. 'Recherches' (Beirut: Dar el-mashreq, 1970).

— (ed.), *Nusus sufiyya ghayr manshura. Trois œuvres inédites de mystiques musulmans: Shaqiq al-Balkhi, Ibn 'Ata', Niffari*, coll. 'Recherches' (Beirut: Dar el-Machreq, 1973).

Qushayri, Abu l-Qasim, *al-Risala al-qushayriyya* (Beirut: Dar al-jil, 1990).

Razi, Fakhr al-Din, *al-Tafsir al-kabir*, 16 vols. (Beirut: Dar al-kutub al-'ilmiyya, 1990).

Sabuni, Nur al-Din, *al-Bidaya min al-kifaya fi l-hidaya fi usul al-din*, ed. F. Kholeif (Alexandria: 1969).

Sarraj, Abu Nasr, *Kitab al-Luma' fi l-tasawwuf* (Cairo: Dar al-kutub al-haditha, 1960).

Schimmel, Annemarie, *Mystical Dimensions of Islam* (Chapel Hill: University of North Carolina Press, 1975).

— *And Muhammad Is His Messenger* (Chapel Hill: University of North Carolina Press, 1985).

Shahrastani, Muhammad, *Kitab al-Milal wa l-nihal*, tr. D. Gimaret, J. Jolivet and G. Monnot, with introduction, notes and commentary, as *Shahrastani: Livre des Religions et des Sectes*, 2 vols. (Paris: Peeters/ UNESCO, 1986 (vol. 1) and 1993 (vol. 2).

Singh, David Emmanuel, 'Jesus in Ibn al-'Arabi's mysticism', *Dharma Deepika* 2.1 (June 1996), pp. 43–67.

Smith, Margaret, *Rabi'a the Mystic and her Fellow-Saints*, 2nd ed. (Cambridge: Cambridge University Press, 1984; repr. Felinfach, Dyfeld: Llanerch, 1994).

Stott, John, *The Epistles of John: An Introduction and Commentary* (London: Tyndale, 1964).

Suhrawardi, 'Abd al-Qahir, *'Awarif al-ma'arif*, 2nd ed. (Beirut: Dar al-kitab al-'arabi, 1983).

Sulami, Abu 'Abd al-Rahman, *Tabaqat al-sufiyya*, ed. J. Pedersen (Leiden: Brill, 1960).

Tirmidhi, *Sunan*.

Ward, Hannah, and Wild, Jennifer (comps.), *The Lion Christian Quotation Collection* (Oxford: Lion, 1997).

GENERAL INDEX

'Abd al-Jabbar, al-Qadi 87, 96, 109, 113, 341–342
'Abdullah al-Qurayshi 265
'Abdullah bin Shurayh 184
Abraham (*Ibrahim*) 39, 56, 66 (n. 1), 70, 77 (n. 3), 102–103, 105 (nn. 29, 30), 118, 125, 130–131, 146 (n. 24), 174, 177, 181–184, 188–189, 301, 351
Abu 'Abdillah al-Maghribi 223
Abu 'Ali al-Jubba'i 85–87, 96, 110–112, 155, 161, 178, 180–181, 194 (n. 13), 341–342, 344
Abu 'Ali al-Rudhabari 213
Abu Bakr (1st caliph) 273, 292, 308
Abu Bakr al-Wasiti 221
Abu Hafs al-Haddad 202
Abu Hanifa, al-Nu'man 100
Abu Hashim al-Jubba'i 86, 96, 110, 147 (n. 36), 155, 341–343
Abu l-Hasan Bushanji 221
Abu l-Hudhayl, Muhammad 86–87, 343
Abu l-Husayn al-Maghazili 218
Abu Muhammad Sahl 199, 209
Abu Sa'id bin al-A'rabi 203

Abu Sulayman al-Darimi 30
Abu 'Uthman al-Maghribi 218
Abu 'Uthman Hiri 202
Abu Ya'la, al-Qadi 109, 343–344
Abu Zayd, Nasr 282
Adam 28, 39, 70, 90, 109, 121 (n. 8), 128–131, 135, 146 (n. 23), 167–168, 174, 177–178, 180–181, 188, 194 (n. 15), 204, 210 (n. 12), 240, 244–245, 262–263
Afghanistan 314, 346–348, 350
ahl al-kitab (the People of the Book) 57–58, 298–301
Ahmad al-Antaki 214
Aisha 186, 292
Ajurri, Abu Bakr 97, 100
Aleppo 356 (n. 8)
'Ali (4th caliph) 111, 208, 343
Allam, Mahdi 308–309, 312 (n. 36)
Angels 39, 125, 128, 135–136, 141–142, 180, 182, 305
Ansari, 'Abd Allah 198, 203–204, 206, 208, 213–218, 221–222, 225–226, 314–316, 317 (nn. 2, 4), 318, 348
apokatastasis (universal restoration) 267 (n. 3)

INDEX OF QUR'ANIC REFERENCES

INDEX OF BIBLICAL REFERENCES